The Audubon Society
Field Guide to
North American Birds

A Chanticleer Press Edition

The Audubon Society Field Guide to North American Birds

Western Region

Miklos D. F. Udvardy,
California State University,
Sacramento

Visual Key developed by
Susan Rayfield, Associate Editor,
Audubon magazine

Alfred A. Knopf, New York

This is a Borzoi Book
Published by Alfred A. Knopf, Inc.

Prepared and produced by
Chanticleer Press, Inc., New York.

Color reproductions by Nievergelt
Repro AG, Zurich, Switzerland.
Type set in Garamond by
Dix Type Inc., Syracuse, New York.
Printed and bound in Japan.

Published August 30, 1977
Reprinted twelve times
Fourteenth Printing, May 1988

Library of Congress Catalog Card
Number 76-47938
ISBN 0-394-41410-1

CONTENTS

THE AUTHOR

Miklos D. F. Udvardy is Professor of Biological Sciences at California State University, Sacramento. He taught at the University of British Columbia from 1952 to 1966, has been a visiting professor in the German Federal Republic, in Honduras, and at the University of Hawaii, and has lectured at other universities. He is a Research Associate of the Los Angeles County Museum of Natural History and has been an officer of several North American ornithological associations as well as a member of five international ornithological congresses.

His specialties include biogeography, ecology, and animal behavior, but he is primarily a research ornithologist. He has published over 100 scientific papers and several books, including *Dynamic Zoogeography* (1969).

Acknowledgements: Throughout my many years of scientific research in North America, the bird-watching public and students have contributed richly to my knowledge with their observations, bird counts, nest records, banding work, salvaged specimens, and challenging inquiries. My first thanks must go to them. I feel that with this guide I am repaying only part of the debt I owe them.

My wife Maud made this undertaking

possible, not only by taking on herself a great share of my other burdens, but also by her assistance and advice. I am also grateful for criticism and troubleshooting by my friends and fellow ornithologists, Dean Amadon, John Farrand, Jr., John Bull, Joseph R. Jehl, Jr., McTaggart Cowan, Robert T. Orr, and Robert J. Smith. Kimball Garrett and Jon Dunn added many of the descriptions of voice. Susan Rayfield assembled and organized the pictures, and she as well as Cloe Mifsud, Ronald A. Ryder, and Peter Alden contributed to the species descriptions. Range maps were researched by David Ewert, Kimball Garrett, and John Dunn and coordinated by Jill Farmer.
The staff of Chanticleer Press all contributed above and beyond the call of duty, and it was a special pleasure to work with the publisher, Paul Steiner, and with Gudrun Buettner, Carol Nehring, Kathy Ritchell, Mary Suffudy, and Helga Lose. This book, however, owes most of all to the vision, know-how, tact, and contagious enthusiasm of Milton Rugoff.

M.D.F. Udvardy

INTRODUCTION

Ancient Roman bird-watchers formed a society of *augurs* or priests and told the future from various *auspices* or signs such as the flight and appearance of certain birds. Remnants of the lore of augury are reflected in such modern English phrases as "under good auspices." Today, however, most bird-watchers are simply urbanized men and women with a desire to return to nature and enjoy the beauty, song, grace, and charm of birds. This book is meant for such enthusiasts.

Among the oldest existing pictures of birds are those of the early Egyptians, who decorated obelisks and pyramid chambers with colored images that were masterpieces of art. Today we utilize the last word in twentieth-century pictorial communication—color photography. The editors of this book and its companion volume on the birds of eastern North America spared neither time nor cost in gathering the best examples of such photography, especially those that show a bird in a characteristic pose and in its natural habitat. In this respect and in its compact size, flexible format, and organization, this guide is meant to serve as your companion in the field: stuff it into your pocket, and may the birding be good wherever you go!

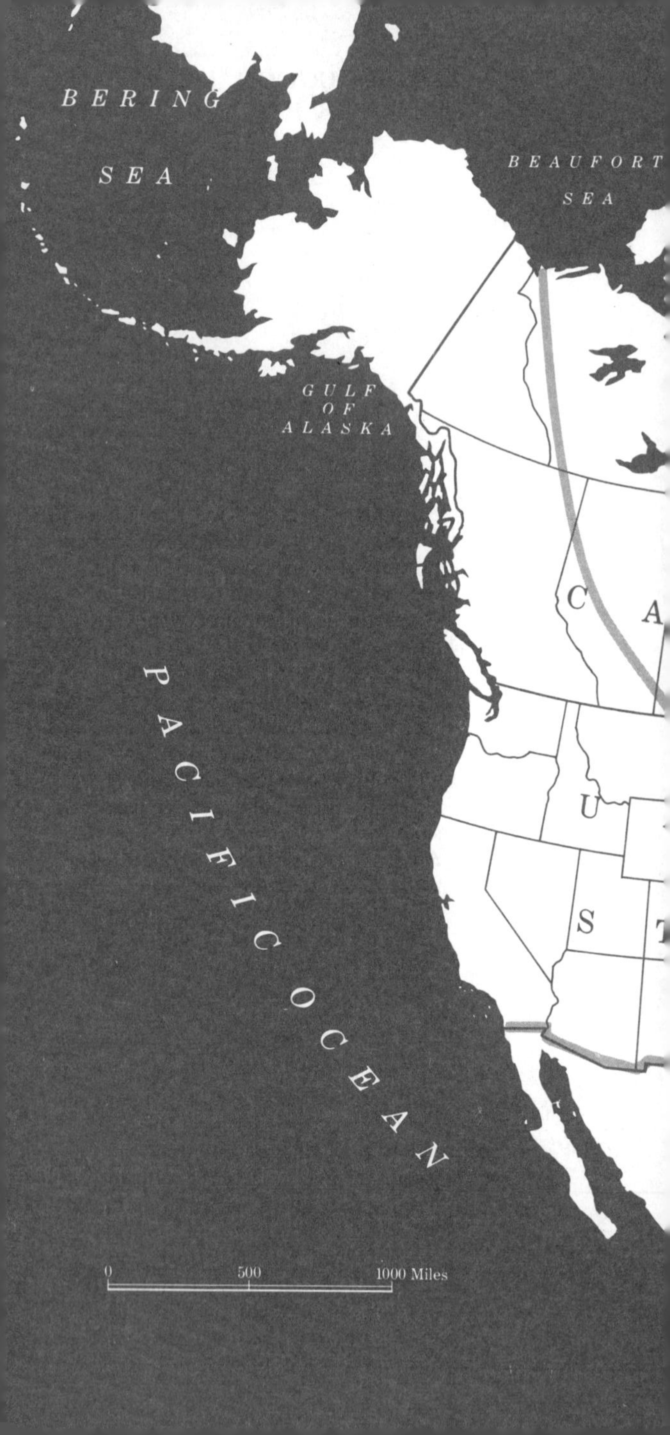

BERING SEA

BEAUFORT SEA

GULF OF ALASKA

PACIFIC OCEAN

C A

U S

S T

0   500   1000 Miles

GREENLAND
BAFFIN BAY
HUDSON BAY
NADA
ITED
ATES
ATLANTIC
OCEAN
GULF OF MEXICO
CUBA
XICO
CARIBBEAN SEA

Geographical Scope This guide covers the birds of western North America. The chain of the Rocky Mountains serves as a convenient natural division of the vast North American continent, separating the mountainous, forested regions of the· West and the arid areas of the Southwest from the more uniform expanses of the East. This dividing line (see map) runs somewhat to the west of the geographic middle of the continent. Thus the eastern boundary of the area covered in this guide lies along the eastern foothills of the Rockies, from the far northern Canadian territories, through British Columbia and Alberta, southeastward to Colorado, and south along the 100th meridian, cutting through the Oklahoma panhandle but west of the Edwards Plateau and the lower Rio Grande Delta of Texas. The southern boundary runs west along the border between the United States and Mexico to the Pacific Coast.

The area covered embraces Alaska, parts of the Yukon, most of British Columbia and Alberta, and part or all of the thirteen western states of the United States.

Altogether, 508 species are described and illustrated; in addition, a small number of "accidental" or marginally occurring species are listed in the back of the book.

Photographs as a Visual Guide No matter how a bird guide is organized, its illustrations must form the basis of bird identification. This book uses photographic illustrations rather than the paintings or drawings common in traditional guide books because photographs add a new dimension in realism and natural beauty. Fine modern photographs are closer to the way the human eye usually sees a bird and, moreover, they are a pleasure to look at.

This guide also departs from the standard grouping of birds by scientific families, that is, according to structural features. It does so simply because a novice would probably not know the family of a bird seen in the wild and would have to search at random through the pages of a conventional guide until he hit upon a picture that looked like the bird he had glimpsed; even an experienced birder must follow this trial-and-error procedure. The illustrations in this book have thus been organized not by families but by clearly visible characteristics. They have been grouped according to an obvious similarity in shape or appearance among certain birds, as, for example, in the group here called "Gull-like Birds," or according to a shared behavior pattern, as in the group called "Tree-clinging Birds," or in a combination of shape and behavior, as in "Long-legged Waders." All of these categories are hardly perfect—nature does not always lend itself to neat classifications—but they will surely prove very useful as a first step in identifying a bird.

In addition, to aid in distinguishing between very similar birds, such as the Horned Grebe and the Eared Grebe, their photographs are placed close to each other. Quite a few photographs showing birds in flight or engaged in some characteristic behavior have also been included.

Because the species we call the "Perching Birds"—technically known as the passerines and popularly called songbirds—make up a very large group, they have been broken down according to their most prominent color, whether an overall color (such as the blue in a Bluebird) or a distinctive patch (as the red patches on a Red-faced Warbler). As in grouping birds by shape or behavior, so in classifying the perching birds by color, a few arbitrary judgments had to be made. Such judgments are, after all, influenced by variable factors such as how the light falls on a bird, the angle from which a bird is seen, and, of course, individual conceptions of color. But many of the decisions were easy to make and all birders will find that this arrangement according to color helps greatly in identification.

Captions under each pictured species include the plate number, the size of the bird, and the number of the page on which the species is described. If the photograph is not of a breeding male, that is also indicated.

Groups   The color-plate groups are as follows:

    Long-legged Waders
    Gull-like Birds
    Upright-perching Waterbirds
    Duck-like Birds
    Sandpiper-like Birds
    Chicken-like Marsh Birds
    Upland Ground Birds
    Owls
    Hawk-like Birds
    Pigeon-like Birds
    Swallow-like Birds
    Tree-clinging Birds
    Hummingbirds
    Perching Birds

Silhouette and   So the bird-watcher using this guide
Thumbprint   can see at a glance the typical shapes of
Guides   the birds in each category, silhouettes of those shapes are shown on the pages immediately preceding the entire section of color plates. To make it easy to locate the group of photographs for each category of birds, a silhouette typical of the category has been inset as a "thumbprint" on the left edge of each double-page of photographs; Long-legged Waders, for example, are represented by the silhouette of an ibis. Most of the photographs in this book are of adult males, since they are generally the most colorful and conspicuous and thus the easiest to identify. The females are usually a

duller, less colorful version of the male,
and many birders can identify a female
only after they know the male. Females
and immatures are shown only when
they are significantly different from the
male. Photographs of birds in flight or
in different color phases are included
only when they will be particularly
helpful. In a relatively few instances—
generally of an uncommon species or of
one with a very limited range—no
satisfactory photograph was available.
Such species are, however, fully
described in the text and the
description is accompanied by a
drawing.

Text Arranged by Habitat In general, most birds leave their
nesting habitat when conditions there
deteriorate, and shift to an alternate
habitat. Jays visit oaks for acorns, gulls
follow the plow of the farmer in the
field, waxwings move to town for the
berries. In this way almost every bird
has several preferred habitats. For the
purpose of identification, we have
considered the primary habitat of a
species the one where most observers
encounter it—even if this is not its
breeding habitat. Thus, many breeders
of the inaccessible Far North have been
listed, for example, under "Seashore."
This grouping of the descriptions by
habitats gives the reader an additional
check on the identification process
begun in the picture section. Twenty
habitat groups are recognized; they are
as follows:

Open Ocean
Seashore
Sea Cliffs
Salt Marshes
Freshwater Marshes
Lakes, Ponds, Rivers
Wet Tundra
Desert Scrub and Mesquite
Grasslands and Savannas
Alpine Meadows

Fields
Cities, Parks, Suburbs
Chaparral
Sagebrush
Pinyon-Juniper Woodlands
Oak Woodlands
Deciduous Woods
Coniferous Forests
Upland Tundra
Inland Cliffs and Canyons

Of course, birds have great mobility
and most of them can tolerate a variety
of habitats, especially when on
migration. One may therefore be
surprised to find a bird entirely out of
its normal habitat, as did the author
when he came upon a Great Blue Heron
peering at the goldfish in a backyard
pond.

Before setting out on a field trip to a
particular habitat, the reader should
look through the section describing the
species generally found in that habitat.
Knowing what to expect will make
initial recognition much easier. As an
additional aid (under the title "How to
Use the Keys"), we give an example of
the steps to be taken in using this book
to identify a particular bird.

Species   Our bird descriptions start with the
Descriptions: bird's vernacular or common name and
English and   its scientific name; thus the common
Scientific Names   name of one species of falcon is
of Birds   Peregrine Falcon and its scientific name
is *Falco peregrinus*. It has a scientific
name because its common name differs
from country to country and sometimes
even from one region of a country to
another. For instance, the bird now
called the Dipper was once called the
"Water Ouzel" (which is the name
of a related but different bird in
England).

The English, or common, names of
birds are those accepted in the 1957
edition of the American Ornithologists'
Union's *Check-list of North American*

Birds, as revised in the 32nd supplement in 1973, and in the 33rd supplement in 1976. Where a bird's name has been changed recently by the A.O.U. we have included its former name in quotation marks.

The scientific name consists of two Latin or Greek words. The first word, always capitalized, indicates the group, called genus, to which the bird belongs; and the second word, the species within the genus. Both words are generally in italics. Thus the Peregrine Falcon is the species *peregrinus* within the genus *Falco.* This remarkable system, worked out by the Swedish naturalist Linnaeus in the eighteenth century, enables scientists all over the world to know exactly which species of animal or plant is being referred to in any instance. Often the scientific name as well as the common name of a bird incorporates the name of a famous ornithologist. Just as there are usually several species in a genus, so there are often several genera that have anatomical characteristics in common and are grouped in one "family." Thus all the genera of falcons (and all the species within them) make up the family known as Falconidae. All family names are capitalized (and never set in italics) and can be recognized by the Latin plural ending "-idae." The families of all North American birds are described in the back of the book.

When a reference is made to any bird not described in this book, both its common and scientific names are given.

The description of each species covers all or almost all of the following:

Size It is hard to say exactly how large a given bird is because such a measurement depends on its posture at a particular moment. The measurement given here is the length from tip of tail to tip of bill of an average museum specimen as it lies in a cabinet drawer. Even this is only an approximation, for specimens may have been stretched out of shape, tails may be worn down, and so forth. In many instances a more general impression is given by a comparison with a well-known bird such as a sparrow or a Robin. Wingspread (W.) measurements are given for the largest birds. These measurements are also approximate since the apparent wingspread of a bird soaring in the air depends on how high it is; even experts have great difficulty in judging the wingspread of a bird flying at a considerable height. Tallness has been given only for birds that are noted for their height, such as cranes and larger herons, but this measurement also depends on variables such as whether the bird is standing stiffly erect or in a more relaxed posture.

Description: Next, the shape, plumage color, and
Shape and   other distinguishing "field marks" are
Plumage   described, with the outstanding features italicized to facilitate quick identification. The appearance of a bird may serve various purposes such as to hide it from enemies or to signal its presence. Thus the male is often conspicuous, enabling him to attract attention, while the female generally blends with the background and achieves effective camouflage. The color of a young bird is normally similar to that of the female. Natural selection has produced some quite marvelous adaptations to the seasonally changing need to be seen or to be hidden. In the most complex cases there are seasonal, sexual, and age changes in the appearance of plumage, tufts, crests, plumes, and even bills. If a bird has two distinctly different plumages, an effort has been made to illustrate both. We have used familiar language

wherever possible, but the use of certain technical terms for the parts of a bird's body was unavoidable. A captioned diagram of a bird in these pages serves to explain these; and all technical terms are defined in the Glossary.

Voice The great majority of birds are very vocal. Their repertoire includes feeding calls to their young or to a mate, alarm calls to warn against predators, mating calls, calls to maintain contact with mate, family, or group, calls or songs to proclaim their presence, and many others. Some are used only in certain seasons, or by one sex or age group; others are modified by distance, the height of the bird's perch, the density of intervening vegetation, and dampness in the air. Add to these the individual differences in bird-watchers' hearing, mood, and ear for sounds, and one can understand why the rendering of bird vocalizations is, at best, variable. An expert phonetic transcription helps, but the best way to learn a bird's call is to see the bird as it utters the call or to have an experienced birder identify the sound.

Habitat Even though we have grouped birds into habitat preference groups, the reader will discover that birds are extremely adaptable. It is quite common for a species to utilize several different types of habitat, if these have in common some feature or features that the bird finds essential. In the case of migratory birds, the breeding habitat is often very different from the one occupied during the non-breeding season.
Each habitat is defined and described on the pages preceding the text.

Nesting The information given here concerning the number and color of eggs, the location of the nest and the type of

nest, should help the reader relate the bird to its nest site and young. Where a bird is said to nest on the ground in a "scrape" made by the bird, or in a natural depression, this implies that no nest is built. In the few instances in which a species does not nest in our area, as, for example, seabirds which regularly visit the West during their migration from the South Seas, few or no details of breeding are given.
The size of the clutch, that is, the number of eggs laid, varies widely in almost every species. Thus the clutch tends to be larger toward the North in many widespread species: summer is shorter in those latitudes, but a very long day enables the birds to feed and raise twice as many young as they might do along, say, the Mexican border. The figures for clutch size therefore usually represent an average. In a few species, the clutch size is fixed no matter where they live: pigeons and doves lay two eggs at a time but attempt to raise several broods in sequence during one summer. Other widespread species vary in the number of broods raised in a given season.

Range   The description of the geographic distribution of each species concentrates on the distribution in the West but may also include details of distribution elsewhere in North America and on other continents. The range of widespread and common species is described more briefly than that of more restricted species. Most descriptions proceed clockwise from the northern boundary eastward, then south, and finally westward. Where winter range is not mentioned, the species is not migratory or generally does not move out of the breeding range during winter.

Range Maps   In addition to a statement of the geographic range, a range map is

provided for species of more than
irregular or casual occurrence within
the area covered by this book. No range
maps are provided for exclusively
oceanic species. On these maps the
following designations are used:

Breeding range

Winter range

Areas in which a species occurs in both
winter and summer are indicated by
cross-hatching.

Permanent range

Notes
and Comment

At the end of each species description a
paragraph or two is devoted to some
interesting aspect of the appearance, life
history, habits, or origin of the bird, its
relationship to kindred species, its
survival status, or its other names in
English.

For information on bird-watching
equipment, lists of casual or accidental
species, and descriptions of all families
of birds that appear in North America,
the reader should consult the
appendixes at the back of this book.

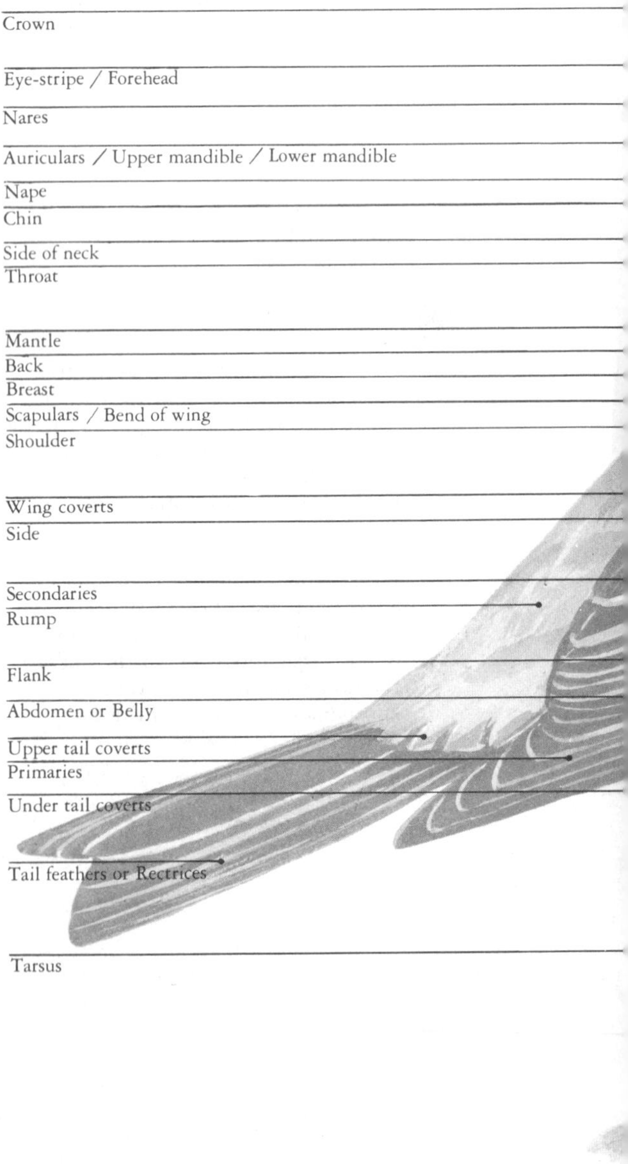

Crown

Eye-stripe / Forehead

Nares

Auriculars / Upper mandible / Lower mandible

Nape

Chin

Side of neck

Throat

Mantle

Back

Breast

Scapulars / Bend of wing

Shoulder

Wing coverts

Side

Secondaries

Rump

Flank

Abdomen or Belly

Upper tail coverts

Primaries

Under tail coverts

Tail feathers or Rectrices

Tarsus

Keys to the Color Plates

The color plates in the following pages
are divided into fourteen groups:

Long-legged Waders
Gull-like Birds
Upright-perching Water Birds
Duck-like Birds
Sandpiper-like Birds
Chicken-like Marsh Birds
Upland Ground Birds
Owls
Hawk-like Birds
Pigeon-like Birds
Swallow-like Birds
Tree-clinging Birds
Hummingbirds
Perching Birds

Thumb Prints To make it easy to locate a group, a
typical outline of a bird from that
group is inset as a thumb print at the
left edge of each double-page of plates.
Thus you can find the Long-legged
Waders by flipping through the color
pages until you come to a series of
thumb prints showing the outline of a
typical wading bird.

Silhouettes of To help you recognize birds by their
the Families in general shape, the color plates are
Each Group preceded by pages showing you
silhouettes of the families in each
group. If the bird you saw looks like
one of these silhouettes, you will find
the bird in that group.

Captions The caption under each photograph
gives the common name of the bird, its
size, and the page number on which it is
described. The color plate number is
repeated in front of each description as
a cross reference.
Most of the photographs show birds in
typical breeding plumage. Certain birds,
as indicated in the caption, are also
shown in distinctive immature or winter
plumage.

Symbol	Category
	Long-legged Waders
	Gull-like Birds

Group Symbols		Plate Numbers
	herons, egrets	1–10, 15
	bitterns	11–12
	storks	13
	ibises	14
	cranes	16
	gulls	17–24, 26–40
	fulmars, shear-waters, albatrosses	25, 65–73

Symbol	Category
	Gull-like Birds
	Upright Perching Waterbirds

Group Symbols		Plate Numbers
	terns	41–52
	skuas, jaegers	53–55, 58
	tropicbirds	56
	frigatebirds	57
	boobies	59–61
	storm-petrels	62–64
	cormorants	74–77

Symbol	Category
	Upright Perching Waterbirds
	Duck-like Birds

Group Symbols		Plate Numbers
	auks, murres, puffins	78–89
	diving ducks	90–95, 98–99, 103–110, 112–113, 115, 130–134, 136–145
	surface-feeding ducks	96–97, 114, 117–121, 123–125, 135, 146–153
	mergansers	100–102, 126, 128–129
	coots	111
	stiff-tailed ducks	116, 127
	whistling-ducks	122
	pelicans	154–155
	swans	156–157

Sandpiper-like Birds

Chicken-like Marsh Birds

Group Symbols		Plate Numbers
	geese	158–165
	loons	166–173
	grebes	174–181
	plovers	182–187, 189–190, 221–222, 227–231, 233
	sandpipers	188, 191–199, 206–217, 223–226, 232, 234–235, 239–240
	phalaropes	200–205, 236–238
	oystercatchers	218
	avocets	219–220, 241
	rails, gallinules,	242–247

Symbol	Category

Symbol Category

Upland Ground Birds

Owls

Hawk-like Birds

Group Symbols		Plate Numbers
	nightjars	248–251
	grouse	252–263, 268–275
	roadrunners	264
	pheasants, quails, partridges	265, 267, 276–285
	turkeys	266
	true owls	286–301, 303
	barn owls	302
	ospreys	304, 334

Symbol	Category
	Hawk-like Birds
	Pigeon-like Birds

Group Symbols		Plate Numbers
	caracaras	305
	vultures	306–307, 336–338
	hawks, (buteos, accipiters)	308, 310–316, 324–327, 339–343
	falcons	309, 318, 320–323, 328–331
	harriers	317
	kites	319
	eagles	332–333, 335
	pigeons, doves	344–351

Symbol	Category
	Swallow-like Birds
	Tree-clinging Birds

Group Symbols		Plate Numbers
	swallows	352–359
	swifts	360–361
	woodpeckers	362–385
	nuthatches	386–387, 389
	creepers	388
	hummingbirds	390–407

Symbol	Category
	Perching Birds

Group Symbols		Plate Numbers
	buntings, finches, sparrows	408, 417–418, 430–431, 442, 452–453, 459–465, 479–480, 483, 501, 522, 524–525, 553–554, 563–564, 568–570, 572–573, 575–579, 583–584, 586–591, 593–602, 604–606
	wood warblers	409–416, 419, 438–441, 456, 458, 478, 511–512, 542, 552, 608–609
	flycatchers	420–421, 451, 469, 474, 490, 513, 517–521, 546–549, 551, 610
	titmice	422, 485–489, 544–545
	meadowlarks	423–424
	wagtails, pipits	425, 571
	cardinals, grosbeaks	426, 429, 443, 448, 466–468, 481, 498, 550, 567, 582

Symbol	Category
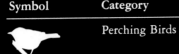	Perching Birds

Group Symbols		Plate Numbers
	orioles, blackbirds	427–428, 435–437, 446–447, 556–561, 581, 607, 612, 614–615, 618–623
	tanagers	432–434, 449–450, 454–455
	thrushes	444–445, 476, 482, 496–497, 499–500, 538–541, 543
	trogons	457
	jays, magpies	470–471, 502, 505–507, 616–617
	shrikes	472–473
	mockingbirds, thrashers	475, 477, 533–537
	wrentits	484

Symbol	Category
	Perching Birds

Group Symbols		Plate Numbers
	silky flycatchers	491, 613
	dippers	492
	becards	493
	gnatcatchers, kinglets	494–495, 509–510
	kingfishers	503–504, 523
	vireos	508, 514–516
	wrens	526–532
	starlings	555, 611
	cuckoos	562

Symbol	Category
	Perching Birds

Group Symbols		Plate Numbers
	waxwings	565–566
	larks	574, 603
	weaver finches	580, 585, 592
	crows, ravens	624–627

The color plates on the following pages are numbered to correspond with the description of each species in the text. Most of the birds shown are adult males but also shown are some distinctive females and immatures and a few instances of seasonal changes in plumage.

Long-legged Waders

These are medium to large-sized water birds with long legs adapted for wading in fresh or salt water. Most of these species, such as herons, egrets, cranes, ibises, spoonbills, and flamingos, are conspicuously patterned and many are entirely white. Others are pink but some have concealing colors which make them difficult to detect.

1 Snowy Egret breeding plumage, 20–27″, p. 418

2 Snowy Egret non-breeding plumage, 20–27″, p. 418

3 Great Egret breeding plumage, 37–41″, p. 419

4 Great Egret non-breeding plumage, 37–41″, p. 419

5   Cattle Egret breeding plumage, 20″, p. 408

6   Cattle Egret non-breeding plumage, 20″, p. 408

7 Green Heron, 16–22″, p. 460

8 Black-crowned Night Heron, 23–28″, p. 420

9   Green Heron imm., 16–22″, p. 460

10   Black-crowned Night Heron imm., 23–28″, p. 420

11 Least Bittern, 11–14", p. 420

12 American Bittern, 23–34", p. 421

13   Wood Stork, 40–44″, p. 422

14   White-faced Ibis, 19–26″, p. 423

15　Great Blue Heron, 42–52″, p. 424

16　Sandhill Crane, 34–48″, p. 425

Gull-like Birds

 These waterbirds spend much of their time in flight. All have long, pointed wings. Gulls, terns, gannets, and boobies are predominantly white, while frigatebirds are black. Most of these birds occur along seacoasts or on the ocean, but some of the gulls and terns are found on inland waters.

17 Thayer's Gull, 22½–25″, p. 352

18 Herring Gull, 22½–26″, p. 352

19 California Gull, 20–23″, p. 460

20 Glaucous Gull, 26–32″, p. 380

21 Glaucous-winged Gull, 24–27″, p. 353

22 Western Gull, 24–27″, p. 354

23 Mew Gull, 16–18″, p. 355

24 Ring-billed Gull, 18–21″, p. 461

25 Northern Fulmar, 17–20″, p. 338

26 Black-legged Kittiwake, 16–18″, p. 381

27 Red-legged Kittiwake, 14–15½″, p. 382

29 Bonaparte's Gull, 12–14″, p. 462

30 Sabine's Gull, 13–14″, p. 340

31 Franklin's Gull, 13½–15½″, p. 463

32   Bonaparte's Gull winter plumage, p. 462

33   Black-legged Kittiwake winter plumage, p. 381

34   Franklin's Gull winter plumage, p. 463

35   Mew Gull second year, 16–18″, p. 355

36   Glaucous-winged Gull second year, 24–27″, p. 353

37   California Gull first year, 20–23″, p. 460

38   Herring Gull first year, 22½–26″, p. 352

39   Western Gull first year, 24–27″, p. 354

40   Heermann's Gull first year, 18–21″, p. 356

41   Gull-billed Tern, 13–14½", p. 409

42   Least Tern, 8½–9½", p. 357

43   Black Tern, 9–10¼", p. 426

44 Common Tern, 13–16″, p. 464

45 Forster's Tern, 14–16¼″, p. 464

46 Arctic Tern, 14–17″, p. 340

47 Caspian Tern, 19–23″, p. 465

48 Royal Tern, 18–21″, p. 358

49 Elegant Tern, 16–17″, p. 359

50   Aleutian Tern, 13½–15″, p. 359

51   Royal Tern non-breeding plumage, 18–21″, p. 358

52   Forster's Tern winter plumage, 14–16¼″, p. 464

53 Parasitic Jaeger, 16–21″, p. 492

54 Long-tailed Jaeger, 20–23″, p. 756

55 Pomarine Jaeger, 20–23″, p. 493

56 Red-billed Tropicbird, 24–40″, p. 360

57 Magnificent Frigatebird, 37½–41″, p. 361

58 Skua, 20–22″, p. 341

59   Red-footed Booby, 26–30″, p. 362

60   Brown Booby, 28–32″, p. 362

61   Blue-footed Booby, 32–34″, p. 363

62   Leach's Storm-Petrel, 7½–9″, p. 383

63   Least Storm-Petrel, 5½–6″, p. 342

64   Ashy Storm-Petrel, 7½″, p. 384

65   Pink-footed Shearwater, 20″, p. 343

66   Sooty Shearwater, 16–18″, p. 344

67   Manx Shearwater, 12½–15″, p. 344

68   Flesh-footed Shearwater, 19½", p. 345

69   Short-tailed Shearwater, 13–14", p. 346

70   New Zealand Shearwater, 16½–18", p. 347

71 Laysan Albatross, 32″, p. 347

72 Black-footed Albatross, 28–36″, p. 348

73 Northern Fulmar dark phase, 17–20″, p. 338

Upright-perching Water Birds

These birds are usually seen perching on rocks or trees at the edge of the water. In most cases, their feet are located far back on the body, which gives the birds a distinctive upright posture when perching. The auks, murres, and puffins are patterned in black-and-white, while the cormorants and anhingas are largely or entirely black.

74   Pelagic Cormorant, 25–30″, p. 385

75   Red-faced Cormorant, 28–30″, p. 386

76 Double-crested Cormorant, 30–36″, p. 466

77 Brandt's Cormorant, 33–35″, p. 387

78   Thick-billed Murre, 17–19″, p. 388

79   Common Murre, 16–17″, p. 389

80 Pigeon Guillemot, 12–14", p. 390

81 Common Murre winter plumage, 16–17", p. 389

82   Tufted Puffin, 14½–15½″, p. 390

83   Horned Puffin, 14½″, p. 391

84   Tufted Puffin swimming, 14½–15½″, p. 390

85   Rhinoceros Auklet, 14½–15½″, p. 392

86　Crested Auklet, 9½–10½″, p. 393

87　Cassin's Auklet, 8–9″, p. 394

88 Parakeet Auklet, 10″, p. 395

89 Least Auklet, 6″, p. 396

Duck-like Birds

Included here are the many ducks, geese, and swans, as well as other birds that, like the ducks, are usually seen swimming. Many of the male ducks, and breeding-plumaged loons and grebes, are boldly patterned, while female ducks and winter-plumaged loons and grebes are clad in modest browns and grays.

90   Ring-necked Duck, 14½–18″, p. 427

91   Tufted Duck, 17″, p. 409

92 Lesser Scaup, 15–18½″ p. 410

93 Greater Scaup, 15½–20″, p. 411

94   Redhead, 18–22″, p. 428

95   Canvasback, 19½–24″, p. 428

96 Northern Shoveler, 17–20″, p. 429

97 Mallard, 20½–28″, p. 431

98   Oldsquaw, 19–22½″, p. 494

99   Oldsquaw winter plumage, 19–22½″, p. 494

100 Red-breasted Merganser, 19½–26″, p. 467

101 Common Merganser, 22–27″, p. 468

102 Hooded Merganser, 16–19″, p. 468

103 Bufflehead, 13–15½″, p. 469

104 Barrow's Goldeneye, 16½–20″, p. 470

105 Common Goldeneye, 16–20″, p. 471

106   King Eider, 18½–25″, p. 495

107   Spectacled Eider, 20½–22″, p. 496

108 Steller's Eider, 17–18½″, p. 496

109 Common Eider, 23–27″, p. 365

110   Black Scoter, 17–20½″, p. 366

111   American Coot, 13–16″, p. 432

112 White-winged Scoter, 19–23½", p. 367

113 Surf Scoter, 17–21", p. 368

114 Wood Duck, 17–20½″, p. 472

115 Harlequin Duck, 14½–21″, p. 473

116 Ruddy Duck, 14½–16″, p. 432

117 Cinnamon Teal, 14½–17″, p. 434

118 European Wigeon, 16½–20″, p. 434

119 American Wigeon, 18–23″, p. 435

120 Blue-winged Teal, 14½–16″, p. 436

121 Green-winged Teal, 12½–15½″, p. 437

122   Fulvous Whistling-Duck, 18–21″, p. 438

123   Mexican Duck, 21–23″, p. 439

124 Pintail, 25–29″, p. 439

125 Gadwall, 18½–23″, p. 440

126   Hooded Merganser ♀, 16–19″, p. 468

127   Ruddy Duck ♀, 14½–16″, p. 432

128 Common Merganser ♀, 22–27", p. 468

129 Red-breasted Merganser ♀, 19½–26", p. 469

130 Barrow's Goldeneye ♀, 16½–20″, p. 470

131 Common Goldeneye ♀, 16–20″, p. 471

132　Lesser Scaup ♀, 15–18½″, p. 410

133　Greater Scaup ♀, 15½–20″, p. 411

134   Ring-necked Duck   ♀, 14½–18″, p. 427

135   Wood Duck   ♀, 17–20½″, p. 472

136   Redhead ♀, 18–22″, p. 428

137   Canvasback ♀, 19½–24″, p.428

138 Black Scoter ♀, 17–20½″, p. 366

139 Oldsquaw ♀, 19–22½″, p. 494

140   White-winged Scoter ♀, 19–23½″, p. 367

141   Surf Scoter ♀, 17–21″, p. 368

142   Spectacled Eider ♀, 20½–22″, p. 496

143   Bufflehead ♀, 13–15½″, p. 469

144 King Eider ♀, 18½–25″, p. 495

145 Common Eider ♀, 23–27″, p. 365

146　Mallard ♀, 20½–28″, p. 431

147　Gadwall ♀, 18½–23″, p. 440

148　Pintail ♀, 20½–22½″, p. 439

149　American Wigeon ♀, 18–23″, p. 435

150 Green-winged Teal ♀, 12½–15½″, p. 437

151 Northern Shoveler ♀, 17–20″, p. 429

152 Cinnamon Teal ♀, 14½–17″, p. 434

153 Blue-winged Teal ♀, 14½–16″, p. 436

154   White Pelican non-breeding plumage, p. 474

155   Brown Pelican, 45–54″, p. 399

156 Whistling Swan, 47–58″, p. 412

157 Trumpeter Swan, 60–72″, p. 441

158   Ross' Goose, 21–25½", p. 442

159   Snow Goose white phase, 25–31", p. 443

160 Emperor Goose, 26–28″, p. 369

161 Snow Goose blue phase, 25–31″, p. 443

162   Canada Goose, 22–45″, p. 444

163   White-fronted Goose imm., 26–34″, p. 445

164 Brant, 23–26″, p. 370

165 White-fronted Goose, 26–34″, p. 445

166   Red-throated Loon, 24–27″, p. 371

167   Arctic Loon, 23–29″, p. 371

168   Yellow-billed Loon, 33–38″, p. 497

169   Common Loon, 28–36″, p. 475

170   Arctic Loon winter plumage, 23–29″, p. 371

171   Red-throated Loon winter plumage, 24–27″, p. 371

172 Yellow-billed Loon winter plumage, p. 497

173 Common Loon winter plumage, 28–36″, p. 475

174   Western Grebe, 22–29″, p. 476

175   Red-necked Grebe, 18–22″, p. 477

176 Pied-billed Grebe, 12–15″, p. 478

177 Pied-billed Grebe, immature, 12–15″, p. 478

178 Eared Grebe winter plumage, 12–14″, p. 479

179 Horned Grebe winter plumage, 12–15¼″, p. 480

180   Eared Grebe, 12–14″, p. 479

181   Horned Grebe, 12–15¼″, p. 480

Sandpiper-like Birds

This is a large group of small to medium-sized birds that have long legs and slender bills and are usually seen foraging on the beach or along the margins of lakes, ponds, marshes, or streams. Although these birds are collectively called "shorebirds," a few, such as the Killdeer, are often found on bare ground, far from water. Many of these birds are cryptically colored, but some, like the American Oystercatcher and the avocets and stilts, are boldly patterned in black-and-white.

182   Snowy Plover, 6–7″, p. 372

183   Semipalmated Plover, 6½–8″, p. 373

184   Killdeer, 9–11″, p. 481

185 Ruddy Turnstone, 8–10″, p. 400

186 Ruddy Turnstone, 8–10″, p. 400

187 Killdeer displaying, 9–11″, p. 481

188   Dunlin, 8–9″, p. 374

189   American Golden Plover, 9½–11″, p. 756

190   Black-bellied Plover, 10½–13½″, p. 758

191　Solitary Sandpiper, 7½–9″, p. 481

192　Spotted Sandpiper, 7½–8″, p. 482

193　Sanderling, 7–8¾″, p. 374

194   Western Sandpiper, 6–7″, p. 759

195   Least Sandpiper, 5–6½″, p. 498

196   Semipalmated Sandpiper, 5½–6¾″, p. 499

197   Baird's Sandpiper, 7–7½″, p. 759

198   Pectoral Sandpiper, 8–9½″, p. 483

199   Sharp-tailed Sandpiper, 8¼″, p. 375

200   Wilson's Phalarope imm., 8–10″, p. 445

201   Red Phalarope, 7½–9″, p. 376

202   Northern Phalarope, 6½–8″, p. 377

203   Wilson's Phalarope ♀, 8–10″, p. 445

204   Red Phalarope ♀, 7½–9″, p. 376

205   Northern Phalarope ♀, 6½–8″, p. 377

206   Lesser Yellowlegs, 9½–11″, p. 688

207   Greater Yellowlegs, 12½–15″, p. 688

208   Upland Sandpiper, 11–12½″, p. 528

209   Lesser Yellowlegs, 9½–11″, p. 688

210   Marbled Godwit, 16–20″, p. 528

211   Rock Sandpiper, 8–9″, p. 401

212   Short-billed Dowitcher, 10½–12″, p. 413

213   Long-billed Dowitcher, 11–12½″, p. 500

214   Common Snipe, 10½–11½″, p. 446

215 Willet, 14–17", p. 447

216 Whimbrel, 15–18¾", p. 760

217 Long-billed Curlew, 20–26", p. 529

218   Black Oystercatcher, 17–17½″, p. 402

219   Black-necked Stilt, 13–16″, p. 448

220   American Avocet, 15½–20″, p. 448

221 Black Turnstone, 9″, p. 403

222 Surfbird, 10″, p. 403

223 Red Knot, 10–11″, p. 762

224   Surfbirds winter plumage, 10″, p. 403

225   Black Turnstone winter plumage, 9″, p. 403

226   Wandering Tattler winter plumage, p. 404

227 Surfbirds, 10″, p. 403

228 Semipalmated Sandpiper winter plumage, p. 499

229 Sanderling winter plumage, 7-8¾″, p. 374

230 Red Knot imm., 10–11", p. 762

231 Dunlin winter plumage, 8–9", p. 374

232 Spotted Sandpiper winter plumage, p. 482

233 Mountain Plover winter plumage, 8–9½", p. 576

234 Black-bellied Plover winter plumage, p. 758

235 American Golden Plover winter plumage, p. 756

236 Red Phalarope winter plumage, p. 376

237 Northern Phalarope winter plumage, p. 377

238 Wilson's Phalarope winter plumage, p. 445

239   Long-billed Dowitcher winter plumage, p. 500

240   Willet winter plumage, p. 447

241   American Avocet winter plumage, p. 448

Chicken-like Marsh Birds

These are small to medium-sized marsh birds, most of which keep themselves well concealed in the reeds or marsh grasses. The bill may be long and slender, as in the Clapper Rail or Virginia Rail, or stubby and chicken-like, as in the Sora. The two gallinules, allied to the modestly plumaged rails that make up the rest of this group, are more often seen in the open and are more brightly colored.

242　Virginia Rail, 8½–10½″, p. 449

243　Clapper Rail, 14–16½″, p. 413

244 Yellow Rail, 6–7½″, p. 450

245 Sora, 8–9¾″, p. 451

246   Common Gallinule, 12–14¼", p. 452

247   Black Rail, 5–6", p. 414

Upland Ground Birds

This group contains the familiar game birds—grouse, quails and pheasants— as well as certain other cryptically colored birds of woodlands, such as the woodcocks, snipe, and the nightjars. Many of these birds are difficult to detect against a background of dead leaves or grass until they flush unexpectedly into the air.

248 Whip-poor-will, 9–10″, p. 634

249 Poor-will, 7–8½″, p. 606

250   Common Nighthawk   ♀, 8½–10″, p. 530

251   Lesser Nighthawk   ♀, 8–9″, p. 504

252 Sharp-tailed Grouse displaying, 15–20″, p. 531

253 Sage Grouse displaying, 26–30″, p. 606

254   Greater Prairie Chicken displaying, 17–18″, p. 531

255   Lesser Prairie Chicken d

256   Sharp-tailed Grouse, 15–20″, p. 531

257   Sage Grouse ♀, 26–30″, p. 606

258   Greater Prairie Chicken, 17–18″, p. 531

259   Lesser Prairie Chicken, 16–18″, p. 532

260   Blue Grouse displaying, 15½–21″, p. 689

261   Blue Grouse , 15½–21″, p. 689

262 Spruce Grouse, 15–17″, p. 690

263 Ruffed Grouse, 16–19″, p. 635

264   Roadrunner, 20–24″, p. 504

265   Ring-necked Pheasant ♀, 21–25″, p. 576

266 Turkey ♂, ♀ , p. 620

267 Ring-necked Pheasant, 30–36″, p. 576

268 Willow Ptarmigan fall plumage, 15–17″, p. 763

269 Willow Ptarmigan summer plumage, 15–17″, p. 7

270 Willow Ptarmigan winter plumage, 15–17″, p. 763

272   Rock Ptarmigan, 13–14″, p. 764

273   White-tailed Ptarmigan, 12–13″, p. 568

274 Rock Ptarmigan winter plumage, 13–14″, p. 764

275 White-tailed Ptarmigan winter plumage, p. 568

276   Gambel's Quail ♀, ♂, 10–11½″, p. 505

277   Mountain Quail, 10½–11½″, p. 594

278 California Quail, 9–11″, p. 594

279 California Quail ♀, 9–11″, p. 594

280   Bobwhite ♀, 8½–10½″, p. 533

281   Chukar, 13–15½″, p. 595

282 Bobwhite, 8½–10½″, p. 533

283 Montezuma Quail, 8–9½″, p. 620

284   Scaled Quail, 10–12″, p. 534

285   Gray Partridge, 12–14″, p. 577

Owls

This well-known group of birds scarcely needs a description. They are small to large birds with large round heads, loose, fluffy plumage and disk-like faces. Many are nocturnal, and are usually seen roosting quietly in trees during the day, but a few, such as the all-white Snowy Owl or the Short-eared Owl, often hunt by day and may be seen in open country.

286 Screech Owl red phase, 7–10″, p. 621

287 Screech Owl gray phase, 7–10″, p. 621

288 Great Horned Owl, 18–25″, p. 635

289 Long-eared Owl, 13–16″, p. 636

290　Great Gray Owl, 24–33″, p. 691

291　Short-eared Owl, 13–17″, p. 452

292   Hawk-Owl, 14½–17½", p. 692

293   Spotted Owl, 16½–19", p. 693

294   Elf Owl, 5–6″, p. 506

295   Pygmy Owl, 7–7½″, p. 693

296 Ferruginous Owl, 6½–7″, p. 507

297 Flammulated Owl, 6–7″, p. 694

298 Saw-whet Owl, 7–8½″, p. 695

299 Saw-whet Owl imm. 7–8½″, p. 695

300 Boreal Owl, 8½–12″, p. 696

301 Burrowing Owl, 9–11″, p. 534

302   Barn Owl, 14–20″, p. 535

303   Snowy Owl, 20–27″, p. 765

Hawk-like Birds

The hawks and their allies range in size from the American Kestrel, scarcely larger than a Blue Jay, to the huge eagles and vultures. All have sharply hooked bills for tearing their prey, and many are often seen soaring high in the air. The wings may be rounded, as in the Red-tailed and Sharp-shinned Hawks, or pointed, as in the falcons and some of the kites.

304 Osprey, 21–24½″, p. 484

305 Caracara, 21–25″, p. 507

306 Black Vulture, 23–27″, p. 536

307 Turkey Vulture, 26–32″, p. 537

308 Swainson's Hawk, 19–22″, p. 538

309 Gyrfalcon black phase, 20–25″, p. 378

310 Rough-legged Hawk, 19–24″, p. 765

311 Harris' Hawk, 17½–29″, p. 508

312   Red-shouldered Hawk, 17–24″, p. 637

313   Red-shouldered Hawk imm., 17–24″, p. 637

314 Red-tailed Hawk, 19–25″, p. 538

315 Ferruginous Hawk, 22½–25″, p. 539

316   Rough-legged Hawk light phase, 19–24″, p. 765

317   Marsh Hawk, 17½–24″, p. 453

318 Gyrfalcon white phase, 20–25″, p. 378

319 White-tailed Kite, 15–17″, p. 540

320 Prairie Falcon, 17–20″, p. 776

321 Peregrine Falcon imm., 15–21″, p. 776

322 Aplomado Falcon, 15–18″, p. 541

323 Peregrine Falcon, 15–21″, p. 776

324   Sharp-shinned Hawk, 10–14″, p. 696

325   Sharp-shinned Hawk imm., 10–14″, p. 696

326 Goshawk, 20–26″, p. 697

327 Cooper's Hawk ♀, 14–20″, p. 638

328   Merlin ♀, 10–13½″, p. 698

329   Merlin imm., 10–13½″, p. 698

330 American Kestrel, 9–12″, p. 542

331 American Kestrel, ♀, ♂, 9–12″, p. 542

332   Golden Eagle, 30–41″, p. 543

333   Bald Eagle imm., 30–43″, p. 485

334 Osprey, 21–24½″, p. 484

335 Bald Eagle, 30–43″, p. 485

336 Turkey Vulture, 26–32″, p. 537

337 California Condor, 45–55″, p. 777

338   Black Vulture, 23–27″, p. 536

339   Black Hawk, 20–23″, p. 638

340   Gray Hawk, 16–18″, p. 639

341   Zone-tailed Hawk, 18½–21½″, p. 640

342   Red-tailed Hawk, 19–25″, p. 538

343   Swainson's Hawk, 19–22″, p. 538

Pigeon-like Birds

This group includes the familiar Rock Dove or city pigeon and its allies. These are small to medium-sized birds, small-headed, and clad in soft browns and grays. On the ground they walk with a characteristic mincing gait.

344 Ground Dove, 6–6¾″, p. 509

345 Inca Dove, 7½–8″, p. 584

346 Rock Dove, 13″, p. 584

347 Band-tailed Pigeon, 14–15½″, p. 699

348 White-winged Dove, 11–12½″, p. 510

349 Mourning Dove, 11–13″, p. 544

350 Ringed Turtle Dove, 10–12″, p. 585

351 Spotted Dove, 13″, p. 585

Swallow-like Birds

Included here are the swallows and martins and the similar but unrelated swifts. These are small birds that spend most of their time in the air, flying gracefully about in pursuit of their insect prey. They have pointed wings and often gather in large flocks.

352   Barn Swallow, 5¾–7¾″, p. 778

353   Cliff Swallow, 5–6″, p. 779

354 Rough-winged Swallow, 5–5¾", p. 486

355 Bank Swallow, 4¾–5½", p. 486

356 Tree Swallow, 5–6″, p. 487

357 Violet-green Swallow, 5–5½″, p. 700

358 Purple Martin, 7¼–8½″, p. 701

359 Purple Martin ♀, 7¼–8½″, p. 701

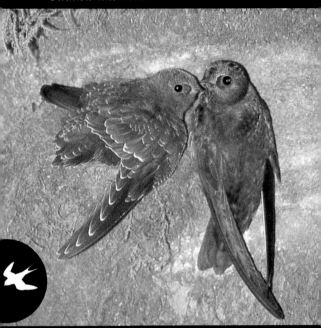

360   Black Swift, 7–7½″, p. 781

361   Chimney Swift, 4¾–5½″, p. 641

Tree-clinging Birds

The woodpeckers, nuthatches, and creepers are usually seen climbing about on the trunks of trees, in search of insects hidden in the bark. Most of the woodpeckers are clad in black-and-white, although a few, like the Common Flicker, are mainly brown. The nuthatches are soft gray above and whitish or rusty below, and the creepers are brown and streaked.

362   Downy Woodpecker ♀, 6–7″, p. 641

363   Hairy Woodpecker ♀, 8½–10½″, p. 702

364 Downy Woodpecker, 6–7″, p. 641

365 Hairy Woodpecker, 8½–10½″, p. 702

366 Ladder-backed Woodpecker ♀, 6–7½″, p. 510

367 Nuttall's Woodpecker ♀, 7–7½″, p. 623

368 Ladder-backed Woodpecker, 6–7½″, p. 510

369 Nuttall's Woodpecker, 7–7½″, p. 623

370   Common ("Red-shafted") Flicker, 12½–14″, p. 642

371   Common ("Red-shafted") Flicker ♀, p. 642

372 Common ("Yellow-shafted") Flicker, p. 642

373 Common ("Gilded") Flicker, 12½–14", p. 642

374   Golden-fronted Woodpecker, 8½–10½″, p. 643

375   Gila Woodpecker, 8–10″, p. 511

376 Acorn Woodpecker, 8–9½″, p. 623

377 Lewis' Woodpecker, 10½–11½″, p. 624

378 "Red-naped Sapsucker," 8–9", p. 644

379 "Red-breasted Sapsucker," 8–9", p. 644

380 Arizona Woodpecker, 7–8″, p. 625

381 Pileated Woodpecker, 16–19½″, p. 703

382   Northern Three-toed Woodpecker, 8–9½″, p. 704

383   Black-backed Three-toed Woodpecker, p. 705

384 Williamson's Sapsucker, 9½", p. 706

385 White-headed Woodpecker ♀ 9" p. 706

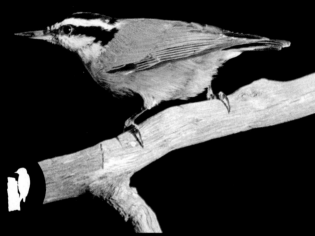

386 Red-breasted Nuthatch, 4½–4¾″, p. 707

387 White-breasted Nuthatch, 5–6″, p. 708

388   Brown Creeper, 5–5¾″, p. 709

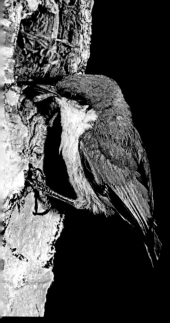

389   Pygmy Nuthatch, 3¾–4½″, p. 709

Hummingbirds

 These tiny to small perching birds have rather short tails and long, thin bills. Metallic, flashy colors are displayed especially on head and throat (*gorget*) of male. Their display flights are often spectacular. Flying with a hum of fast-beating wings, they move forward or backward with equal ease. They hover over flowers, sucking nectar and taking insects from the flower, and they defend food sources with noisy calls and much chasing about.

390   Allen's Hummingbird, 3–3½″, p. 596

391   Rufous Hummingbird, 3–4″, p. 710

392 Allen's Hummingbird, 3–3½″, p. 596

393 Broad-tailed Hummingbird, 4–4½″, p. 568

394   Broad-billed Hummingbird, 3¼–4″, p. 512

395   Rivoli's Hummingbird, 4½–5½″, p. 645

396 Blue-throated Hummingbird, 4½–5″, p. 646

398 Black-chinned Hummingbird, 3¼–3¾", p. 569

399 Anna's Hummingbird, 3½–4", p. 597

400 Calliope Hummingbird, 2¾–4″, p. 711

401 Costa's Hummingbird, 3–3½″, p. 513

402 Broad-tailed Hummingbird ♀, 4–4½″, p. 568

403 Blue-throated Hummingbird ♀, 4½–5″, p. 646

404   Rivoli's Hummingbird imm. ♂, p. 645

405   Broad-billed Hummingbird ♀ 3¼–4″ p. 512

406 Rufous Hummingbird ♀, 3–4″, p. 710

407 Calliope Hummingbird ♀, 2¾–4″, p. 711

Perching Birds

This very large group includes nearly all of the songbirds, as well as cuckoos, kingfishers and hummingbirds, which, while unrelated, resemble songbirds rather closely. They range in size from the three- or four-inch hummingbirds and kinglets, to the large crows and ravens. They occur in a great variety of habitats and show an even greater variety of patterns and colors.

408   American Goldfinch, 4½–5½″, p. 578

409   Wilson's Warbler, 4½″, p. 648

410   Yellow Warbler ♀, 4½–5¼″, p. 649

411   MacGillivray's Warbler, 4¾–5½″, p. 650

412   Nashville Warbler, 4–5″, p. 651

413   Yellow-breasted Chat, 6½–7½″, p. 652

414 Yellow-rumped ("Audubon's") Warbler, p. 714

415 Townsend's Warbler, 4¼–5″, p. 715

416 Hermit Warbler, 4½″, p. 716

417 Lesser Goldfinch, 3½–4″, p. 544

418 Lawrence's Goldfinch, 4–4½″, p. 653

419 Common Yellowthroat, 4½–5¾″, p. 454

420   Tropical Kingbird, 8–9½″, p. 654

421   Western Kingbird, 8–9″, p. 545

422   Verdin, 4–4½″, p. 514

423 Western Meadowlark, 8½–11″, p. 547

424 Eastern Meadowlark, 8½–11″, p. 548

425 Yellow Wagtail, 6½″, p. 766

426 Evening Grosbeak, 7–8½", p. 717

427 Scott's Oriole, 7½–8¼", p. 614

428 Yellow-headed Blackbird, 8–11", p. 455

429 Evening Grosbeak ♀, 7–8½", p. 717

430 American Goldfinch ♀, 4½–5½", p. 578

432   Hepatic Tanager ♀, 7–8″, p. 719

433   Summer Tanager ♀, 7½–7¾″, p. 656

434   Western Tanager ♀, 6–7½″, p. 719

435   Hooded Oriole ♀, 7–7¾", p. 586

436   Northern ("Bullock's") Oriole ♀, 7–8½", p. 657

437   Scott's Oriole ♀, 7½–8¼", p. 614

438   American Redstart ♀, 4½–5¾″, p. 658

439   Wilson's Warbler ♀, 4½″, p. 648

440   Common Yellowthroat ♀, 4½–5¾″, p. 454

441 American Redstart, 4½–5¾", p. 658

442 Rufous-sided Towhee, 7–8½", p. 598

443 Black-headed Grosbeak, 6½–7¾", p. 659

444 Varied Thrush, 9–10″, p. 720

445 American Robin, 9–11″, p. 587

446 Northern ("Bullock's") Oriole, 7–8½″, p. 657

447 Hooded Oriole, 7–7¾″, p. 586

448   Cardinal, 7½–9″, p. 660

449   Summer Tanager, 7½–7¾″, p. 656

450   Hepatic Tanager, 7–8″, p. 719

451 Vermilion Flycatcher, 5½–6½", p. 516

452 Red Crossbill, 5¼–6½", p. 721

453 White-winged Crossbill, 6–6¾", p. 722

454 Western Tanager, 6–7½″, p. 719

455 Summer Tanager imm. ♂, molting, p. 656

456 Painted Redstart, 5″, p. 626

457 Coppery-tailed Trogon, 11–12", p. 660

458 Red-faced Warbler, 5¼", p. 723

459 Gray-crowned Rosy Finch, 5¾–6¼", p. 571

460   House Finch, 5–5¾", p. 588

461   Purple Finch, 5½–6¼", p. 723

462   Cassin's Finch, 6–6½", p. 724

463 Common Redpoll, 5–5½″, p. 769

464 Hoary Redpoll, 5–5½″, p. 770

465 Brown-capped Rosy Finch, 5¾–6½″, p. 572

466　Pine Grosbeak, 8–10″, p. 725

467　Cardinal ♀, 7½–9″, p. 660

468　Pyrrhuloxia, 7½–8″, p. 517

469   Scissor-tailed Flycatcher, 11–15″, p. 548

470   Clark's Nutcracker, 12–13″, p. 726

471   Gray Jay, 10–13″, p. 727

472 Loggerhead Shrike, 8–10″, p. 549

473 Northern Shrike, 9–10¾″, p. 728

474 Eastern Kingbird, 8–9″, p. 550

475 Mockingbird, 9–11", p. 589

476 Townsend's Solitaire, 8–9½", p. 729

477 Gray Catbird, 8–9¼", p. 661

478   Virginia's Warbler, 4–4¼", p. 626

479   Yellow-eyed ("Mexican") Junco, 5½–6½", p. 730

480   Gray-headed Junco, 5½–6", p. 730

481 Pine Grosbeak ♀, 8–10″, p. 725

482 Wheatear, 5½–6″, p. 770

483 Dark-eyed ("Oregon") Junco, 5–6¼″, p. 731

484 Wrentit, 6–6½″, p. 599

485 Bushtit, 3¾–4″, p. 662

486 Plain Titmouse, 5–5½″, p. 627

487   Black-capped Chickadee, 4¾–5¾″, p 663

488   Mountain Chickadee, 5–5¾″, p. 733

490   Gray Flycatcher, 5½″, p. 607

491   Phainopepla ♀, 7–7¾″, p. 517

492   Dipper, 7–8½″, p. 488

493 Rose-throated Becard, 6″, p. 664

494 Black-tailed Gnatcatcher, 4½–5″, p. 518

495 Blue-gray Gnatcatcher, 4–5″, p. 628

496 Mountain Bluebird, 6½–8″, p. 734

497 Mountain Bluebird ♀, 6½–8″, p. 734

498 Blue Grosbeak, 6–7½″, p. 665

499 Bluethroat, 4¾″, p. 772

500 Western Bluebird, 6–7″, p. 629

501 Lazuli Bunting, 5–5½″, p. 666

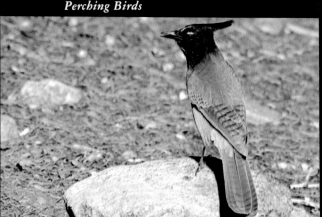

502　Steller's Jay, 12–13½″, p. 735

503　Belted Kingfisher, 11–14½″, p. 488

504　Belted Kingfisher ♀, 11–14½″, p. 488

505 Scrub Jay, 11–13″, p. 630

506 Mexican Jay, 11½–13″, p. 631

507 Pinyon Jay, 9–11¾″, p. 615

508   Bell's Vireo, 4¼–5″, p. 667

509   Golden-crowned Kinglet, 3¼–4″, p. 735

510   Ruby-crowned Kinglet, 3¾–4½″, p. 736

511   Orange-crowned Warbler, 4½–5½″, p. 668

512   Tennessee Warbler, 4½–5″, p. 738

513   Western Wood Pewee, 6–6½″, p. 740

514   Warbling Vireo, 4½–5½″, p. 669

515   Red-eyed Vireo, 5½–6½″, p. 670

516   Solitary Vireo, 5–6″, p. 670

517 Hammond's Flycatcher, 5–5½″, p. 740

518 Willow Flycatcher, 5¼–6¾″, p. 672

519 Alder Flycatcher, 5¼–6″, p. 673

520 Wied's Crested Flycatcher, 8½–9½", p. 519

521 Say's Phoebe, 7–8", p. 782

522 Painted Bunting ♀, 5–5½", p. 674

523 Green Kingfisher ♀, 7–8½″, p. 489

524 Green-tailed Towhee, 6¼–7″, p. 600

525 Painted Bunting, 5–5½″, p. 674

526 Bewick's Wren, 5–5½″, p. 675

527 Winter Wren, 4–4½″, p. 741

528 Long-billed Marsh Wren, 4–5½″, p. 456

529　House Wren, 4½–5″, p. 676

530　Canyon Wren, 5½–5¾″, p. 783

531　Rock Wren, 5–6″, p. 784

532   Cactus Wren, 7–8¾″, p. 520

533   Sage Thrasher, 8–9″, p. 608

534   Bendire's Thrasher, 9–11″, p. 531

535 Curve-billed Thrasher, 9½–11½″, p. 521

536 California Thrasher, 11–13″, p. 600

537 Le Conte's Thrasher, 10–11″, p. 522

538   Swainson's Thrush, 6½–7¾″, p. 676

539   Gray-cheeked Thrush, 7–8″, p. 742

540   Veery, 6½–7¾″, p. 677

541 Hermit Thrush, 6½–8″, p. 743

542 Northern Waterthrush, 5½–6½″, p. 678

543 American Robin imm., 9–11″, p. 587

544   Boreal Chickadee, 5–5½″, p. 744

545   Chestnut-backed Chickadee, 4½–5″, p. 744

546   Dusky Flycatcher, 5¼–6″, p. 601

547 Olive-sided Flycatcher, 7–8″, p. 745

548 Ash-throated Flycatcher, 7½–8½″, p. 615

549 Western Flycatcher, 5½–6″, p. 746

550   Blue Grosbeak ♀, 6–7½″, p. 665

551   Vermilion Flycatcher ♀, 5½–6½″, p. 516

552   Yellow-rumped ("Audubon's") Warbler ♀, p. 71

553   Red Crossbill ♀, 5¼–6½″, p. 721

554   White-winged Crossbill ♀, 6–6¾″, p. 722

555   Starling imm., 7½–8½″, p. 590

556 Yellow-headed Blackbird ♀, 8–11″, p. 455

557 Red-winged Blackbird ♀, 7–9½″, p. 456

558 Brown-headed Cowbird ♀, 6–8″, p. 679

559 Bronzed Cowbird ♀, 6½–8¾″, p. 579

560 Brewer's Blackbird ♀, 8–10″, p. 551

561 Rusty Blackbird ♀, 8½–9¾″, p. 747

562 Yellow-billed Cuckoo, 11–13½″, p. 680

563 Brown Towhee, 8–10″, p. 602

564 Abert's Towhee, 8–9″, p. 524

565 Bohemian Waxwing, 7½–9″, p. 747

566 Cedar Waxwing, 6½–8″, p. 748

567 Pyrrhuloxia ♀, 7½–8″, p. 517

568　Grasshopper Sparrow, 4½–5″, p. 552

569　Savannah Sparrow, 4½–5¾″, p. 555

570　Lark Bunting ♀, 6–7½″, p. 556

571   Water Pipit, 6–7″, p. 572

572   Fox Sparrow, 6–7¼″, p. 680

573   Song Sparrow, 5–7″, p. 681

574   Skylark, 7–7½″, p. 580

575   Vesper Sparrow, 5–6½″, p. 609

576   Lapland Longspur ♀, 6–7″, p. 502

577 Lark Sparrow, 5½–6¾", p. 557

578 Clay-colored Sparrow, 5–5½", p. 558

579 Snow Bunting ♀, winter plumage, p. 772

580   House Sparrow ♀, 5¾–6¼″, p. 592

581   Bobolink ♀, 6–8″, p. 558

582   Black-headed Grosbeak ♀, 6½–7¾″, p. 659

583 Purple Finch ♀, 5½–6¼", p. 723

584 Cassin's Finch ♀, 6–6½", p. 724

585 House Finch ♀, 5–5¾", p. 588

586   White-crowned Sparrow, 5½–7″, p. 682

587   White-throated Sparrow, 6–7″, p. 749

588   Golden-crowned Sparrow, 6–7″, p. 750

589 Tree Sparrow, 5½–6½", p. 581

590 Chipping Sparrow, 5–5¾", p. 751

592   House Sparrow, 5¾–6¼″, p. 592

593   Black-throated Sparrow, 4¾–5½″, p. 524

594   Harris' Sparrow, 7–7¾″, p. 751

595 McCown's Longspur, 5¾–6", p. 559

596 Smith's Longspur, 5¼–6½", p. 773

597 Chestnut-collared Longspur, 5½–6½", p. 560

598 Pine Siskin, 4½–5¼″, p. 752

599 Lincoln's Sparrow, 5–6″, p. 683

600 Brewer's Sparrow, 5″, p. 609

601 Black-chinned Sparrow, 5–5½", p. 604

602 Sage Sparrow, 5–6", p. 610

603 Horned Lark, 7–8", p. 561

604   McKay's Bunting, 7″, p. 774

605   Snow Bunting, 6–7¼″, p. 772

606　Lark Bunting, 6–7½″, p. 556

607　Bobolink, 6–8″, p. 558

608 Black-throated Gray Warbler, 4½–5″, p. 617

609 Blackpoll Warbler, 5–5¾″, p. 753

610   Black Phoebe, 6–7″, p. 490

611   Starling, 7½–8½″, p. 590

612   Yellow-headed Blackbird, 8–11″, p. 455

613   Phainopepla, 7–7¾″, p. 517

614　Red-winged Blackbird, 7–9½″, p. 456

615　Tricolored Blackbird, 7½–9″, p. 457

616   Yellow-billed Magpie, 16–18″, p. 563

617   Black-billed Magpie, 17½–22″, p. 564

618 Common Grackle, 11–13½″, p. 684

619 Great-tailed Grackle, 16–17″, p. 564

620   Brown-headed Cowbird, 6–8″, p. 679

621   Bronzed Cowbird, 6½–8¾″, p. 579

622   Brewer's Blackbird, 8–10″, p. 551

623   Rusty Blackbird, 8½–9¾″, p. 747

624 Northwestern Crow, 16–17″, p. 754

625 Common Crow, 17–21″, p. 685

626 Common Raven, 21½–27″, p. 685

627 White-necked Raven, 19–21″, p. 526

Part II
Habitat Key

The number preceding each species
description in the following pages
corresponds to the number of the
illustration in the color plates section.
If the description has no number there
is no color plate but in that case a
drawing accompanies the description.

Open Ocean

Pelagic waters, not visible from the coast. The waters off the coast cover the Continental Shelf and are therefore relatively shallow and well lit and yield much plankton, which provides food for fish, seabirds, or fish-eating seabirds. Truly pelagic birds spend their lives on the open ocean and do not return to land—even at night—except during the breeding season, when they seek out islands and undisturbed headlands for nesting. The birds treated in this section may nest in areas remote from North America and are attracted to our coasts by the rich food supply in the cold, California current. Other birds, including gulls, cormorants, alcids, and petrels, also feed in these waters but are treated in the Sea Cliff or Seashore habitat, where they are more commonly encountered.

25, 73   **Northern Fulmar**
"Fulmar"
(*Fulmarus glacialis*)
Shearwaters (Procellariidae)

Description: 17–20" (43–51 cm). Resembles a
medium-sized gull, but *stockier*.
Rounded yellow bill with fused tube-like
nostrils. Sexes look alike. There are two
color phases. *Light phase: head and
underparts white;* otherwise light gray
above. Legs vary, but are never pink.
Dark phase: overall smoky gray with light
patch at base of primaries visible in
flight.

Voice: A grunting *kek kek kek*. Usually silent
on winter grounds.

Habitat: Open ocean.

Nesting: 1 white egg; in colonies on sea cliffs
along the Arctic coasts, where the
greatest concentrations of seabirds in
the Northern Hemisphere occur.

Range: Circumpolar on Arctic coasts. In winter
along the Pacific Coast south
occasionally to Baja California.

The Northern Fulmar is stockier than
its shearwater relatives and seems to
have somewhat shorter wings, but the
stiff-winged flight of both is similar.
The fulmar's flight pattern, several flaps
and a glide, banking and skimming in
stiff-winged fashion low over the water,
is quite different from the steadier
flapping of the gull. This buoyant
swimmer has pushed its breeding
stations southward in the North
Atlantic to Canada and the British
Isles, responding to increased human
activity in those areas. Fulmars
consume offal and follow whaling ships
for spoils of blubber and flesh. Formerly
called "Fulmar."

Ross' Gull
(*Rhodostethia rosea*)
Gulls (Laridae)

Description: 11–14″ (28–36 cm). Small gull with short bill. About the size of Bonaparte's Gull. Distinguished by its *wedge-shaped tail*. Adults have white underparts and pale gray wings (darker gray below) with white trailing edge, lacking black wing tips. In breeding plumage, *pinkish body with thin black collar and red legs.* Nonbreeding adults have white body, gray wings and may not have black collar. Immatures similar to immature Kittiwakes, with black "M" on upper surface of wings, but lack dusky nape band of Kittiwakes and have wedge-shaped tail. Buoyant, tern-like flight.

Voice: Various melodious cries, described as *a-wo, a-wo a-wo, claw-claw-claw,* and in alarm, *via, via, via.* On the whole, higher-pitched than those of other gulls.

Habitat: Arctic waters, especially amid drift ice.

Nesting: 3 olive green eggs with brown spots, in a nest of grass, twigs, and lichens on boggy tundra; in small colonies. Other water birds nest close by, probably attracted by the protection that noisy gulls offer.

Range: Northeastern Siberia. Winters in Arctic Ocean north of the U.S.S.R., Alaska, Canada, and Greenland.

In early fall these gulls migrate in large numbers through the coastal waters north of Alaska; nonbreeding birds have been seen near the North Pole. In summer this species includes insects in its diet; in winter it feeds mostly on various small fish and crustaceans.

30 Sabine's Gull
(*Xema sabini*)
Gulls (Laridae)

Description: 13–14" (33–36 cm). Small gull, with gray mantle, white body and *forked white tail.* In summer, head of adult slate gray. *Black outer primaries,* and *white triangle in midwing* create a striking pattern in flight. Bill black with yellow tip, feet black. Winter adults and juveniles lack dark head. Juveniles retain the pattern of adult plumage, but have pale brown mantle and black, triangular terminal band on tail.

Voice: A single loud, harsh grating note, described as *kier.*

Habitat: Wet tundra during breeding season; a bird of the open ocean when not breeding.

Nesting: 3 olive, brown-spotted eggs in a scanty grass nest; mostly in colonies.

Range: The extreme High Arctic tundra in North America as well as in Siberia. On migration, fairly common off the west coast, rarely recorded inland. Winters on the open ocean at tropical latitudes.

In flight the Sabine's Gull resembles a tern in that it seldom sails, and it swoops down, in the fashion of a tern, to pick food from the surface of a marsh. It runs around on mud flats like a shorebird.

46 Arctic Tern
(*Sterna paradisaea*)
Gulls (Laridae)

Description: 14–17" (36–43 cm). Back and wings gray, face and underparts white, and cap black. Primaries edged with dusky, blackish color (lacking in Forster's Tern) form thin dark line on trailing edge of wing. Adults after breeding have dusky black behind eyes and on nape, but white lores and forehead. In all plumages similar to Common Tern, but shorter-necked, with a round-headed appearance and shorter legs. Thin dark trailing edge of the primaries and the translucent "windows" formed by the flight feathers help identify an Arctic Tern overhead. Arctic Terns have *a wholly red bill*, whereas the other two, more southern species have a black bill tip. Aleutian Tern is darker gray but has a black bill and white forehead the year round.

Voice: A high-pitched *kik-kik-kik*.

Habitat: Rocky shores with coves, islets with sandbanks, and other sheltered areas, but also tundra marshes.

Nesting: 2 light olive, irregularly spotted eggs in a scrape, which may be lined with dry vegetation; in colonies or in single pairs.

Range: High Arctic seabird, circumpolar on all northern shores facing the North Pole; extends south with cold currents to the Aleutian Islands and southeastern shore of Alaska and to Massachusetts in the East. To avoid the dark northern winter these terns undertake a tremendous migration well offshore to the cold-water zone near Antarctica.

Their harsh, rasping, high-pitched cry makes the ternery a noisy place. All members assemble to mob an intruder. The nests and eggs left unattended during an attack are so well camouflaged that a predator is not likely to find them. These terns attack so fiercely that a human observer has to protect himself in the colonies.

---

58 **Skua**
(*Catharacta skua*)
Jaegers (Stercorariidae)

Description: 20–22″ (51–56 cm). About as long as Pomarine Jaeger, but much larger and stockier with short, broad, wedge-shaped (not elongated) tail. Adults and juveniles resemble a stocky juvenile Western Gull: *overall dark brown,* but with bill heavier and more hooked than in a gull. In light phase, body gray-brown, head pale. A central band of *white across base of primaries* is visible on the open wings.

Voice: A scream transcribed as *skerr;* on the breeding ground it utters another call, *uk uk uk.* Otherwise silent.

Habitat: Open ocean when visiting the Pacific Coast.

Nesting: 2 or 3 brown-blotched eggs in a scrape; nests in the vicinity of other skuas but not in dense colonies.

Range: Uniquely bipolar. One population nests on the coasts of northern Europe, several others on and around Antarctica. Visitors to the North Pacific Coast come from the Antarctic continent. Many believe that these "South Polar Skuas" are a species distinct from the North Atlantic breeders.

At sea off the North American coasts it robs other seabirds of their prey. On its southern breeding grounds it is a coastal scavenger and preys on seabird eggs and young. This large bird is deceptively fast; it can outfly any gull and often forces it to drop or disgorge its food.

63 Least Storm-Petrel
"Least Petrel"
(*Halocyptena microsoma*)
Storm-Petrels (Hydrobatidae)

Description: 5½–6" (14–15 cm). Sparrow-sized seabird. Long wings; *short wedge-shaped tail.* Black overall, including bill and feet. Flies with strong deep wingbeats.

Voice: A harsh, scraping 7-noted call is given on breeding grounds. Silent at sea.

Habitat: Open ocean; nests on rocky islands.
Nesting: 1 white egg in a crevice on bare rock.
No nest. Nocturnal at nesting colonies.
Range: Breeds on islands off both coasts of Baja
California. Visits southern California
waters in late summer and fall.

All other western black petrels have a
forked tail and are much larger. The
Least Storm-Petrel, formerly called the
"Least Petrel," has a wedge-shaped tail.

---

65 **Pink-footed Shearwater**
(*Puffinus creatopus*)
Shearwaters (Procellariidae)

Description: 20″ (51 cm). Gull-sized. *Dark gray-
brown above, white below;* underwings
white with dark borders. Straw-colored,
black-tipped bill and pink feet.
Voice: Silent except on southern breeding
grounds, where it utters grunts and
moaning calls.
Habitat: Open ocean, seldom seen from the shore.
Nesting: 1 white egg in a burrow; parents
abandon the young before it fledges.
Nocturnal on breeding grounds.
Range: Off the Pacific Coast of North America
in migration; breeds on smaller islands
off the Chilean coast.

Shearwaters occur from spring to fall,
but are seen most commonly in fall,
when thousands congregate at favored
places, such as Monterey Bay or outside
San Francisco's Golden Gate. They fly
close to the water, using several deep
wingbeats followed by a long glide,
searching for surface food such as small
fish and crustaceans. They alight and
dip their bills or even dive.

66 Sooty Shearwater
(*Puffinus griseus*)
Shearwaters (Procellariidae)

Description: 16–18″ (41–46 cm). *Black* except for
pale silvery wing linings seen in flight.

Voice: A din of nasal, squealing, and crooning
notes is heard on the breeding grounds;
otherwise silent.

Habitat: Open oceans, but in stormy weather
they are driven landward, approaching
prominent coastal points, such as Point
Roberts, Washington.

Nesting: 1 white egg in underground burrows.
In large colonies.

Range: From its breeding grounds in
southeastern Australia, New Zealand,
and southern South America to the
North Pacific, where it spends the non-
breeding season and perhaps the first
two years of life. Millions of these birds
migrate or summer off the coast from
Alaska to California.

Although shearwaters feed during
daylight, they are strictly nocturnal in
their breeding colonies. They are the
"Moaning Birds" that sailors on South
Sea islands heard after dusk as the birds
sat outside their burrows and wailed
and yammered in territorial disputes.
Most shearwaters leave their single
offspring before it fledges, but the
chick has been fattened and overfed to
give it the resources necessary to grow,
develop flight feathers, and leave the
colony. Adult and young thus fly north
separately, yet all follow the ancestral
routes to the Pacific Coast.

67 Manx Shearwater
(*Puffinus puffinus*)
Shearwaters (Procellariidae)

Description: 12½–15″ (32–38 cm). Smallest
shearwater among regular visitors to
western American shores. Contrasting

colors: *uniform blackish above, white below, including wing linings.* Bill black, feet pink. The race occurring off the west coast has *black undertail coverts* and was formerly regarded as a separate species: "Black-vented Shearwater."

Voice: Croons noisily in the breeding colony; usually silent at sea.

Habitat: High seas, but often comes close to shore as well.

Nesting: 1 white egg in a burrow or a crevice; no nest. In colonies.

Range: Breeds in the North Atlantic, the Mediterranean, and islands off Baja California; in fall and winter north occasionally to British Columbia.

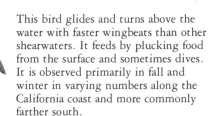

This bird glides and turns above the water with faster wingbeats than other shearwaters. It feeds by plucking food from the surface and sometimes dives. It is observed primarily in fall and winter in varying numbers along the California coast and more commonly farther south.

68 Flesh-footed Shearwater
"Pale-footed Shearwater"
(*Puffinus carneipes*)
Shearwaters (Procellariidae)

Description: 19½" (50 cm). W. 39" (1 m). Largest and stoutest dark-bodied shearwater of the North Pacific. *Sooty black overall;* heavy *straw-colored bill* with dark tip; *feet flesh-colored.*

Voice: High-pitched, reedy squeal. Generally silent away from breeding grounds.

Habitat: Open ocean.

Nesting: 1 white egg in a burrow. In colonies.

Range: Breeds on islands off southwestern Australia, Lord Howe Island, and New Zealand. Visits the North Pacific during summer; seen regularly but not in large numbers off the coast of the Pacific Northwest to British Columbia; more casual off California.

Fishermen report that this shearwater
follows boats for offal and fights over
discarded salmon entrails. Its flight,
like that of other shearwaters, consists
of several quick flaps of the long, stiff
wings followed by a low glide over the
surface of the waves. Formerly called
"Pale-footed Shearwater."

---

69   **Short-tailed Shearwater**
     "Slender-billed Shearwater"
     (*Puffinus tenuirostris*)
     Shearwaters (Procellariidae)

Description: 13–14″ (33–36 cm). Dark shearwater,
appearing black overall, including bill
and feet. Wing linings vary from light
gray brown to dusky, usually lacking
flashing silvery color of those of the
similar Sooty Shearwater. Bill and tail
are smaller than in the Sooty.

Voice: Silent at sea. Hoarse calls heard
sparingly even on the breeding
grounds.

Habitat: High seas.

Nesting: 1 white egg in a rounded chamber at
the end of an excavated burrow up to 5
feet long; in large colonies. All activity
around the nesting colony takes place at
night. The parents thus protect
themselves and their young from gulls,
against whom they have little defense
on land.

Range: Breeds in Tasmania and neighboring
islands off the Australian coast; visits
the northeastern Pacific, where it is
common in the Aleutian, Alaskan, and
British Columbian waters; seen farther
south along the California coast in late
fall, on return migration to its breeding
grounds.

In Tasmania and Australia, the young
of this shearwater are exploited for oil
and meat on the breeding grounds.
(This species is known there as the
"Mutton Bird".) Its post-breeding

migration resembles a great figure 8: first through the Micronesian islands toward Japan, then up to the Alaskan area; in fall it flies southward along the Pacific Coast of North America to central California, and crosses its northward path at the Fiji Islands before returning to Tasmania. Formerly called "Slender-billed Shearwater."

---

70 New Zealand Shearwater
(Puffinus bulleri)
Shearwaters (Procellariidae)

Description: 16½–18″ (42–46 cm). Gull-sized with wedge-shaped tail. *Dark gray above, with a darker cap, white below* and underwing. In flight, dark bar on upper-wing and lower back creates *M-shaped pattern of darker color,* the points of the "M" coming at the bend of the wing.

Voice: Silent when at sea. A mewing chorus is heard in the colony at night.

Habitat: Open ocean, seen offshore where attracted by food concentrations.

Nesting: 1 white egg in a burrow. In colonies.

Range: Nests in New Zealand, and after the nesting season ranges in the North Pacific, especially from Monterey Bay in central California north to Washington (where it is rather common) and to British Columbia.

Its flight, somewhat slower than that of the other shearwaters, is characterized by less frequent wing flapping and longer gliding periods with wings arched.

---

71 Laysan Albatross
(Diomedea immutabilis)
Albatrosses (Diomedeidae)

Description: 32″ (81 cm). W. 78″ (2 m). *Large, black-and-white seabird with very long wings* and short tail. Black wings, tail, and back; white head, neck, breast, and rump. Underwing is white with black edging and irregular black patches. Thick, hooked bill; feet are fleshy gray. At close range conspicuous dark patch around eye.

Voice: Silent at sea; occasional throaty grunts when squabbling over food.

Habitat: Open ocean, usually well offshore.

Nesting: 1 buffy white egg in a shallow sandy depression on a sea island. In colonies.

Range: Nests on mid-Pacific islands, chiefly in the Hawaiian chain. Rare visitor to offshore waters of the North Pacific and the Gulf of Alaska.

Although the Laysan Albatross occurs less frequently than the Black-footed off the west coast, the Laysan is regularly observed from northern California to Alaska. Unlike the Black-footed, it pays little attention to offal from ships, but feeds mainly on squid. Sailors and Pacific islanders know albatrosses as "Gooney Birds."

72 **Black-footed Albatross**
(*Diomedea nigripes*)
Albatrosses (Diomedeidae)

Description: 28–36" (71–91 cm). W. 78–84" (2 m). Large seabird. *Dusky black overall* with white area encircling dark bill and light streaking in primaries; some adults have white undertail coverts. Long narrow wings; stiff shearwater-like wingbeat and gliding pattern.

Voice: Screeches and grunts. In courtship display, whistles, quacks, and bill-clapping noises.

Habitat: Open ocean, rarely seen near shore.

Nesting: 1 white egg, sometimes blotched, in a sandy depression on a sea island. In extended colonies.

Range: Along the entire Pacific Coast of North America. Breeds on mid-Pacific islands, including northwestern Hawaiian Islands.

Albatrosses take 10 to 12 years to mature. The young roam the Pacific, seldom returning to their birthplace before they are 6 or 7 years old. These birds take squid and surface fish; they often follow ships and feed on refuse.

Seashore

Rocky or sandy beaches, rocky
headlands, the intertidal zone, and
adjacent waters.
This is the habitat of inshore seabirds—
those that feed near land and are usually
visible from shore—as well as the
waders in the intertidal areas. Grebes,
loons, ducks, gulls, and other species
that breed in inland areas but occur
along the shore in their non-breeding
season are considered under their
breeding habitats.

17 Thayer's Gull
(*Larus thayeri*)
Gulls (Laridae)

Description: 22½–25″ (57–64 cm). Almost identical
to Herring Gull. *Mantle slightly darker
gray, and black area of wing tips smaller,
paler, with larger white "windows"* and
tips. Yellow bill with red spot on lower
mandible; *brown eye,* with purple-red
ring around it; pink feet. In immature
plumages, very similar to Herring
Gulls of the same age but slightly
smaller with proportionately smaller
bill; overall coloration somewhat paler,
especially the wing tips.

Voice: A long, mewing call, *hiyah,* and a
warning call, *gah-gah-gah,* like those of
the Herring Gull.

Habitat: Seabird of the Arctic; coastal rocks and
rocky headlands. In winter, among
other gulls on the Pacific Coast.

Nesting: 2 or 3 olive-brown, heavily blotched
eggs in a grass nest in colonies on sea
cliffs.

Range: Central Canadian Arctic archipelago
and adjacent areas. Winters from
British Columbia to Baja California.

The Herring, Thayer's, Glaucous,
Glaucous-winged, and Western gulls
arose from the splitting up of a single
northern gull species during glacial
epochs. They occasionally hybridize
where their ranges meet, yet different
eye, eye-ring, and foot colors usually
keep them from interbreeding.

18, 38 Herring Gull
(*Larus argentatus*)
Gulls (Laridae)

Description: 22½–26″ (57–66 cm). Large white bird
with gray back and wings. *Wing tips
black with white spots;* bill yellow with
red spot on lower mandible, feet pink.
Eyes pale yellow with yellow eyelid

ringing eye. In winter red spot on bill darkens to dusky, and head is suffused with dusky color. Juveniles similar to those of Western Gull, but slightly paler; they gradually acquire lighter plumage of the adult.

Voice: A loud series, *ke-yah, ke-yah . . .* Various squealing cries.

Habitat: Tundra, other wetlands, and coasts as long as nesting islets or cliffs are nearby; coastal areas in winter.

Nesting: 2 or 3 brown or olive, blotched eggs in a grass or seaweed nest in a depression; in colonies on islets.

Range: Widespread in Eurasia; in North America from central Alaska east to north central Canada and south to British Columbia, the Great Lakes, and Long Island. In winter along the Pacific Coast to northern Mexico, and along the Atlantic and Gulf coasts.

Originally a beach scavenger and surface-fishing bird, this gull greatly increased its Atlantic Coast populations by availing itself of man-made sources of food such as harbors, seafood canneries, and city dumps. In the West, the wintering population from the Far North forms a minority among the other large gulls.

21, 36 **Glaucous-winged Gull**
(*Larus glaucescens*)
Gulls (Laridae)

Description: 24–27″ (61–69 cm). Large *white gull with pearly gray mantle and wings.* Gray primaries show a white "window" near tip of each feather; yellow bill with red spot on lower mandible, light brown or silvery eyes, pink feet. In winter red spot on bill becomes a diffuse black; head and nape look dusky. First-year birds gray-brown overall, with wing tips same color as mantle. Black bill, dark eyes and feet. Second-year birds acquire more gray and are generally paler.

Voice: Similar to the "long call" of the Western Gull: a raucous series of similar notes on one pitch. Other calls include a series of dull *ga-ga-ga* notes uttered when intruders appear, as when a boat approaches the breeding colony.

Habitat: Rocky or sandy beaches, harbors, dumps, open ocean.

Nesting: 2 or 3 light olive-brown eggs with dark speckles in a grass or seaweed nest in a depression on remote islets or headlands. In colonies. Males actively defend the nesting territory from other males, females from other females, while nonbreeding birds remain on the periphery of the colony.

Range: From the Aleutians and Bering Sea south to Oregon, where it mingles and hybridizes with the Western Gulls in a few colonies along the boundary area.

Like other large gulls, this species feeds mainly along the shore. Over water it picks up edibles such as dead or dying fish and squid; over the beach it feeds on dead seabirds, seals, whales, starfish, clams, and mussels. In harbors and towns it scavenges on garbage. One banded female was observed to make daily trips from her nest to a garbage dump over 42 miles away.

22, 39 Western Gull
(*Larus occidentalis*)
Gulls (Laridae)

Description: 24–27″ (61–69 cm). Large gull. *Snowy white, with dark slaty back and wings.* Yellow eye and bill; breeding adult has a red dot near tip of lower mandible. *Pinkish or flesh-colored feet.* In winter, head and nape light dusky. First-year immatures are dark gray-brown with dark, almost black primaries, contrasting with lighter areas on nape and rump; bill dark.

Voice: Most commonly utters a raucous series
of similar notes. Also loud squealing
calls.

Habitat: Coastal waterways, beaches, harbors,
dumps; open ocean.

Nesting: 3 light buff, blotched eggs in a grass or
seaweed nest in a depression, protected
and slightly isolated by broken terrain.
In colonies on rocky headlands, islets,
or dikes in the tideland, but mainly on
offshore islands such as the Farallon
Islands off San Francisco, where there
are now over ten thousand pairs. The
male is the chief provider and defends
the territory and nest; the female
defends the chicks.

Range: Nests on the Pacific Coast from
Washington to Baja California and
through the Gulf of California.
Regularly occurs in winter along the
coast of British Columbia.

The large gulls of the Pacific Coast had
a common ancestor but evolved
separately in isolation during past Ice
Ages. The Glaucous-winged Gull
resembles the Western Gull in size and
habits, but its coloration is extremely
light, as befits a gull living among the
ice floes of Alaska today or among
glaciers of the Pacific Northwest in the
past. A distinct population of Western
Gulls that breeds through the Gulf of
California has bright yellow feet; it
wanders to the Salton Sea in small
numbers in summer. It is considered by
some a distinct species, the "Yellow-
footed Gull."

23, 35 Mew Gull
(*Larus canus*)
Gulls (Laridae)

Description: 16–18″ (41–46 cm). Medium-small
gull. White with gray mantle, black
wing tips, and greenish-yellow legs.

Bill is small compared to that of larger gulls and is *unmarked* greenish-yellow. Juvenile similar to young Ring-billed Gulls but generally darker with less crisply marked tail band.

Voice: A high mewing *kee-yer*.

Habitat: Nests along rivers and lake shores as well as seacoasts.

Nesting: 2 or 3 olive eggs with brown or black blotches and scrawls in a grass nest, on beaches and riverbanks; also in treetops or on stumps and pilings; almost always in colonies, often among other gulls.

Range: Alaska east to central Mackenzie and south to northern Saskatchewan and along the coast to southern British Columbia. Winters on Pacific coast. Also along the boreal forest belt of Eurasia.

This small gull is as versatile a feeder as the larger species of gulls, but its egg-stealing in seabird colonies is less destructive. It often eats insects, sometimes from swarms in the air.

28, 40 Heermann's Gull
(*Larus heermanni*)
Gulls (Laridae)

Description: 18–21″ (46–53 cm). Medium-sized gull. *Predominantly dark.* Bill *red; snow-white head* blends into gray on neck, back, and rump; slate black on wings and tail, with white terminal band on tail and secondaries. Juveniles dusky with throat lighter and tail trimmed with white; bill dark.

Voice: A high *see-whee*. Also a low-pitched *kuk-kuk-kuk*.

Habitat: Coastal waters, islands, and beaches.

Nesting: 2 or 3 eggs in a scrape; in large colonies on offshore islands.

Range: Breeds on islands (mainly Isla Raza) in the Gulf of California and on the San Benito Islands off the west coast of Baja

California. Some migrate northward from July to October, spending the winter on the Pacific Coast north to Vancouver Island; others migrate southward as far as Panama. Nonbreeders are found year-round on the coast of California, but adults leave by January.

This gull demonstrates that all migration is not necessarily southward in fall and northward in spring in the Northern Hemisphere. On its breeding grounds, Heermann's Gull commonly follows fishing boats and robs fish from Brown Pelicans. Farther north, it scavenges along beaches and feeds on herring eggs.

42 **Least Tern**
(*Sterna albifrons*)
Gulls (Laridae)

Description: 8½–9½" (22–24 cm). Smallest North American tern. White with gray back and wings. *Crown black, forehead white; in winter, crown also white. Outer primaries dusky; feet yellow; yellow bill tipped with black.* Tail slightly forked. Immatures have blackish primaries and white secondaries; back dusky rather than pearl gray.

Voice: A sharp *kit, kit* or *kseek.* Frequently repeats a two-syllable *dee-dee* at the ternery.

Habitat: Beaches bordering shallow water, along rivers, lakes, or coasts.

Nesting: 2 or 3 light buff, sparsely speckled eggs in a scrape in beach debris; in colonies, sometimes associated with other tern species.

Range: Cosmopolitan; in North America it breeds along the coast of California and Baja California, along major rivers in the interior United States, and along the Atlantic and Gulf coasts.

Due to the destruction of its habitat by human activities, it is an endangered species in California; along the coast south of San Francisco, only 20 colonies with a total of fewer than 700 pairs remained in 1973.

48, 51   Royal Tern
(*Sterna maxima*)
Gulls (Laridae)

Description: 18–21″ (46–53 cm). Larger than the very similar Elegant Tern, with which it shares beaches. Large *orange bill;* black crest is smaller than Elegant's; black cap present only during brief courtship period, thus usually has white forehead. In nonbreeding plumage the eye of the Royal stands out in its white face. In the Elegant the black of the hind neck extends forward to include the eye. The larger Caspian Tern has a red bill and the undersides of the primaries are black.

Voice: *Kee-rer,* lower-pitched than in the Elegant Tern.

Habitat: Sandy beaches along seacoast; bays and estuaries.

Nesting: 1 egg; color and markings and blotchings vary. In colonies on sandbars and flat desert islands.

Range: Breeds along northwest coast of Mexico—rarely north to San Diego, California. Also along coast from Virginia to Texas and Mexico; the West Indies; West Africa. As a winter visitor, not uncommon along the California coast, north to Morro Bay.

The major nesting area for both Royal and Elegant terns is on Isla Raza in the Gulf of California, where thousands breed together.

49 Elegant Tern
(*Sterna elegans*)
Gulls (Laridae)

Description: 16–17" (41–43 cm). Medium-sized tern. *Orange;* white with gray mantle and wings; *black cap ending in long crest;* deeply forked tail. In nonbreeding plumage forehead becomes white, but crown, crest, and eye area remain black.

Voice: A loud, grating *kar-eek.*

Habitat: Lagoons and beaches.

Nesting: 1 egg, often buffy (but the color is variable), in a scrape on a sandy beach, preferably on an island; in colonies.

Range: Breeds in Gulf of California and at San Diego. Winters both to the south and north, some going down to Chile and Peru but others regularly visiting the northern California coast.

The nesting of the Elegant Tern is restricted mostly to Isla Raza, a small flat island in the northern part of the Gulf of California, where it has several colonies of hundreds of nests. Since terneries are crowded, with each female just out of bill range of her neighbors, and coastal winds obliterate landmarks that help adults find their nests, the individual color and markings of the single egg help parents recognize their own. When the eggs hatch, the color pattern of the hatchling serves the same purpose. The population was seriously depleted by Mexican egg-dealers, but the breeding island is now protected and the species is increasing.

50 Aleutian Tern
(*Sterna aleutica*)
Gulls (Laridae)

Description: 13½–15" (34–38 cm). Mantle and wings dark gray, *cap black, but forehead white;* forked tail white; grayish below.

Voice: Scold note is a high squeal. Also a shorebird-like high whistle of three notes.

Habitat: Open beaches, marshes, neighboring shallow bays, and oceans.

Nesting: 2 olive or buff eggs in a scrape on high, dry land, safe from tides, on small islands off the coast and in coastal meadows; in colonies of 50–60 pairs.

Range: Spotty distribution and rare, in southern and western Alaska and on Sakhalin Island northwest of Japan. Winters in the high northern seas.

Little is known about this tern, but such seabirds are being increasingly studied in Alaska.

---

56 Red-billed Tropicbird
(*Phaethon aethereus*)
Tropicbirds (Phaethontidae)

Description: 24–40″ (61–102 cm). Gull-sized, but appears larger because of *long tail* with elongated trailing central feathers up to 18″ (45 cm) long. *Largely white,* but *outer edge of wing and stripe behind eye black;* mantle finely checkered with black. *Bill large and red.*

Voice: Rasping screams at the nest; a loud, rattling cry in the air.

Habitat: Offshore; feeds on the open ocean.

Nesting: 1 pale reddish, finely scrawled and marked egg, without a nest, in sheltered niches of cliffs, on islets or rocky headlands.

Range: Tropical seabird which irregularly visits southern California waters; most often seen in summer and fall, generally far offshore.

In flight, tropicbirds with their light-colored wings and long tails are unmistakable. Near breeding colonies they habitually display in the air with tail and feet spread, soaring and circling up and down. They have very short legs and are rarely seen at rest on land except on cliffs and at burrow entrances.

57 Magnificent Frigatebird
(*Fregata magnificens*)
Frigatebirds (Fregatidae)

Description: 37½–41" (96–104 cm). W. 84–96" (2.1–2.4 m). Large tropical seabird with *long, sharply hooked bill* and *long, deeply forked scissor-like tail,* opened up only during maneuvering in flight. *Exceptionally long, angled wings* allow spectacular soaring. Male iridescent black with inflatable red throat pouch displayed during the breeding season. Female has white breast. Immatures have white head and underparts.

Voice: Mostly silent, but in courtship the male warbles and utters a rattling noise as he inflates a conspicuous balloon-like throat pouch and shakes it rhythmically.

Habitat: Along seacoasts, seldom far from land. Perches on isolated sea cliffs and bushes, never on water.

Nesting: 1 white egg in a loosely made platform of sticks and twigs placed on the top of low bushes, in crotches of limbs, or on mangroves; breeds in loose colonies, often among boobies and other seabirds.

Range: Tropical Atlantic, Gulf of Mexico, and eastern Pacific; rare but regular on the southern California coast, the Salton Sea, and the lower Colorado River in summer. In the United States breeds locally on islets in Florida Bay.

Frigatebirds are superb aerial pirates; they will attack and harass a gorged booby or other seabird until it disgorges its prey, which is then snatched in midair or retrieved from the surface of the water or from the beach. Relative to its weight, the Magnificent

Frigatebird has the largest wing expanse
of any bird.

59 **Red-footed Booby**
(*Sula sula*)
Boobies (Sulidae)

Description: 26–30" (66–76 cm). Smallest of the
boobies. Most adults are *white, with
black primaries and secondaries,* bluish
bill, pink face, and *bright red feet.* In its
dark phase, brown with only the belly,
rump, and tail whitish. All immatures
are pale brownish.

Voice: Silent at sea. Loud quacks and grunts
make the breeding colony noisy; males
utter a high-pitched, females a lower-
pitched *rah-rah-rah-rah.*

Habitat: Oceans; islands.

Nesting: 1 chalky pale blue egg in a stick nest
on trees or shrubs on tropical islands
and atolls. In colonies.

Range: Islands throughout the tropical seas. In
the United States it nests on Hawaiian
Islands.

Though brown and white variants may
interbreed and intermediate forms
occur, including brown-tailed adults,
the red feet are always diagnostic. The
only Red-footed Booby seen in the
western United States was sighted on
the Farallon Islands, California.

60 **Brown Booby**
(*Sula leucogaster*)
Boobies (Sulidae)

Description: 28–32" (71–81 cm). Large, dark
booby. Adults *dark chocolate brown, with
sharply defined white breast and belly,* and
white underwing lining. *Yellow bill and
feet.* Immatures brownish below.

Voice: Usually silent at sea, but raucous in the
colony; male's call is a high-pitched

hiss, female's a low quack.

Habitat: Offshore seabird; roosts on island cliffs and breakwaters.

Nesting: Usually 2 chalky pale blue eggs in a scanty nest of sticks and debris; on cliffs in undisturbed coastal situations, or on the ground on islands. In colonies but may also nest singly.

Range: Tropical seas; closest to the United States on Mexico's Pacific Coast. Occasionally seen in southern California at the Salton Sea; accidental on the Pacific Coast.

Boobies fish from a height, and their dives into the water are a spectacular sight. Frigatebirds often harass boobies, forcing them to disgorge their prey, which the pirate catches in midair. When on the wing, but not fishing, boobies will often fly in lines close to the surface of the waves and may resemble shearwaters.

61 Blue-footed Booby
(*Sula nebouxii*)
Boobies (Sulidae)

Description: 32–34″ (81–86 cm). Large seabird, with long, pointed bill, wings, and tail. Head and neck pale brown. Wings, mantle, tail dark brown; white patches on upper back; rump and underparts white. Immature's back and rump are slightly mottled. *Bright blue webbed feet.*

Voice: Generally silent except on breeding grounds, where they make trumpeting and whistling noises.

Habitat: Islands and open sea.

Nesting: 2 or 3 chalky pale blue eggs on the ground. In colonies on islets or on cliff heads.

Range: Breeds from the Gulf of California south to Peru. After breeding, a few stray to the Salton Sea or, infrequently, the southern California coast.

Boobies fly fairly high over the ocean
with steady, rapid, even strokes,
followed by a short glide. When
fishing, they plunge headlong into the
water with wings folded.

Kittlitz's Murrelet
(*Brachyramphus brevirostris*)
Auks (Alcidae)

Description: 7½–9″ (19–23 cm). Smaller than a
Robin but chubbier. *In summer dusky
above with buff marbling, foreparts buff
with dark barring,* belly whitish. *In
winter white below, slate gray above* and on
top of head, face white. A white patch
on the dark wings is sometimes visible
on the swimming murrelet and always
visible in flight. Short stubby bill.

Voice: Undescribed.

Habitat: Nests on talus slopes of high
mountains; otherwise it is a bird of
ocean waters and glacier bays.

Nesting: Little known; but the single egg, olive
with heavy markings, has been found
on mountain slopes among rock slides.

Range: The coasts of the Bering Sea, Aleutians
and southeastern Alaska. Rarely farther
south in winter.

It may be distinguished from the
Marbled Murrelet during the breeding
season by its grayer, lighter colors and
shorter bill. In winter, the white of the
lower side extends to the face above the
eyes. One of the least-known North
American birds.

Marbled Murrelet
(*Brachyramphus marmoratus*)
Auks (Alcidae)

Description: 9½–10″ (24–27 cm). Chubby Robin-
sized seabird with very short neck and

tail. In summer, *brown above, light brown-and-gray-marbled below*. In winter, *black above, white below* with white wing patch and incomplete white collar.

Voice: Birds flying to and from nesting sites give plaintive cries: *keer, keer, keer*.

Habitat: Breeds in coastal rain forests; in shore waters at other times.

Nesting: The nesting of this bird was solved only recently. Most alcids use burrows or ledges on coastal cliffs, but Marbled Murrelets, burdened with fish, take off from the sea at twilight and disappear inland. Some weeks later one finds feathered young bobbing on the water. The first clues were found in Kamchatka in 1963 by a Siberian ornithologist who reported a nest in a huge tree. In 1974 a nest was discovered in a Douglas fir in the Santa Cruz Mountains of California, about 135 feet from the ground and set in a depression lined with live moss. It contained pale green, heavily marked eggshell fragments and a buffy gray downy nestling. It is now assumed that these murrelets nest high up in trees, up to several miles from the sea.

Range: From Sakhalin Island to the Kamchatka coast on the Asian side and from Alaska's Kodiak Island south to central California on the American side of the North Pacific.

On the water Marbled Murrelets move about in small groups. They dive for fish and other aquatic animals.

109, 145 **Common Eider**
(*Somateria mollissima*)
Ducks (Anatidae)

Description: 23–27″ (58–69 cm). Large sea duck. Short neck; long sloping bill creates a distinctive profile. Male with *white back, neck, and breast; black below. White*

head with light green nape, *black cap,*
and *orange bill.* Female mottled
brown.

Voice: The male gives a loud moaning or
cooing call on the breeding grounds;
the female utters a grating *gog-gog-gog.*

Habitat: A true sea duck, it breeds near salt
water; winters along seacoasts.

Nesting: 4–7 buffy eggs in a down-lined hollow,
away from water, usually on rocky islets
inaccessible to Arctic Foxes; often in
colonies.

Range: Circumpolar, mostly on the northern,
Arctic coasts, with extensions
southward: in the eastern Pacific area it
breeds south to the Kenai Peninsula of
Alaska. Winters along Alaska's
southern coast. Rare south of
Vancouver Island.

Down from the female's breast is used
for expensive sleepings bags and
pillows. Most eiderdown comes from
Scandinavia, where artificial nest sites
entice the hens and permit easy access
to the down. Once robbed, the female
furnishes a second plucking. At
hatching time the owner of an "eider
farm" collects the used down and
carries the hatched ducklings to sea,
where they join another hen, who
eagerly adopts them.

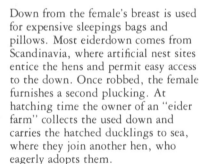

110, 138 Black Scoter
"Common Scoter"
(Melanitta nigra)
Ducks (Anatidae)

Description: 17–20½" (43–52 cm). Medium-sized
sea duck. *Male black overall with bright
orange spot on upper mandible.* Female
dark brown, head light grayish with
contrasting dark cap.

Voice: More vocal than other scoters; during
display male gives a peculiar whistling
note, *coar-loo.*

Habitat: Tundra and boreal woodland

interspersed with lakes or rivers; in
winter, along seacoasts and in inshore
waters.

Nesting: 6–10 pinkish-buff eggs in a down-lined
nest in a sheltered place on the ground
near water.

Range: Circumpolar; in North America it
breeds in the coastal regions of far
western Alaska and inland in
northeastern Canada. Winters on both
coasts, although it is uncommon south
of northern California. Judging from
subtle differences in the bill, Pacific
Coast birds come only from Alaska.

Black Scoters, like Surf Scoters, are
gregarious; the two species often feed
near each other, but separately, in coves
along the Pacific Coast. The mating
display of both occurs on sunny days
during the winter. Whereas the male
Surf Scoter dives and flies up while
displaying around the female, the male
Black Scoter splashes and whistles.
Formerly called "Common Scoter."

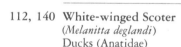

112, 140 White-winged Scoter
(Melanitta deglandi)
Ducks (Anatidae)

Description: 19–23½" (48–60 cm). One of largest
ducks. Male *black with white eye-patch*
that curves back and up; female dark
brown with two light cheek-patches,
much like female Surf Scoter. Both
sexes have a *white speculum,* usually
visible even when wings are folded.

Voice: A hoarse croak.

Habitat: Muskeg and bog of the boreal forest
belt in summer; seacoasts in winter.

Nesting: 9–14 pinkish eggs in a down-lined
hollow in tall vegetation near water.

Range: Across Scandinavia, the Siberian taiga,
Aleutian Islands, and on ponds from
forested Alaska to southern Manitoba
and North Dakota. Winters on the
coasts and, rarely, on the Great Lakes.

Scoters dive for shellfish. At sea, where they winter, this species seems more solitary than other sea ducks. White-winged Scoters, Surf Scoters, Black Scoters, scaups, and Oldsquaws fly in long, wavering lines over water. Such a formation, when settled on the water, is called a "raft." When a raft disperses and starts to dive, the White-winged Scoters seem to drift apart, while the other species of scoters stay together.

113, 141 Surf Scoter
(*Melanitta perspicillata*)
Ducks (Anatidae)

Description: 17–21″ (43–53 cm). Male *black with white patches on forehead and nape.* Big swollen *bill has a bright white-black, red-orange pattern.* Female dark brown with two light cheek patches like those of White-winged Scoter, but white wing patches distinguish the latter.

Voice: A low grating croak and other grunting notes. Usually silent on winter grounds. In courtship flight, wings produce a whirring sound.

Habitat: Tundra and forest bogs during breeding season; coastal waters during winter.

Nesting: 5–9 creamy buff eggs in a scrape lined with down on the tundra. The down insulates the nest from the marshy ground and is used to cover the eggs when the female is going off to feed.

Range: From Aleutian Islands and western Alaska to western Labrador, but its distribution is not completely known. Winters on both coasts and, rarely, on the Great Lakes.

The commonest scoter of the Pacific Coast in winter, it spends most of the year there and only a short season on its Arctic breeding grounds. These scoters stay some distance from shore, taking shellfish, especially mussels. In deeper water the colorful males and dark brown females dive with their wings partially open, and swim underwater with feet and wings, using the alula, or false wing, as stabilizer. Displays of several males around a single female may be seen from early winter on, especially in sunny weather. Single birds, usually young males, may spend their second summer on the sea.

160 Emperor Goose
(*Philacte canagica*)
Ducks (Anatidae)

Description: 26–28″ (66–71 cm). As large as Snow Goose or White-fronted Goose. Body and wings *silver-gray;* black-and-white feather margins give a scaled, bluish appearance. *White head,* hindneck, and tail, *black throat and foreneck,* flesh-colored bill, bright orange legs and feet. Juveniles gray overall.

Voice: Loud musical notes, *cla-ha, cla-ha, cla-ha.*

Habitat: Seacoasts, mud flats, marshes, and tundra.

Nesting: 5 or 6 creamy white eggs in a down-lined ground nest, on islets of the tundra marsh or among driftwood on the coast.

Range: Islands and marshy coasts of the Bering Sea, Aleutian Islands. In winter, frost and pack ice drive it south of the Aleutian chain. Casual winter visitors appear south along the North Pacific Coast and in inland valleys.

The head and neck of these geese take on a deep rust stain from the iron in stagnating waters, for they feed with head and neck submerged, grazing on bottom vegetation. The black pattern on the throat distinguishes this species from the "Blue Goose" (the blue phase of the Snow Goose) which is relatively rare in the West.

164 **Brant**
"**Black Brant**"
(*Branta bernicla*)
Ducks (Anatidae)

Description: 23–26" (58–66 cm). Mallard-sized
goose. On water it seems *entirely dark
except for a white collar;* in flight it shows
a black-and-white pattern. Head, neck,
chest, back, wings, and tail black; sides
of chest appear lighter; lower belly,
flanks, and undertail snow white.

Voice: A series of soft *ruk-ruk* calls.

Habitat: An entirely marine bird breeding on
coastal tundra. Bays and estuaries in
winter.

Nesting: 4 or 5 buff or cream eggs in a down-
lined nest close to the water.

Range: Circumpolar on the Arctic shores of
Eurasia and North America. On
the Pacific Coast it winters from
Vancouver Island to Baja California.
Concentrations occur in winter in
Washington's Puget Sound and in
California's Humboldt and Morro bays.

Brant from the central and eastern
Canadian Arctic that migrate to the
Atlantic Coast have a grayish-brown
breast and belly contrasting with a
black neck and chest, whereas those
that breed in Alaska and northwestern
Canada and winter on the Pacific Coast
have darker undersides (as described
above) and were formerly called "Black
Brant." Because their chief food is
eelgrass and sea lettuce, brant rarely
stray to inland waters. Many are shot
by hunters each year, but a greater
danger to the species is the steady loss
of winter habitats to encroaching
civilization.

166, 171   Red-throated Loon
(*Gavia stellata*)
Loons (Gaviidae)

Description: 24–27" (61–69 cm). Smallest loon.
Slender upturned bill. In summer, gray
above with a chestnut throat patch; in
winter, mottled gray on back (lighter
than other loons) with white throat and
foreneck. Sexes look alike.

Voice: Silent except on breeding grounds,
where it utters a rather long series of
quacking notes.

Habitat: Small, shallow, partly vegetated lakes;
generally seen along seacoasts in
winter.

Nesting: 2 olive-to-brown eggs with darker spots
in a depression amid vegetation, usually
on the shore of a lake. Both parents
incubate and feed the young on fish or
aquatic insects.

Range: More completely circumpolar than
other loons. In America it breeds in
Aleutians and along Arctic coasts, also
inland on tundra, and south along
Pacific Coast to southern British
Columbia. Winters on both coasts and
also on the Great Lakes.

These loons often gather in flocks of
several dozen. In Arctic Alaska, Eskimo
ceremonial cloaks are made from their
skins, alternated with skins of the
Yellow-billed Loon. In 1763 the
Danish naturalist Erik Pontoppidan
imagined that he saw a brilliant red star
in the throat patch of this loon and
named it *stellata,* meaning "the starred
one."

167, 170   Arctic Loon
(*Gavia arctica*)
Loons (Gaviidae)

Description: 23–29" (58–74 cm). Small loon with
slender bill. In summer, similar to
Common Loon but *light gray head and*

neck contrasts with darker gray back; black shield on throat flanked with white stripes marks the elegant breeding plumage of both sexes. In winter, two-toned like all loons, darker above than Red-throated Loon. Its straight bill also distinguishes it from Red-throated Loon, and its smaller size from Common Loon.

Voice: Largely silent except on breeding grounds, where a barking *caw wow* is uttered. Also a variety of wailing and honking notes.

Habitat: Lakes in woods or tundra; winters along seacoast.

Nesting: 2 deep brown eggs with darker markings, in a nest near water on shore or islet.

Range: Circumpolar. Breeds in the western and central Arctic of North America. Winters along the Pacific Coast to the Gulf of California.

This loon is believed to migrate only during the day. It flies in loose formations, presenting a long, slender gray outline, with the feet stretched backward and the neck held straight or bent downward in an arc.

---

182 Snowy Plover
(Charadrius alexandrinus)
Plovers (Charadriidae)

Description: 6–7″ (15–18 cm). A small pale plover with an *incomplete breast band;* also an *incomplete eye-line;* bill and feet dark as compared with the dark yellow feet of the Semipalmated.

Voice: A low-pitched *krut.* Also a whistled *ku-wheet.*

Habitat: Sandy or alkaline shores.

Nesting: 3 buff, spotted eggs in a scrape; tended by both parents alternately.

Range: Cosmopolitan, but occurring only on riverbanks, sand dunes, alkali flats, or coral beaches. A casual visitor in

Canada. In the United States it breeds in various western states with suitable pale-colored surroundings and along the Pacific Coast from Washington southward, wintering there as well.

This small, sand-colored plover has a perfect camouflage on sandy shores. As soon as it stops running it seems to disappear, blending into its surroundings. The eggs also blend with dry sand or salty barren soil, and are almost impossible to find once the incubating bird slips off them.

183 Semipalmated Plover
(*Charadrius semipalmatus*)
Plovers (Charadriidae)

Description: 6½–8" (17–20 cm). Larger than a plump sparrow. Short neck and rounded head; *dark sandy brown above, white below with single black breast band.* Black eye-stripe, white forehead and eyebrow; legs dark yellow; bill dark yellow with black tip.

Voice: A mellow whistled, *chu-whee.*

Habitat: Breeds on tundra; winters on seashore, favoring sandy beaches and tidal flats.

Nesting: 4 buff or whitish eggs in a scrape, on tundra or beach pebbles.

Range: North American tundra from Alaska to Labrador, south along the Pacific Coast to the Queen Charlotte Islands. Winters from central California coast to Patagonia.

When feeding, these birds hunt littoral life exposed by the tide. Their feeding method is a quick run, followed by a sudden stop, and a lightning-swift jab at a tiny crab or beach hopper. The front toes are joined by a small web; hence the name *semipalmated,* meaning "possessing half a palm."

188, 231 Dunlin
(*Calidris alpina*)
Sandpipers (Scolopacidae)

Description: 8–9″ (20–23 cm). Medium-sized
sandpiper. Smaller than Red Knot but
larger than Western Sandpiper. *Bill
longer than head and slightly curved.* In
spring and summer, *cinnamon red back,*
white below with *black belly.* In winter
uniform gray upperparts and gray
breast. Immatures brown above, buff
below with brownish streaks on breast
and sides.

Voice: A low, grating *kerrr.*

Habitat: Wet tundra in summer; seacoasts in
winter.

Nesting: 4 greenish or buff, brown-marked eggs
in a grass nest in a scrape on tundra.

Range: Holarctic; in North America along
coast from Alaska to Hudson Bay.
Winters on coasts; in the West from
British Columbia to Baja California.

Large flocks are found on mud flats
from autumn to spring. They spread
out at low tide, but if a hawk flushes
them, they cluster in a tight group of
several hundred birds, twisting and
swirling in the air. Few birds of prey
would risk entering this flying mass,
but an old, sick, or handicapped bird
may lag behind to become easy prey.

193, 229 Sanderling
(*Calidris alba*)
Sandpipers (Scolopacidae)

Description: 7–8¾″ (18–22 cm). Small, plump
sandpiper. In breeding plumage, back,
head, and upper breast are mottled
gray-and-white with rust-colored tones;
white on belly. Easy to recognize in
winter plumage, when it is the palest of
all small sandpipers: *light gray above,
white below;* bill and feet black. In
flight, shows bold white wing stripe.

Voice: A sharp, high *kit*, sometimes given in series.

Habitat: Nests on dry, stony tundra; migration and through winter, sandy beaches.

Nesting: 4 olive, spotted eggs in a well-concealed, grass-lined depression on dry tundra.

Range: Circumpolar; on the tundras of North America and northern Eurasia. Sandy beaches of all continents during the winter.

On their Arctic Canadian or Greenland nesting grounds, incubating Sanderlings may be observed from as close as 2 or 3 feet. Unlike most sandpipers, they are quite tame even during winter and are a delight to watch as they retreat and advance with the breaking waves. Sanderlings generally feed by probing, but also take small invertebrates that wash ashore. Whereas "peeps" such as the Western Sandpiper feed in large loose flocks on the mud flats, flocks of Sanderlings feeding on the beach spread out in long lines along the water's edge and run in small groups of twos or threes.

199 Sharp-tailed Sandpiper
(*Calidris acuminata*)
Sandpipers (Scolopacidae)

Description: 8½" (22 cm). Resembles its close relative the Pectoral Sandpiper in size and behavior. *Brownish overall* but more rust brown than in Pectoral; *cap redder* and buffy *breast lighter* with faint streaking limited to the sides in immatures, and breast pattern is less sharply contrasted with the white belly than in the Pectoral.

Voice: Call is a sharp *whit-whit*.

Habitat: Grassy areas of coastal marshes and tidal flats.

Nesting: 4 buffy eggs spotted with brown in a grass nest on the ground.

Range: An eastern Siberian tundra bird, it
occurs in very small numbers along the
Pacific Coast of North America in fall
and is seen most regularly in the
Northwest, but occasionally elsewhere.
Accidental in the interior western
states.

Sharp-tailed Sandpipers observed in
western North America are generally
immatures.

201, 204, 236 Red Phalarope
(*Phalaropus fulicarius*)
Phalaropes (Phalaropodidae)

Description: 7½–9″ (19–23 cm). A slim shorebird
with smallish head and dainty bill. In
spring bright rust red below with buffy
mottled back and white face. Female
has black lores and crown; male smaller
and less colorful. Bill yellow with black
tip. In fall and winter unstreaked gray
above, head and underparts white, bill
darker; dark eyeline is common in all
phalaropes in winter plumage.

Voice: A sharp *kip.*

Habitat: A tundra breeding seabird, it passes
offshore along the coast in fall and
spring. Winters on high seas.

Nesting: 4 greenish-buff eggs, heavily spotted,
in a scrape on the tundra, in wet and
dry areas, always well concealed. The
male cares for eggs and young.

Range: Circumpolar; in North America breeds
on Arctic coasts from Alaska across
Canada to Greenland. Winters in open
oceans of both hemispheres, but usually
not in very cold regions; rarely north of
central California on the Pacific coast.

Phalaropes feed on the surface; they
swim in tight circles with the body
held high, the head bobbing, paddling
with lobed toes, in search of plankton
or small marine invertebrates.

202, 205, 237 **Northern Phalarope**
(*Phalaropus lobatus*)
Phalaropes (Phalaropodidae)

Description: 6½–8″ (17–20 cm). Bluebird-sized. In
spring male dark gray with *white throat*
and *buffy neck;* female has bright rusty
neck. Bill dark, thinner than in Red
Phalarope. In fall and winter darker
backed than Red Phalarope with *dark
ear and crown markings* contrasting with
white head. Shows pronounced wing
stripe in flight.

Voice: A high, sharp *kip.*

Habitat: Breeds near ponds on wet tundra;
winters on high seas.

Nesting: 4 olive-buff, thickly spotted eggs in a
scrape on the tundra, near the edge of
water. The roles of the sexes are
reversed. The female is brighter in color
since she does the courting and
advertises and defends the breeding
territory, while the male tends the eggs
and offspring.

Range: Circumpolar; in North America on
tundra from Aleutians and Alaska to
Labrador. In migration, common off
Pacific Coast; also occurs on lakes
of all western states and provinces.
Majority winter on oceans of Southern
Hemisphere, but some stay in extreme
southern California.

Northern Phalaropes, like the Red
Phalarope but unlike other shorebirds,
prefer to swim rather than wade, which
enables them to spend the winter on
the high seas. They float buoyantly and
pick small creatures from the surface of
the water, often while swimming in
circles and gyrating.

309, 318 Gyrfalcon
(*Falco rusticolus*)
Falcons (Falconidae)

Description: 20–25″ (51–64 cm). *Largest falcon. Three color phases occur: white, gray, and black.* Dark birds similar to smaller Peregrine Falcon, but mustache mark indistinct. It flies very fast, but measured wingbeats cause it to seem more deliberate.

Voice: Low harsh *kak kak kak* cries. Generally silent away from the breeding grounds.

Habitat: On the tundra near cliffs, or in mountains, also on sea cliffs. In winter, various open habitats, but chiefly seen at the coast.

Nesting: 3 or 4 creamy eggs with a rufous tinge or blotches. It may use a raven's nest or build a scanty one of its own on rocky crags or shelves.

Range: Circumpolar Arctic breeder; extends somewhat south along the high mountains of Alaska and British Columbia. In winter, irregularly south to northern tier of states.

On occasion it is seen harrying flocks of sandpipers and waterfowl. When a Gyrfalcon appears, all birds except the diving ducks take to flight and group together for protection.
The prized companion of the medieval falconer, it was considered the most graceful and skillful falcon and its use became a royal privilege.

Sea Cliffs

Rocky shorelines, cliffs, and offshore islands or islets.

These areas provide good feeding opportunities for some shorebirds, and seabirds dive and feed in currents around the rocks. Some of the birds considered here use the rocks as nest sites, others burrow in the soil, and a few nest in flat areas atop the cliffs or islands. The Black Turnstone and the Surfbird, for example, nest in other habitats and use the rocky shores only in winter. Although the storm-petrels are commonly considered birds of the open ocean, we have included four of them in this habitat because they breed on cliffs along islands. Bald Eagles, gulls, ducks and other water-associated birds may occur in this habitat, but they are dealt with in other habitats.

20 Glaucous Gull
(*Larus hyperboreus*)
Gulls (Laridae)

Description: 26–32″ (66–81 cm). Large gull. Adult *white, with pale gray mantle.* Legs and feet pink, bill of breeding bird yellow with red spot. Juveniles are palest of all Pacific area gulls, with primaries of wings lighter than buff upperside; second-year birds white overall. Bill of juveniles flesh-colored at base, black at tip.

Voice: Loud double notes rendered as *cart-lage;* hoarser and deeper than those of other gulls, and somewhat like a raven's voice.

Habitat: As varied as in other gulls, ranging from sea cliffs and coastal tundra to garbage dumps.

Nesting: 2 or 3 olive or buff eggs with brown blotches, in a bulky nest of sod, moss, or seaweed. Nests in colonies on rocks, preferring somewhat sheltered ledges or depressions; also on the tundra, often surrounded by water.

Range: Circumpolar; in North America on the coasts and islands of Alaska and the Canadian Arctic. Moves south in winter, but only small numbers reach as far as the Pacific Northwest and even fewer get to California, the Hawaiian Islands, and Texas. A casual visitor in the inland western states.

Around the North Atlantic this gull is known as the "Burgomaster," the chief magistrate or toll-taker of Arctic seabird colonies. It preys on eggs, on unattended young, and even on adult auklets. It forces diving eiders to disgorge the food they have gathered.

26, 33 Black-legged Kittiwake
(*Rissa tridactyla*)
Gulls (Laridae)

Description: 16–18″ (40–46 cm). Small gull of the open ocean. White with gray back and gray wings with *ink-black wing tips;* wing linings white. Yellowish bill similar to that of Mew Gull, but its *black legs* are distinctive. In winter, has large gray patch on back of head. Juveniles have black terminal tail band that emphasizes the slight fork of the tail; dark bill, dusky nape band, and black zigzag "M" across open wings.

Voice: Among its many cries the commonest is *kittiwake,* which gives the bird its name.

Habitat: Open waters of Arctic Ocean and neighboring seas, with cliffs on islands or headlands for nesting.

Nesting: 2 buff or greenish-olive, blotched eggs in an orderly nest of seaweed; mud holds the nest material together. In colonies on narrow ledges where predators can get no foothold.

Range: Circumpolar. Breeds on coastal cliffs of Arctic Ocean and neighboring seas. In winter, migrates southward; many get as far as Mexico.

Commonest gull of the Arctic. Colonies of many thousands occupy the steepest cliffs, the breeding pairs looking like pearls on a necklace. They may be so tightly packed that there is room only for one parent at the nest at a time. In one colony on Alaska's Pribilof Islands, rock walls 1000 feet high were covered with these nests on every ledge for 5 miles—probably totaling several million birds. They feed at sea even in the roughest weather since they can snatch food from the top of the water.

27 **Red-legged Kittiwake**
(*Rissa brevirostris*)
Gulls (Laridae)

Description: 14–15½″ (36–39 cm). Small gull, similar to closely related Black-legged Kittiwake. Bill short, slightly curved, and yellow; mantle *gray. Lining of the open wing gray* (Black-legged Kittiwake has white wing lining), red legs. Wing tips black.

Voice: Said to be similar to that of the Black-legged Kittiwake: a sound like its name, *kittiwake*.

Habitat: Seabird of the open ocean; nests on ledges of sea cliffs.

Nesting: 2 eggs, buff or creamy, marked with brown, in a grass and mud nest on a ledge.

Range: Bering Sea. Restricted to two island groups, the Commander Islands off eastern Siberia and the Pribilof Islands.

This bird has one of the most limited distributions in the West, but the Pribilof Islands gullery is perhaps the most spectacular seabird colony in the world; every ledge is packed with tens of thousands of kittiwakes, murres, fulmars, and other seabirds.

Fork-tailed Storm-Petrel
"Fork-tailed Petrel"
(*Oceanodroma furcata*)
Storm-Petrels (Hydrobatidae)

Description: 8–9″ (20–23 cm). Blackbird-sized *gray* petrel, pale below; all other Pacific storm-petrels are dark and blackish-looking.

Voice: A twittering note and squeaking may be heard around the nesting burrows.

Habitat: Open ocean, but common in enclosed waters in summer. Storm-petrels are seabirds, usually seen from land only during heavy storms.

Nesting: 1 white egg with spots around the large

end, in a burrow or other cavity. In colonies. It has been suggested that the musky smell of the burrow may guide the parent home.

Range: Distributed around the Pacific in an arc from the Kurile Islands to northern California islands.

Formerly called "Fork-tailed Petrels," they feed during daylight at sea, sometimes in groups of hundreds, by picking small animals from the surface or by a shallow dive. They visit the nesting colony in the evening. The birds dig burrows close together in soft ground, forming a network. Their long wings, forked tails, and habit of fluttering and hovering over the water surface when feeding have earned this species, as well as other storm-petrels, the name "Sea Swallow" in many languages.

62 Leach's Storm-Petrel
"Leach's Petrel"
(*Oceanodroma leucorhoa*)
Storm-Petrels (Hydrobatidae)

Description: 7½–9″ (19–23 cm). Blackbird-sized black petrel, with black body and forked tail. North Pacific populations breeding south to central California are identified by *white rump*. Farther south, in southern California, white on rump virtually disappears. *Wings have brown crossbar*.

Voice: Silent at sea, but can be detected at night by subdued ticking and trilling notes and twitterings coming from the rock piles where they nest and, at courtship time, from the air when they circle over the nesting burrows.

Habitat: Open ocean.

Nesting: 1 white egg on bare ground in a chamber at the end of a burrow or in a crack or tunnel among rocks.

Range: Pacific Ocean is the center of its

distribution. Nests widely in scattered colonies on both sides of the North Pacific south to Japan and Baja California. Also around the North Atlantic. Winters mainly in tropical seas.

Until recently called "Leach's Petrel." Storm-petrels flutter close to the water to pick up tiny fish, crustaceans, or other surface plankton. In a colony at night and against a moonlit sky, storm-petrels look like bats.

---

64   **Ashy Storm-Petrel**
"Ashy Petrel"
(*Oceanodroma homochroa*)
Storm-Petrels (Hydrobatidae)

Description: 7½" (19 cm). Blackbird-sized black petrel with forked tail. *All black,* although at close range the ashy brown color of head and neck and the light mottling on underwing lining may be seen.

Voice: A squeaking twitter may be heard from the nest burrow. Silent at sea.

Habitat: Open ocean; feeds offshore.

Nesting: 1 white egg laid in rock slides or other dark crevices or in burrows; no nest.

Range: Nests on islands from the northern side of the Golden Gate of San Francisco south through the Channel Islands into northern Baja California.

A major nesting colony on Southeast Farallon Island off San Francisco contains about 4000 birds. Like other petrels, these small birds return to nesting islands at night to avoid predators, such as Western Gulls, which can easily catch the tiny petrel. The Ashy Storm-Petrel feeds on plankton in the surface water of the cold current that washes the California coast. Formerly called "Ashy Petrel."

Black Storm-Petrel
"Black Petrel"
(*Oceanodroma melania*)
Storm-Petrels (Hydrobatidae)

Description: 9" (23 cm). Smaller than Robin and a bit larger than Purple Martin. *All black, with rather long, forked tail,* long, slender wings, a tube-nosed bill hooked at the end, and long legs with webbed feet. Smoother, less fluttery flight than other storm-petrels.

Voice: Silent at sea, but its strong *tuck-a-roo* call reverberates in its nesting colonies.

Habitat: Open ocean; nests on rocky islands.

Nesting: 1 white egg without a nest, in rock crevices; in colonies.

Range: Islands in the Gulf of California and off the western coast of Baja California, with all but one nesting colony in Mexico. Ranges in Pacific Ocean from coast of northern California to South America.

Like other storm-petrels, this species obtains its food from the sea surface. It tends to feed closer to shore than Leach's Storm-Petrel and returns to its nesting burrows earlier in the evening. Previously known as "Black Petrel."

74 Pelagic Cormorant
(*Phalacrocorax pelagicus*)
Cormorants (Phalacrocoracidae)

Description: 25–30" (64–76 cm). Smallest of Pacific Coast cormorants. Slim bill with hook at tip; slender head and neck. *All black.* At the onset of the courtship period, it acquires a bright *white patch on its flanks.* Two crests visible at close range. *Red pouch under bill,* green eyes, and blue-green mouth lining. In flight it is long-necked, black with a green gloss. Immatures dark brown.

Voice: Groaning and hissing notes around the breeding colonies.

Habitat: Coastal waters, bays. Nests in colonies
on sea cliffs and rocky islets, and may
feed inshore or far offshore.

Nesting: 3–7 long bluish eggs with a chalky
wash in a flimsy nest of seaweed,
feathers, sticks, and debris.

Range: A North Pacific seabird; breeds from
Japan around the Pacific arc to central
California, and into the Bering Strait.

When all three cormorant species breed
together, the Pelagic nests on a cliff
face, while Brandt's often selects a
gentle slope, and the Double-crested a
cliff top. Pelagic Cormorants nest on
ledges so narrow that they must alight
and take off facing the cliff. By
contrast, Double-crested and Brandt's
colonies nest on broader ledges and can
turn and face the sea in taking off.

75   **Red-faced Cormorant**
(*Phalacrocorax urile*)
Cormorants (Phalacrocoracidae)

Description: 28–30″ (71–76 cm). Somewhat larger
version of Pelagic Cormorant: mainly
*bottle-green with conspicuous red facial skin
extending to forehead.* During courtship
and breeding season it has *white plumes
and two crests* on crown and on nape,
and white patches on flanks. Young and
yearling birds are brownish.

Voice: A low *korr.* Hoarse, deep croaking
notes at the breeding colonies.

Habitat: Pelagic, with cliff ledges serving as its
breeding colonies.

Nesting: 3 or 4 pale bluish eggs with a white,
chalky material almost obliterating the
blue in nests of seaweed or grass. In
colonies.

Range: The Aleutian Islands, the Pribilof
Islands, and a few others. In the Bering
Sea and on the northern Siberian coast.

Male and female share equally in the
parental duties; the bird on the nest is

dominant and has to be appeased by the incoming parent with an elaborate display. This display closely resembles that of the Pelagic Cormorant, evidence of the common ancestry of these species.

---

77 **Brandt's Cormorant**
(*Phalacrocorax penicillatus*)
Cormorants (Phalacrocoracidae)

Description: 33–35″ (84–89 cm). Almost as big as Double-crested Cormorant. Dark, somewhat iridescent seabird, but lacks crest. *Cobalt blue throat* pouch visible only in breeding season, but is difficult to observe. *Buffy band around pouch* is more easily discernible. Both sexes have slender white plumes on face and back early in breeding season. Immatures dark brown with lighter underparts.

Voice: Guttural croaks and grunts heard around the breeding grounds. Otherwise generally silent.

Habitat: Colonial seabird; nests on coastal or offshore rocks next to the waters where it fishes.

Nesting: 3–6 chalky, bluish eggs in a large nest of seaweed, other vegetation, or whatever can be stolen from gull nests. In colonies on coastal cliffs or remote rocky islands.

Range: Restricted to northeastern Pacific Coast, from southern British Columbia to Baja California.

Brandt's Cormorants often gather in flocks of several hundred and fly to feeding grounds in long straggling skeins. They dive together, forming a living net.

78 Thick-billed Murre
(*Uria lomvia*)
Auks (Alcidae)

Description: 17–19″ (43–48 cm). Slightly stockier than similar Common Murre; thicker, pointed bill with *white line along its base in all plumages.* In summer *black above, white below* with black throat and neck. Similar in winter but with white throat and neck. The area above and behind eye remains black, whereas in the Common Murre it whitens in winter.

Voice: Usually silent, except on breeding cliffs, where it utters various bleating and croaking notes; the noise in a colony is like the roar of a storm, with thousands of murres uttering their *arr-rr-rr-r, awk-awk-awk,* or *uggah.*

Habitat: Sea cliffs and rocky islands; dives for food offshore.

Nesting: On rocky ledges with the birds so tightly packed that only one breeding adult in a pair has room to warm the single greenish, dark-blotched egg.

Range: High Arctic, breeding on the shores of Alaska (from Anchorage west and north), the Bering Sea, northern Canada, Greenland, Iceland, and the northern fringes of Eurasia. Winters south to southern Alaska in the West and Nova Scotia in the East. A casual visitor in winter as far south as New Jersey and central California.

Murres are so conservative that photographs of nesting cliffs taken decades apart show the same number of nesters on each ledge, and where the two species of murres mix, even the proportion of the two seems to remain similar—usually a sign of keen competition for nest sites. They fly with fast wingbeats on a steady course, but alight with a "stall" and an ungraceful thumping down almost vertically. They take off by plunging from a cliff, or, on water, by pattering over the sea like heavy ducks.

79, 81 Common Murre
(*Uria aalge*)
Auks (Alcidae)

Description: 16–17" (41–43 cm). One of the larger alcids. A *black-and-white* seabird. Cheek, throat, and neck white in winter with *thin black downcurved line* curving down behind the eye and extending into white portion of cheek. Entire head and neck black in summer; always white below. On land it stands upright, penguin-fashion. In flight, *slender head and pointed bill* suggest a small loon.

Voice: Its common name echoes its call: its breeding colony resounds with a "murring" noise, a moaning *aarr-r-r,* among other calls.

Habitat: Open sea and gulfs. Murres fish away from land and return only for nesting.

Nesting: 1 egg, variable in color: blue, green, or buffy with darker blotches. The egg is very long and exaggeratedly pear-shaped; thus, when struck it rolls in a tight semicircle instead of falling off the ledge. On inaccessible cliff tops or ledges, especially on rocky islets or headlands. Each pair has barely enough space for a single egg and one incubating parent standing upright.

Range: All coasts of the Northern Hemisphere where cold currents or upwellings nourish a multitude of fish. In the West they nest in colonies in western Aleutians and from Arctic Alaska to central California.

When half grown, the young jump 30 to 50 feet into the sea, and accompany the parents, first swimming, then flying, often hundreds of miles, to wintering waters. Apart from having their nests plundered for the eggs, murres of the Pacific Coast have been safe from human intrusion, though potential oil spills now pose a threat to whole colonies.

80 **Pigeon Guillemot**
(*Cepphus columba*)
Auks (Alcidae)

Description: 12–14″ (30–36 cm). Pigeon-sized. In
breeding plumage, *black with large white
wing patch* interrupted by two black
stripes. In winter head and upperparts
lighten slightly, giving dusky mottled
effect; underparts are white with buffy
barring on flanks. In all seasons feet and
bill lining are brilliant red.

Voice: Quite vocal around its breeding cliffs in
spring; high thin whistles given singly.

Habitat: Rocky coastal areas, with shallow
inshore waters as its feeding grounds;
rock crevices and earthen holes serve as
nest cavities.

Nesting: 1 or 2 whitish or greenish, dark-spotted
eggs in a crevice or burrow.

Range: A common inshore alcid along the
Pacific Coast from Aleutian Islands and
Alaska to Southern California. Winters
well offshore.

The least social of all auks. Where
coastal cliffs allow only one nesting
cavity, only one pair will occupy it.
Elsewhere, territories are laid out like
beads on a string. They feed by diving,
taking mostly small fish. Its eastern
relative the black guillemot (*Cepphus
grylle*), which has a large white wing
patch, has been found nesting along the
arctic Alaskan coast.

82, 84 **Tufted Puffin**
(*Lunda cirrhata*)
Auks (Alcidae)

Description: 14½–15½″ (37–39 cm). Pigeon-sized.
Mostly seen sitting upright on a sea
cliff. *Black stubby body, white face,
downcurved yellowish tufts hanging behind
eyes, and large, orange-red, parrot-like bill.*
In winter colored bill plates are molted
and bill is smaller, duller, face turns

dusky, tufts disappear. Immatures
dusky above, light gray below, with
small bill. In flight, the large, webbed,
red feet serve as brakes.

Voice: Silent except for occasional growling
notes uttered around the nest site.

Habitat: Vertical sea cliffs; in colonies or singly.
Feeds at sea.

Nesting: 1 white or, frequently, spotted egg in a
burrow; the chick is raised on fish
brought by the parents during the day.
Grassy slopes and headlands of the Far
North are densely covered with
burrows; where it uses rock crevices this
puffin is less colonial, though usually
found in the company of hundreds or
thousands of other seabirds.

Range: Sizable colonies nest on Siberian,
Alaskan, and British Columbian coasts.
A few nest on the California coast.

In most mixed seabird colonies a strict
social order prevails within each
species. Each seems to have adapted to
a specific niche, occupying the terrain
most suited to it, thus reducing
competition between species but
sharpening it within each species.

83 Horned Puffin
(*Fratercula corniculata*)
Auks (Alcidae)

Description: 14½" (37 cm). Pigeon-sized. Chunky,
tailless body. *Black above, white below.
White face* makes head appear big; *large,
parrot-like bill bright yellow with brilliant
red* at tip. Red eyelids and small, black
upturned "horn" above eye visible at
close range. In winter face darker,
feathers brownish, bill smaller, and
base sooty-colored. Juveniles are even
darker-faced, with narrow, sooty-brown
bills.

Voice: Usually silent, but utters harsh notes
from its burrow.

Habitat: Cold ocean waters, sea cliffs, and rocky

or grass-covered islets and rocks.

Nesting: 1 large egg, whitish with small, dark spots; in colonies, in crevices of cliffs or in deep holes among boulders. More rarely it burrows in soft soil.

Range: Bering Sea and its islands, North Pacific coasts to Japan and the Alaskan panhandle. Winters irregularly south to California.

The relatively huge bill is useful in catching and holding small fish, enabling the parents to bring 3 or 4 fish at a time to the young. It is also used as a signal to mate or neighbor, especially during breeding time in crowded colonies. The colonies may contain thousands of these birds, yet in the Aleutians and other places where they nest among the Tufted Puffins, they are lost among the tens of thousands of the latter species.

85 Rhinoceros Auklet
(*Cerorhinca monocerata*)
Auks (Alcidae)

Description: 14½–15½″ (37–39 cm). Pigeon-sized. Dark above with lighter gray throat and breast, white underparts. Slender, pale yellow bill, white eye. In breeding plumage, short, upright *"horn" at base of bill* with white drooping *whiskers* at either side; white plume above eye. Immatures dark gray above, light below with duller, smaller bill and dark eye.

Voice: Growling and mooing cries of adults and shrill piping of young are heard on the breeding grounds at night.

Habitat: Feeds on fish offshore; digs deep burrows in grassy or timbered headlands.

Nesting: 1 white, often spotted egg in a burrow; in colonies, sometimes in large numbers.

Range: Japan and southeastern Alaska south to

central California. Winters off the west coast south to Baja California.

"Auklet" is a misnomer since this bird is not a close relative of the small, plankton-feeding seabirds called auklets, but is actually related to the brighter-colored, parrot-billed puffins. These birds feed on the open sea during the day but may be seen at sunset in summer among Pacific Coast inlets and islets. They swim and bob with a beakful of fish, waiting for nightfall before feeding their young in the burrows.

86 Crested Auklet
(*Aethia cristatella*)
Auks (Alcidae)

Description: 9½–10½" (24–27 cm). Shorter than Robin, a chubby bird without much visible tail. *Slate black above, brownish-gray below.* In breeding season, *white plume* behind white eye and prominent *forward-curving black crest. Bill red,* with an extra red plate on side of face. In winter crest shorter, and lacking in juveniles; dullish brown.

Voice: A variety of loud honking and grunting notes are given on the breeding grounds. Otherwise silent.

Habitat: Talus slopes on islands for nesting, and nearby sea for feeding.

Nesting: 1 white egg among boulders in coastal and island cliff areas where sliding rocks form a talus slope, with the largest boulders at the bottom and bare cliff at the top. In colonies.

Range: Aleutians and islands and coasts around the Bering Sea area and adjacent Arctic coasts of Siberia.

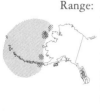

Like other auklets, it feeds on planktonic crustaceans, filling a special sac under its tongue with food for its single young.

Whiskered Auklet
(*Aethia pygmaea*)
Auks (Alcidae)

Description: 7–7½″ (18–19 cm). Sparrow-sized. In all plumages, *dusky gray* above, lighter gray below. Adults have forward-curling, quail-like gray topknot and *three white ornamental plumes* projecting backward from face like grotesque mustaches; short bill red during summer, brown in winter. Immatures dark with traces of three white head stripes.

Voice: Not yet described in detail, but one of its common calls probably is *choo-chirr-eck,* similar to the name given it by the Aleuts of Attu Island.

Habitat: Rock slides and cliffs for nesting; the neighboring sea for feeding.

Nesting: 1 white egg in rock crevices; in colonies.

Range: Very restricted; on the Aleutian and Kurile islands.

The most restricted and rarest of the four Alaskan auklets, it resembles in appearance and habits the larger Crested Auklet.

87   **Cassin's Auklet**
(*Ptychoramphus aleuticus*)
Auks (Alcidae)

Description: 8–9″ (20–23 cm). Stocky, Robin-sized seabird. Dark, *slate gray above,* lighter gray below, white belly. Eyes dark brown during first year, they then lighten and are white in breeding adults. Stubby *bill has white spot* at base of each side of lower mandible. No seasonal change in plumage.

Voice: Their weak, croaking song becomes a mighty chorus on windy, foggy nights.

Habitat: Open ocean. Nests on sea cliffs and isolated headlands.

Nesting: 1 white egg mainly in burrows but also

in cavities among rocks; in colonies.

Range: Aleutians to central Baja California. Colonies irregularly distributed; over 100,000 birds nest on the Farallon Islands, near San Francisco.

The parents take 24-hour watches while incubating the chick. During the nesting season they grow a pouch under the tongue and fill it with food. The island birds fly to sea long before dawn, after which they run the risk of being pursued and devoured by Western Gulls. They feed on planktonic shrimp by day and approach the colony only after dark. Most seabirds abandon the nest site as soon as the young fledge, but on the Farallon Islands, Cassin's Auklets remain. From December to March, birds occupy the island so densely that vacated burrows (the owners presumably dead) are promptly taken over by others. It is believed that this "housing shortage" compels the auklets to defend burrows year round.

88 Parakeet Auklet
(*Cyclorrhynchus psittacula*)
Auks (Alcidae)

Description: 10" (25 cm). Robin-sized, but short tail and *chubby body* make it look larger. *Sooty black above, white below.* In summer *white, mustache-like plume* extends from below eye to lower neck. *Stubby, red upturned bill.* In winter, white plume missing, throat and underparts white, bill duskier.

Voice: Generally silent but utters a clear, tremoloed whistle in breeding colonies.

Habitat: Open ocean; it requires coastal or island cliffs for nesting and rather deep water for feeding.

Nesting: 1 white, oval egg in cliff crevices and among boulders.

Range: The Bering Sea islands and some nearby

coasts. Aleutians. A rare winter visitor on the Pacific Coast south to California.

This auklet, common on its Alaskan home grounds, does not form large colonies but mainly nests scattered among the puffins and Pigeon Guillemots that prefer the same habitat. On approaching a mixed seabird colony from the sea, we note the chubby Parakeet Auklets sitting high up on the cliff, each on watch near its nesting cavity while its mate is down below incubating or tending the young. In the morning or afternoon it leaves the cliff to feed, diving for krill, a kind of shrimp, which it scoops from near the bottom.

89 Least Auklet
(Aethia pusilla)
Auks (Alcidae)

Description: 6″ (15 cm). *Sparrow-sized. Black above, white below.* In summer white plume behind eye; *dark markings on sides and breast (often forming breast band) set off white throat;* bill orange with yellow tip. In winter plume smaller; unmarked white below; bill dark; white patch on wing. Intermediate plumaged birds often present on breeding grounds.

Voice: Various twittering notes are given around the breeding colonies.

Habitat: Seabird; nesting in rock crevices of talus slopes under cliffs; feeds at sea.

Nesting: 1 white egg in a small crevice. Huge colonies, with tens of thousands of inhabitants, occupy rocky slopes.

Range: Islands of the Bering Sea and the Aleutian chain. In winter south to the northwestern Pacific.

In winter vast numbers of Least Auklets leave their Arctic islands before the sea freezes and return in June when the slopes are still snow-clad. One study noted that in June certain birds came back daily from their diving and feeding and sat on the snow in a certain pattern. Photos made from a blind showed that the "snow sitters" sat on their future nest site and took possession as soon as the snow melted. Perhaps oriented by a few large boulders, they were apparently able to locate the nest site they had used the previous season.

Xantus' Murrelet
(*Endomychura hypoleuca*)
Auks (Alcidae)

Description: 9½–10½" (24–27 cm). Robin-sized but slender, resembling a tiny murre. *Black above,* with no distinctive pattern; *white cheek, throat, and underparts. Underwing coverts white.* Bill is thin, narrow pincers, good for catching small fish or shrimp. No seasonal change in plumage.

Voice: High thin whistles, usually in a quick series.

Habitat: Ocean; nesting in colonies on rocky sea islands.

Nesting: 1 or 2 buffy eggs with brown markings among boulders and in crevices off island beaches. Both parents incubate and brood the young. The hatchlings go to sea with the adults when they are 2 to 3 days old.

Range: Breeds on offshore islands of Baja California and southern California, occasionally wanders north to Vancouver Island.

Murrelets are so called because they resemble tiny murres. At sea, they are often seen in pairs. This species was named for its discoverer, Hungarian explorer John Xantus, who pioneered on the west coast in the 1860s.

Craveri's Murrelet
(*Endomychura craveri*)
Auks (Alcidae)

Description: 8½–10″ (22–25 cm). *Black above, white
              below,* with black extending down neck
              to form partial collar. Underwing
              grayish. Black of face extends below
              bill on Craveri's but not on Xantus'.

      Voice: In breeding season, a trilling whistle
              heard near the colony at sea.

    Habitat: Offshore seabird.

    Nesting: 2 white eggs in a rock crevice or under
              boulders.

      Range: Breeds on islands in the Gulf of
              California and off Baja California north
              to the San Benitos Islands. After
              breeding, it wanders to southern
              California coast and occasionally farther
              north.

As with many other species that nest in
the Gulf of California, Craveri's
Murrelet wanders northward in fall to
feeding grounds in the California
Current. Its habits are similar to those
of Xantus' Murrelet.

Ancient Murrelet
(*Synthliboramphus antiquus*)
Auks (Alcidae)

Description: 9½–10½″ (24–27 cm). Quail-sized.
              Black head, gray back, white below,
              white plume over eye, and small white-
              barred area at side of neck. *Bill white.*
              In winter, wide white area on throat
              and face, back solid slate gray; similar
              Marbled Murrelet has white patch on
              flanks, dark bill.

      Voice: A low shrill whistling note; may give a
              piping whistle at sea.

    Habitat: Open ocean; nesting on oceanic islets
              with enough soil for a burrow, often
              under heavy timber.

    Nesting: 2 brown-to-green eggs spotted with
              brown and lavender; incubated by both

parents in 72-hour shifts. Large colonies occur where birds can easily dig burrows at night. The chick goes to sea with its parents soon after hatching, and feeds on fish and on crustaceans, called krill, that are found in great masses in northern waters.

Range: Offshore islets of the North Pacific and mainland shores south to central British Columbia. Some winter there, but others occur south to southern California.

Russian explorers who discovered this bird thought its white plumes similar to an old man's white locks; hence its Latin (*antiquus*) and English names. By moving to and from land at twilight, these birds escape most predators with the exception of Peregrine Falcons. Ancient Murrelets are not strong flyers, and heavy storms may carry them as far inland as the Great Lakes or wash masses of dead bodies ashore on the Pacific Coast.

155 Brown Pelican
(*Pelecanus occidentalis*)
Pelicans (Pelecanidae)

Description: 45–54″ (114–137 cm). Large, heavy seabird. *Huge, dark bill and large throat pouch;* adults *grayish-brown* with white head; immatures dark-headed, pale below. In flight, it is easily recognized by its alternate flapping and gliding of broad powerful wings, short tail, and S-shaped neck. Breeding birds have dark chestnut hindneck extending to crested nape.

Voice: Groaning and screaming sounds are uttered by young around breeding colonies. Adults generally silent.

Habitat: Oceans, inshore waters; stands on pilings or rocks.

Nesting: 2 or 3 white eggs, but if food shortages develop, only 1 or 2 young are raised, with the last hatchling starving or crowded to death by siblings. A bulky nest of sticks lined with fresh green vegetation; on islands.

Range: In the United States, Pacific and southeastern coastal areas. Also Central and South America. Occasionally reaches Vancouver Island.

These social, colonial birds fly in single file low over the water; on sighting prey they plunge from heights of up to 30 feet but surface to swallow fish. They also use their pouch, which expands under water, to suck in small fish. Pelicans have a history of at least thirty million years but were threatened with extinction in the early 1970s because they are sensitive to chemical pollutants, absorbed from the fish they eat. The pollutants affect calcium metabolism, resulting in thin-shelled eggs that break when moved by the incubating bird. Breeding improved sharply after DDT was banned.

185, 186 Ruddy Turnstone
(*Arenaria interpres*)
Sandpipers (Scolopacidae)

Description: 8–10″ (20–25 cm). About as large as Killdeer but has shorter legs. Very colorful; breeding adults are white with *orange-red mantle* and *irregular black "V" on breast,* extending forward in halter-like pattern across white face. *Bright orange legs and feet.* Tail white with broad black band. In flight, wings flash bright black-white-rust pattern. Even in winter, this pattern immediately distinguishes them from similar-sized plovers and sandpipers.

Voice: Common call is a low *cut-cut-cut.* Also a guttural rattle.

Habitat: Beaches and other flat, open areas near the water's edge; sometimes on rocks and breakwaters.

Nesting: 4 grayish-green, spotted or streaked eggs in a scant nest in a depression in the open, usually near water.

Range: On Arctic shores of Eurasia and North America. In North America breeds only in Alaska, Greenland, and the northernmost Canadian Arctic archipelago. Migrates along both coasts; common in winter on Hawaiian and other Pacific islands. Rare inland.

On its territory, neighbors often display head to head, the harlequin pattern of the face and black-and-white fanned tail serving like colorful banners. This sandpiper is found most commonly on beaches, where it uses its bill to turn seaweed, rocks, or other debris in search of food.

211 Rock Sandpiper
(*Calidris ptilocnemis*)
Sandpipers (Scolopacidae)

Description: 8–9″ (20–23 cm). Small sandpiper; most frequently seen in winter. *Slate gray* head, breast, and upperparts with indistinct white eye-stripe, chin, and wing-stripe, *dark rump and tail. Feet yellowish or greenish.* Indistinct white wing bar. Spring breeding plumage resembles that of Dunlin; brown mottled crown and less rust color on back, higher and smaller dusky black breast blotch, and less breast streaking.

Voice: Trilling calls on the nesting grounds.

Habitat: Breeds on upland tundra; rocky shores in winter.

Nesting: 4 buff-olive eggs with brown spotting, in a mossy depression on the tundra.

Range: The High Arctic of the Bering Strait, Aleutians, areas of Alaska and Siberia. Winters along the northern Pacific shores of North America; common in British Columbia and Washington, scarcer in California.

Dark gray birds feeding in loose flocks at the waterline or on exposed, alga-covered surfaces at low tide may be Rock Sandpipers, Black Turnstones, or Surfbirds. All are similarly camouflaged to match wet, dark rocks. In flight, the three are easily distinguished: the Rock Sandpiper has a dark tail, the Surfbird has a white tail terminating in a black triangle, and the Black Turnstone has its checkered black-and-white pattern.

218 Black Oystercatcher
(*Haematopus bachmani*)
Oystercatchers (Haematopodidae)

Description: 17–17½″ (43–44 cm). Large shorebird. *Black with long, stout, red bill;* flesh-colored legs and feet; light eyes. Sexes look alike.

Voice: Their loud ringing notes carry above the crashing of the surf; a whistled *wheeee-whee-whee-whee.*

Habitat: Rocky seacoasts.

Nesting: 2 or 3 large, olive-buff eggs with brownish-black blotches, among pebbles in a shallow rocky depression or in a scrape on the beach. Both parents care for the young.

Range: Cool Pacific shores from the Aleutians south to Baja California. Midway in Baja California, the black-and-white American Oystercatcher (*Haematopus palliatus*) replaces it.

Before nesting, the birds undertake conspicuous long courtship flights, screeching loudly as they turn and twist, emphasizing each cry with a peculiar wingbeat, as if flying in slow motion. The flat, strong bill is used to open oysters or pry limpets off rocks. After breeding, the birds may flock together, up to 40 or 50 often gathering on a flat rock at low tide.

221, 225 Black Turnstone
(*Arenaria melanocephala*)
Sandpipers (Scolopacidae)

Description: 9" (23 cm). Resembles Ruddy
Turnstone in general patterns. In
breeding plumage *upperparts, head,
and breast black;* large white spot in
front of, and white line above, the eye;
fine white spotting from nape across
side of breast; white belly. Winter
plumage is dusky black with
unstreaked white belly. Legs dark. Bill
short and slightly upturned. In flight,
flashes a *black-and-white pattern.*

Voice: A distinctive grating *kr-re-e-e-e-r*
uttered in flight.

Habitat: Nests in marshy, coastal tundra in
summer; visits seaweed-covered rocky
shores of the Pacific Coast in fall and
winter.

Nesting: 4 yellowish-olive eggs with darker olive
and brown markings, in a scrape
without a nest; on open, pebbly ridges,
or gravel bars in wet tundra.

Range: Breeds on western and southern coasts
of Alaska. Winters all along the coast
south to Baja California and Sonora.

Turnstones are territorial only on the
breeding grounds. On the coast they
live in flocks, the bright wing pattern
probably aiding in keeping the group
together in flights from one rocky islet
to another. They turn over pebbles with
the bill in search of crabs, beach
hoppers, and sand fleas.

222, 224, 227 Surfbird
(*Aphriza virgata*)
Sandpipers (Scolopacidae)

Description: 10" (25 cm). Slightly larger than Black
Turnstone, with which it mixes. In
winter, dark gray head, breast, and
upperparts; *white rump; white tail with
black terminal triangular pattern;* white

wing stripe. Light lores, throat, and
belly with gray-streaked flanks. *Bill and
legs yellow.* In breeding plumage, heavy
black-brown mottling above, and
strong black mottling on white
underparts.

Voice: On their winter grounds they utter a
shrill *ke-week* in flight.

Habitat: Nests above timberline in dry open
areas of the alpine tundra zone; in
winter, rocky shores, headlands, and
islets.

Nesting: 4 buffy eggs, spotted with various
colors, among broken rocks and on
talus slopes. No nest.

Range: Breeds on the mountain tundra of
Alaska. Winters along the Pacific Coast
from southern Alaska to southern South
America.

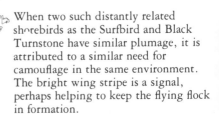

When two such distantly related
shorebirds as the Surfbird and Black
Turnstone have similar plumage, it is
attributed to a similar need for
camouflage in the same environment.
The bright wing stripe is a signal,
perhaps helping to keep the flying flock
in formation.

226 Wandering Tattler
(Heteroscelus incanus)
Sandpipers (Scolopacidae)

Description: 11″ (28 cm). Medium-sized sandpiper.
In winter uniformly *dark gray above,*
paler below; light areas at throat and
belly; *dark bill slightly longer than head.*
Summer tattlers have fine black cross-
barring below. Dark eye-line framed by
lighter eye-stripes above and *yellow legs*
remain constant in all seasons.

Voice: Call is 3 to 4 clear whistles in rapid
succession, usually as it takes to flight.

Habitat: Mountain streams in summer; coastal
rocks, shell beaches, and rocky coves
from fall to late spring.

Nesting: 4 greenish eggs with some spotting in a

finely built nest of roots, twigs, and dry leaves; on gravel bars in mountain streams above timberline.

Range: Breeds in mountain areas of south-central Alaska and northwestern British Columbia. Winters on both Pacific Coasts (in U.S. from southern California southward).

The Surfbird, Bristle-thighed Curlew, Kittlitz's Murrelet, and Wandering Tattler all breed scattered about above the timberline in Alaska's rugged mountains, and their nests were among the latest to be discovered; the Tattler's nest was first found in 1922. They are easier to approach in their wintering places on the southern coasts, because they do not fear man. When very low tides expose rocky bottoms, several tattlers come into sight but each feeds alone.

Salt Marshes

Tidal marshes occur in low, shallow
bays and especially in estuaries, where
silt deposited by rivers may provide
extensive areas for plant growth. Salt
water floods these areas at high tide.
The salt and brackish (half salt, half
fresh) water is nutritious, but few kinds
of plants can tolerate it.
Relatively few birds nest in tidal
marshes, but many species appear there
in fall and winter. These marshes are
also important wintering places for
waterfowl and shorebirds that nest on
the Arctic tundra, as well as for those
that breed in the freshwater marshes of
the interior.

5, 6 Cattle Egret
(*Bubulcus ibis*)
Herons (Ardeidae)

Description: 20″ (51 cm). *Small white heron.* At a
distance resembles Snowy Egret but has
shorter, thicker neck and orangish bill
and legs. Breeding adults have buff-
orange mantle, breast and crown.
Immatures are white with yellow bill
and dark legs.

Voice: Various croaking notes are heard around
the nest.

Habitat: Extensive marshes or pastures; during
roosting and breeding they fly in
wavering lines to wooded areas in
marshes.

Nesting: 3–5 bluish eggs in a twig nest. A very
social species, dozens or even hundreds
may nest in the same tree.

Range: Prime example of greatly expanding
distribution. Originally from the Old
World tropics, some were seen in the
last century in British Guiana. A few
were found breeding in Florida in 1953
and soon formed huge nesting colonies
there. The first in California appeared in
1964; now they are also breeding there
(commonly at the Salton Sea), and
pioneers have been sighted as far north
as southern Canada.

Cattle Egrets have always been seen
perching on the backs of African
animals; now they may be observed in
the United States around or on top of
cattle, catching grasshoppers and other
insects stirred up by the animals. The
claim that they disturb gamebirds or
crowd out native heronries is being
studied.

41 Gull-billed Tern
(*Gelochelidon nilotica*)
Gulls (Laridae)

Description: 13–14½″ (33–37 cm). Pigeon-sized.
White with long wings, silvery gray
back, and *black crown.* Resembles
several other terns, such as Forster's,
Common, and Arctic, but has stout
black bill, black legs, slightly forked tail,
and whiter overall coloration. In fall, it
has white crown with dusky streaks,
dark patch behind eye.

Voice: A harsh nasal cry that some hear as
catydid, catydid; also a gull-like alarm
rattle.

Habitat: Salt marshes, seashore.

Nesting: 2 or 3 buff, brown-marked eggs in a
scrape, sometimes with a lining of
shells, pebbles, or dry grass; in
colonies.

Range: Cosmopolitan, with disjunct range on
certain coasts of the world; in the
western United States breeds only at
the Salton Sea in California.

This marsh tern often forages for insects
in fields around lagoons where it nests,
or hawks for them in the air as they
swarm over the marsh. Even when
feeding on fish it does not plunge below
the surface. Its flight is heavier than
that of many terns.

91 Tufted Duck
(*Aythya fuligula*)
Ducks (Anatidae)

Description: 17″ (43 cm). Old World bird similar to
Ring-necked Duck. Breeding male has
iridescent green on *black body* and
violet-black head, contrasting with
*white flanks and underside. Long, slender
crest* dangles backward from crown; eyes
are yellow. Female is dusky, often with
white ring around bill, as in female
scaup, and white under tail. Both sexes

have blue bill and, like Greater Scaup, white streak along length of open wing.

Voice: A low *korr, korr, korr* resembling the calls of a scaup. Courting males give a weak whistle.

Habitat: Seashore and coastal lagoons during autumn and winter.

Nesting: 7–10 greenish eggs, in a grass bowl, lined with down, usually near water.

Range: Across the taiga belt of northern Eurasia. A rare straggler to the northeast and northwest coasts of North America.

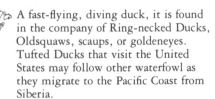

A fast-flying, diving duck, it is found in the company of Ring-necked Ducks, Oldsquaws, scaups, or goldeneyes. Tufted Ducks that visit the United States may follow other waterfowl as they migrate to the Pacific Coast from Siberia.

92, 132 **Lesser Scaup**
(*Aythya affinis*)
Ducks (Anatidae)

Description: 15–18½″ (38–47 cm). Darkish diving duck. Male resembles Greater Scaup, but sheen on *head purple* rather than green, and *sides not as white;* bill bluish-gray. Head narrow and pointed rather than rounded as in Greater Scaup. Female similar to female Greater: dull brown with a *white facial patch at base of bill. White stripe* on hind wing mostly confined to speculum; shorter than in Greater.

Voice: Like the Greater Scaup.

Habitat: Prairie and forest marshes; in winter in salt marshes, estuaries, and lakes. More often on inland ponds and lakes than Greater.

Nesting: 9–12 olive-brown eggs in a hollow with some grasses and down lining in tall vegetation, not too far from water. On leaving the nest, the female covers the eggs with down to keep them warm as well as to conceal them.

Range: From central Alaska east to Manitoba, south to Montana, North Dakota. Breeds in smaller numbers in interior British Columbia, Oregon, Idaho, Colorado, and Iowa. Winters along all coasts, the Mississippi Valley, and throughout Central and northern South America.

Both the Lesser and Greater are popularly called "Bluebills." They are hunted in the East, but seashore hunting is not as popular in the West, where the inland dabbling ducks are preferred.

93, 133 Greater Scaup
(*Aythya marila*)
Ducks (Anatidae)

Description: 15½–20″ (39–51 cm). Medium-sized duck. *Midbody* of male *is white below,* and light with wavy gray lines above. Head, breast, and tail are black with green *sheen on head*. In flight, its *long, white wing stripe* distinguishes it from Lesser Scaup. Bill bluish-gray. Female is dull brown with *white facial patch* encircling base of bill.

Voice: Females give a low *arrr;* courting males, a soft, cooing whistle.

Habitat: Wet tundra, lakes and rivers; boreal forests south of tundra. In winter on the sea near the coast.

Nesting: 7–10 pale olive-brown eggs in a down-lined depression; near water in dense vegetation.

Range: Circumpolar; in North America, in low arctic tundra marshes in a belt from western and central Alaska through northern Canada. Winters on all three coasts, at some of the Great Lakes and the Mississippi valley.

For most birders the Greater Scaup is either a winter duck or a rarity. It is

found in flocks, or rafts, often mixed
with other diving ducks. It feeds on
oysters, small clams, and rock crabs in
sheltered bays and inshore waters, but
also consumes quantities of buds and
seeds of submerged plants.

156 Whistling Swan
(Olor columbianus)
Ducks (Anatidae)

Description: 47–58″ (119–147 cm). Large white
swan; habitually holds neck straight
and stiff; black bill usually with a small
yellow spot near eye. Immatures light
gray-brown, with pinkish bill.

Voice: A high-pitched, whistling *wow-wow,*
often heard long before the birds can be
seen in the sky.

Habitat: Tundra in nesting season; in winter,
tidal and freshwater marshes.

Nesting: 4 or 5 white eggs in a huge nest of
plant debris on small islets of tundra
lakes and marshes. The family moves
south together before the waters freeze.

Range: Breeds near the Arctic coast between
the Bering Sea and Hudson Bay and in
the central Canadian Arctic. Winters
on the Atlantic and Pacific coasts.

In one study, swans were marked with
colored neck bands at Chesapeake Bay
and their migration was followed to
their Alaskan breeding grounds. One
"Whistler," banded on the Atlantic
seaboard the previous winter, was
sighted in the Central Valley of
California in March 1974. This Arctic
breeder alternately visited the Atlantic
and Pacific coasts of the huge North
American continent, surely something
of a record for birds.

212 Short-billed Dowitcher
(*Limnodromus griseus*)
Sandpipers (Scolopacidae)

Description: 10½–12" (27–30 cm). Snipe-like, *long-billed shorebird with white lower back and rump, black-and-white-checkered tail, dark bill, green legs.* Smaller than the Long-billed Dowitcher. In summer: salmon below, with dark spotting (barring on the Long-bill) on breast. In winter: gray overall except for light eyebrow stripe, white lower back and rump.

Voice: Its call distinguishes it from its long-billed cousin; a mellow *tu-tu-tu*, as opposed to the thin *keek* of the latter.

Habitat: Marshes or edge of wet tundra in summer; mud flats and shallow ponds the rest of the year.

Nesting: 4 greenish, brown-spotted eggs in a depression.

Range: Southern Alaska through taiga region of Canada east to Labrador. Winters locally along the southern coasts of United States and south to South America.

These are among the first shorebirds to migrate south, the adults leaving as early as July and the young following in August. In fall and winter, this species is found mainly on coastal mud flats, whereas the Long-bill prefers fresh-water ponds.

243 Clapper Rail
(*Rallus longirostris*)
Rails (Rallidae)

Description: 14–16½" (36–42 cm). Chicken-sized. Grayish-brown with *tawny breast* and *barred flanks*, long legs, and *fairly long, slightly decurved bill.*

Voice: A loud *kik-kik-kik-kik* that carries far even in dense reeds.

Habitat: Densely vegetated salt marshes; locally in fresh or brackish marshes.

Nesting: 5–14 buff eggs spotted with dark
brown in a platform nest of dead plant
material constructed in clumps of
marsh grasses arched over by
surrounding grasses to form a roof.

Range: Along the Atlantic and Gulf coasts, and
from the central California coast south
to Baja California and to South
America.

Rails are secretive, seldom coming out
into the open. The population in the
western United States has been
endangered by the gradual destruction
of marsh habitat. Its stronghold is San
Francisco Bay (with fewer than 3000
birds in the early 1970s). A freshwater
population (Yuma Clapper Rail),
containing fewer than 1000 birds, is
found along the lower Colorado River of
California, Arizona, and Mexico.

---

247 **Black Rail**
(*Laterallus jamaicensis*)
Rails (Rallidae)

Description: 5–6″ (13–15 cm). Sparrow-sized.
Blackish with *chestnut nape,* white
speckling on back, and short black bill.

Voice: A rolling *ki-ki-doo,* the last syllable
lowest in pitch.

Habitat: Freshwater and saltwater marshes.

Nesting: 4–8 white or buffy, thickly spotted
eggs in a domed nest hidden among
vegetation.

Range: Coastal marshes from San Francisco Bay
area south to Baja California; also along
lower Colorado River; more widespread
in the East.

The small Black Rail is often confused
with chicks of other rails because, like
them, it is black with longish legs, and
swims or creeps swiftly over the mat of
salt-marsh plants or freshwater lily
pads. One gets only glimpses of this
secretive rail. Threatened by the

destruction of its coastal-marsh habitat, it is on the official list of rare birds in California. The size of the remaining population is unknown.

Freshwater Marshes

Where the water in lakes or quiet bends
of lowland rivers covers the land
shallowly, marshy vegetation springs
up: lily pads in deep water, bulrushes
and cattails in shallower places, reeds
and sedges where marsh merges into
wet meadow.

Swamps are marshes with tree growth.
In the swamps of the North, which
take the form of bogs and muskegs, the
main vegetation is sphagnum moss; a
bog may have open water, whereas a
muskeg does not.

Marshes often include open waters
attractive to lake birds such as White
Pelicans and grebes. Where the
vegetation is short, sandpipers nest, but
since we see them most often on the
seashore in winter, we have included
them in that habitat.

1, 2 Snowy Egret
(Egretta thula)
Herons (Ardeidae)

Description: 20–27" (51–69 cm). Medium-sized
heron. *Snow-white plumage, black bill,
dark legs,* and *yellow feet.* White plumes
on head are usually spread when bird
alights; plumes also present on foreneck
and back during breeding. Immatures
have yellowish stripe along back of leg.
Cattle Egret has pale bill, legs, and feet
(adults), dark legs and feet
(immatures). Much larger Great Egret
has yellow bill, black legs and feet.

Voice: A low croak.

Habitat: Marshy areas, near freshwater lakes or
estuaries.

Nesting: 3–6 pale blue eggs in a platform nest
on willows in marshes or on nearby
trees; in colonies.

Range: Widespread in North and South
America. In the West, breeds
commonly in California and in the
wetlands of Nevada, Utah, Colorado,
and the southwestern states. Winters in
California and farther south.

When the sexes look alike, as in the
Snowy Egret and all other herons, their
roles in courtship and in parental care
are often similar. Snowy Egrets use the
veil of fine plumes in their courtship
display, which both partners perform
face to face in exactly the same way. As
the mates alternate on the nest, the
bird which happens to be on the egg or
young has to be greeted by the other
parent lest it be attacked; the greeting
consists of deep bows with the head
plumes erected.

3, 4 Great Egret
"Common Egret"
(*Casmerodius albus*)
Herons (Ardeidae)

Description: 37–41″ (94–104 cm) and over 30″ (76 cm) tall. Large heron; in the West next in size to Great Blue Heron. Body *snow white,* back of breeding birds enveloped in a magnificent veil of white plumes. *Yellow bill, black legs and feet,* and size distinguish it from other white herons.

Voice: A low, growling croak.

Habitat: Marshes where deeper water is edged with low, vegetated banks. Nesting colonies may be in reeds or cattails, but more commonly in trees.

Nesting: 3–5 pale blue eggs in a large platform nest of sturdy sticks and stems. Old nests are reused after repair. Both parents feed fish, frogs, and snakes to the young.

Range: All continents; shuns only cold northern tracts or desert expanses. In the West, breeds chiefly from southern Oregon and Idaho southward. Winters in all southwestern states and south to Colombia.

Heron plumes, especially the white ones, were once in great demand for women's hats. By 1900 the Great Egret and other plume-bearing birds were close to extinction throughout much of their range. Legal protection under international law proved only partly effective; a ban on imports and guarding of American nesting colonies finally succeeded in saving the birds, but the Great Egret, formerly called the "Common Egret," now faces a loss of its habitat due to the draining of wetlands.

8, 10   Black-crowned Night Heron
(*Nycticorax nycticorax*)
Herons (Ardeidae)

Description: 23–28″ (58–71 cm). *Medium-sized heron. Short, thick neck; glossy blackish-green* crown and back, *gray wings* and tail; *face and underparts white,* including three fairly large plumes at nape; large red eyes. Immatures buff and brown with light spots above; pale with olive and brown streaks below; eyes pale yellow to orange.

Voice: Call is a loud, barking *kwok!*

Habitat: Freshwater habitats, also brackish marshes.

Nesting: 3–5 pale bluish-green eggs in a stick or cane nest lined with small twigs in a tree. Its heronries often contain other species.

Range: Worldwide except in Australia and in taiga and tundra belts. In the New World, from southern Canada through South America.

At a heronry the plumage of immature birds blends so well with the background that there appear to be many more adults than young, but when the birds take flight one may see many more immatures than adults.

11   Least Bittern
(*Ixobrychus exilis*)
Herons (Ardeidae)

Description: 11–14″ (28–36 cm). A small marsh-dwelling heron. Male has black crown and *black back with two light stripes;* head and back of neck reddish tan, *wings reddish with large buff patches,* whitish below. In female, black is replaced by purplish-chestnut.

Voice: A low, very rapid *coo-coo-coo-coo,* given most often at night during the breeding season. Also a *kuk, kuk, kuk . . .*

Habitat: Densely vegetated marshes.

Nesting: 4 or 5 pale bluish-green eggs laid in a platform nest, sometimes an old nest of another species.

Range: Breeds from Oregon south to Baja California; east of the Rockies from southernmost Canada south into South America. Winters from southern United States southward.

The observer in a hurry will rarely see this bittern. After waiting patiently on a levee or marsh edge, one may catch a brief glimpse of it as it flushes from the reeds.

12 American Bittern
(*Botaurus lentiginosus*)
Herons (Ardeidae)

Description: 23–34" (58–86 cm). A large, stocky heron, somewhat larger than the Black-crowned Night Heron. Brownish with longitudinal streaks and faint markings matching the color of dry reeds; *broad black sideburns*. When approached, it freezes with neck and head pointing skyward like a cattail stalk. In the air, blackish flight feathers and fast wingbeat distinguish it from the juvenile Black-crowned Night Heron.

Voice: A "pumping" call (described below).

Habitat: Heavily reeded, often inaccessible areas in marshes or bogs.

Nesting: 3–7 olive eggs. A most asocial heron, it nests in single pairs in a territory defended by the male; the female builds a platform nest in heavy cover.

Range: Widespread in North America, nesting from the Great Slave Lake and Hudson Bay to Newfoundland and south to the lower Colorado River and lower Mississippi Valley and Florida. Migratory in the North.

Wherever people have had long association with marshes, the bittern's eerie call has made it famous in

superstition and fable. In spring and
early summer the twilight or darkness
reverberates with its repeated *pump-er-
lunk* call. The sound is best described as
like that of an old-fashioned pump
along with a stake being hammered
into the ground.

---

13 Wood Stork
"Wood Ibis"
(*Mycteria americana*)
Storks (Ciconiidae)

Description: 40–44" (102–112 cm). *White, with black
flight feathers and tail.* Long legs; thick
decurved dark bill; long neck, but
unfeathered black upper half of neck
and head reduce apparent length of
neck, making it look stockier than it
actually is. By contrast, juvenile has
lighter neck and yellow bill. Older
birds have a horny, dirtyish-looking
plate on crown, like a cap.

Voice: Silent on its visits to the western
United States. Gives a harsh croak on
the nesting grounds.

Habitat: Tropical swamps and marshes,
especially those with tree growth, such
as mangrove swamps.

Nesting: 2 or 3 white eggs in bulky stick nest.
In colonies in trees.

Range: Gulf and southern Atlantic and Pacific
coasts of North America and Central
and South America. Florida has the
only nesting colonies in the United
States. Regular nonbreeding summer
visitor to the Salton Sea, California; a
casual visitor elsewhere in the
Southwest.

Ibises and storks are close relatives, and
this species was formerly called the
"Wood Ibis." It is larger, though, than
the ibises, and has a thicker and less
curved bill; these and other
characteristics resemble those of the
celebrated White Stork of Eurasia. It

flies with slow wingbeats, neck and legs extended; the black tail and wing tips are especially conspicuous when it soars over the rookery. It forages in muddy waters for fishes, frogs and snakes.

14 White-faced Ibis
(*Plegadis chihi*)
Ibises (Threskiornithidae)

Description: 19–26″ (48–66 cm). Long legs, long neck, and long curved bill. *Chestnut brown,* with a green and violet sheen on upperparts. In breeding plumage both sexes have a *conspicuous white marking around chin and eye,* distinguishing them from widespread Glossy Ibis, a close relative. Juveniles lighter below and lack sheen.

Voice: A low quacking call given in flight.

Habitat: Large marshes, with nesting colony hidden in inaccessible reedbed or willow-covered area.

Nesting: 3 or 4 pale greenish eggs on a large stick platform built in low trees or in dense standing vegetation near or over marshes. Breeds in colonies and readily joins rookeries of other marsh birds.

Range: Its breeding range has contracted as it seems to flee civilization. Still breeds in the West, from California across to southern Idaho, Nevada, Utah, Colorado, and the Texas coast. Also in South America. Winters in southernmost California and in Mexico.

Feeding ibises are versatile, wading and probing in mud for crayfish but also walking through wet meadows to take grasshoppers and frogs. In flight to and from the roost they present an unforgettable view as long, wavering lines of large, dark, curlew-like birds speed toward the horizon.

15 Great Blue Heron
(*Ardea herodias*)
Herons (Ardeidae)

Description: 42–52″ (107–132 cm) and 48″ (122 cm) tall. A large blue-gray heron. Back and *wings blue-gray; underparts whitish* with black streaking on belly, *head white with black stripe* ending in black plumes behind eye; black-and-white foreneck and chest end in gray plumes in the breeding adult. Juveniles lack plumes and are more brownish.

Voice: Herons call mainly when startled or alarmed, uttering a loud, raucous *grak* or *kraak*.

Habitat: Wetlands where tall trees, rock ledges, or extensive reeds provide a safe site for the heronry. It readily makes 20–30-mile round trips to feed.

Nesting: 3–7 bluish-green eggs in a stick nest; in colonies, often with many nests in the same tree.

Range: Widespread in North America except the northern tundra and forest belts, and extending to northern South America. Migratory where waters freeze.

Because of the gray body and long legs and neck, Great Blue Herons are often miscalled cranes, but herons have a longer bill and fly with neck folded back on the shoulder, extending it only when about to alight or when under attack. Herons stand in water or on a bank; cranes stand in marshes or dry fields, and are more wary. In late summer, young herons disperse widely and may be encountered at small ponds, mountain waters, or even in backyard pools, wherever fish are plentiful.

16 Sandhill Crane
(*Grus canadensis*)
Cranes (Gruidae)

Description: 34–48″ (86–122 cm). Over 36″ (90 cm) tall. Large bird with long legs and neck but relatively short bill; *color of ash or wet sand, with red cap on forehead.* Like all cranes, flies with neck and legs outstretched. Great Blue Heron is slimmer, lighter-bodied, longer-billed, and flies with neck folded.

Voice: In flight formation some utter a *krooo-ooo* or *garooo-a* call incessantly, audible at great distances; when disturbed, the whole flock calls.

Habitat: Breeds in marshes; in the North on tundra, prairies, and muskegs.

Nesting: 2 olive, brown-spotted eggs on a large mound in a remote marshy area. Both parents incubate the eggs and tend the young.

Range: Breeds from northeastern Siberia across coastal Alaska to the central Canadian Arctic, south to northeastern California, Nevada, Colorado, South Dakota, and Michigan. Also from southern Mississippi through Florida to Cuba. Winters from California to western Texas and south to central Mexico.

A similar bird, the rare Whooping Crane (*Grus americana*), is much larger, white, with black primaries. Only about 50 survive and these breed in northern Alberta, wintering at the Aransas refuge on the Texas coast. The Sandhill is still common at some places in the North, but the nesting population in British Columbia and the United States is decreasing due to loss of its habitat. In winter the Sandhill chooses not only marshes but also extensive prairies and fields, where it thrives on spilled grain. Families fly together in groups of 20 to 100 birds in "V" formation, usually during early afternoon when the air is warmest. The cranes soar on outstretched wings in a rising column of air, called a thermal, until almost out of sight, then form a "V" again and glide to the next thermal. The small tundra subspecies is also known as the "Little Brown Crane."

43 Black Tern
(*Chlidonias niger*)
Gulls (Laridae)

Description: 9–10¼" (23–26 cm). In summer, *entirely dark, except under the tail.* In fall, lighter gray above, except for wings; white below, with white head but black nape and eye-line. Tail only slightly forked.

Voice: A high, sharp *kip* and *k-seek.*

Habitat: Marshes with open water, and tall tules, reeds, or other vegetation surrounding a colony of nests. Rice fields.

Nesting: 2 or 3 buffy eggs, heavily marked with brown, in nests, generally floating, set close together and made from pieces of cattail and other dead marsh vegetation.

Range: Widespread in temperate latitudes of North America and Eurasia, such as the Canadian prairies and also bogs in the taiga belt south to marshes in the Western states, including California, Nevada, and Colorado. Winters south of the United States.

In Central Europe this dainty bird is considered the "black-veiled fairy" of the wetlands. It is constantly on the move like a swallow, circling and hovering with head down, occasionally swooping to pick up a damselfly from the surface of the water. When mayflies break the surface, flocks of Black Terns dance above them like butterflies, catching them as they rise. When a colony is disturbed dozens rise up, protesting loudly, from flimsy

platforms of cattail stems with small
eggs balanced on them.

90, 134 **Ring-necked Duck**
(*Aythya collaris*)
Ducks (Anatidae)

Description: 14½–18" (37–46 cm). Size of a Lesser
Scaup, with which it often associates in
winter. In breeding plumage *male has
black back,* gray sides with vertical
white marks before the wings,
iridescent purple head, and blue-gray
bill with two white vertical bars.
Chestnut brown neck band of male is
seldom discernible. *In flight, dark wing
coverts* provide contrast with lighter
gray primaries and secondaries. Female
is brown and lacks white facial ring of
the scaups, but has thin white ring near
tip of bill, pale lores, and eye-ring.

Voice: Relatively silent. Males give soft
whistling notes during courtship.

Habitat: A freshwater diver, it rarely takes to the
sea. Frequently winters near coast on
lakes, small streams, and marshes.

Nesting: 8–12 dark olive eggs in a grass or reed
nest.

Range: Broadly distributed in interior western
Canada and in valleys and prairies of
northcentral states to the Great Lakes,
also east to the Maritime Provinces of
Canada. Winters as far north as
Vancouver, British Columbia, east to
the Chesapeake Bay, and south to Cuba
and Guatemala.

This bird is considered very edible but
is little hunted because it does not
gather in large winter flocks but spreads
out on small watercourses and in
marshes.

94, 136   Redhead
(*Aythya americana*)
Ducks (Anatidae)

Description: 18–22" (46–56 cm). Medium-sized diving duck. Male has *large round chestnut-red head, black breast* and black under tail, *gray body*. Bill blue with dark tip. Canvasback male has same red-black-gray pattern but much paler back and sides and longer, slimmer black bill. Females uniformly brown, darkest on back, with light patch at base of bill and chin, pale eye-ring and line behind eye. Pale bill with dark tip.

Voice: Male gives a loud cat-like *meow* as a courting call; females rather silent.

Habitat: Feeds on submerged vegetation in prairie sloughs and lakes; marshy habitats of boreal forest belt.

Nesting: 10–15 pale olive or creamy eggs in a nest of reeds and down, in marshes where vegetation is dense and deep water close by.

Range: Breeds locally in central Alaska, from British Columbia east to Manitoba, and Minnesota; and south, then, locally, to California, Arizona, and Colorado. Winters from southern British Columbia east to Massachusetts and south to Mexico in tidewater areas or inland marshes with open water.

A sizable bird, and a good flyer, it is prized by hunters. Its decline in the eastern parts of its range is due mainly to draining of marshes. It is still abundant in the West.

95, 137   Canvasback
(*Aythya valisineria*)
Ducks (Anatidae)

Description: 19½–24" (50–61 cm). One of the largest diving ducks. Similar to the Redhead, but with dark, longer black bill and *shallow sloping forehead,* which

gives a unique shape to its head. Male's
midbody whitish; front and rear look
black from a distance, *head chestnut-red.*
Female has brown head and breast,
lighter near eye and throat, gray-brown
back, grayish sides, and has same
distinctive profile.

Voice: Male gives a cooing call during
courtship; otherwise rather silent.

Habitat: Prairie and parkland lakes with
emergent vegetation; open marshes
adjacent to boreal forest.

Nesting: 7–9 dark grayish-olive eggs in a nest
placed just below the high-water level
in dense marsh vegetation near open
waters with enough depth for diving
and abundant bottom vegetation and
fauna.

Range: Breeds in British Columbia, Alberta,
Saskatchewan, southern Manitoba, and
the states directly to the south, with
Oregon, northern Utah, Colorado,
Nebraska, and Minnesota forming
southern boundary of breeding range.
Winters on both coasts from southern
British Columbia and Massachusetts
south to central Mexico.

These wary birds stay in the middle of
large lakes, bays, and flooded marshes
in the winter; their summer haunts are
also quite inaccessible. A favorite
gamebird, it is kept under observation
by game management authorities to
prevent its numbers from decreasing.

96, 151 Northern Shoveler
"Shoveler"
(*Anas clypeata*)
Ducks (Anatidae)

Description: 17–20″ (43–51 cm). A large-sized teal,
identified by *large shovel-shaped bill* and
relatively *short neck.* Breeding male has
green head like Mallard but much
larger bill; lower neck and breast snow
white, belly and flanks chestnut, but

white in front of black tail. Females, molting males, and juveniles are drab and mottled, but their open wings show the same bright pattern seen in Blue-winged and Cinnamon teals: light cobalt-blue inner forewing with a white band separating it from metallic-green speculum.

Voice: Females give a harsh quack, sometimes in diminuendo series; males generally silent, but give rattling notes during courtship.

Habitat: Freshwater marshes; tidal bays in winter.

Nesting: 8–12 olive-green eggs laid in early spring in a simple nest lined with down, often found under bushes or weeds not far from water.

Range: Circumpolar. Breeds in North America from Alaska through western Canada, mainly south of the tundra to Manitoba; south from eastern Washington; east to northeastern Kansas and Wisconsin; also in central California. Winters from Puget Sound south along Pacific and Gulf coastal states and Mexico.

This species, formerly called the "Shoveler," needs shallow open water where the birds can use their large bills to sieve the water, mostly for animal matter. The male wears drab summer plumage until February, in contrast to other ducks such as the Mallard and Pintail, which molt in early or mid autumn. The Northern Shoveler's courtship is correspondingly limited to a short period in spring. The Northern Shoveler and other marsh ducks have become relatively abundant because game departments in Canada, the United States, and Mexico and private hunting organizations have purchased breeding as well as wintering habitats for them to ensure annual replacement and survival.

97, 146 Mallard
(*Anas platyrhynchos*)
Ducks (Anatidae)

Description: 20½–28" (52–71 cm). From fall through winter and in breeding season, male has *green head, white collar, deep chestnut breast,* purplish-blue speculum bordered in front and back by black-and-white stripe. White tail, flanked by black, is topped by curled tail coverts. At other times only his yellow-green bill distinguishes him from female. Both have mottled brownish-buff bodies with dark crown and eye-stripe. Bill of female is orange with black mottling.

Voice: The female utters a loud quack or *quack-wack-wack;* the male *rab-rab-rab.*

Habitat: From large marshes to small river bends, bays, and even ditches and city ponds.

Nesting: 8–10 light olive-green eggs in a nest often placed away from water, sometimes even in a tree. Males linger while their mates incubate, but later gather in sheltered lakes to molt, losing the power of flight for a few weeks. The females also lose their flight feathers but remain with their young.

Range: The most widespread duck species throughout the Northern Hemisphere; occurs wherever there are wetlands, but in North America it is absent in most high Arctic, Atlantic coastal, and all southeastern areas.

The Mallard is the ancestor of our domestic duck, with which it often mingles and interbreeds in cities. Hybrids, flying with wild Mallards, may have heavier bodies and varying amounts of white in their plumage.

111 **American Coot**
(*Fulica americana*)
Rails (Rallidae)

Description: 13–16″ (33–41 cm). Chicken-sized.
Dark slate body, with ivory-colored bill
and frontal shield, reddish at upper
edge; head and neck black, long toes
with lobes on the sides, which serve for
swimming and for walking over lily
pads.

Voice: Low croaking notes and a higher cackle.
Also various "laughing" notes, such as
ka-ha-ha.

Habitat: Marshes and vegetated ponds, river
bends with two feet or more of open
water.

Nesting: 8–12 eggs on a platform nest in a
marsh, usually on the edge of open
water. Old nests are used throughout
the year for resting and preening.
Young chicks have a red-and-blue
frontal shield, which seems to be a
signal organ: when parents see the color
pad, they hold out a billful of
pondweed to the chick.

Range: Widespread in North America from
British Columbia to Massachusetts
south to Baja California and the Gulf
Coast states and Mexico. Winters where
waters do not freeze; found even on salt
water if there is submerged vegetation
to feed on.

Coots feed mainly by diving to the
bottom, but they also dabble from the
surface, or graze on lawns when they
winter in urbanized coastal areas.

116, 127 **Ruddy Duck**
(*Oxyura jamaicensis*)
Ducks (Anatidae)

Description: 14½–16″ (37–41 cm). Small duck,
easily recognized. Male is in breeding
plumage from spring until end of
summer: entire body *bright chestnut* with

black cap; face and underparts white; broad, *sky-blue bill.* In display (not commonly seen) *stiff tail uptilted,* making the bird look like a tiny, floating saddle. More often, especially when wary, it carries its tail on or below the water surface. In fall and winter male is dark above, light below, and has white cheek patch; bill gray. Female similar to winter male but with dark stripe on face. In flight, Ruddies show long tail and no speculum.

Voice: Males utter a thumping note and weak croaks during courtship, otherwise silent.

Habitat: Mainly prairie marsh; in winter, also in coastal salt marshes.

Nesting: 6–10 or more large, whitish eggs in a well-constructed, woven nest. Both sexes care for the ducklings.

Range: From northwestern Canada and valleys of the Pacific coastal areas sporadically throughout the western United States, south to California and east to Texas; south in Mexico, West Indies, and Colombia. Also locally in east-central North America. Winters on fresh or salt water from southwestern British Columbia southward.

Ruddy Ducks differ from other ducks in many ways. They are deep-water divers, but mainly vegetarian, feeding from the bottom even as hatchlings whereas other diving ducks begin by picking food from the surface. For this feeding method they require clear, deep-water areas, but for retreat and nesting they need tall, dense reeds. When disturbed, they retreat under water like grebes. They fly close to the surface, with rapid beats of their short wings. The long tail is an aid in swimming, but is also used in courtship displays.

117, 152 Cinnamon Teal
(*Anas cyanoptera*)
Ducks (Anatidae)

Description: 14½–17" (37–43 cm). Small duck
closely related to the Blue-winged Teal.
Male bright *cinnamon* from October to
June, with richest color on head; large
pale blue patch on forewing. Female
mottled brown with bluish patch on
forewing visible in flight; virtually
indistinguishable from female Blue-
winged Teal.

Voice: Female has a high quacking note; male
utters a rattling note during courtship.

Habitat: Marshes and vegetated shallow ponds,
or river bends.

Nesting: 10–12 or more white or buffy eggs, a
little distance from water, in bulrushes,
other marsh vegetation, or even dense
rushes above water.

Range: Its distribution is oddly discontinuous:
bulrush marshes in the West, from
southern British Columbia to the
southern end of the Mexican Plateau,
with another population breeding in
southern South America.

At hatching, young Cinnamon Teals,
like all ducklings, are "imprinted" by
the mother's appearance and call and
follow her closely. This trait is useful,
for as soon as the brood enters the water
it encounters many kinds of waterfowl,
including other teals. By closely
following their mother and heeding her
warning notes, the young survive many
of the perils that beset ducklings.

118 European Wigeon
(*Anas penelope*)
Ducks (Anatidae)

Description: 16½–20" (42–51 cm). Resembles
American Wigeon in size, general
pattern, and female's coloration. In
breeding colors, male has *fox-red head*

and neck, *creamy forehead, wine-colored breast,* finely vermiculated gray body. Large white patch on wing, undertail black. Dark red head makes it appear much darker on the water than American Wigeon. Female may have rust tinge on head and underparts.

Voice: Male has a sharp descending whistle; the female, a whirring call.

Habitat: Coastal marshes, ponds, in water mixing with other ducks; a grazing duck found in parks, lakes, golf courses, and other grassy areas.

Nesting: 7 or 8 buffy eggs in grass nest.

Range: Across northern Eurasia, but scarce winter visitor to the Pacific and Atlantic coasts of North America.

This wigeon is usually found associating with flocks of American Wigeon.

119, 149 **American Wigeon**
(*Anas americana*)
Ducks (Anatidae)

Description: 18–23" (46–58 cm). Male has *brown body, grayish head, white crown* (hence the popular name "Baldpate") and *green face patch. Extensive flashing white forewing of male* distinguishes the species; speculum green. Female is *drab brown,* with *finely flecked grayish head.*

Voice: Males give a distinctive softly whistled *wheew-whew;* females quack.

Habitat: Open marshy areas, tundra, and prairie.

Nesting: 8–10 glossy, creamy white eggs in a ground nest in a marsh, but away from water.

Range: Alaska and the Northwest Territories south to the central Canadian mountain provinces and the western states. On the Pacific Coast it winters in tidal and valley marshes from Vancouver Island south through Mexico. Also winters along the East Coast and in the Gulf Coast states.

In many parts of their range, flocks of wigeons and coots winter together. Both feed on bottom vegetation, wigeons dabbling in the shallows, coots diving in deeper waters. When food that the wigeons reach becomes scarce, they steal food out of the bills of the coots, causing the latter to work double-time to satisfy themselves as well as the ducks. Wary and alert, wigeons present a delightful sight on an open marsh, whole flocks rising in unison at the slightest disturbance. In the air they form tight, swiftly turning flocks and their whistling calls enliven the scene.

120, 153 Blue-winged Teal
(*Anas discors*)
Ducks (Anatidae)

Description: 14½–16″ (37–41 cm). A small duck. Male has bluish-gray head with *white crescent before eye;* body dull mottled brown above; pinkish-buff with black spots below. Female mottled buff brown and almost indistinguishable from female Cinnamon Teal. In flight males and females of both species show large pale blue patch on forewing, with green speculum.

Voice: Females utter a high quack; courting males, a high whistled note.

Habitat: Marshes.

Nesting: 10–12 or more dull white eggs in a delicate nest of dry grass stalks close to the shore of a pond.

Range: Breeds from forest-tundra bogs in central Canada south to northern California, Nevada, Utah, and Colorado, and east to the Atlantic. Some winter along the Gulf Coast, many more in Central America and northern South America.

In past decades when great numbers of these ducks left the prairies on

migration, they were heavily hunted,
and their population was drastically
reduced. They are in less danger today
because the hunting season opens after
most of the birds have migrated. Fast
flyers and wary, they fly in small groups
or flocks, turning in unison, flashing
the blue area of the wing. They arrive
latest of all ducks at their breeding
ground and leave early in the fall.

121, 150 **Green-winged Teal**
including "Common Teal"
(*Anas crecca*)
Ducks (Anatidae)

Description: 12½–15½" (32–39 cm). Very small
duck with green, glossy speculum.
Male's *chestnut head has dark green
patch* around eye and ear; buff breast
with dark speckles, *gray sides with
conspicuous, vertical white stripe* in front
of folded wing and cream-colored patch
under dark tail. Female speckled light
and dark brown.

Voice: Male gives a high *dreep;* female, a low
quack.

Habitat: Marshes and lakes.

Nesting: 10 or more eggs, varying from dirty
white to olive, in a hollow lined with
down and grass, located near water.

Range: Circumpolar across the tundra and
boreal forest of North America and
Eurasia. Breeds in Aleutians and from
the Yukon Delta to Newfoundland,
south to California and Arizona in the
West and Pennsylvania in the East.
Winters from southern Canada to
northern Mexico, wherever it finds open
water in marshes.

This duck gathers by the hundreds on
its winter grounds and staging areas.
Flocks describe beautiful maneuvers in
the air, accompanied by a whistling
chorus from the males. When the ducks
settle on water, the flock breaks up into

small groups often consisting of one
female courted by several males.
Eventually the female pairs up and the
chosen male wards off other suitors.
This phase of the courtship is similar in
several species of ducks. The European
population formerly was called
"Common Teal."

---

122 **Fulvous Whistling-Duck**
     (*Dendrocygna bicolor*)
     Ducks (Anatidae)

Description: 18–21" (46–53 cm). Body *deep tan* or
             fulvous-colored, with dark back and
             wings conspicuous in flight. Long,
             goose-like neck, with white throat
             streakings (not always visible), long,
             slate blue legs and feet. In flight, the
             tail shows a black-white-black pattern.
             Sexes look similar.
      Voice: A whistled *pe-cheea*.
    Habitat: Richly vegetated marshes with areas of
             open water.
    Nesting: 15–20 buffy or whitish eggs, along
             marsh ponds in dense vegetation.
      Range: Mexico, with breeding area extending
             from Louisiana west to southern
             Arizona and California's Imperial and
             San Joaquin valleys, but lately scarce in
             the latter; also in southern Florida.
             Populations live in parts of India, East
             Africa, and South America.

These ducks are mainly vegetarian,
preferring rich waters with abundant
plant life and a muddy bottom, but
they also feed in grainfields. In flight
their long necks and outstretched legs
give them an almost heron-like
appearance. When swimming, they
look more like miniature geese than
ducks.

123 Mexican Duck
(*Anas diazi*)
Ducks (Anatidae)

Description: 21–22″ (53–56 cm). Plumage of both
sexes in all seasons resembles that of
female Mallard: dark, *streaked buff
overall with blue speculum bordered in front
and back with white.* Bill of male is
yellow-green; female's, dusky orange.
No white in tail.

Voice: Resembles that of the Mallard: the male
utters a *kwek-kwek-kwek-kwek;* the
female, a loud quack.

Habitat: Marshes.

Nesting: 8–10 olive eggs in a down-lined nest in
marshes, brush, or hollows.

Range: Northeastern Mexico and adjacent parts
of Arizona, New Mexico, and western
Texas.

This smaller, darker version of the
Mallard is a nonmigratory form. Some
ornithologists are undecided about its
status as a full species. A 1966 census
counted fewer than 300 Mexican Ducks
in the United States. A breeding
program is underway to boost the
numbers of this endangered species.

124, 148 Pintail
(*Anas acuta*)
Ducks (Anatidae)

Description: Male 25–29″ (64–74 cm), female 20½–
22½″ (52–57 cm). Long-necked slender
duck. Male has *brown head and white
neck* and underparts, grayish back and
sides and *long black pointed central* tail
feathers. Speculum metallic brown and
green with white rear border which
shows in flight. Feet gray. Female has
brownish head, gray bill, and
somewhat pointed tail.

Voice: As in most ducks, the male has the
higher-pitched voice, uttering a high
dreep-eep; females give a low quack.

Habitat: Marshes of the tundra and boreal forests as well as prairie marshes; in winter most freshwater marshes and lakes.

Nesting: 6–12 olive eggs in a nest close to water, in a marsh, meadow, or tilled field.

Range: Throughout the Northern Hemisphere; in North America breeds from Aleutians, Alaska to Hudson Bay and south to California and Colorado.

A banding project on the Hawaiian Islands revealed that the few thousand Pintails that winter there hatched as far away as California's Sacramento Valley, a Saskatchewan marsh, and even the Siberian tundra. Pairing takes place in late fall and winter in the southern wintering areas. The male then follows his new mate to her breeding area, regardless of where he was born or spent the previous summer. Thus the Pintail population undergoes a steady mixing, keeping the species uniform everywhere.

125, 147   **Gadwall**
(*Anas strepera*)
Ducks (Anatidae)

Description: 18½–23" (47–58 cm). Smaller than the Mallard. Drab, grayish-brown dabbling duck; only duck with *white speculum* having black outer and inner margins. Breeding plumage of male is *gray with contrasting black stern* and brown forewing. Female is mottled overall like Mallard female but with yellowish bill; has white speculum like male.

Voice: Male utters low *rreb* notes and a high whistle; females, a low flat quack.

Habitat: Marshes and ponds; shallow, wide waters rich in bottom vegetation; alkali or salt lakes and marshes; in late summer, in stubble fields.

Nesting: 7–13 whitish eggs in a well hidden nest lined with down.

Range: Circumpolar; in North America breeds

in many scattered marshes from the Alaska Peninsula to Long Island, N.Y.; more concentrated breeding areas in northern prairie provinces and states and in the West from southern British Columbia to California and northern Utah. Winters in the West where waters do not freeze, in south central and eastern seaboard states.

Gadwalls are dabbling ducks; they feed on the bottom in shallow water by tipping forward so that the tail sticks up.

157 **Trumpeter Swan**
(*Olor buccinator*)
Ducks (Anatidae)

Description: 60–72″ (150–180 cm). One of North America's largest birds. Adult male weighs up to 28 pounds (over 12.5 kg). *Snow white* with large black bill; immature dusky, gray-brown and has pink bill with black base and tip. Mute Swan (*Cygnus olor*), an introduced species and a tame pond bird, is smaller with a black knob at the base of its orange bill. Mute Swans hold their necks in a graceful curve with bill pointing down, whereas the native Trumpeter and Whistling swans swim with straight necks and horizontal bills.

Voice: A booming, horn-like *ko-hoh,* lower in pitch than the Whistling Swan's call.

Habitat: Marshes, lakes, or rivers with dense vegetation.

Nesting: 4–6 whitish eggs in a huge nest on a bulrush-covered island or beaver lodge. Since they do not breed until at least four years of age, replacement is slow.

Range: Breeds in southern Alaska, northern British Columbia, western Alberta, Oregon, Idaho, Montana, and Wyoming. Winters in southeastern Alaska, western British Columbia, and open water areas of United States breeding range.

Draining of marshes, hunting, and other disturbances brought the Trumpeter Swan close to extinction. From a very small number in the 1930s, conservation measures have allowed it to increase to more than 1000 on each of two remaining nesting areas, one in Alaska and northern Canada and the other in Montana and nearby states. Reintroduction into formerly inhabited marshes has been successful and the population in the 1970s has exceeded 3000.

158 Ross' Goose
(*Chen rossii*)
Ducks (Anatidae)

Description: 21–25½″ (53–65 cm). Like Snow Goose but Mallard-sized. *White with black wing tips; stubby bill pink with a dark base,* lacks dark margin found in Snow Goose.

Voice: A weak cackling note.

Habitat: Tundra in summer; freshwater marsh in winter.

Nesting: 3–6 eggs in a down-lined nest near water. While the female incubates, the male stands by to ward off enemies; later he shares in leading the young to water and pasture.

Range: The small population of this species (totaling about 32,000) nests in a limited area of the central Canadian Arctic. Winters mainly in California's Sacramento Valley, mixing with White-fronted and Snow geese.

This relatively rare bird is carefully monitored by both Canadian and United States game biologists, but some hunting is allowed on its winter grounds.

**159, 161 Snow Goose
including "Blue Goose"**
(*Chen caerulescens*)
Ducks (Anatidae)

Description: 25–31" (64–79 cm). Smaller than the
domestic goose. Those that nest in
northeastern Siberia and in the Arctic
tundra of western North America are
pure white with black wing tips, pink feet,
and stout *pink bill with black margin.*
Juveniles mottled with brownish-gray
and have dark bill. In the eastern Arctic
most individuals are white, but a blue
phase occurs (formerly considered a
separate species, the "Blue Goose"):
upperparts bluish-gray, underparts
brownish-gray, head and upper neck
white. Blue phase birds have spread
westward in recent decades and are now
found among the thousands of white
Snow Geese wintering in California.
Voice: A rather high, nasal *how-wow.*
Habitat: Tundra and marsh.
Nesting: 4–8 white eggs in a nest sparsely lined
with down on the tundra.
Range: Arctic areas of Asia and North
America.

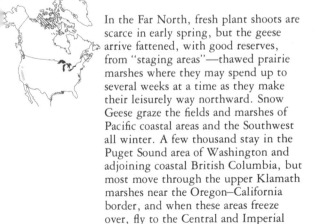

In the Far North, fresh plant shoots are
scarce in early spring, but the geese
arrive fattened, with good reserves,
from "staging areas"—thawed prairie
marshes where they may spend up to
several weeks at a time as they make
their leisurely way northward. Snow
Geese graze the fields and marshes of
Pacific coastal areas and the Southwest
all winter. A few thousand stay in the
Puget Sound area of Washington and
adjoining coastal British Columbia, but
most move through the upper Klamath
marshes near the Oregon–California
border, and when these areas freeze
over, fly to the Central and Imperial
valleys of California, where they graze
in marshes and stubble fields.

162 Canada Goose
(*Branta canadensis*)
Ducks (Anatidae)

Description: 22–45" (56–92 cm). *Long black neck,*
black head and bill, white cheek patches.
Body grayish-brown; lower belly, upper
and undertail coverts white; tail and
rump black.

Voice: The "contact call," uttered in flight or
when a bird is separated from the flock,
is a deep, hollow, musical *ah-honk;*
smaller subspecies only cackle.

Habitat: Varied: marsh and lake country,
tundra, forest bog, and prairie sloughs.

Nesting: 4–8 large, white eggs, usually in a
marsh, also on a lakeshore or on a
haystack.

Range: Breeds across northern North America
from Alaska to Labrador, south to mid-
Atlantic states, Kansas, and California.
Introduced in many areas. Size and
coloration vary: the largest birds, males
weigh up to 13 pounds, are from the
northern prairies, the Pacific
Northwest, and coastal British
Columbia; the smallest race, the
Cackling Goose, weighs only 2½–3
pounds and breeds from western Alaska
east to the Yukon.

In Vancouver's Stanley Park, geese nest
on cedar stumps 10–15 feet high.
Hatchlings are led by both parents to
grazing meadows and lakes or ponds.
The adults molt all their flying feathers
simultaneously, becoming flightless for
a few weeks. After completing the
molt, families migrate in flocks to the
southwestern or Pacific coastal states.
On the winter grounds geese of various
areas mix, but in spring each returns to
its ancestral breeding grounds.
Knowledge of migratory routes and
seasonal homes is passed on by the
parents to the offspring during a single
migration.

163, 165 White-fronted Goose
(*Anser albifrons*)
Ducks (Anatidae)

Description: 26–34″ (66–86 cm). Smaller than a domestic goose. Gray-brown with *white patch on face* at base of pink bill; *feet orange*. Irregular *black spots* or black areas on the gray belly prompted hunters' names: "Specklebelly" or "Speck." Immatures gray without face patch or speckled belly.

Voice: A cackling quite different from the high-pitched barking of the Snow Goose or the deep honking of Canadas. A ringing *gli-gli* or *gla-gla-gla* call.

Habitat: Tundra during breeding season. Migrates through marshy areas and river estuaries to winter on freshwater marshes from early October to May.

Nesting: 4–8 creamy white eggs in a nest of dry plants lined with down; built by female in a shallow depression on wet tundra.

Range: The commonest Arctic goose from northern Russia across the Siberian tundra, and from Alaska to the western Canadian Arctic and Greenland. Winters regularly in the western United States, particularly in the Central Valley of California.

These geese migrate and winter in large flocks; each flock contains many smaller family units consisting of two speckled adults and up to five unspeckled young.

200, 203, 238 Wilson's Phalarope
(*Steganopus tricolor*)
Phalaropes (Phalaropodidae)

Description: 8–10″ (20–25 cm). Largest phalarope, with *long thin bill*. Summer female is more colorful than male, with *black eye-stripe; rust-colored neck stripe*, extending across back; *head gray and white*. Male is smaller and duller, with white spot on nape. Both sexes have white tail, *lack wing stripe* of other phalaropes. Legs black in breeding season, otherwise greenish-yellow. In fall, back, crown, and eye-stripe are pale bluish-gray; underparts white. Immatures buffy-gray above with light-edged feathers.

Voice: A low grunting, *ca-work;* very different from the high *kik* notes of the other two phalaropes.

Habitat: Freshwater marshes with shallow, open water surrounded by low vegetation.

Nesting: 4 buff, spotted and blotched eggs in a grass-lined depression near water.

Range: Central British Columbia and prairie provinces in Canada; throughout the western interior of the United States; eastward to Ontario. Winters in Argentina.

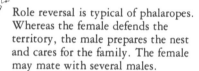

Role reversal is typical of phalaropes. Whereas the female defends the territory, the male prepares the nest and cares for the family. The female may mate with several males.

214 **Common Snipe**
"Wilson's Snipe"
(*Capella gallinago*)
Sandpipers (Scolopacidae)

Description: 10½–11½" (26–29 cm). A long-billed shorebird of inland marshes, usually seen in flight. *Zigzag flight, brown-mottled body, and striped head* are distinctive.

Voice: A raspy *zhak* given when flushed. On its breeding grounds, a hollow sound is produced by the tail feathers as the bird circles overhead. It also gives a prolonged series of short calls from an elevation in its territory.

Habitat: Marshes and bogs.

Nesting: 4 olive-brown, mottled eggs in a grass-lined depression in a clump of vegetation in the marshes.

Range: Widespread in the Northern Hemisphere; in North America from

subarctic tundra south to California and New Jersey. In the West it nests everywhere but the southern Rocky Mountain states. Winters from southern United States to northern South America.

This snipe, formerly called "Wilson's Snipe," is a favorite gamebird; it stays well hidden in ground cover, flushes abruptly, and zigzags sharply in flight. It probes deeply in the mud to feed on small animals.

215, 240 Willet
(*Catoptrophorus semipalmatus*)
Sandpipers (Scolopacidae)

Description: 14–17" (36–43 cm). *Large, long-legged, and fairly long-billed, light sand-gray bird with gray legs.* When flushed, it shows startling broad white wing bar and white base of tail contrasting with black posterior margin of its wings. In spring, mottled brown on chest; in fall and winter, grayish.

Voice: A loud *kreer-reer-reerr* or *pee-wee-wee.*

Habitat: Muddy shores and wet meadows for nesting; in the East, coastal marshes.

Nesting: 3 or 4 spotted, buffy eggs in a grass cup or in a scrape hidden in grass.

Range: Breeds in Great Basin and northern prairie states and Canadian provinces and along Atlantic and Gulf coasts. Winters on southern coasts of United States and south to South America; very common on California beaches and adjacent salt or freshwater marshes.

These are conspicuous and noisy birds, with several distinctive calls. They separate when feeding but remain in loose contact. if several are forced into the air by the approach of bathers, they usually fly together, calling back and forth, landing farther along the beach.

219 **Black-necked Stilt**
(*Himantopus mexicanus*)
Avocets (Recurvirostridae)

Description: 13–16″ (33–41 cm). Medium-sized shorebird. Black above, white below, *with very long reddish legs* and long thin black bill.

Voice: An incessant *keek-keek* or *yip-yip*.

Habitat: Alkali flats, open seashore, or lake shores. It needs shallow water for feeding and adjacent flats for breeding.

Nesting: 4 buff, brown-spotted eggs in a depression on open ground or in grass.

Range: Breeds locally from southern Oregon, northern Utah, Nebraska, southern Texas, and Delaware, south to Peru. Winters mainly south of the United States, but also in southern California.

The Black-necked Stilt is spectacular both in appearance and in its noisy mobbing of intruders. Its numbers have been decreasing largely because of the destruction of its habitat.

220, 241 **American Avocet**
(*Recurvirostra americana*)
Avocets (Recurvirostridae)

Description: 15½–20″ (41–51 cm). Large shorebird, with *very long legs and long upcurved bill.* Wings and back black-and-white; underparts and tail white. Head and neck light cinnamon in breeding plumage; white with some light dusky in winter.

Voice: A ringing *kleep, kleep.*

Habitat: Marshes, shallow lakes, freshwater or alkali ponds and sloughs with muddy, thinly vegetated margins and an unobstructed horizon.

Nesting: 4 blotched, olive eggs in a shallow hollow in mud or grass such as a dried cow track. Each pair occupies a separate territory within which the nest is

located. When approached by a
predator, the screaming parents alarm
other avocets, which mob the intruder,
often driving it away.

Range: Breeds mainly in open marshes of the
Great Basin and Canadian prairie
regions but also in the Central Valley of
California and on open shores of lakes
in the prairie states from the Dakotas to
Oklahoma.

Avocet populations may decrease
because of the draining of marshes and
the abandonment of salinas, the salt-
producing ponds in California. They
feed in shallow pools, catching tiny
shrimp-like crustaceans with a
sweeping movement of the bill.

---

242 Virginia Rail
(*Rallus limicola*)
Rails (Rallidae)

Description: 8½–10½″ (22–27 cm). *Long-billed*,
small rail. Quite colorful but the colors
blend in a camouflage effect: *gray face
with white throat;* cinnamon wings and
breast; back cinnamon with black
mottling; belly barred black-and-white.
White undertail area conspicuous when
tail is raised; this seems to be an
important signal among rail-like birds,
for it is well marked in all of them.

Voice: Attracts attention with its loud calls,
usually described as a grunting,
descending *wak-wak-wak,* or *kick, kick,
kid-ick, kid-ick, kid-ick.*

Habitat: A common rail of marshes.

Nesting: 5–12 eggs in a woven nest of marsh
plant stalks lined with finer material
and fastened to vegetation above water
level; on almost any body of fresh water
as long as dense vegetation and open
water are present. The downy young are
black.

Range: Wetlands from coast to coast; from
southern Canada to the southern United

States. Winters mainly in southern
United States and Mexico, but may be
found throughout range where marshes
do not freeze.

The best time to see this rail is in a
marsh in a blind or boat at dawn, for it
is then and at dusk that rails forage
briefly in the open. In California it has
been found nesting as high as 6800 feet.

244 Yellow Rail
(*Coturnicops noveboracensis*)
Rails (Rallidae)

Description: 6–7½″ (15–19 cm). Sparrow-sized,
short-billed rail. *Yellow-tan,* mottled
with black on back and black-and-
white barring on flanks. *In flight, white
secondaries are conspicuous;* fine white
cross-barring on feathers of back
distinguishes it from immature
plumage of much larger Sora.

Voice: A series of ticking notes in twos and
threes: *tick-tick, tick-tick-tick,* endlessly
repeated, at night.

Habitat: Wet grassland or meadows for nesting;
on migration it stops in grainfields and
haying meadows.

Nesting: 7–10 buff, brown-spotted eggs in grass
or other vegetation, often over water,
with tules or dead plants forming a
natural canopy over a cup-shaped grass
nest.

Range: Across the Canadian provinces east of
the Rockies, extending into some
neighboring states. Formerly nested in
northeastern California but now mostly
a rare transient there and in other
western states. Winters along the Gulf
and southern Atlantic coasts.

All rails live in dense vegetation in
marshes or meadows and are difficult to
observe or even flush, but this tiny rail
is especially elusive. It is said to be
active mainly toward evening. It feeds

amid grass and weeds, but also climbs up stems in search of insects and snails. In doing so it often jerks up its tail, as if to improve its balance. If flushed, it flies feebly, just above the vegetation and for a short distance.

---

245 Sora
(*Porzana carolina*)
Rails (Rallidae)

Description: 8–9¾" (20–25 cm). Robin-sized with *short bill*. Brown-mottled on back, *gray on head, neck, and breast* with black-and-white barring on belly and white undertail coverts. *Black face patch and bib. Yellow bill* and feet. Immatures and winter birds are a plainer, buffy color.

Voice: A rising whistled *ner-wee?* Also a squeal followed by a descending series of whistled notes, suggesting a whinny: *kweee-wi-wi-wi.* . . .

Habitat: Freshwater marshes; also tidal marshes in winter.

Nesting: 8–13 buffy, brown-spotted eggs in a basket nest woven of stalks, set in a wet marsh over water, or in a simple nest in grass.

Range: Most of temperate North America; in the West from British Columbia and the Canadian prairie provinces to Baja California and the southwestern border states, but rarely in Texas. Winters from southern United States to northern South America.

The Sora is the commonest rail, its whinny familiar to anyone who has watched birds in a marsh. Even long-time rail-watchers have seldom seen a rail fly except when it comes close to a blind and the occupant makes a movement or noise, flushing it. It undertakes sustained flights in spring and fall, when it migrates at night.

246   Common Gallinule
(*Gallinula chloropus*)
Rails (Rallidae)

Description: 12–14¼" (30–37 cm). Smaller and
more slender than the American Coot.
Slate gray head, neck and underparts,
back and wings deep brown. *Bright red
frontal shield and bill* with yellow tip.
*Conspicuous white undertail coverts and
stripe along sides.* Feet and enormously
long toes greenish. Immatures lighter-
colored and lack the frontal shield.

Voice: Loud cackling notes; commonly, a
croaking *kar-ruck*.

Habitat: Freshwater marshes and lakes with
reeds or cattails.

Nesting: 9–12 buffy, dark-spotted eggs in a nest
built of rushes at water's edge or in
water on a platform of fallen reeds.

Range: Cosmopolitan; in the Western
Hemisphere from northern California,
central Arizona and New Mexico east to
Nebraska and southern Canada, south
to southern South America. Winters
from southern California, Arizona and
the Gulf States south.

This bird owes its wide distribution to
its choice of a common habitat: open
water with a tiny stand of reeds. The
Gallinule—"Moorhen" to the British—
is omnivorous, feeding on mosquitoes,
spiders, tadpoles, insect larvae, fruits,
and seeds. Its long, lobed toes enable it
to swim in water or walk on tules with
equal ease. Gallinules and coots pump
their heads as they walk or swim.

291   Short-eared Owl
(*Asio flammeus*)
Owls (Strigidae)

Description: 13–17" (33–43 cm). Medium-sized
owl, *short "ears"* close together and
seldom noticeable. Paler than Long-
eared Owl, more buffy, with light

brown streaking below, darker above. Face mask and wing linings are also light, the bird appearing pale in flight.

Voice: A sharp, barked *kyow!*

Habitat: Open country with short vegetation, whether tundra, taiga bog, marsh or meadow with thickets, or forest clearing.

Nesting: 5–7 or more creamy white eggs in a grass-lined depression on the ground, usually well hidden in tall grass, weeds, or thick willow clumps.

Range: Almost cosmopolitan; widespread throughout the West, except for the driest areas, but transients and winter visitors occur even in Arizona, New Mexico, and Texas.

This owl hunts for field mice and other small rodents on cloudy days long before sundown, slowly patrolling the grassland, in a wavering flight, or taking up a watching post on a stump. When cornered on its nest, it resorts to the usual owl bluff, humping its back and stretching its wings in a wide arch so that it appears large. Its yellow eyes glow fiercely, and it snaps its bill repeatedly in menacing fashion.

317 Marsh Hawk
(*Circus cyaneus*)
Hawks (Accipitridae)

Description: 17½–24" (45–61 cm). Slim, with *long wings, tail, and legs.* Male is light gray above, white underparts with reddish spotting; in flight, black wing tips and barred tail. Female is brown above with some brown streaks below. *Both sexes have white rump.* Immature is brown above, cinnamon below. Slow, hesitant flight and intermittent, tilting glide on wings held in a shallow "V" are characteristic.

Voice: Generally silent. It may utter a short chatter around the nest.

Habitat: Marshes, meadows, and fields.
Nesting: 4–6 white eggs in a grass nest on the
           ground in marshes. After breeding,
           families gather together on ground
           roosts for the night.
Range: From coast to coast, ranging from the
           southern tundra to freshwater marshes
           in the desert belt, excluding the
           southeastern seaboard and the South.
           Winters mainly in western, central,
           and southern United States.
           Widespread in Eurasia.

"Harriers," the old English name of
these hawks, are specialized mousers in
tall vegetation; their owl-like disk-
shaped face mask directs the squeaks of
field mice to their sensitive ears. They
surprise small waterfowl or the young
of other birds among the reeds.

419, 440   Common Yellowthroat
"Yellowthroat"
(*Geothlypis trichas*)
Wood Warblers (Parulidae)

Description: 4½–5¾" (11–15 cm). Adult male has
               black mask edged toward crown with
               white. *Olive green above, bright yellow
               below,* fading into dull white on belly.
               Female lacks mask, is brownish-olive
               above, buffy below with some yellow,
               especially on throat. Immature male
               dull-colored, often some black on face.
Voice: Song is a repeated *whichity-whichity-
               whichity,* sometimes with an additional
               which. Call is a low *djip.*
Habitat: Meadows, fields, edges of thickets,
               streams, marshes, and other places with
               open, low vegetation.
Nesting: 3–5 white eggs with markings around
               the larger end, in a bulky nest of woven
               plant material with a lining of fine
               grasses and sometimes hair. Hidden in
               weeds or grass on or near the ground.
Range: Widespread from coast to coast and
               from the treeline to southern Mexico.

This meadow bird, formerly called "Yellowthroat," is common throughout North America, but we get a glimpse of it only when the male climbs the tallest stalk and utters his abrupt song. To foil predators, the parents drop down into the thick of the grasses or weeds, secretly approach the well-hidden nest, deliver the food, and depart by another route.

428, 556, 612 **Yellow-headed Blackbird**
(*Xanthocephalus xanthocephalus*)
Orioles (Icteridae)

Description: 8–11″ (20–28 cm). Male *all black with yellow head and breast;* in flight shows white wing patch. Female is smaller, browner, with dirty yellow on chest, throat, and face; lacks white wing marks.

Voice: Call is a throaty *krruck.* Song is a loud, nasal *oka-wee-wee,* which, coming from hundreds of individuals, blends into a loud, wavering chorus.

Habitat: Freshwater marshes.

Nesting: 3–5 whitish, brown-speckled eggs in a nest woven around several strong stalks, basket-fashion; in colonies in tall marsh vegetation over water.

Range: Throughout the West, extending east into the prairie states and provinces. Migrates to the southern United States and Mexico.

Water provides safety for this bird but often limits available nesting space and causes crowding. One study found about 25 nests in an area of 15 square feet. In a colony, some males are always in display flight, with head lowered, feet and tail dropped, wings beating slowly. Others quarrel with neighbors about boundaries. Approaching predators are mobbed by clouds of Yellow-heads, with neighboring Red-wings joining in.

528   Long-billed Marsh Wren
(*Cistothorus palustris*)
Wrens (Troglodytidae)

Description: 4–5½" (10–14 cm). Small wren;
brown, with barring on wing and tail,
solid brown cap, white eye-stripe, black-
and-white stripes on back.

Voice: The strongly territorial males sing a
loud, variable, chattering, bubbling
song. Call note is a sharp *chick-chick.*

Habitat: No other wren lives in dense, low
marsh vegetation in the West, whether
salt marshes, reeds, cattails, and grass
tules of freshwater marshes, or borders
of rivers and ponds.

Nesting: 5 or 6 dark brown, spotted eggs in a
domed nest fastened to stems of marsh
stalks. Mock or "dummy" nests are also
built by the male.

Range: Widespread in marshes over most of
United States and southern Canada.
Where marshes freeze, it is migratory.

This wren feeds entirely on insects it
takes from plants as well as the surface
of water. It is a secretive bird; even the
singing territorial male remains well
hidden, briefly climbing a cattail for a
look at an intruder.

557, 614   Red-winged Blackbird
(*Agelaius phoeniceus*)
Orioles (Icteridae)

Description: 7–9½" (18–24 cm). *Male black with red
and buffy yellow epaulets,* may be
confused in California with its close
relative, the Tricolored Blackbird,
which has red-and-white shoulder
patches. Female is streaked brown.
Immature males resemble female but
are darker, with faint epaulets. Freshly
molted fall males have tan feather
edges. Shoulder patches of adult males
in the Central Valley of California are
pure red.

Voice: A loud, liquid, ringing *ok-a-lee!* Call is a low *chuck* and a thin *teeyee*.

Habitat: Marshes, but not so partial to emergent aquatic vegetation as is the Yellow-headed Blackbird, preferring a narrow edge of cattails, tall weeds, and even blackberry tangles, surrounded by open meadows or fields.

Nesting: 3–5 pale blue-green, heavily marked eggs in a woven cup. Nests are far apart, with males defending a sizable territory; one male sometimes mates with several females.

Range: Widespread from subarctic Canada to the tropical swamplands of Central America and Cuba. Migratory in the northern United States and Canada.

Red-wings form the nucleus of the huge flocks of mixed blackbird species that feed in fields, pastures, and marshes from early fall to spring. Although blackbirds are often considered pests because they consume grain in farmers' fields, farmers benefit because the birds consume harmful insects during the nesting season.

---

615 Tricolored Blackbird
(*Agelaius tricolor*)
Orioles (Icteridae)

Description: 7½–9″ (19–23 cm). Similar to Red-winged Blackbird. Male is black but with *dark red epaulets,* very *broadly margined with white. Female more slate-colored* than the brownish-dusky Red-wing and lacks streaks on the rump and belly.

Voice: Calls rather similar to those of the Red-wing but song is more nasal, less musical.

Habitat: Cattail marshes, marshy meadows, and rangeland.

Nesting: 3 or 4 greenish eggs, covered with brown scrawls, in a nest woven onto reed stems or blackberry vines. More colonial than the Red-winged Blackbird, its territories are crowded, with nests often less than 5 or 6 feet apart. Colonies in the Central Valley contain thousands of birds. Breeding usually occurs in late May, but when early fall rains refresh the California marshes, some colonies nest in October.

Range: A California bird, it is restricted to the Klamath marshes at the Oregon border, California west of the Sierra, and the coast to northern Baja California. Not seasonally migratory, but moves its nesting colonies to wherever more food is available.

During the late-summer drought, grasshoppers abound and support the wandering hordes of Tricolored Blackbirds; in winter, rice fields and marshes provide food. Until recently, some colonies were estimated to contain 1–2 million birds; today the total population is down to about 750,000 due to the draining of marshes.

Lakes, Ponds, Rivers

Open water that supports birds that swim, dive, snatch food from above the water, or feed along a shore.

Many species (ducks, grebes) nest in sheltered areas along the edge of lakes. Some (Kingfisher, swallows) burrow in sandy banks. Others (Osprey, cormorants) build bulky stick nests in trees near water, and a few (Wood Duck, Tree Swallow) nest in cavities in these trees.

Swans, loons, and ducks nest on lakes in the Far North, but since most birders see them only during the winter in saltwater and freshwater marshes, we have included them in those habitats.

7, 9   Green Heron
(*Butorides striatus*)
Herons (Ardeidae)

Description: 16–22″ (41–56 cm). *Dark, crow-sized heron.* Crown black, *back and wings dark grayish-green* (although, despite its name, it doesn't always appear green); thick *chestnut-colored neck.* Bill dark; legs bright orange; immatures have streaked neck, breast, and sides.

Voice: Call is a piercing *kyowk.*

Habitat: Breeds in freshwater marshes with clumps of trees. Feeds along the banks of any body of water.

Nesting: 3–6 bluish-green eggs in a crow-like stick nest built in a tree or dense thickets.

Range: In the West from the Fraser River delta of British Columbia south to California and Arizona and throughout Mexico. The eastern North American population reaches Texas and southern New Mexico. Migratory in the North.

Toward the end of summer, before migrating southward, young herons and other birds often wander far from their breeding areas. If one finds a suitable spot, it will return there the following spring rather than to its birthplace. Green Herons are rather solitary, which is unusual for herons. They fish singly, and breeding pairs nest in a tree by themselves.

19, 37   California Gull
(*Larus californicus*)
Gulls (Laridae)

Description: 20–23″ (51–58 cm). Similar to Herring Gull, but smaller, with *darker gray mantle, dark eye, reddish eye-ring, and greenish legs;* bill of breeding birds has red spot overlapped by black. Winter and immature birds have black subterminal bar on bill and lack red eye-ring of adults. A common *inland* gull.

Voice: A shuddering, repetitive *kee-yah*.

Habitat: In breeding season, on interior lakes and marshes; in winter, mostly on seacoast.

Nesting: 2 or 3 heavily blotched, buff-olive eggs in a nest made of grass, dead weeds, and sticks. Large colonies are found on islands in shallow inland lakes, often together with Ring-billed Gulls, though each species remains with its own kind.

Range: Northern prairie provinces east to North Dakota, south to northwestern Wyoming and Utah, west to northeastern California. Winters mainly on the Oregon, Calfornia, and Baja California coasts; in lesser numbers inland.

The California Gull attained fame when great numbers arrived at the Mormon colony near the Great Salt Lake and devoured a locust swarm that threatened the settlers' first crop. A statue in Salt Lake City commemorates the event.

24 Ring-billed Gull
(*Larus delawarensis*)
Gulls (Laridae)

Description: 18–21″ (45–53 cm). Adult looks like a small Herring Gull but has reddish eye-ring, greenish-yellow legs, and a *blackish band ringing both mandibles of yellow bill.* Adult plumage is acquired in 3 years, with mottled-brown juvenile plumage gradually lightening and tail losing black subterminal band.

Voice: High, shrill squeals; a shrill *ky-eow*.

Habitat: Breeds on islands in inland lakes; in winter along seacoasts.

Nesting: 3 buffy eggs with dark blotches in a nest of grass and stalks. In colonies with California Gulls.

Range: Prairie and lake country in Canada and

midwestern states; also sparsely in the northern Great Basin area down to the northeastern corner of California. In winter, in the west it is found on the Pacific Coast and on reservoirs of the Southwest.

Misnamed "sea gull," this bird follows farm plows or scatters over meadows after heavy rains to feast on drowning earthworms. The eye of the slightly larger, darker-mantled California Gull is *dark brown;* whereas eye of Ring-bill is *yellow.*

29, 32 Bonaparte's Gull
(*Larus philadelphia*)
Gulls (Laridae)

Description: 12–14″ (30–36 cm). Small white, gray-backed, *black-headed* gull. *In winter head is white* with only *ear patch dark; feet bright red* in summer, pale pink in winter; bill blackish in both plumages. Best distinguished from Franklin's Gull by long triangle of white on leading edge of outer wing. Juveniles resemble winter adults but have diagonal brownish-black lines across inner wing and dark subterminal tail bands.

Voice: A low, nasal *cherr* contact call, constantly uttered.

Habitat: In summer muskegs and lakes; in winter at sea.

Nesting: 2 or 3 small olive, dark-blotched eggs in a well-constructed nest; in trees, such as spruce. Sometimes loosely colonial.

Range: Boreal forest belt from Alaska and the Yukon and from British Columbia to Hudson Bay. Passes through the Northwest in fall and spring. Winters off Pacific Coast of the United States and Mexico. Also Atlantic, Gulf coasts.

Flocks of these dainty gulls make a graceful spectacle as they fly tern-like along the seashore or over salt ponds. When swimming, they float high with wingtips crossed over the tail. Along the Pacific Coast, at peak migration time, jaegers accompany them and rob them of fish.

31, 34 Franklin's Gull
(*Larus pipixcan*)
Gulls (Laridae)

Description: 13½–15½" (34–39 cm). Small gull. Breeding adults have gray back, *white underparts and black head;* in flight show gray wings with black-and-white wing tips, a *distinct white bar separating the black areas from the gray;* red bill and feet. From September to April or May head is white, washed with slate gray on nape and ear regions. Immatures have brownish-gray above and white below, with a black tail band, and acquire at least a partial hood by spring although they don't breed for 2 years.

Voice: *Kuk-kuk-kuk.* Also a nasal *karrr.*

Habitat: Open country around prairie lakes.

Nesting: 3 brownish, buff, or olive eggs. Some colonies as large as 15,000–20,000 pair. Other waterbirds such as Eared Grebes nest in these gulleries, apparently benefiting from the protection provided by the wary, bold, and noisy gulls.

Range: Throughout the prairies. Colonies have been found from Alberta to Manitoba in the North and from Montana and Oregon to Iowa in the South. They migrate south for the winter. Some winter on the Gulf Coast; most go on to South America.

These gulls are considered beneficial since they feed mainly on insects, including those that damage crops. In late fall they feed on grasshoppers and dragonflies until the birds leave for the Pacific Coast of South America.

44 Common Tern
(*Sterna hirundo*)
Gulls (Laridae)

Description: 13–16" (33–41 cm). Grayish seabird
with *long forked tail, black cap, red bill
with black tip.* Long wings with dark tips.
In non-breeding plumage forehead is
white; dark smudge on nape and crown.
Resembles Forster's which has *silvery
primaries;* Arctic Tern has *all red bill* in
breeding season.

Voice: Call is a loud, distinct, rolling *tee-arr* or
kree-err. When a predator or bird-
watcher approaches, this chorus changes
to a screaming, rattling *kik kik kik.*

Habitat: Marshes, lakes, rivers, seacoasts.

Nesting: 2 or 3 eggs, ranging from greenish to
buff, with brown markings, in a scrape
on a sandbar or beach; in colonies.

Range: Nearly circumpolar. In the West, in
the prairie provinces of Canada and
in adjacent states. Migrates along the
Pacific Coast to winter south of
the United States. Also common on
Atlantic Coast.

This bird flies with deliberate
wingbeats over the water, head turned
down at a right angle to the body.
When it sights a fish or tadpole, it
dives much like a booby to catch its
aquatic prey.

45, 52 Forster's Tern
(*Sterna forsteri*)
Gulls (Laridae)

Description: 14–16¼" (36–41 cm). Medium-sized
tern. White with light silvery-gray
mantle, *primaries silvery; tail light
gray.* In summer *black cap, bright orange-
red bill with black tip.* In winter black
cap molts to white but black patch
remains around eye; bill black.

Voice: A low, nasal *ky-yarr* and a harsh, nasal,
buzzy *zraa.*

Habitat: Marshes near open shallow water.

Nesting: 3 or 4 buffy, spotted eggs. Nesting habits vary. In the West floating debris serves as a platform, and a neat nest is built of old cattails; elsewhere it is built on the beach. All American terns nest in colonies.

Range: From the Canadian prairies south to south-central California (and San Diego) and across to Colorado; also on the southeastern Atlantic (north to southern New Jersey) and Gulf coasts. Winters to Central and South America.

Terns have forked tails and longer, more slender wings than gulls. They feed almost entirely by plunge-diving on fish, pointing the bill downward; whereas gulls do not dive but usually feed from the surface of the water.

47 **Caspian Tern**
(*Sterna caspia*)
Gulls (Laridae)

Description: 19–23″ (48–58 cm). North America's largest tern. Resembles medium-sized gull, with black cap and *oversized red bill;* moderately forked tail. Cap has slight crest; white streaking on forehead and crown in winter; undersurface of primaries extensively blackish.

Voice: Loud, grating *kar-rreeow* or *ga-ga-gaaah;* immature birds utter a high, whistled *whee-you.*

Habitat: Inland lakes and rivers; coastal waters.

Nesting: 2 or 3 rather large eggs in a scrape; in colonies.

Range: Virtually cosmopolitan from the tropics to the Far North, but discontinuously distributed. Breeds in terneries on several lakes in west-central Canada and in the Great Basin area and California. Winters from the southern Pacific coast of United States to Central America; also southern Atlantic and Gulf coasts.

A lone fisher, it patrols a chosen area, suddenly plunging headlong after its prey. Its courtship is typical of terns. The male seizes a fish crosswise in his bill and offers it to the female or lays it beside her. She may ignore it or join him in a courtship flight, during which she follows him as he carries the fish and rises high into the air. In winter it is often seen resting on sandbars along with Royal and other terns.

76 Double-crested Cormorant
(*Phalacrocorax auritus*)
Cormorants (Phalacrocoracidae)

Description: 30–36" (76–91 cm). Goose-sized. Adults black; immatures light brownish, lightest on breast and neck; bill straight, with hooked tip. Adults and young have *bare patch of orange skin underneath bill*. Breeding adults have two inconspicuous tufts (white in one western race) on both sides of crown.

Voice: Usually silent, except for grunting calls in the nesting colony.

Habitat: Freshwater lakes, rivers, and the sea; generally requires trees for nesting but does well on treeless islands such as those in the Gulf of California; settles only around large, deep bodies of water that provide good fishing.

Nesting: 3 or 4 long, chalky bluish eggs. The naked nestlings are black. In colonies like all cormorants and usually in trees; nest is made of sticks even when built on rocks or on bare sand.

Range: Widespread in North America. In the West it breeds on islands along Pacific Coast and on inland lakes. Winters on seacoast and on inland waters.

The only cormorant nesting inland in the West. Cormorants perch upright and often dry their wings by spreading them. Double-cresteds following a coastline often take shortcuts over land, whereas Brandt's and the Pelagic always fly over water.

100, 129 Red-breasted Merganser
(*Mergus serrator*)
Ducks (Anatidae)

Description: 19½–26" (50–66 cm). Medium-sized duck, smaller than Common Merganser. Thin *double crest* on back of head. Breeding *male has green-black head, reddish bill, black mantle, gray flanks, reddish-brown mottled breast. Rufous head of female blends into gray throat and neck.* In flight, both sexes show large white patch on inner wing.

Voice: On the breeding grounds, displaying males utter a *yeow-yeow* note; females have a harsh *karrr* note.

Habitat: Lakes and rivers with clear water and abundant fish. Usually winters on salt water.

Nesting: 8–10 olive-buff eggs in a nest low but well hidden among roots, rocks, or burrows of other creatures.

Range: A more northern bird than the Common Merganser; in Eurasia as well as North America it lives in the northern coniferous forest and woodland tundra belt. Breeds in Alaska and northern Canada, barely reaching the northern forested region of the western United States, but extends east to the lake forest areas, the Maritime Provinces, and New England. Winters on all United States seacoasts.

This is the most common winter merganser on the Pacific Coast where rocky shores with clearwater coves provide good fishing. The species can often become fairly tame and is often observed around fishing piers.

101, 128   Common Merganser
(*Mergus merganser*)
Ducks (Anatidae)

Description: 22–27″ (56–69 cm). Largest merganser, Mallard-sized. Breeding male has *black-and-white body and wings, shiny green-black head* (brown during the nonbreeding season), *red bill*. Female is gray overall and *slightly crested rufous head sharply contrasting with white of throat and breast.*

Voice: On the breeding grounds, the male utters a twanging note; the female, a harsh *karrr*.

Habitat: Mountain and subarctic lakes and rivers; prefers fresh water in winter.

Nesting: 6–12 pale buff, unspotted eggs. Prefers tree holes, but will nest in an opening among boulders and roots, on cliffs, in breeding boxes hung near waters rich in food. In British Columbia, it commonly nests along coastal streams, but rears its young at sea.

Range: Northern North America and Eurasia; in the West from southwestern Alaska to Manitoba, the Sierra Nevada, and the Rocky Mountain states. Winters mainly on unfrozen fresh water.

This large duck dives and pursues its aquatic prey under water. Its narrow bill, with hooked upper mandible and saw-like teeth along the edges, is specialized to catch swimming prey such as small fish and insects.

102, 126   Hooded Merganser
(*Lophodytes cucullatus*)
Ducks (Anatidae)

Description: 16–19″ (40–48 cm). Smallest North American merganser. Has *white crest with black hind border* usually depressed backward but sometimes opened fan-like in a unique and startling display. Breeding male shiny black above, white

below; cinnamon-colored flanks. When swimming with lowered hood it may look like the male Bufflehead, but latter is smaller, has white head patch without margins, and white sides. Female dark, small, and has a bushy, warm brown crest. In flight, both sexes show a small white patch on the inner wing.

Voice: Generally silent except for a rolling, croaking note uttered by the courting male.

Habitat: Breeds near clear-water ponds surrounded by woods.

Nesting: 8–12 white eggs; often competes with Wood Ducks or goldeneyes for nesting holes.

Range: North America exclusively; from southern Alaska to the Atlantic Coast and west across the northern United States but mainly restricted to the areas shown on map. Winters on both coasts, generally on fresh water.

Small wintering groups live on fresh water throughout the West. Males perform a beautiful courtship display and, once mated, swim energetically around the female in further ritual displays. This duck's diet includes aquatic invertebrates, minuscule frogs, newts, and polliwogs.

103, 143 **Bufflehead**
(*Bucephala albeola*)
Ducks (Anatidae)

Description: 13–15½″ (33–39 cm). Smallest North American duck. Breeding male white with shiny black back and with *large white patch* on head conspicuous against green- and purple-glossed black forehead and nape. Female dark overall with pale breast, blackish head with well-defined white oval below and behind eye. Both sexes show white patch on inner wing in flight.

Voice: Male gives a squeaky whistle; female, a low quack.

Habitat: Boreal forest with small ponds and bogs surrounded by open water and trees.

Nesting: 8–12 pale buff eggs in a tree hole such as those made by woodpeckers.

Range: Alaska to northern Ontario and south through British Columbia to northern California. In winter, in most of America where waters remain open and on Pacific and Atlantic coasts.

These sprightly, beautiful ducks fly fast and usually close to the water. They are quite tame; when flushed, they often circle back and settle in their original places. In winter they visit even the smallest ponds or ditches as long as there is sufficient animal food. They also like rocky shores. Displaying males float high, alternating forward rushes with head-bobbing and chin-up displays with the head feathers erected.

104, 130 Barrow's Goldeneye
(*Bucephala islandica*)
Ducks (Anatidae)

Description: 16½–20″ (42–51 cm). Male differs from the Common Goldeneye in having *white crescent in front of eye*. Flattened, blocky profile with low, abrupt forehead; *black head glossed with purple* with more of a crest than in Common Goldeneye, and sides extensively black. In flight, both sexes show less white on inner wing than Common Goldeneye. Female has brown head, white collar, grayish body; *bill usually orange-yellow* during mating season, whereas Common Goldeneye female shows this color only on tip of bill.

Voice: Generally silent except for a whining sound produced by its wings in flight. Clicking, grunting, and whistling notes are uttered during courtship or brood care.

Habitat: Breeds near forested lakes. Winters on bays and along the coast.

Nesting: 9 or 10 pale greenish-white eggs in a down nest in holes in trees.

Range: Southwestern Alaska, British Columbia, southward in mountains to northern Wyoming; also in far northeastern Canada, Greenland, and Iceland. Winters with Common Goldeneyes or other diving ducks along the northwestern Pacific Coast and, sparingly, on open waters of the Rocky Mountain states.

This duck's family life is identical to that of the Common Goldeneye. Mating displays occur all winter. The male dips his bill in the water, then raises his head straight up and arcs it over his back while uttering a peculiar whistle. Even if the two goldeneye species spend the entire winter together, the slight differences between them prevent the female from choosing a mate not of her own species.

105, 131 **Common Goldeneye**
(*Bucephala clangula*)
Ducks (Anatidae)

Description: 16–20" (41–51 cm). Medium-sized diving duck closely resembling Barrow's Goldeneye. In spring, male has black back and tail; white neck, sides, and underparts; *head shiny green-black* with large, *round white spot in front of eye*. Plumage of summer male, female, and juvenile is gray with darker gray wings and tail; large head is brown with white collar separating it from gray neck. *Solid-white wing patch* visible in flight (in Barrow's the patch is divided by a black line).

Voice: Courting male produces a shrill *jeee-ep;* female may utter a low quack.

Habitat: Lakes and bogs in coniferous forests.

Nesting: 8–15 greenish-white eggs in rotted-out

stumps, woodpecker holes, and other cavities, sometimes far from water.

Range: From Alaska through forested Canada and northern United States, but mainly east of the Rockies. Also boreal forests of Eurasia. Winters on coasts or on rivers and deep lakes from southeastern Alaska to Gulf Coast and California.

Goldeneyes fly swiftly, usually in small flocks. The males' wingbeat produces a whistle (hence the ducks' colloquial name, "Whistler"). Density on the breeding grounds on lakes or muskegs depends on the presence of old, hollow snags or abandoned holes of Pileated Woodpeckers. The area where the male meets the incubating female is her territory, as is the vicinity of the nest hole, often far from the lake territory. When the brood hatches she may lead them to a third territory, with shallow water where the ducklings dive for water beetles, wigglers, and other animal food and occasionally for soft plants.

114, 135   Wood Duck
         (*Aix sponsa*)
         Ducks (Anatidae)

Description: 17–20½″ (43–52 cm). Medium-sized, but in flight its long tail makes this duck appear larger. It floats higher on water than similar ducks. Male is brightly colored with a *long, downswept crest. Head glossy green and purple, with white stripes* and throat; breast *chestnut;* upper parts gray with black-and-white stripes, back *black.* Female grayish-brown with smaller crest, white patch around eye, and white throat.

Voice: Male utters a clear, rising whistle; female a low *wook.*

Habitat: Backwaters of rivers and streams; woodland lakes.

Nesting: 10–15 eggs in a down-lined tree hole,

often high above the ground. Soon after hatching, ducklings jump from the nest cavity and follow the female to water.

Range: Southern British Columbia and Montana (also in southern Alberta, where it was introduced) through Washington and the northern half of California. Breeds sporadically elsewhere in the West. Common east of the Rocky Mountains from southern Canada to the Gulf Coast. Western populations winter in Pacific coastal states.

Not only does the Wood Duck nest in tree cavities, but the mated pair often perches in trees, especially when searching for a nesting site. Both the Wood Duck and its relative the Asian Mandarin Duck (*Aix galericulata*) are seen often on park ponds. While the two females are hard to tell apart, the Mandarin male is even brighter than the Wood Duck, being vivid olive-brown and buff, with a long crest striped with white.

115 Harlequin Duck
(*Histrionicus histrionicus*)
Ducks (Anatidae)

Description: 14½–21″ (37–53 cm). Rather small. Breeding male is *slate blue with bright chestnut flanks and bold white markings* outlined in black—as on a clown or harlequin—most conspicuous on head and wings. Female and nonbreeding male dark with two or three small white patches on head; male also shows some white on wing.

Voice: Mostly silent. Male utters high, squealing notes; female, a harsh croak.

Habitat: Near rushing water around boulders; in mountain streams during the nesting season and, in winter, around partly submerged ledges of rocky seashores.

Nesting: 6 or 7 creamy eggs in a down-lined

grass nest hidden among boulders or grass under a tree. The downies can dive quickly and negotiate rapids and racing waters easily.

Range: Baffin Island; Greenland, Iceland, mountainous Pacific North America; Alaska to California and Wyoming. Eastern Siberia. In the West, it winters along the Pacific Coast.

In the Georgia Strait— Puget Sound area of Washington and British Columbia—these ducks may be seen all year among rocky headlands and islets where currents have created great surges. They dive daily for snails, chitons, and crabs. The earliest breeders leave for coastal streams on the nearby mainland in April. The males return at the end of June or later, when other males are still courting their females at sea, and waiting for their Rocky Mountain home streams to thaw, at which time they can nest.

154   White Pelican
(*Pelecanus erythrorhynchos*)
Pelicans (Pelecanidae)

Description: 54–70″ (137–178 cm). W. 108″ (2.7 m). *Very large. White with black primaries and outer secondaries;* large, *yellow pouched bill.* In breeding season has short, yellowish crest on back of head, and triangular horny plate on upper mandible.

Voice: Generally silent. In breeding colonies it may utter low grunting and groaning calls.

Habitat: Large, shallow bodies of water rich in fish, with flat islets, inaccessible to predators, for nesting.

Nesting: 2 whitish eggs in a large nest mound; in colonies. The young are naked at first, and parents must shield them from the sun. They congregate in large groups after leaving the nest.

Range: A North American bird, nesting in the prairies and adjacent large Canadian lakes; also in the marshes west of the Rockies. Winters in California and Mexico, on the Gulf Coast and Florida.

White Pelicans are a magnificent spectacle as they maneuver in the air, soaring against blue sky on motionless wings, often so low that each black wing feather is visible. Unlike the Brown Pelican, individual birds do not dive for prey but cooperate with others to surround fish in shallow water, scooping it into their enormous bill pouches. A vanishing species, the White Pelican is a victim of insecticide poisoning and shooting by hunters who confuse it with the Snow Goose. Many nesting colonies are decreasing due to careless visitors who scare these birds off at midday, causing the death of many young from overexposure to the sun.

169, 173 Common Loon
(*Gavia immer*)
Loons (Gaviidae)

Description: 28–36" (71–91 cm). Large bird, about the size of a Canada Goose. Breeding birds have dark bodies spotted with pearl-white marks, especially visible on back; head and neck glossy green-black with white necklace. In winter, *gray-brown above, white below. Dark bill heavy and straight,* whereas similar Yellow-billed Loon has upturned bill.

Voice: Yodeling call given on breeding grounds; less commonly, on migration. Its tremolo, uttered at night in the still northern woods, is a thrilling sound. Generally silent on its wintering grounds.

Habitat: Coniferous forest belt of the North, lakes or rivers with deep water, and vegetation reaching the waterline to hide the nest. In winter loons are found on lakes and large rivers as well, but the majority prefer bays and coves along the coast.

Nesting: 2 dark olive-brown eggs on a mound of vegetation at water's edge. Both parents care for eggs and young.

Range: Aleutians, Alaska, Canada, northern border states of the United States, Greenland, and Iceland. Winters along all coasts of North America.

In the words of naturalist Sigurd Olson, the loon's wild, laughing tremolo is "the sound that more than any other typifies the wilderness." Loons are powerful divers and have been caught in fishermen's nets 200 feet below the surface. Seldom do dives last more than 30 seconds, but these birds have been known to stay under as long as 2 or 3 minutes. Their legs are set far back and within the body, so that only the ankles are visible. Unlike most other birds, they have almost solid bones with a specific gravity close to that of water, enabling them to submerge effortlessly.

174   Western Grebe

(*Aechmophorus occidentalis*)
Grebes (Podicipedidae)

Description: 22–29″ (56–74 cm). Largest North American grebe. *Long neck.* Head, neck, and body *slate-blackish above, white below;* long, *yellow bill.* Long white wing stripe shows in flight. Sexes look alike year round.

Voice: A rolling *kr-r-rick!,* given most often on its breeding grounds, but frequently heard from wintering birds as well.

Habitat: Large lakes with tules or rushes for breeding; in winter, mainly an inshore seabird.

Nesting: 3–5 bluish-white or brownish, stained eggs on nests close together in reeds, floating but anchored to rush stalks.

Both sexes care for the young. To reach feeding waters, parents bypass defended territories of other nesting pairs by diving off the nest and swimming underwater.

Range: Breeds on prairie lakes and other big lakes of the West from British Columbia south to southern California and sparsely to Mexico, east to Lake Winnipeg. Winters from the central British Columbia coast south to central Mexico, and on some inland waters.

The mating display of these grebes is spectacular. Hundreds of paired birds display together, both sexes dancing and posturing like mirror images as they race across the surface of the water. In migration, they fly in loose flocks but spread out to feed during the day. These grebes are very susceptible to oil spills and to insecticides that have accumulated in their food and thus affected their breeding success.

175 Red-necked Grebe
(*Podiceps grisegena*)
Grebes (Podicipedidae)

Description: 18–22″ (46–56 cm). Medium-sized, *stocky grebe. Rufous neck in summer* with black crown and gray face outlined in white. Two small black ear tufts are visible where crown and nape meet. In winter gray neck and face with white crescent from throat to ear. Afloat, it looks short-bodied and heavy-headed, with rather long, stout yellow bill. In flight it shows double white patch on inner wing. Sexes look alike.

Voice: Generally silent except on breeding grounds, where a sharp *kack* and wailing courtship call may be heard.

Habitat: During summer marshy ponds and bays of lakes; in winter deeper open waters, especially along the coast.

Nesting: 4 or 5 whitish eggs in a floating, anchored nest.

Range: Mainly a northwestern bird, nesting on lakes from the Aleutians and Alaskan taiga and northern tundra, east to Minnesota and south from central Washington to southern Wisconsin. In winter common on the Pacific Coast south to central California; less common on the Atlantic Coast; also in Europe and eastern Asia.

The Red-necked Grebe migrates from its coastal wintering grounds to inland lakes, dispersing to nest on the vegetation in larger ponds. It eats small aquatic vertebrates such as fish, tadpoles, and newts. Like other grebes it swallows feathers, probably to strain out fish bones and other undigested remnants, which it periodically regurgitates.

176, 177 Pied-billed Grebe
(*Podilymbus podiceps*)
Grebes (Podicipedidae)

Description: 12–15″ (30–38 cm). Small, drab brown grebe with thick, short, chicken-like bill, no crest. White beneath tail; *black bill ring and throat in summer,* white throat and bill in winter. Very rarely seen in flight. Sexes look alike.

Voice: A low, hollow, yelping *eeow-eeow-eeow-keeowm-kowm-kowm.*

Habitat: Marshes, ponds, and ditches with shallow water and dense marsh vegetation; open water of any size in winter or on migration.

Nesting: 5–7 whitish-blue or green eggs in a large floating nest of marsh plants anchored to protective vegetation. Whenever the parents leave the nest, they cover the eggs with nest materials. In the water hatchlings grab the tail of either parent and climb onto the back, where they are carried and fed; the parent even dives with the young clinging to it.

Range: Breeds throughout the Americas, except the subarctic and subantarctic regions. Winters in central British Columbia and all western and southern states with open water. Also on seacoasts.

The Pied-billed Grebe may mix with other waterfowl, but it is usually solitary; breeding pairs are secretive and sometimes only one pair is found on a pond. It is able to sink with barely a ripple, only its head popping up, like a periscope, at a distance before it dives again.

178, 180 **Eared Grebe**
(*Podiceps nigricollis*)
Grebes (Podicipedidae)

Description: 12–14″ (30–36 cm). Teal-sized bird, a bit smaller than the Horned Grebe. Breeding birds rufous below with black head and neck, golden ear tufts (neck of Horned Grebe is rufous). In winter plumage, *dark neck* and *dark ear region* contrasting with whitish face distinguish it from the Horned Grebe; bodies of both dusky above, white below. At close range, *bill upturned;* that of Horned Grebe is straight. Both have red eyes.

Voice: On the breeding grounds, a loud *ker-yeep!*

Habitat: Large lakes and sloughs where part of the water is overgrown with emergent vegetation.

Nesting: 3 or 4 whitish eggs in a depression on a floating platform lined with decaying algae; in colonies. Both of the parents incubate the eggs and care for the young.

Range: Southwestern Canada through the western United States south to the desert belts. Also in the Old World. Winters south to Mexico.

Adult and young alike feed on insects. These birds migrate at night, and large congregations may be seen at lakes or seaside coves, where they dive for tiny crustaceans. Breeding in colonies is thought to provide a synchronized timetable for mating, egg laying, and rearing of young. So many eggs and chicks available simultaneously provide an oversupply of food for predators, allowing most eggs to escape predation.

179, 181 **Horned Grebe**
(*Podiceps auritus*)
Grebes (Podicipedidae)

Description: 12–15¼" (30–39 cm). Breeding birds of both sexes have rufous lower parts and neck, black head, and two buffy tufts on head. In winter gray above, white below; short, thin neck and much *white on face, ear area, and neck,* contrasting with blackish cap. *Straight bill.*

Voice: A high squeal and a sharp *ka-raa* heard on the nesting grounds. Otherwise generally silent.

Habitat: Small lakes and ponds. Coastal bays, oceans in winter.

Nesting: 4 or 5 bluish-white eggs on a floating nest built of anchored, decayed vegetation; in groups of two or three pairs or, often, a single breeding pair.

Range: From the Yukon Delta east to Hudson Bay, and east-central Ontario, and North Dakota west to Idaho, Washington, and British Columbia; also Old World. Winters on both coasts.

In contrast to the Eared Grebe, this bird primarily eats fish and tadpoles rather than insects. Horned Grebes are solitary or form loose aggregations, wintering mainly on the coasts.

184, 187 Killdeer
(*Charadrius vociferus*)
Plovers (Charadriidae)

Description: 9–11″ (23–28 cm). Robin-sized, larger than Semipalmated Plover. Grayish-brown above, white below with *two black breast bands* and long, predominantly tan tail, most evident in flight or in distraction display.

Voice: Repeats its name, a shrill *kill-deer, kill-deer.*

Habitat: Fields and pastures, occasionally breeding on flat graveled roofs. After breeding, frequents coastal fields, inland beaches, or lawns.

Nesting: 4 buff, spotted eggs in a nest or scrape with a few pebbles. Like other plovers, both parents incubate and care for the young.

Range: Throughout temperate North America. Migratory; winters inland where climates are mild; common along the East and West coasts.

If a predator approaches, the killdeer performs a conspicuous distraction display, dragging itself, often on one foot, with its wings appearing broken and with tail fanned toward the intruder. This "injury-feigning" is effective in leading the predator away from the vicinity of nest or young.

191 Solitary Sandpiper
(*Tringa solitaria*)
Sandpipers (Scolopacidae)

Description: 7½–9″ (19–23 cm). Slightly smaller than a Robin. *Dark gray back with light spotting;* lighter on head with white eye-ring; white below with *greenish legs.* In flight, shows dark wings and flashy tail, dark in center, cross-barred white on sides. Bill straight and rather long.

Voice: High, clear *pee-weet* or *hueet* calls as it flushes.

Habitat: Breeds in muskegs and lakes in the
northern forest; during nonbreeding
season, along muddy shores of pools.

Nesting: 4 pale green or buffy eggs, heavily
spotted with brown, in abandoned nest
of Robins and other birds; in trees in
muskeg.

Range: In coniferous forests north to Alaska
and from treeline in Alaska to central
Canada. Transient across the West in
migration. Winters in Central and
South America.

Well named, this species does not
migrate in flocks. It feeds along the
edges of irrigation canals and small
ponds, especially where cattle are
watered. When disturbed, it bobs its
head and flies up with loud calls. Its
habit of occupying nests of other birds
is unique among North American
shorebirds, which usually do not make
a nest but use a scrape on the ground.

192, 232   **Spotted Sandpiper**
(*Actitis macularia*)
Sandpipers (Scolopacidae)

Description: 7½–8″ (18–20 cm). Small sandpiper.
*Flesh-colored or yellowish legs; white wing
stripe* shown in flight distinguishes it
from larger Solitary Sandpiper which
has uniformly dark wings and more
white in tail. In autumn unmarked
olive-brown above, with olive wash
across sides of upper breast, white
below, with light eye-stripe and white
eye-ring. In spring, *underparts are
heavily marked* with large, dark spots.
Almost always first identified by
teetering habit and manner of flight
(see below).

Voice: Utters a sharp *peet-weet* or a repeated
weet-weet-weet.

Habitat: Streams, lakes, reservoirs, or almost any
body of water that is surrounded by
vegetation and woods.

Nesting: 4 buffy, blotched eggs in a depression in grass or gravel near water.

Range: Very widespread; breeds in almost all of North America except the southeastern seaboard. In the southern part of its range, it breeds in mountains. Winters in milder areas of United States south to South America.

Often, when I come to a creek or a forest pool, whether in familiar places close to home in California or in faraway parts of Eurasia and Africa, the small birds fly out from underfoot, make an arc over water on stiffly vibrating wings, alight a little farther on, and make jerky dashes along the shore, bobbing almost continually. These are the Spotted Sandpipers, or their Old World counterpart, Common Sandpipers (*Actitis hypoleucos*). Some consider them one species.

198 Pectoral Sandpiper
(*Calidris melanotos*)
Sandpipers (Scolopacidae)

Description: 8–9½" (20–24 cm). Male is Robin-sized, female smaller. *Brown, mottled and striped above, including throat and breast; streaking below ends abruptly at white belly.* Legs yellowish-green. No prominent wing stripe; dark rump and tail.

Voice: A low, grating *churr* note.

Habitat: Breeds on tundra; tidal marshes and wet fields in migration.

Nesting: 4 greenish or buffy brown-marked eggs in a scrape in the grass.

Range: Nests in northern Siberia and from northwestern Alaska to Hudson Bay. Migrates mainly eastward, and thus not very common in the West. Some follow the Pacific Coast in the fall, but most fly through the interior plains or along the Atlantic Coast. Winters mainly in southern South America.

During the breeding display, the male inflates his throat and makes a hollow booming sound that carries far over the tundra; this proclaims his presence in the mating territory. The name "pectoral," comes from the Latin word *pectus*, meaning "breast."

304, 334 Osprey
(*Pandion haliaetus*)
Ospreys (Pandionidae)

Description: 21–24½" (53–62 cm). *Large hawk. Dark brown above, white below. Head is white with dark line through eyes.* In flight, shows a distinctive bend in its wing at the elbow.

Voice: High, whistled *k-yewk, k-yewk, k-yewk* calls.

Habitat: Coasts and inland lakes and rivers.

Nesting: 2–4 buffy, brown-blotched eggs in a large stick eyrie, reused year after year, on top of any height near water, on a Douglas fir snag in the Northwest, a rock pinnacle in Yellowstone, a cactus tree in coastal deserts, even a bridge. The down of the young is white, as in all birds of prey.

Range: Truly cosmopolitan; occurring on every continent, at least as a winter visitor. Nests throughout North America. Winters from southern United States, south.

Called the "Fish Eagle" in many countries because, unlike other birds of prey that feed on small mammals and birds, it feeds entirely on fish. It catches fish by hovering, then plunging talons-first into the water. Like the Bald Eagle, its nesting success has decreased in many areas because the fish it eats are contaminated with toxic chemicals. It requires active measures to ensure its conservation.

333, 335 Bald Eagle
(*Haliaeetus leucocephalus*)
Hawks (Accipitridae)

Description: 30–43" (76–109 cm). W. 78–96" (2–2.4 m). Adult, over 5 years old, has *snow-white head, neck, and tail; brownish-black body. Yellow bill.* Immatures brown, except for whitish wing linings and, usually, whitish blotches on underparts. Head and tail gradually whiten with each molt as birds attain adulthood.

Voice: A thin, chittering note, quite weak for so magnificent a bird.

Habitat: Most often on or near seacoasts; also large lakes and rivers where fish are abundant.

Nesting: 1–3 white eggs in large nest of sticks usually placed in tall trees, especially conifers. In the Northwest this bird will choose a nesting tree that is obscured by a dense stand of younger trees. Nests are renovated year after year, increasing in size until they break off or the whole tree falls in a winter storm.

Range: Formerly bred throughout North America, but now breeds only in Aleutians, Alaska, parts of northern and eastern Canada, northern United States, and Florida. In winter, along almost any body of water, especially larger rivers in the interior of the continent.

Although the Bald Eagle eats carrion and sometimes catches crippled waterfowl, it is primarily a fish-eater. Its beachcombing role has been its downfall, for it accumulates pesticides in its own body from contaminated fish and wildlife. Hunting, poaching, and the encroachment of civilization have diminished its populations drastically except in the rain forest coasts of Alaska and northern and central British Columbia

354 Rough-winged Swallow
(*Stelgidopteryx ruficollis*)
Swallows (Hirundinidae)

Description: 5–5¾″ (13–15 cm). Pale brown above, white below with *dingy brown throat.* Similar but smaller Bank Swallow has white throat, brown breast band.

Voice: A low, unmusical *br-r-ret,* more drawn-out than the call of the Bank Swallow, and often doubled.

Habitat: Riverbanks. It flies over water, pastures, or whatever land is near nest site. Prefers a drier site than the Bank Swallow.

Nesting: 4–8 white eggs in a burrow or cavity. Not highly colonial; often nests singly. Will utilize ready-made cavities in bridges, culverts, or other streamside masonry.

Range: Widespread, from central British Columbia and Alberta, the southern parts of the Canadian prairie provinces, and the Great Lakes, through Central and South America.

The outer primary has tiny hooklets on the outer vane (flat part of a feather) near the end of the shaft, visible only under a magnifying glass. Their function is unknown.

355 Bank Swallow
(*Riparia riparia*)
Swallows (Hirundinidae)

Description: 4¾–5½″ (12–14 cm). Smallest swallow in North America. Resembles Rough-winged Swallow, brown above, *white below* with a distinct *band of brown across upper breast.*

Voice: Sharp, unmusical *pret* or *trit-trit.*

Habitat: Banks of rivers, creeks, and lakes; seashores.

Nesting: 4–6 white eggs in a grass-and-feather nest in a chamber at the end of a deep tunnel which it digs near the top of a steep bank. Since it breeds in large colonies, nesting banks may sometimes appear riddled with holes.

Range: Throughout North America except in deserts and in rain forests of the Northwest. Also Eurasia, where it is known as the "Sand Martin." Migratory.

The Bank Swallow is a sporadic breeder in the West, perhaps because the soft earth that it needs for nesting is scarce. Since it also forages near the nesting colony, bank and suitable feeding area must be near each other.

---

356 Tree Swallow
(*Iridoprocne bicolor*)
Swallows (Hirundinidae)

Description: 5–6" (13–15 cm). *Metallic blue-black* above; underparts white. Juveniles are gray-brown above, sometimes with indistinct dusky partial breast band.

Voice: Calls are variations on a liquid *chweet*.

Habitat: A variety, including mountain meadows, marshland, parkland forest, but always near water.

Nesting: 4–6 white eggs in a soft, feather-lined cup nest in a woodpecker hole, natural cavity, or nesting box.

Range: Coast to coast in North America from Alaska to California across to mid-Atlantic states. Winters in southern United States and Central America.

Hole-breeders such as this often face a housing shortage and must fight to get into, or keep, woodpecker holes or other sought-after space. By means of breeding boxes, the numbers of these birds may be greatly increased. The Tree Swallow almost invariably nests in the immediate vicinity of water.

492 Dipper
(*Cinclus mexicanus*)
Dippers (Cinclidae)

Description: 7–8½" (18–22 cm). Uniformly *slate gray, wren-shaped* bird with stubby tail; feet yellowish.

Voice: Vigorous singers, their loud bubbling song carries over the noise of rapids. Call is a sharp *zeet*.

Habitat: Near clear fast streams with rapids.

Nesting: 3–6 white eggs in a relatively large, insulated nest of moss, with a side entrance, built under roots, in a rock crevice or bank side area along the home stream.

Range: From Alaska to mountains of Central America, and from Pacific Coast to eastern slope of the Rockies. It may move to lowlands in winter.

The "Water Ouzel"—its British name—feeds on insect life of streams. Where water is shallow and runs over gravel, the dipper appears to "water-ski" on the surface. At deeper points it dives into the water and runs along the bottom with half-open wings.

503, 504 Belted Kingfisher
(*Megaceryle alcyon*)
Kingfishers (Alcedinidae)

Description: 11–14½" (28–37 cm). *Large head; very long, heavy bill; crest.* Male *bluish-gray above with white underparts* and bluish-gray breast band. Female similar but with rufous band below the bluish-gray one.

Voice: A loud, dry rattle, often prolonged.

Habitat: Banks of rivers and lakes; seashore; near clear fishing waters.

Nesting: 5–8 white eggs at the end of a long tunnel excavated in a bank. The birds construct no nest; regurgitated fish bones build up under the clutch by the time the eggs hatch.

Range: Aleutians, central Alaska, across Canada, south to Mexico and the Gulf Coast. Winters north to the limit of unfrozen fresh water and south to Central America and Caribbean islands.

While searching for fish, it perches conspicuously on a limb over a river or lake. On sighting a fish it flies from its post and hovers over the water before plunging after its prey. When flying from one perch to another, often a good distance apart, it utters a loud rattle.

523 Green Kingfisher
(*Chloroceryle americana*)
Kingfishers (Alcedinidae)

Description: 7–8½″ (18–22 cm). *Sparrow-sized,* with flicker-like bill. Dark metallic-green above, white below, on side of neck and throat. Wing speckled with white; flanks spotted with green. *Male has broad red breast band;* female lacks this, but green spots on flanks form loose band across breast.

Voice: A *cheep* in flight; a repeated *tick* near the nest.

Habitat: Along streams, rivers, slow-flowing or stagnating branches of estuaries, and mangrove swamps.

Nesting: 4–6 white eggs in a burrow dug in a bank; no nest.

Range: Central and South America, southern Texas, and an infrequent visitor to Arizona and New Mexico.

Prefers shaded rivulets, where pairs can fish on both sides of the main river and along the rivulet. Their watching posts are low above the water.

610 Black Phoebe
(*Sayornis nigricans*)
Tyrant Flycatchers (Tyrannidae)

Description: 6–7" (15–18 cm). *Slate black except for white belly and undertail coverts and outer tail feathers.* Its *tail-wagging,* erect posture, and insectivorous feeding habits are helpful in field identification.

Voice: Song is a repetition of the phrase *fee-bee,* the second syllable alternately lower and higher in pitch. Call is a sharp, downslurred *chip.*

Habitat: Shady watered areas, streams, pond and lake banks; in winter, city parks, open chaparral.

Nesting: 3–6 white eggs, with a few faint speckles, in a mud, moss, and grass nest lined with soft material, often feathers or cow hair. Nests are found under bridges, on ledges, in crevices of old buildings, and among hanging roots near the top of embankments close to water.

Range: Southwestern United States and western Mexico south to Argentina.

Black Phoebes are territorial and solitary nesters, often remaining year round in an established territory. The wanderers found in atypical winter habitats (chaparral or grassland) are thought to be first-year, nonbreeding birds.

Wet Tundra

In the Arctic, the upper layers of soil
thaw in June or early July, but the
subsoil remains permanently frozen. On
low ground above this permafrost,
meltwater creates boggy areas,
sometimes of vast expanse.
The shallow, warm water breeds
countless mosquitoes, midges, and
other insects that are the main food for
shorebirds. When the tundra freezes,
waterbirds must migrate southward to
new food supplies. Loons, eiders,
jaegers, and several other species that
nest in wet tundra are more likely to be
encountered by most birders in aquatic
habitats farther south.

53 **Parasitic Jaeger**
(*Stercorarius parasiticus*)
Jaegers (Stercorariidae)

Description: 16–21″ (41–53 cm). Resembles medium-sized long-tailed gull, but flies like a falcon. Light phase brown above, white below; *black cap,* yellowish cheeks; gray-brown wash on chest. Dark phase uniformly brown. Both phases show *white flash* near tip of wing formed by white bases of primaries. There are three species of jaegers, best distinguished (in adults) by tail shape. Parasitic has *two long central tail feathers* extending 2–4 inches beyond tip of tail. The dusky, barred immatures of the three species––predominating among fall and winter visitors––lack longer central tail feathers and are difficult to distinguish.

Voice: On the tundra, it utters a wailing cry, *ka-aaow* or *ya-wow*. When attacking a seabird or a flock, piercing *tok-tok* or *tick a tick tick* cries frighten the intended victims.

Habitat: Tundra for nesting; open ocean during the rest of the year.

Nesting: 2 spotted brown eggs in a nest formed of a few lichens, or simply in a depression on the tundra.

Range: Circumpolar Arctic breeder of the North American and Eurasian tundra. In winter it roams the seas, including the North Pacific; north to California, but mostly in Southern Hemisphere.

The American name for these birds, jaeger, comes from the German word for hunter. During the short Arctic summer this species feeds mainly on birds and lemmings. Upon leaving the Arctic, jaegers become pirates, robbing seabirds by harassing them until they disgorge their captured prey. They can often be seen pursuing flocks of terns on migration.

55 Pomarine Jaeger
(*Stercorarius pomarinus*)
Jaegers (Stercorariidae)

Description: 20–23″ (51–58 cm). Largest jaeger, stockier than other species, but similar in coloration. Light phase dark above, white below, *dark cap,* yellow wash on face. Often shows strong to incomplete *dark breast* band; *coarse barring on flanks.* *White wing* flash larger than in other species. Dark phase uniformly blackish except for *wing* flash. Broad, *twisted* central tail feathers extend 3–5 inches beyond rest of tail in adults. Immatures brownish, strongly barred with black.

Voice: Various squealing and squeaky notes, a harsh *which-you,* and a querulous chatter. Generally silent during migration.

Habitat: Tundra breeder; on the open ocean after the breeding season.

Nesting: 2 brown eggs with blotches in a depression lined with moss and grass.

Range: Circumpolar on Arctic tundras. In the West it may be seen on its breeding grounds in western and northern Alaska and northern Canada. It is common off the Pacific Coast during fall and spring. Winters on open ocean from Hawaii and California south to South America.

Its flight is steadier, with slower, heavier wingbeats, than that of the Parasitic Jaeger; in pursuit of gulls or terns, however, it makes lightning-fast dives, chasing them until they disgorge their food, which it then catches in the air. Along the West Coast the Pomarine is the most common jaeger. On the tundra it feeds almost exclusively on lemmings.

98, 99, 139 Oldsquaw
(*Clangula hyemalis*)
Ducks (Anatidae)

Description: 19–22½″ (48–57 cm). Medium-sized
sea duck, but male looks larger due to
long central tail feathers. Most variable of
all American ducks, wearing three
plumages annually. Winter male is
white on head, back, underside, and
elongated shoulder feathers and has
black on ear, breast, wing, and central
tail feathers; in late spring mainly
black, with chestnut–buff on mantle,
white flanks, gray patch surrounding
eyes; summer male has, in addition,
gray flanks and sides, more buff on
wings. Female corresponds to male but
with shorter tail; black crown in winter
plumage, white semicollar in spring
and summer plumages. In flight, both
sexes show dark wings.

Voice: The displaying male has a repertoire of
gurgling, gabbling calls, some
sounding like *ow-owly, owly, owly* or *ah,
ah, ah,* and *ong.*

Habitat: Breeds on tundra ponds and marshes;
winters on inshore waters with shallow
mussel banks.

Nesting: 6–8 olive or buffy eggs in a down-lined
depression near water on the tundra.

Range: Circumpolar on the Arctic coasts of
northern continents with extensions
southward. In the West, breeds on
Aleutian Islands and Alaskan and
Canadian tundra. Winters along Pacific
Coast, south mainly to Washington.

When they arrive at wintering waters,
Oldsquaws search for mussel banks
where they will feed. Studies show that
adults lead the immatures to feeding
grounds; eventually the young learn the
locality. In courting, several males
display around a female, calling noisily.
This phase of the courtship behavior
gave rise to their American name; the
British call them "Long-tailed Ducks."

106, 144 King Eider
(Somateria spectabilis)
Ducks (Anatidae)

Description: 18½–25" (47–64 cm). Male similar to
Common Eider with white head, neck,
and breast (tinged pink during
breeding season), and black below, but
has a *black back.* Bill has *enormous orange
swelling* at base of upper mandible,
light green face, light gray cap. Black
wings flash smallest white shoulder
patch of all the eiders. *Female buff* and
similar to female Common but shorter
bill does not extend up forehead, thus
head profile more rounded, less sloping.

Voice: Usually silent. Females utter loud,
hollow *gog-gog-gog* notes; courting males
have various cooing calls.

Habitat: Ponds on High Arctic tundra and,
when not breeding, coastal waters.

Nesting: 4–7 olive eggs in a down-lined scrape,
covered with down when the female
leaves the nest; inland on the tundra.

Range: Circumpolar on coastal tundra along
the northern coasts and islands of
Eurasia and North America. In winter
south along Aleutian chain and
southern coast of Alaska peninsula,
rarely farther south; on the east coast to
New Jersey.

The traveler who braves northern waters
between the polar ice and mainland
coasts gets a spectacular view of these
birds gathering to leave for the South.
Males migrate first, abandoning the
incubating females and gathering in
enormous flocks to molt at a few
sheltered areas where mussels and
crustaceans abound. Females and their
offspring follow, usually skirting the
coasts because eiders avoid flying over
land. In spring, each homeward-bound
flock may contain tens of thousands of
individuals all hurrying to take
advantage of the short Arctic summer.

107, 142   Spectacled Eider
(*Somateria fischeri*)
Ducks (Anatidae)

Description: 20½–22″ (52–56 cm). Breeding male
has white neck and back, black breast
and belly. Bright, light olive green head
and large white, *black-rimmed spectacles*
around eyes distinguish it. Female is
mottled buff, with *light buff spectacles*
and with *large bill feathered halfway
down.*

Voice: As in the other eiders: females utter a
loud *gog-gog-gog* note; males are
generally silent.

Habitat: Coastal tundra during the breeding
season; inshore waters for the rest of the
year.

Nesting: 5–9 greenish, olive-buff eggs in a
down-lined depression in the tundra,
near fresh or brackish water.

Range: Coasts of Arctic Siberia and Alaska,
including the northern Bering Sea area.
In winter, down to the Aleutians.
Scarce along the southern Alaska coast
and accidental further south.

Although this eider feeds on aquatic
insects and vegetable matter on the
tundra ponds where the young are
raised, at sea it is a diving duck,
staying offshore over mollusk-laden
banks. Apparently it has never been a
common species.

108   Steller's Eider
(*Polysticta stelleri*)
Ducks (Anatidae)

Description: 17–18½″ (43–47 cm). Very small
eider, the size of a goldeneye. Male is
*pale rufous below, bright black-and-white
above;* head white with black ring
around eye and small black-and-green
crest on nape. Female is mottled brown
like other eiders. Both sexes have
purple speculum bordered in front and

back with white, noticeable in flight.

Voice: Male has a weak croon similar to Common Eider's; female, a low, growling *qua-haa* note. As in goldeneyes, the wings produce a whistling noise in flight.

Habitat: Coastal tundra and adjacent coastal waters.

Nesting: 6–10 light olive or greenish eggs in a depression in moss lined with eider down on flat tundra.

Range: The Arctic coasts of Siberia and Alaska, and the Bering Sea. Winters in the Aleutians and southwest to the Kodiak Island area. Accidental to coast of British Columbia.

This fast-flying, beautiful duck dives for crustaceans, insect larvae, and even waterweeds and their seed. It has been observed to feed on crowberries, a staple tundra fruit preferred by several kinds of waterfowl.

168, 172 Yellow-billed Loon
(*Gavia adamsii*)
Loons (Gaviidae)

Description: 33–38″ (84–97 cm). *Largest loon,* goose-sized. In summer, black upper side dotted with white, with pearl-like marks on flanks and back, arranged in rows on mantle. Neck and head deep black with purplish-green gloss; two incomplete white collar marks. *Bill conspicuously ivory yellow,* and at close range straight upper mandible and upturned outline of lower mandible makes whole bill seem upturned. Since its plumage in summer and winter is similar to Common Loon's, only its slightly larger size and the color and shape of its bill distinguish it. In winter, head and neck usually paler than Common Loon, with dark patch behind ear. Sexes look alike.

Voice: The loud, laughing call is similar to

that of the Common Loon.

Habitat: Estuaries and bays on the coastal tundra; lakes. In winter sheltered coves and bays.

Nesting: 2 olive-brown eggs in a grass-and-moss nest, hidden in vegetation on a small island or placed on land near water.

Range: Nests on the High Arctic lakes of North America and Eurasia. In the West it winters on the Pacific Coast south of Alaska.

In recent years this large loon has been seen regularly (but rarely) along the Pacific Coast of the United States, south to Monterey Bay and (once) in Baja California.

195 Least Sandpiper
(*Calidris minutilla*)
Sandpipers (Scolopacidae)

Description: 5–6½" (13–17 cm). Smaller than Western Sandpiper. *Short thin* dark *bill, yellowish legs,* light brown breast, and striped brown underparts. Least Sandpipers appear warm brown; in winter they look drab or gray; but leg color does not change.

Voice: A high *preeep* or *pree-rreeep.*

Habitat: Nests in tundra marshes, bogs; tidal mud flats, grassy pools, and flooded fields in winter.

Nesting: 4 pale buff, brown-marked eggs in a depression sparingly lined with dry grass, or in a scrape in boggy, marshy tundra.

Range: Low Arctic tundra from Alaska to Labrador, even bogs in the Maritime Provinces. Visits the Pacific and other coastal states in great numbers in winter, though some flocks proceed south to Central and South America.

A very common sandpiper of mud flats and wet grassy areas. It is tame in the presence of man. As a tightly bunched flock twists and turns in unison, the birds alternately flash white bellies and dark backs.

196, 228 **Semipalmated Sandpiper**
(Calidris pusilla)
Sandpipers (Scolopacidae)

Description: 5½–6¾" (14–17 cm). Slightly larger than the Least Sandpiper. In all plumages, grayer above with less streaked breast than other "peeps." *Black feet and short, black bill,* the bill appreciably stouter than in Least Sandpiper.

Voice: A sharp *cheh,* not as drawn-out as the notes of the Least and Western sandpipers.

Habitat: Tundra in breeding season. Salt water mud flats, often among flocks of other small sandpipers in migration and in winter.

Nesting: 4 olive-buff eggs with darker spots in a leaf-lined scrape on the tundra.

Range: The majority of these Low Arctic birds migrate east of the Rockies to the Gulf and south Atlantic Coast and down to South America.

The name "semipalmated" refers to the front toes, which are partially joined by webbing into a "palm" that helps support these birds on soft mud.

Rufous-necked Sandpiper
(Calidris ruficollis)
Sandpipers (Scolopacidae)

Description:  6½" (17 cm). Small sandpiper. In breeding plumage *face, neck, and upper breast are cinnamon-rufous,* rest of underparts white; above, cinnamon and brown with black blotches. Wing stripe white, rump dark, bill and feet black. In fall, when most of the red hues are replaced by gray, it is virtually indistinguishable from the Semipalmated Sandpiper.

Voice: A thin *chit-chit;* a simple *pip.*

Habitat: Marshy tundra in summer; mud flats and sewer ponds in winter and on migration.

Nesting: 4 cream-colored eggs, marked with brown, on dry willow leaves in a depression in the tundra.

Range: Eastern Siberian Arctic and the western edge of Alaska. Accidental in the Pacific states. Winters in southeastern Asia, Australia, and New Zealand.

This sandpiper breeds on inaccessible coasts. Due to the difficulty of distinguishing it from other "peeps," as small sandpipers have been nicknamed, its status as a stray in North America is unknown.

213, 239 Long-billed Dowitcher
(*Limnodromus scolopaceus*)
Sandpipers (Scolopacidae)

Description: 11–12½" (28–32 cm). *Very long-billed* sandpiper. In spring, brown above, rust-colored below with transverse *black barring.* In winter *grayish* above, *whitish* below. Immatures brownish above and mottled buff below. Has *white lower back* and *rump,* barred tail. Difficult to distinguish from the Short-billed Dowitcher, but the Long-bill is somewhat darker and has bars rather than spots on breast.

Voice: The Long-billed Dowitcher gives a high sharp *keek;* the Short-bill utters a low, mellow *tu-tu-tu.*

Habitat: Wet tundra; in winter, freshwater ponds.

Nesting: 4 eggs, greenish with brown markings, in a scrape in a tundra marsh.

Range: On adjacent coasts of Siberia and western Alaska, east to the Mackenzie District of Canada. Winters in the

south, along both coasts of North and Central America.

Both species of dowitchers are social shorebirds; small flocks feed in mud in shallow waters all winter, taking off swiftly with loud whistles and twisting and turning in flight. The Long-bill prefers pond habitats while the Short-bill usually keeps to tidal mudflats.

Bar-tailed Godwit
(*Limosa lapponica*)
Sandpipers (Scolopacidae)

Description: 15–18″ (38–46 cm). Large shorebird. Long legs; long, *slightly upturned bill.* In spring, head, neck, and unbarred underparts are cinnamon; dusky above with cinnamon and light spotting; in fall and winter, striped brownish-gray, light below. In both plumages the distinguishing mark is *white rump and white, cross-barred tail.*

Voice: A loud *kew-wew* and various other notes. Noisy on its limited breeding grounds in North America.

Habitat: Tundra marshes in summer; estuarine mud flats and lake edges in winter and in migration.

Nesting: 4 greenish eggs with small brownish spots, in a scant nest in a hollow.

Range: Eurasian tundra and isolated spots in western Alaska. Migrates across the ocean to Pacific islands as far south as Australia and New Zealand. The only godwit regularly seen in Alaska. A rare stray in migration along Pacific and Atlantic coasts.

Godwits wade in open water and probe deeply for worms and crustaceans. This species is abundant in many parts of the Old World.

576 Lapland Longspur
(*Calcarius lapponicus*)
Finches (Fringillidae)

Description: 6–7" (15–18 cm). In breeding plumage
male has *black head, throat, and upper
breast; chestnut nape;* broad buffy eye-
stripe and white border between nape
and bib. Belly white with slight black
side streaking. Brown back and wings
with sparrow-like streaking. Male in
winter plumage has brown, striped
head, ill-defined black breast blotch,
and faint chestnut wash at nape. Female
is sparrow-like, with *dark tail and white
outer tail feathers.*

Voice: Flight song is a jingling, high-pitched
see, serilee-aw, serilee-ee, serileeaw. Alarm
call is *peer.* Contact call in flight is *dir-
it.*

Habitat: Swampy tundra and wet meadows; in
winter, fields, prairies, lakeshores.
Often found flocking with Snow
Buntings, Horned Larks, or other
longspurs.

Nesting: 4–7 variable, pale olive to buffy brown,
spotted and blotched eggs in a feather-
lined nest depression in the tundra.

Range: Circumpolar in the Eurasian and North
American tundra. Winters from east to
west coast as far south as Florida,
southern California, and northern
Mexico.

Both the Lapland Longspur and the
Snow Bunting have a long hind toenail.
These birds run or walk rather than
hop, as finches normally do. The
commonest small bird in the vast
expanses of sedgy, moist tundra, the
Lapland Longspur is bold in the
breeding territories, but wintering
flocks are wary.

Desert Scrub and Mesquite

A desert region where more than half of the ground is bare and the vegetation consists of thorny, waxy, or cactus-like shrubs, many without leaves except after the rare rain. Mesquite sometimes grows to tree size; other conspicuous desert vegetation includes yuccas and Joshua trees, saguaro and organpipe cacti, paloverde, and creosote bush. Desert birds such as the Common Raven, House Finch, and Burrowing Owl also occupy other types of habitats and are described there. Desert oases attract straying migrants, and birds from any habitat may appear there during their migration.

251 Lesser Nighthawk
(*Chordeiles acutipennis*)
Nightjars (Caprimulgidae)

Description: 8–9″ (20–23 cm). Similar to but
smaller than Common Nighthawk, but
white wing patch (buff in female) is
nearer tip of wing (visible in flight).
Both sexes have buffy cast to
underparts. Male's throat white;
female's buffy. Whereas Common
Nighthawk hunts and calls from high
up, Lesser Nighthawk flies low and
utters no loud aerial calls.

Voice: Call is a soft, sustained, tremolo
whirring; very difficult to locate.

Habitat: Dry, open scrub; desert valleys; prairies
and pastures.

Nesting: 2 light gray, spotted eggs on the open
ground.

Range: Southwestern United States (mainly
southern California, Arizona, parts of
Nevada, Utah, New Mexico, and
Texas) south to Brazil. Winters mainly
south of the United States.

The Lesser is more nocturnal than the
Common Nighthawk, and it hunts its
insect prey flying low above the canopy
of trees or the brush and grass of open
plains. During courtship flight display,
the male pursues the female close to
the ground, flashing his white throat
as he calls.

264 Roadrunner
(*Geococcyx californianus*)
Cuckoos (Cuculidae)

Description: 20–24″ (51–61 cm). Magpie-sized.
Brown with green sheen, streaked with
black and white above; buff below with
brown streaks on breast; oversized *heavy
bill and crest;* long graduated tail, which
it occasionally flicks up; white-tipped
outer tail feathers. Runs rapidly on
strong feet, seldom flies.

Voice: "Song" is a mournful series of low cooing notes, dropping in pitch: *cooo cooo cooo cooo-ah coo-ah.*

Habitat: Chaparral, desert scrub, and other arid brush.

Nesting: 3–6 white eggs in a neat, shallow saucer nest in a mesquite bush, large cactus, or shrub in chaparral. Young hatch at intervals; if food becomes scarce, the largest seize all that parents bring, leaving the smaller ones to starve.

Range: From the Central Valley of California throughout the Southwest, Colorado, into the southern part of the prairie states. and south to Mexico.

Famous for its rather unusual behavior. It is a reticent bird that when surprised on a road runs rapidly away (hence its name), vanishing into cover. It feeds on a wide variety of desert life including insects, scorpions, lizards, and snakes; it also takes rodents and young of ground-nesting birds.

---

276 Gambel's Quail
(*Lophortyx gambelii*)
Pheasants (Phasianidae)

Description: 10–11½" (25–29 cm). Desert counterpart of California Quail. *Buffy white, unscaled belly* with *central black patch* on male (black lacking in female) and *more chestnut on crown and flanks* (rather than grayish-brown) distinguish it from California Quail. Teardrop-shaped head plume, in both sexes, is peculiar to these two quails.

Voice: Cackling calls are similar to those of the California Quail, but slightly higher in pitch and have 1 or 2 notes more often than 3 notes.

Habitat: Desert thickets; arid country.

Nesting: 10–20 buffy eggs, with dark markings in a ground scrape well shaded by cactus pads. Large coveys, numbering

from 20 to over 100 birds, break up in
February or March, and pairs disperse
for nesting. Both parents care for the
young. These birds suffer great losses;
more than half the nests are said to be
taken by predators.

Range: Southwestern United States to
northwestern Mexico; introduced on a
small scale elsewhere.

An ingenious watering device has been
invented to fill the main environmental
need of these quail: a slanting metal
roof open to the cool night air of the
desert accumulates dew, which drips
down into a trough, providing water
during the heat of the day.

---

294   **Elf Owl**
       (*Micrathene whitneyi*)
       Owls (Strigidae)

Description: 5–6″ (13–15 cm). *Smallest American
               owl,* sparrow-sized. No ear tufts; white
               eyebrows, yellow eyes; underparts
               faintly streaked with buff. *Short tail*
               extending only to wing tips; row of
               white spots above shoulder.

Voice: The calls, high-pitched for an owl,
         consist of various whistles and
         whinnies, most typically a downslurred
         kew kew kew.

Habitat: Southwestern saguaro deserts, arid
           scrub, and wooded canyons.

Nesting: 3 or 4 white eggs in an abandoned
           woodpecker hole in a saguaro cactus or
           a tree.

Range: Breeds from southeastern California to
         Texas, and southward to Central
         Mexico.

At night in the desert this tiny
nocturnal owl is most often located by
means of its tremulous call. It feeds
entirely on large insects.

296 Ferruginous Owl
(*Glaucidium brasilianum*)
Owls (Strigidae)

Description: 6½–7" (17–18 cm). Resembles Pygmy Owl, but more rust-colored. Especially characteristic is *red, faintly cross-barred tail.* Crown streaked with white, underside streaked with red-brown, and white-bordered black patch on either side of nape. Like Pygmy Owl, undulating flight recalls that of a shrike.

Voice: Monotonous, repeated, harsh whistle, *poip,* and other whistles.

Habitat: Saguaro desert; mesquite or other streamside growth.

Nesting: 3 or 4 white eggs in a hole in a saguaro cactus or tree.

Range: From the desert of southern Arizona and the woods of the lower Rio Grande River Valley of Texas south through Central and South America. Rare and local.

The male calls incessantly in spring at a rate of 90–150 times a minute (one is reported to have called for three solid hours). This tiny tropical owl is rare and local in the United States, and the small population around Tucson, Arizona is a great attraction to bird-watchers.

305 Caracara
(*Caracara cheriway*)
Falcons (Falconidae)

Description: 20–25" (51–64 cm). W. 48" (122 cm). A long-legged hawk often seen on ground. Dark above and below, with black cap, white face, neck, and brown-barred breast. Facial skin red. In flight, appears long-necked and long-tailed, with conspicuous white head, wing patches, and base of tail. Immatures browner.

Voice: Generally silent except for a cackling cry from which its name is derived.

Habitat: Open or semi-open country, brushland, seashore, plantations with scattered tall trees, desert scrub; often perches on tall cactus.

Nesting: 2 or 3 brown eggs with darker blotches, in a large stick nest at a safe height.

Range: Tropical Americas, reaching its northern limit just inside the United States in Arizona, Texas, and Florida.

An omnivorous raptor, it feeds on small vertebrates as well as carrion. This bird, magnificent in flight, is the "Mexican eagle" of the flag of Mexico. The Mexican peso coin shows the Caracara hacking a wriggling rattlesnake to death with its beak. It has become much rarer in western Mexico, perhaps due to pesticides.

311 **Harris' Hawk**
(*Parabuteo unicinctus*)
Hawks (Accipitridae)

Description: 17½–29" (44–74 cm). W. 42–45" (1–1.1 m). Slim, medium-sized hawk. Dark, with *chestnut shoulder, wing linings, and thighs* (hence sometimes called "Bay-winged Hawk"). Long tail is black with white terminal band and flashy white tail coverts, and in flight appears white with broad black band. Juveniles paler and streaked below.

Voice: Call is a harsh squeal.

Habitat: Mesquite shrub and desert areas; requires trees for nesting and prefers those in woods in river bottoms.

Nesting: 3–5 whitish eggs in a small stick platform nest in yucca, mesquite, or a low tree.

Range: A tropical or semitropical hawk, widespread from the border areas of the United States (the lower Colorado River Valley of California east to southern

Texas) south to central Chile and
Argentina.

During incubation and brooding, the
smaller male single-handedly supplies
the whole family with food.

344 Ground Dove
(Columbina passerina)
Pigeons (Columbidae)

Description: 6–6¾" (15–17 cm). A tiny dove. Short
*black tail and rufous primaries, most
noticeable in flight.* Light brown like
Mourning Dove; adult male has blue
crown; much purplish on neck-shield
area and shoulders, and is slightly
"scaled," i.e., feathers have a somewhat
darker edge. Folded wings are
patterned with *big black spots.*

Voice: Rapidly repeated *woo-oo,* the two
syllables often blending.

Habitat: Mesquite, brushy areas, roadsides,
edges of woods.

Nesting: 2 white, rounded eggs in a flimsy flat
nest placed low in a bush, vine, cactus,
small tree, or even on the ground.

Range: Widespread in tropical America,
extending into the border areas of the
United States from southern California
through southern Arizona and New
Mexico east to the Gulf Coast, Florida,
and South Carolina.

The Ground Dove flies incredibly fast,
with its short wings beating rapidly,
almost like those of a quail. When it
walks, it nods like a pigeon. It searches
for seeds on the ground, but requires
low brush for nesting and roosting.
Most of its courtship behavior takes
place on the ground, the male pursuing
the female, bobbing his expanded neck
in rhythm with his monotonous cooing.

348 White-winged Dove
(*Zenaida asiatica*)
Pigeons (Columbidae)

Description: 11–12½" (28–32 cm). Length of
Mourning Dove but tail is much
shorter and body is larger. *Drab brown
body* with a purplish sheen on crown,
neck, and shoulder. Primaries charcoal
gray; *white upper wing coverts*
conspicuous in flight. Tail is rounded
with white-tipped outer tail feathers.

Voice: A harsh cooing reminiscent of a
crowing rooster; sometimes represented
as *who cooks for you-all?*

Habitat: Desert scrub and fields, cottonwoods
along watercourses and willow thickets,
suburbs.

Nesting: 2 buffy eggs in a flimsy stick nest low
in cactus or trees.

Range: Southern California, Arizona, New
Mexico, and Texas south to South
America.

Many northern species of pigeons and
doves are seed-eaters, but tropical
species feed primarily on fruit. The
White-winged Dove enjoys both: in the
desert its main seasonal fruit is that of
cactus; elsewhere it supplements its
seed diet with berries. These fast-flying
birds are gamebirds.

366, 368 Ladder-backed Woodpecker
(*Picoides scalaris*)
Woodpeckers (Picidae)

Description: 6–7½" (15–19 cm). *Zebra-backed* like
Nuttall's Woodpecker, but with
slightly smaller black ear patch and face
stripe, usually separated from black of
nape and back by white band. Male's
red cap usually more extensive than
Nuttall's. Best identified by voice and
habitat.

Voice: The sharp *pik* call is unlike the rolling
notes of the similar Nuttall's

Woodpecker. During encounters with rivals it utters a harsh *jeee jeee jeee.*

Habitat: Deserts and their borders; also mesquite, pinyon-juniper woodland, and scrub oaks.

Nesting: 4 or 5 white eggs in the tall (up to 30 feet high) dry stalk of a century or agave plant; occasionally in a hole chiseled in a yucca, a cottonwood tree, or even a fence post.

Range: Southern California, Utah, and Colorado south to Baja California, northern Mexico; locally to Nicaragua.

This "agave woodpecker" lives in an unusual microcosm. After pollinating the century plant, the agave beetle lays eggs in the flower stalk, where its larvae consume some of the growing seed. The woodpecker eats the larvae, thus controlling their number. After the century plant seeds mature and the plant dies, the stalk serves as a nest site for the woodpecker.

375 Gila Woodpecker
(*Melanerpes uropygialis*)
Woodpeckers (Picidae)

Description: 8–10" (20–25 cm). Medium-sized woodpecker. Similar to the Golden-fronted Woodpecker but with different head pattern and checkered, not white upper tail coverts. *Male has small red cap.* Head and underparts gray-brown; back has black-and-white "zebra back" pattern. Female and juvenile similar but lack red cap and thus resemble juvenile Golden-fronted. White wing patches are prominent in flight.

Voice: Has a vibrato call, a rolling *churrr,* as well as one like a barnyard hen.

Habitat: Low desert scrub with saguaro and mesquite trees for nesting; also farther south in tropical deciduous thorny bush and forest, often interspersed with organ-pipe cactus.

Nesting: 3–5 white eggs in a hole in giant
saguaro or trees.

Range: From southeastern California through
the Sonora Desert to Central Mexico.

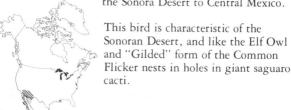

This bird is characteristic of the
Sonoran Desert, and like the Elf Owl
and "Gilded" form of the Common
Flicker nests in holes in giant saguaro
cacti.

394, 405 Broad-billed Hummingbird
(*Cynanthus latirostris*)
Hummingbirds (Trochilidae)

Description: 3¼–4″ (8–10 cm). Male dark green
above and below, with bright *metallic-
blue gorget.* Bright *red-orange* bill with
black tip. Female's *unmarked gray throat
and underparts* and *red-orange bill*
distinguish her from other female
hummers of the same size.

Voice: Call is a rapid, scratching *chi-dit,* like
the note of a Ruby-crowned Kinglet.

Habitat: Desert canyons; mesquite and other
thickets in arid country.

Nesting: 2 white eggs in a loosely woven, rough
cup nest on a vertical branch of a
streamside tree.

Range: A Mexican species of both eastern and
western Sierra Madre mountain ranges,
extending into the United States
in the low desert areas of southeastern
Arizona, southwestern New Mexico,
and western Texas.

It is said to be quieter and less active
than most hummers, often sitting on a
high perch for long periods. However,
its flight is more irregular and jerky
than that of other hummers in the same
habitat.

401 **Costa's Hummingbird**
(*Calypte costae*)
Hummingbirds (Trochilidae)

Description: 3–3½″ (8–9 cm). Tiny hummingbird.
Male's *violet-purple crown and gorget,*
which is *flanked with very long,*
conspicuous side feathers, distinguish it
from the Black-chinned Hummingbird.
Female is indistinguishable from female
Black-chinned. Costa's preference for
more arid terrain and habit of soaring
between flower clusters is helpful in
distinguishing it.

Voice: In display male's outer tail feathers
produce a very high-pitched whine,
highest in pitch and intensity in the
middle. Call notes include a light *chip*
and high tinkling notes.

Habitat: Low desert and, in California and Baja
California, chaparral.

Nesting: 2 white eggs in a delicately woven cup
with leaves or lichens fastened to the
outside, built low on a protected
branch of a bush or small tree.

Range: Southwestern desert states extending
south from central California and
southern Nevada to northwestern
Mexico.

Hummingbirds feed both on insects
and on nectar. Although
hummingbirds in North America
encounter many nectar-bearing flowers
on their migrations, they have a
decided preference for red flowers. In
southern and central California, Costa's
feeds extensively on the red
beardtongue. Since this plant is found
mainly in habitats where Costa's is the
only resident hummingbird, it is
probably the plant's chief pollinator.

Lucifer Hummingbird
(*Calothorax lucifer*)
Hummingbirds (Trochilidae)

Description: 3¾" (10 cm). Small hummingbird, the only one with a *decurved bill.* Male iridescent green with *green crown* and *purple gorget;* white below with some buff on flanks; forked tail. Female buff below; has decurved bill, lacks forked tail. Costa's Hummingbird has a similar gorget but also has purple on the forehead and a tail that is rounded, not forked, and lacks the decurved bill.

Voice: Males utter a shrill shriek.

Habitat: Open arid country; desert vegetation, especially agave.

Nesting: 2 white eggs in a small cup nest of downy plant fibers, cobwebs, and lichens, usually near the ground in agave and other vegetation.

Range: Mexico, rarely extending north into western Texas (where it breeds in the Chisos Mountains in Big Bend National Park). Accidental summer visitor to extreme southeastern Arizona.

In Latin, *lucifer* means light-bearing and was applied in Old English to the morning star. Thus when William Swainson named the bird in 1827 he might have been thinking of the luminous glow of this bird's colors. The male Lucifer's outer tail feathers are hard and narrow, and hum loudly during aerial displays. The male performs a zigzag dance to attract females and repel other males.

---

422   Verdin
(*Auriparus flaviceps*)
Titmice (Paridae)

Description: 4–4½" (10–11 cm). Smaller than a chickadee, as large as Bushtit. *Gray with yellow head and throat;* chestnut patch at bend of wing; white underparts. Juveniles lack both yellow and chestnut coloration of adults and are distinguishable from Bushtit by shorter tail.

Voice: The call most often heard is a single sharp *seep!* Its infrequent song is a 3-note *kleep-er-zee!,* the final note being highest.

Habitat: Low desert, containing brush and taller shrubs.

Nesting: 3–5 greenish, spotted eggs in a hanging nest built among the prickliest branches of the cholla cactus or in a crotch of mesquite, with an entrance hole in the side.

Range: Southeastern California east to southern Texas and south to northern Mexico.

Verdins behave like their relatives the chickadees and bushtits, feeding on insects, seeds, and berries. The small clutch size may be an adaptation to assure sufficient food in an area of climatic extremes. The thorny protection around most nests probably discourages predators.

Lucy's Warbler
(*Vermivora luciae*)
Wood Warblers (Parulidae)

Description: 4" (10 cm). Small, plain warbler with white eye-ring. Both sexes gray above, creamy white below, with *bright chestnut rump.* Chestnut crown feathers usually concealed, except in display. In fall underside buff but undertail coverts white. Immatures have buff rump.

Voice: Song is reminiscent of Yellow Warbler's: *chit chit chit chit sweeta che-che-che.* Call is a soft *plenk,* often run into a series.

Habitat: Southwestern deserts, especially among cottonwoods and streamside trees and mesquite in washes or canyons.

Nesting: 4 or 5 white, speckled eggs in a well-lined cup nest in a tree under loose bark or in a hole—a rare nest site among warblers.

Range: Desert areas near the Colorado River in California, Nevada, and Utah; southern Arizona and New Mexico south into Mexico.

The only desert warbler, Lucy's is characterized by a flicking tail, rapid motions, and a rich song.

451, 551   Vermilion Flycatcher
(*Pyrocephalus rubinus*)
Tyrant Flycatchers (Tyrannidae)

Description: 5½–6½" (14–17 cm). Male has bright *vermilion head and underparts.* Brownish-black narrow mask, back, wings, and tail. Female and immatures are lighter brown above, lightly streaked on white breast; yellow-tan or pink wash on belly and undertail coverts.

Voice: Generally silent except for springtime aerial displays of the male. In flight, the male utters a stuttering outburst: *pit-pit-pit-pitty-zeee!*

Habitat: Deserts; thickets adjacent to watercourses, subtropical scrub.

Nesting: 2 or 3 whitish, heavily marked eggs in a flat, saucer-shaped nest of twigs lined with animal or plant hair, in the crotch of a horizontal limb.

Range: The Southwest to South America.

Despite its brilliant color, the Vermilion Flycatcher is hard to detect in cottonwoods, willows, or mesquite, since it hunts from the highest canopy and generally remains well concealed. In sparsely vegetated areas, however, it may descend to the ground after insect prey. The male signals his defense of a territory with a prominent aerial display. He flies up singing, his red underparts and cap contrasting with the blue sky. When trying to attract a female, he sings even at night.

468, 567 Pyrrhuloxia
(*Cardinalis sinuatus*)
Finches (Fringillidae)

Description: 7½–8" (19–20 cm). Shaped like
Cardinal, but with *parrot-like bill*. Male
gray wth crimson crest, rose stripe down
middle of breast and belly, with darker
red flashes in wings and tail. Female
more buffy than gray and lacks red
markings except in front of eyes, on
crest, wings, and tail. Bill yellow in
summer, horn-colored in winter, never
pink like that of Cardinal.

Voice: Song like that of a Cardinal, but
thinner and usually downslurred: a clear
tseeu tseeu tseeu tseeu. Call is *quit*.

Habitat: Mesquite scrub, less heavily vegetated
than the Cardinal's habitat.

Nesting: 2–4 small, grayish-white, dotted eggs
in a compact cup nest of weed stalks
and roots, in mesquite or thorny bush.

Range: A Mexican bird, entering the United
States in southern Arizona, New
Mexico, and Texas.

Pyrrhuloxias feed on seeds and insects,
and benefit cotton fields by destroying
great numbers of cotton worms and
weevils. When an observer approaches,
a pair will fly up to a high watch post,
erect their crests, and sound a loud
alarm. Its name comes from Latin and
Greek words meaning "bullfinch with a
crooked bill." As has been suggested
repeatedly, it would be more proper to
call it the Gray Cardinal.

491, 613 Phainopepla
(*Phainopepla nitens*)
Silky Flycatchers (Ptilogonatidae)

Description: 7–7¾" (18–20 cm). Larger than a
sparrow. Slender, elegant bird with
conspicuous crest; longish tail and *upright
posture*. Male *shiny black* with white
wing patch that shows only in flight.

Females and juveniles plain gray with pale wing patch.

Voice: Common calls include an upslurred whistled *hoooeet* and a low *quirk*. The short warbled song is rarely heard.

Habitat: Known as a desert scrub bird, yet it does not have strong preference for desert; it favors hot country with single, tall trees, preferably with mistletoe or other berries available when flying insects are scarce.

Nesting: 2–4 pale greenish speckled eggs in a simple shallow nest in mistletoe-bearing desert trees, such as the mesquite along washes, or in tall trees bordering rivers.

Range: Central California, Arizona (extending into extreme southern Nevada and Utah), east to western Texas; south through arid areas of Mexico. In the more northerly parts of its range, it is migratory.

The Phainopepla is the northernmost of a group of tropical birds that feed on mistletoe. In the Southwest the berries are seasonal, so it supplements them with insects, which it takes from the air in long sallies, like a flycatcher.

494 Black-tailed Gnatcatcher
(*Polioptila melanura*)
Old World Warblers (Sylviidae)

Description: 4½–5″ (11–13 cm). Tiny bird similar to Blue-gray Gnatcatcher. Gray above, whitish below. Male has *black crown* during summer which extends to eyes. *Long black tail with white corners.* Winter male, female, and juveniles duller.

Voice: The common call is a harsh 2- or 3-note wren-like scold: *chee chee chee.*

Habitat: Deserts and arid country; dry washes in the low desert.

Nesting: 3 or 4 pale blue, spotted eggs in a small, smooth cup nest in mesquite or other desert bush or a low tree.

Range: Southern California, Nevada, Arizona, New Mexico, Texas, southward into Mexico.

Identification of gnatcatchers is difficult, particularly in the Southwest, where the ranges of two species, the Black-tailed and the Blue-gray, overlap. The tail of the more widespread Blue-gray is mostly white as seen from underneath, and when fanned, the three feathers on each side have diminishing amounts of white, whereas that of the Black-tailed is black underneath with only one outer white-tipped feather on each side.

---

520 Wied's Crested Flycatcher
(*Myiarchus tyrannulus*)
Tyrant Flycatchers (Tyrannidae)

Description: 8½–9½″ (22–24 cm). Kingbird-sized. Olive-brown above, darkest on crest; two wing bars. Larger size and deeper coloration of its heavy black bill, *pale gray throat* and breast, and brighter sulphur yellow belly distinguish it from Ash-throated Flycatcher. In flight, conspicuous reddish tail and primaries.

Voice: Very loud, with a variety of rolling *prr-rreeep!* notes. Call is a sharp *weep*.

Habitat: Desert where saguaro cactus is available for nest sites; also river groves and woodlands and in sycamore canyons.

Nesting: 3–6 creamy buff eggs, heavily marked with blotches and spots, in a hair- and feather-lined nest in a woodpecker hole or natural cavity.

Range: Southern Arizona east to southern Texas and south to Argentina.

Biologists have found that when closely related similar species such as the Wied's Crested, Ash-throated, and Olivaceous flycatchers occur together, ecological specializations such as differences in size, feeding habits, and vocalizations allow the species to co-exist without competing.

---

532 Cactus Wren
(*Campylorhynchus brunneicapillus*)
Wrens (Troglodytidae)

Description: 7–8¾" (18–22 cm). The largest North American wren; as large as a small thrasher but chubbier. Long *white eye-stripe,* brown head, upperparts striped with white; cross-barred wings and tail, white spotting on outer tail feathers. *Dark spotting* of underparts is concentrated on *upper breast.* Pale rust color on lower belly.

Voice: Calls are low, harsh, and repetitious, and frequently unbirdlike. For example, a harsh *chug chug chug chug . . .* or *ka ka ka ka . . .*

Habitat: Deserts and arid hillsides with clumps of yucca or mesquite.

Nesting: 4–7 pinkish eggs, heavily dotted; the nest is a large, oval, covered structure with a side entrance, usually placed among the prickly joints of the cholla cactus or protected by the dagger-like leaves of yucca trees.

Range: Southwestern United States to central Mexico.

Cactus Wrens forage for food very methodically, searching under leaves and other ground litter. Like other wrens, they build roosting nests and even use them for shelter in rainy weather. They are late sleepers and an early bird-watcher may surprise them still dozing in the snug nest.

534 Bendire's Thrasher
(*Toxostoma bendirei*)
Mockingbirds (Mimidae)

Description: 9–11″ (23–28 cm). Robin-sized. Shorter, less curved bill than other desert thrashers. Body light grayish-brown with *faint streaking on sides of neck and on breast. Yellow eyes.*

Voice: The beautiful song is a clear, melodious warble with some repetition and continuing at length. Call is a low *chuck.*

Habitat: Desert scrub of the Southwest.

Nesting: 3 or 4 pale greenish eggs, with buffy spots, in a stick nest lined with fine, soft material and hidden in a bush such as *Lycium,* paloverde, or cholla cactus.

Range: Sonora Desert, extending from Baja California to southern Utah, southeastern New Mexico and northwestern Oklahoma, south into mainland Mexico. In winter it moves slightly to the south.

This thrasher flies from bush to bush, whereas other desert thrashers almost never fly. However, most of its feeding is done on the ground.

535 Curve-billed Thrasher
(*Toxostoma curvirostre*)
Mockingbirds (Mimidae)

Description: 9½–11½″ (24–29 cm). Robin-sized, with *long curved bill,* pale red-orange eyes, and faint streaking on breast. Grayish-brown above with darker long tail; narrow light wing bars occasionally present.

Voice: Song is a long but halting carol with little if any repetition. Distinctive call is a loud *whit-wheet?*

Habitat: Permanent resident in the cactus desert of the Southwest.

Nesting: 2–4 pale blue-green, spotted eggs in a nest of twigs built in the spiny tangle of a cholla cactus. The nest has been

described by a late-nineteenth-century observer as "ten million cambric needles, set on hundreds of loosely jointed spindles, woven so closely together as apparently to defy penetration of a body however small, but the thrashers go in and out and up and through them with the ease of water running through a sieve."

Range: Southern Arizona to western and southern Texas and south to Mexico.

This bird forages on the ground, tossing aside litter in search of insects.

537 Le Conte's Thrasher
(*Toxostoma lecontei*)
Mockingbirds (Mimidae)

Description: 10–11" (25–28 cm). Palest of the thrashers. *Light sand color* with lighter, unstreaked underparts and darker tail. Dark bill, *dark eyes,* and dark eye-line. During breeding season adults have deep buff undertail coverts.

Voice: Song is a loud, rich melody which recalls that of a California Thrasher but is less harsh and with infrequent repetition of phrases. Calls are a rising *whit* and *tu-weep.*

Habitat: Deserts with scant vegetation (mostly cholla and creosote bush), where the bird blends with the light-colored, sandy soil.

Nesting: 2–4 light blue-green eggs speckled with brown, in a bulky twig nest covered with coarser grasses and lined with fine stems and feathers, placed in a cholla cactus or low thorny bush.

Range: Sonora Desert and neighboring hot areas, the lower San Joaquin Valley of California, southern Nevada and Utah, Arizona, Sonora, and Baja California.

This thrasher is a permanent resident in the Southwest. Like most other desert thrashers, it prefers to escape by scurrying away through the sparse vegetation, but will fly if pressed. It feeds mostly in early morning or just before dark, when insects are most active, and seeks shade in the middle of the hot day.

Crissal Thrasher
(*Toxostoma dorsale*)
Mockingbirds (Mimidae)

Description: 10½–12½" (27–32 cm). Large, dark thrasher, with deeply curved bill. Brown above with *lighter gray-brown, unstreaked underparts; dark mustache line;* eyes yellowish. The undertail area, or crissum, is *chestnut brown;* this undoubtedly gave the bird its common name.

Voice: Call is a rolling *chorilee, chorilee.* The song consists of loud, repeated phrases.

Habitat: Dense underbrush near desert streams; edge of canyon chaparral in the hot, low desert.

Nesting: 2-4 pale blue-green eggs in a rather large twiggy nest well hidden in dense mesquite or other thick desert vegetation.

Range: Southeastern California east through southern Utah to western Texas, and south to Baja California and central Mexico.

Seldom flies in the open, but moves furtively among streamside mesquite thickets, willows, and other tangles. This bird resembles the California Thrasher in its habit of gathering food by hacking the ground with its heavy curved bill, but their ranges do not overlap. Except during the hottest months and briefly after molting, it delivers its loud melodious song year-round.

564 Abert's Towhee
(*Pipilo aberti*)
Finches (Fringillidae)

Description: 8–9″ (20–23 cm). *Grayish-brown* above; slightly paler underparts with buffy belly and tawny undertail. Black facial patch surrounding pale bill.

Voice: Call is a single bell-like note.

Habitat: Along arroyos in desert thickets; associated with cottonwood, willow, mesquite, although it is also found around farms, orchards, and urban areas.

Nesting: 3 or 4 pale blue-green, scrawled eggs in a cup nest close to the ground in a bush or tree.

Range: Arizona, parts of neighboring Utah, New Mexico, and California southward into Baja California and Sonora in Mexico.

This bird, while related to and closely resembling the Brown Towhee, is paler, more secretive, and has a different song. They do not interbreed, even though their ranges overlap.

593 Black-throated Sparrow
(*Amphispiza bilineata*)
Finches (Fringillidae)

Description: 4¾–5½″ (12–14 cm). Gray above, darkest on head, dusky on wings; sooty black tail has white margins and corners. Eyebrow, *mustache,* and a spot below eye are *white; large black bib;* white below. Sexes similar; juveniles lack black bib and have finely streaked breast, thus somewhat resemble Sage Sparrow.

Voice: A quick little song starting with 2 or 3 melodious phrases, ending in a fast, tinkling trill. Calls are various tinkling notes.

Habitat: Driest and hottest cactus and sagebrush desert.

Nesting: 3 or 4 bluish-white eggs in a low, well-concealed loose cup nest lined with plant or animal hair in a low bush, often in a cholla cactus.

Range: From northwestern Nevada and southern Wyoming through the deserts of the Southwest and northern Mexico.

The Black-throated Sparrow is well adapted to the extremes of its habitat. Studies have shown that it has a great tolerance for heat and drought. During the hot months of late summer and early fall, it maintains itself on dry seeds and drinks regularly at water holes. After the rains, these sparrows scatter into small flocks and feed on vegetation and insects, from which they derive all the moisture they need. They raise their young in the dry upland desert. This bird is thus known as the "Desert Sparrow" in the Southwest.

Varied Bunting
(*Passerina versicolor*)
Finches (Fringillidae)

Description: 4½–5½" (11–14 cm). Sparrow-sized. Male is a dark plum *violet* with bright red patch on nape. In poor light it *appears all black*. Females and immatures are unstreaked light brown.

Voice: Call is a hard *chip*. Song is a series of sweet rising and falling phrases, uttered from a high perch.

Habitat: Mesquite and other semi-arid or desert vegetation, often near stream beds.

Nesting: 3–5 bluish-white eggs in a cup nest in a thick bush, tree, or tangle.

Range: Mexico, extending north of the border in Arizona and New Mexico, and in southwestern Texas.

As in other, more common and widespread buntings, the singing male is conspicuous, while the female is secretive and lives hidden in vegetation.

627 White-necked Raven
(*Corvus cryptoleucus*)
Crows (Corvidae)

Description: 19–21" (48–53 cm). Crow-sized, but
with *heavy* bill, *wedge-shaped tail,* and
long, pointed throat feathers. *All black;*
its heavy black ruff conceals white
upper neck feathers, except in display.
It flies with the raven's typical flat-wing
glide.

Voice: Call is a harsh, prolonged *caaaa,* higher
than that of a raven.

Habitat: Yucca desert, mesquite groves, and arid
grasslands. Trees or powerline poles are
required for nesting.

Nesting: 4–7 greenish, blotched eggs in a fur-
lined bowl on a large platform of sticks
or even baling wire; often placed in
mesquite or yucca or on a utility pole.

Range: Scarce from Nebraska south through
the prairie region; more common from
the Oklahoma panhandle south through
Texas, New Mexico, and Arizona across
the open areas of Mexico.

A scarcity of trees may have originally
led to this bird's habit of reusing the
same nest year after year. Gregarious
birds, they feed in groups on
grasshoppers or other insects as well as
carrion. They roost communally, and
soar high in the air in group displays.

Grasslands and Savannas

Natural grassland found on bare spots on hills and mountains where the soil is meager and rainfall is low and periodic. Grassland often covers the lee side of mountain chains as well as California's valleys and foothills where rain falls only in winter.

Once much of the West was covered with lush grass prairies; only a small part of this remains, the rest having been converted mainly to cultivated fields.

Savannas, pastures, and rangeland are forms of grassland. Savanna is a grassland with single trees or scattered groups of trees. Pastures and meadows are smaller areas where the grass is cultivated. Rangeland is native grassland cropped close by domestic stock.

Some perching birds (Black-billed Magpie) are adapted to grasslands but require trees for nesting; these could be included in either grassland or wooded habitats. Others (Prairie Falcon, Barn Swallow) hunt over grasslands but nest elsewhere, and some (Snow Bunting) use the grasslands only in winter.

208 Upland Sandpiper
"Upland Plover"
(*Bartramia longicauda*)
Sandpipers (Scolopacidae)

Description: 11–12½" (28–32 cm). A meadowland sandpiper with *long, yellowish legs,* long thin neck; short bill. *Mottled* above and below; whitish unstreaked belly; *more buffy than other sandpipers of similar size.* It often holds its wings upward briefly on alighting, *exposing black-and-white barring on underwing.*

Voice: Alarm call a mellow *quip-ip-ip-ip.* On its breeding grounds, a long mournful rolling whistle.

Habitat: Prairies, open grasslands, and flat open bogs; frequently perches on fence posts, poles, or stones.

Nesting: 4 eggs, buff or paler, speckled with brown, in tall grass along the edges of clearings, sloughs, or muskegs; nest on the ground lined with dry plant material.

Range: From Alaska through the Canadian prairie provinces and much of northern United States south to Oklahoma and Texas.

Until recently it was called the "Upland Plover." Formerly very common on the prairies, but indiscriminate hunting and the destruction of its habitat reduced its numbers. As a result of land clearing, its breeding range in the East is expanding and the population is increasing.

---

210 Marbled Godwit
(*Limosa fedoa*)
Sandpipers (Scolopacidae)

Description: 16–20" (41–51 cm). Large, long-legged shorebird. *Long, slightly upturned bill.* Mottled buffy brown above; paler, finely vermiculated below, giving

marbled impression; cinnamon wing linings;
bill flesh-colored at base, with black at
tip; feet bluish-gray.

Voice: A loud *karrack* and a laughing *ha-ha.*
Also a rapid *ratica, ratica, ratica.*

Habitat: Prairie grasslands and meadows around
lakes; coastal wetlands, beaches in
winter.

Nesting: 4 olive-buff, spotted eggs in a scrape in
grass.

Range: Western interior provinces of Canada
south to Montana and the Dakotas.
Winters from California and Gulf Coast
to northern South America.

In spring, the aerial displays and noisy
calls of godwits are conspicuous. They
favor prairie meadows for nesting. After
breeding they migrate to coastal
beaches where they probe the mud.

217 Long-billed Curlew
(*Numenius americanus*)
Sandpipers (Scolopacidae)

Description: 20–26″ (51–66 cm). Very large
shorebird with extraordinarily *long
downcurved bill. Cinnamon brown with
dark mottling above,* clear buff below,
with light side streaking on neck and
belly, cinnamon underwing linings,
long neck.

Voice: A far-reaching, loud *cur-lee?,* often
answered by *kli-li-lili-lili.*

Habitat: Salt marshes, mud flats, beaches; nests
on upland prairies.

Nesting: 4 olive eggs heavily spotted with brown
and lavender, in a grass-lined
depression on open ground.

Range: Southern Canada throughout the Great
Basin, east to Texas and northwestern
Oklahoma. Winters from the
southwestern states to the grasslands of
the Mexican plateau and the coastal
lagoons of western Mexico; also Gulf
Coast of United States and southern
Florida.

Although territorial when nesting, curlews are social birds that feed, roost, and migrate in flocks. They avoid cover, feeling safe only in the open. The bill looks almost as long as the body, whereas in the smaller Whimbrel the bill is only about the length of the head and neck. Formerly hunted for their delectable meat, they are now fully protected.

250 Common Nighthawk
(*Chordeiles minor*)
Nightjars (Caprimulgidae)

Description: 8½–10″ (22–25 cm). Robin-sized. Long notched tail and long pointed wings *with broad white wing bar;* mottled brownish-black above and below, perfectly matching the forest floor. Male has white throat patch and white subterminal tail bar. Female has buffy throat patch and no tail bar.

Voice: A nasal call, *peent* or *spee-ik,* heard primarily at dusk. Courtship display involves aerial dives ending in a loud, vibrant buzz.

Habitat: Open woodlands, clearings, fields, towns with roosting trees or fence posts.

Nesting: 2 creamy or olive-gray, finely and densely speckled eggs laid on ground or roof.

Range: Widespread in North America except for tundra and low deserts of the Southwest. Winters in subtropical habitats of Mexico and South America.

This bird has moved into towns where flat roofs provide abundant nest sites and railroad yards, vacant lots, and sports fields offer good feeding opportunities. Discarding the old English term "Goatsucker," pioneer settlers mistook this bird for a hawk because of its swift flight and long wings. It flies in daylight as well as at night but is most in evidence in early evening.

252, 256 Sharp-tailed Grouse
(*Pedioecetes phasianellus*)
Grouse (Tetraonidae)

Description: 15–20″ (38–51 cm). Slightly smaller than female pheasant, which it roughly resembles; mottled buffy coloration overall; slightly lighter underparts. Central tail feathers slightly *elongated*, mottled brown, with graduated *white outer tail* feathers. Tail of male longer than that of female. Male has violet neck patch.

Voice: During courtship, a single low cooing note.

Habitat: Open brushy country; also boggy openings in spruce or pine forest of the northland.

Nesting: 10–13 buff-brown eggs in a grass-lined scrape in tall grass brush.

Range: From interior Alaska to Hudson Bay, south to Utah and Nebraska and east to Lake Huron.

Sharptails, like many grouse, perform elaborate displays on communal grounds called leks, returning to the same spot every year. In one case, when a homestead was built over the lek, the grouse displayed on the farmhouse roof the following spring.

254, 258 Greater Prairie Chicken
(*Tympanuchus cupido*)
Grouse (Tetraonidae)

Description: 17–18″ (43–46 cm). *Medium-sized grouse.* Brownish overall with camouflage barring. *Male has bare-skinned orange air sac* on both sides of neck that show only when inflated during courtship hooting; yellow comb over eyes. *Long, black feathers* (which account for a local name, "Pinnated Grouse") dangle from nape of male and are erected in courting dance. Flared crest and upturned, rounded, black-edged tail give the head and tail of the courting male a similar appearance.

Voice: A deep booming during courtship; it consists of 3 or 4 notes unlike the longer accelerating series of some other grouse.

Habitat: Tall-grass prairie, rangeland, and even brushy fields.

Nesting: 11 or more olive eggs, lightly speckled with brown, in a grass-lined scrape among tall grass.

Range: Becoming very scarce in Canadian prairie provinces, it still occurs in Saskatchewan and Manitoba; more common in the prairie states south to Oklahoma.

Males are polygamous and gather in spring on communal leks or display grounds, strutting and uttering a hollow booming sound. Females mate with the male of their choice but raise their chicks alone.

255, 259 Lesser Prairie Chicken
(*Tympanuchus pallidicinctus*)
Grouse (Tetraonidae)

Description: 16–18″ (41–46 cm). Slightly smaller than the Greater Prairie Chicken. *Neck pouch* of the male is *reddish* rather than orange. Body a mottled *pale buff-brown*, barred with black and brown; rounded tail black in male, brown in female. Male has erectile black-and-white neck feathers and yellow comb over eyes.

Voice: Gurgling, high-pitched, gobbling sounds uttered by males in the mating dance on the lek.

Habitat: Arid short-grass prairies.

Nesting: 11–13 buff, dotted eggs in a scrape

with some grass.

Range: Southern prairie states, including western Oklahoma, eastern New Mexico, and Texas.

With the dwindling of prairies, the range of this spectacular prairie grouse has been reduced. Game management is required to maintain the population.

280, 282 Bobwhite
(*Colinus virginianus*)
Pheasants (Phasianidae)

Description: 8½–10½" (22–27 cm). Small, tawny-brown quail with *white throat and eye-stripe* in male (buffy in female) which extends through nape. Brown or black crown forms slight crest. Stocky gray tail held downward when walking. *Male's dark eye-line connects with chest or throat collar,* cross-barring on belly; contrasting chestnut-streaked sides.

Voice: The male call sounds like *bob-white,* with an emphasis on the rising second syllable.

Habitat: Forest edge, burns, mixed brushy open areas.

Nesting: 10–15 dull white eggs in a grass-lined ground scrape sheltered by grass or brush.

Range: Mainly an eastern and Mexican bird, but also found in foothills of the Rocky Mountains. Introduced Bobwhites thrive in Washington, Oregon, and Idaho.

After the breeding period, the Bobwhite family lives together in a covey, sleeping in low bushes and huddling together in cold weather. When danger threatens they flush out in every direction, and after a short fluttering flight settle into cover. The male calls in spring after the covey breaks up; when a female is attracted and stays, he stops calling and helps raise the family, even incubating the eggs, a practice not common among pheasant-like birds.

284 **Scaled Quail**
(*Callipepla squamata*)
Pheasants (Phasianidae)

Description: 10–12″ (25–30 cm). *White, cottony topknot;* pale unstreaked gray head; bluish-gray feathers of breast and mantle have black semicircular edge, creating *scaled effect;* belly also has brown "scales"; white lines on flanks. Sexes look alike.

Voice: The call is often interpreted as a nasal *pay-cos, pay-cos.*

Habitat: Semi-deserts such as yucca flats, juniper hillocks, canyon bottoms.

Nesting: 9–20 white to buff, pear-shaped eggs speckled with brown, in a well-hidden nest, often among prickly agaves.

Range: Its distribution centers on the Chihuahua Desert of Mexico; it extends north to southeastern Arizona, New Mexico, Utah, southern Colorado, and parts of Texas.

Though birds of arid habitat, Scaled Quails must visit water holes regularly. They nest in the rainy season, when moisture produces some vegetation, and do not breed during extremely dry summers. They often gather in large flocks during nonbreeding periods. They seldom fly, preferring to run from intruders. Locally this bird is called the "Blue Quail" and the "Cotton Top."

301 **Burrowing Owl**
(*Athene cunicularia*)
Owls (Strigidae)

Description: 9–11″ (23–28 cm). Small owl of open country; no ear tufts; generally earth brown with white spots, whitish eyebrows and throat interrupted by a dark collar. *Long legs and short, stubby tail.* It stands upright whether perching or on the ground.

Voice: The alarm note is a cackling sound. Also a mellow rolling *coo-c-o-o.*

Habitat: Open country such as prairies, sagebrush flats, pinyon-juniper slopes, deserts, fallow fields, and seashore dunes; wherever rodent burrows are numerous.

Nesting: 5–7 white eggs in ground squirrel or prairie dog burrows, but the claim that it shares these with rodents or rattlesnakes has never been proved.

Range: Throughout the West; also in Florida and the dry region of South and Central America. Leaves colder areas in winter.

In urban areas it occurs at airports and vacant lots where open spaces resemble those of its natural habitat. Although normally diurnal, during the nesting season the male hunts both day and night to provide food for the young. When agitated, it frequently bobs and bows.

302 Barn Owl
(*Tyto alba*)
Barn Owls (Tytonidae)

Description: 14–20″ (36–51 cm). Medium-sized owl. White, heart-shaped face ringed with tan; back light tan with fine pearl gray streaks; *white below* suffused with tan. Sits upright on long feathered legs.

Voice: A loud rasping hiss, quite unlike the typical hooting of owls. Also a clicking note and, when alarmed, a snapping of the bill.

Habitat: Hunts in rodent-rich savanna, woodlands, farmlands, or suburbs; needs trees for perching.

Nesting: 5–11 round, white eggs on a bare surface, in a natural or man-made cavity, such as a cave, rock shelter, barn, or attic.

Range: Cosmopolitan, it lives in tropical and temperate regions on all continents; absent from coniferous forests in the mountains.

In the glare of auto headlights, a flying Barn Owl looks snow white, often giving the impression that it is a Snowy Owl. Barn Owls are effective mousers and take many rats. Owls do not digest fur and bone, periodically ridding themselves of these in the form of regurgitated pellets. Barn Owl pellets are easily collected from roosts and are a useful source of information about the small mammals in an area.

306, 338   Black Vulture
(*Coragyps atratus*)
Vultures (Cathartidae)

Description: 23–27" (58–69 cm). W. 54–60" (1.4–1.5 m). Somewhat smaller than the Turkey Vulture. *Black, with broad wings in flight showing a whitish "window" near the tip.* Black face is naked but is enveloped in a feathered "hood" that makes head look much larger than the naked, reddish head of the Turkey Vulture. In flight its short, square tail usually does not seem as long as its outstretched legs.

Voice: Generally silent. Croaking or hissing notes when annoyed.

Habitat: Similar to that of the Turkey Vulture: open, broken country.

Nesting: 1–3 whitish, blotched eggs in a hollow tree or rock, a cave, or hidden on the ground. No nest.

Range: Southeastern and, sporadically, southwestern United States and south to South America.

These vultures soar, often in numbers, high in the skies, until one of them

discovers carrion, whereupon all converge on it. It soars in short spurts that alternate with short glides. The Black Vulture is trusting with people, acting as the village sanitary agent, often seen walking, almost underfoot, in the markets and harbors of Caribbean or Mexican towns.

307, 336 Turkey Vulture
(*Cathartes aura*)
Vultures (Cathartidae)

Description: 26–32" (66–81 cm). W. 72" (1.8 m). One of North America's largest birds of prey, next in size after the Condor and the two eagles. Brown-black overall; with unfeathered red head (dark in young); yellow feet. In flight, conspicuously short-necked; broad *wings appear two-toned* with dark gray flight feathers looking lighter than black wing linings. Wings in flight are *held at a slight V angle,* or dihedral, often with primaries separated.

Voice: Rarely gives a soft hiss or groan, but generally silent.

Habitat: Dry open country or along roadsides, where it forages for carrion.

Nesting: 1–3 whitish eggs, blotched with brown, in a sheltered place such as a cave, cliff, hollow log, or even an abandoned barn. No nest.

Range: Common from southern Canada throughout the United States and Mexico. Also widespread through Central and South America. In the West, winters in California (locally) and southern Arizona.

Vultures are often called buzzards, a Western misnomer originally applied to *Buteo* hawks in the Old World. Although many people find the vulture's eating habits repulsive, it fills a useful role by consuming the flesh of dead animals.

308, 343 Swainson's Hawk
(*Buteo swainsoni*)
Hawks (Accipitridae)

Description: 19–22″ (48–56 cm). W. 48–56″ (1.2–
1.4 m). Smaller than Red-tailed Hawk.
Dark brown above, *white throat and body
accentuated by a dark bib-like band* across
breast. Darker gray flight feathers
highlight whitish wing linings. Tail
gray above, light below with dark
border; terminal band has white
trailing edge. In the dark phase, body
and wings uniformly dark.

Voice: Like many other large raptors, usually
silent. Around the nest it may give a
downslurred whistle.

Habitat: Plains, prairies, dry meadows with few
trees, and tundra.

Nesting: 2–4 bluish or white, often spotted eggs
in a stick nest in a tree, bush, or giant
cactus, on a cliff, or on the bare
ground, often renovating the same nest
year after year.

Range: Commonest hawk of Canadian prairies.
Breeds from Alaska south to the
Mexican Plateau. Winters mainly in
Argentina.

This hawk has a slightly dihedral or V–
angled gliding pattern when soaring on
thermal air currents. It perches near the
ground and feeds mainly on rodents
when available; otherwise it takes
grasshoppers and locusts. In migration
it forms huge flocks of several thousand
individuals en route to South America.

314, 342 Red-tailed Hawk
(*Buteo jamaicensis*)
Hawks (Accipitridae)

Description: 19–25″ (48–64 cm). W. 48–54″ (1.2–
1.4 m). Large hawk. Dark brown
above, most typically light below with
a *dark belly band. Rufous tail has a
narrow dark band* and light tip. Finely

streaked grayish tail of immature is often light at base. Plumage variation widespread, including an overall dark brown phase and a pale white-tailed phase.

Voice: A loud, harsh downslurred scream, often quite prolonged *kee-ahrrr*.

Habitat: A variety of habitats from tundra to semi-desert, wherever there are open hunting areas with woodland seclusion for nesting. Its most characteristic habitat is natural savanna or its man-made counterpart, farmlands with woods.

Nesting: 1–4 whitish, faintly marbled eggs in a large stick nest containing a neat cup with fine root lining and fresh green twigs; in a tree or on a cliff.

Range: North and Central America.

Commonly sighted at roadsides, perching atop telephone poles, haystacks, or fence posts, this hawk may sit for hours, then suddenly glide off to surprise a ground squirrel, lizard, or other ground-dwelling prey. It plays an important role in controlling rodent populations. At mating time it soars high in the air with conspicuous flight displays and cries.

315 Ferruginous Hawk
(Buteo regalis)
Hawks (Accipitridae)

Description: 22½–25" (57–64 cm). W. 56" (1.4 m). *Largest Buteo.* Light phase: *rufous above, whitish* below, with rufous wrist patch and leg feathers. Black primary tips. Dark phase (rare): deep rufous above and below. Whitish tail. Legs feathered down to talons. Immatures resemble light-phase adults but lack rufous markings.

Voice: A loud descending *kre-ah;* gull-like *krag* notes.

Habitat: Prairies, brushy open country, badlands.

Nesting: 3–5 white blotched or spotted eggs in a nest of roots, sticks, sagebrush, cow dung, or even old cattle bones. These hawks prefer trees, but will nest in a bush or on the ground on a ledge, riverbank, or hillside.

Range: Nests from the Canadian prairie provinces south to Oregon, Nevada, Arizona, and Oklahoma. Winters in southern half of breeding range and southwestern states from southern California to southwestern Texas.

The clutch is large for a *Buteo* hawk and may reflect fluctuating food supply. These hawks lay more eggs when prey abounds, fewer in years when rodent populations decrease. They feed mainly on prairie dogs and ground squirrels, less regularly on locusts, Jerusalem crickets, and birds.

---

319 White-tailed Kite
(*Elanus leucurus*)
Hawks (Accipitridae)

Description: 15–17″ (38–43 cm). W. 40″ (1 m). Falcon-shaped with gull-like flight. Gray above with *white head and tail* and black shoulder area. White below with small black mark at bend of wing; dark primaries. Immature has rust-colored streaking on breast, browner back, and faint dark narrow band near tip of tail. When perched, its large red eyes are conspicuous.

Voice: Occasionally gives a series of chirps, such as *kewp kewp* . . . Most vocal during courtship displays.

Habitat: Open savanna, grasslands, and fields; requires woods or trees for perching, roosting, and nesting.

Nesting: 3–5 white eggs with brown blotching in a well-concealed nest of dry twigs with lining of roots or grass stalks; nest seldom visible from below. Male prospects for a nesting tree in midwinter or early spring but female makes final selection.

Range: Distribution spotty: the Central Valley and southern coastal areas of California; southern Texas; also eastern Mexico, Central America, and parts of South America.

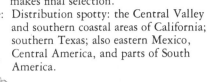

Almost extinct in 1930s and 1940s, these kites have since made a spectacular comeback in California and are now common in suitable lowland habitats. They are very social out of breeding season, congregating at roosts of 10 to 100, and feed principally on mice, which they locate by hovering kestrel-like high in the air. They also eat large insects and reptiles. These kites prefer to rest on treetops or other high lookouts.

322 Aplomado Falcon
(*Falco femoralis*)
Falcons (Falconidae)

Description: 15–18" (38–46 cm). Like a small Peregrine Falcon. Adult *bluish-gray above, with striking striped head.* Black mustache and black stripe behind each eye. *Pale stripe over eye* stretching to rusty nape; white throat, *buff breast,* and *black band on lower breast. Russet thighs and belly* not always visible. Tail black with many white crossbars. Juvenile brown above, streaked on breast, plain brown on flanks.

Voice: A rapid *gacking* cry quickly repeated, quite similar to the call of other falcons of the same size. Also a shrill *eek, eek.*

Habitat: Open arid country, grassland, desert, and savanna.

Nesting: 2 or 3 brown-spotted eggs, in trees; uses nests of desert ravens or other large birds.

Range: Formerly ranged from southeastern Arizona to southern Texas south to Patagonia. Extremely rare and sporadic today in the border country, although fairly common in Latin America. A few may occur in southern New Mexico.

This beautiful falcon strikes its small bird prey in the air, where it also catches large flying insects. It has been known to take ground prey and even fish. In behavior and appearance it resembles a kestrel more than a big falcon. While foraging it flies much lower than a Peregrine Falcon, preferring fast flights nearer the ground. It perches conspicuously in treetops.

330, 331 **American Kestrel**
"Sparrow Hawk"
(*Falco sparverius*)
Falcons (Falconidae)

Description: 9–12" (23–30 cm). W. 22¼–23½" (57–60 cm). Jay-sized. Male has *rufous crown, back, and tail;* blue-gray wings and head; buff breast and nape; white underparts with side spotting. *Black markings behind ear; black mustache and terminal tail band.* The lateral ear markings are said to resemble eyes as seen from above by large hawks. Female's head resembles that of male, but back and wings are darker rufous overall with heavier streaking below.

Voice: A loud, rapid *killy-killy-killy-killy.* Among the most vocal of birds of prey.

Habitat: Partly open country, farmland, forest edges, and cities.

Nesting: 3–5 buffy to grayish-white, lightly spotted eggs in tree holes without a nest; also in niches in buildings and sometimes in magpie nests. The male may help in incubation, which is unusual in raptors.

Range: Throughout the Americas. From Alaska to Tierra del Fuego. Winters throughout range, though northern birds are migratory.

This smallest falcon is commonly seen at roadsides, where it perches atop telephone poles and trees. It often hovers in the air before stooping on its prey. It feeds mainly on grasshoppers and small rodents. Formerly known as "Sparrow Hawk."

332 Golden Eagle
(*Aquila chrysaetos*)
Hawks (Accipitridae)

Description: 30–41" (76–104 cm). W. 76–92" (2–2.4 m). Shaped like a hawk but when soaring its wingspan is much greater; bill also larger, and the "eagle look" of the eye seems more pronounced because of the deep socket. Adult *dark brown overall* with "golden" nape (visible only at close range). Legs feathered down to talons. Immatures in flight show large white wing patch at base of primaries and *white tail with dark terminal band*.

Voice: Rarely heard: soft mewing or yelping notes; sometimes a high squeal.

Habitat: Remote rangeland, alpine tundra, mountainous badlands, and canyons.

Nesting: Normally 2 whitish, blotched eggs; eyrie a large mass of sticks on a crag or ledge or in trees. A pair may alternate between several nests in different years. In Europe, Golden Eagle eyries are known to have been used continually for centuries.

Range: Mountains and rangeland of western North America, from Alaska to Mexico; also in northeastern states and provinces, where rare. Northern populations migratory.

These majestic birds are common in many places in the west. They feed mainly on rabbits and large rodents, and sometimes scavenge dead lambs. The damage attributed to eagles by sheep herders, however, has been exaggerated.

349   Mourning Dove
(*Zenaida macroura*)
Pigeons (Columbidae)

Description: 11–13" (28–33 cm). Light brownish-
gray above, pale buffy below; wings
darker, with black spots along inside
edge; light blue eye-ring, large black
spot at lower base of ear patch;
iridescent light violet neck shield. *Very
long central tail feathers* (shorter in
female), with sharply tapered white-
tipped outer tail feathers.

Voice: Its name comes from the male's
melancholy cooing, the last three notes
lower than the first: *coo-ooh, coo, coo-coo.*
It is uttered from a prominent perch and
followed by a courtship flight which
begins with an upward arc and audible
wing clapping and ends in a glide with
flamboyant tail display.

Habitat: Dry uplands, grain fields, suburban
areas; deserts.

Nesting: 2 white eggs in a loosely constructed
twig nest built on a limb of a tree, low
in a bush, or on the ground. Both
parents feed their young, called squabs,
with "pigeon milk" secreted in the
crop.

Range: Throughout temperate North America,
including Mexico but not in montane
and boreal forests. Migratory in the
North.

The breeding season starts early—in
March in California—and continues to
mid-September. Bird may nest 2–4
times each year. Thus it is easily able to
maintain its numbers even though it is
hunted extensively.

417   Lesser Goldfinch
(*Carduelis psaltria*)
Finches (Fringillidae)

Description: 3½–4" (9–10 cm). Two forms of males:
black-backed and *green-backed;* both have

black crown, white markings on black wing and tail, with *bright yellow underparts*. Nonbreeding black-backed male turns greenish, but both races *retain black cap*. Female is smaller than American Goldfinch though similar, with *dark rump*. Immature is similar to female but with greener underparts.

Voice: Goldfinches are energetic songsters, delivering a rapid jumble of notes from a perch or in flight. The Lesser Goldfinch often combines its own call notes with those of neighboring species.

Habitat: Oak savanna, woodland, suburban gardens.

Nesting: 4–5 pale blue eggs in a twiggy nest in a bush or low tree.

Range: Black-backed races occur from northern Colorado south through Mexico to Central America, and westward to Utah and Arizona. Green-backed races occur from Utah westward to the Columbia River and south into northern Baja California.

Lesser Goldfinches feed on dandelion seeds and raise their young on soft unripe seeds. They adjust the time and place of their breeding to the presence of this staple food. Their Old World cousins, the siskins, goldfinches, serins, and canaries, have been kept as cage birds for centuries, the males singing incessantly all year except during the molt period.

---

421 Western Kingbird
(*Tyrannus verticalis*)
Tyrant Flycatchers (Tyrannidae)

Description: 8–9″ (20–23 cm). *Olive-brown above, yellow below;* gray head, lighter grayish throat and upper breast. Dusky wings and *blackish tail with white margins*. Red crown feathers not normally visible.

Voice: A *whit* call, and shrill calls like those of Eastern Kingbird but on a lower pitch.

Habitat: Arid savanna—natural or man-made
(e.g., alfalfa fields with fences, orchards
alternating with pasture), open chaparral,
pinyon-juniper brushland, roadsides.

Nesting: 3–5 pinkish-white, boldly spotted eggs
in a large well-built nest, usually lined
with matted cow or sheep hair, placed
on a horizontal branch of a tree or on a
bush, telephone pole, or building.

Range: Throughout the West, from southern
Canada south to Mexico, east to Great
Plains. Winters in Central America.

The Western Kingbird is found on
almost every ranch in the West, where
alfalfa and livestock pastures provide
many of the flying insects that make up
the bulk of its diet. After the young
fledge it is not uncommon to see half a
dozen or more kingbirds sally from the
dry upper branches of shade trees to
capture insects. When it has a nestful
of young to defend, it will attack crows
and other larger birds.

Cassin's Kingbird
(*Tyrannus vociferans*)
Tyrant Flycatchers (Tyrannidae)

Description: 8–9" (20–23 cm). Similar to Western
Kingbird but darker; *back* more *olive-
gray, black tail lightly white-tipped* but
lacks white margins. Darker gray breast
makes white throat patch appear
smaller and more clearly defined than
Western Kingbird's.

Voice: A noisy kingbird, its common
utterances are a loud *chi-beer!* and a
rapid *chi-beer, ch-beer-beer-beer-r-r.*

Habitat: Highland counterpart of the Western
Kingbird in savanna, rangeland,
pinyon-juniper woodland.

Nesting: 3–5 white, spotted eggs in a bulky nest
lined with twigs, grass, or animal hair;
on horizontal limb, well hidden.

Range: From southern Montana and Wyoming
to Mexico; also coastal savanna areas of

southern California where some winter as well. Winters in Mexico and Guatemala.

It is often found high on a tree, where it sits quietly as compared with the nervous Western Kingbird.

---

423 Western Meadowlark
(Sturnella neglecta)
Orioles (Icteridae)

Description: 8½–11" (22–28 cm). Robin-sized. *Mottled brown above, bright yellow below, with V-shaped black bib; top of head has black-and-white stripes.* Sexes look alike. Yellow on throat extends farther onto cheek (malar area) than in Eastern Meadowlark; mottled back and tail are lighter brown than Eastern. White tail margins are prominent in flight, and tail flicks open and shut when bird is walking.

Voice: This popular bird has a large repertoire of songs very different from the Eastern Meadowlark. It may utter its loud, melodious flute-like phrases one at a time or repeatedly. The male sings even when migrating or wintering, and at the height of the breeding season may rise in the air while singing *hip, hip, hurrah! boys; three cheers!*; *oh, yes, I am a pretty little bird;* or *u-tah's a pretty place.* Call notes include a harsh *chuck.*

Habitat: Open grassland, savanna, fields with brushy borders.

Nesting: 3–7 heavily spotted white eggs in a grassy, partially domed nest frequently with an entrance tunnel on the side; located in a grassy tussock.

Range: Grassland areas of the western Canadian provinces south through the prairies of all western states and into Mexico; spreading eastward into Midwest.

Its bright colors, fearless behavior, abundance, and above all its loud,

cheerful song make the Western
Meadowlark perhaps the most popular
of western birds.

---

424 Eastern Meadowlark
(*Sturnella magna*)
Orioles (Icteridae)

Description: 8½–11″ (22–28 cm). Dark gray-brown
above with dusky streaks and bars and
with three buff-white stripes on black
crown. *Chin, throat, and breast bright
yellow, interrupted by black crescent on
breast. Entire cheek gray,* whereas
Western Meadowlark has lower half of
cheek yellow. Conspicuous *white patch
on outer tail feathers.*

Voice: Song is a clear whistle rendered as *spring
o' the year;* it is very unlike the
melodious bubbling of the western
species. Call is a sharp *spit.*

Habitat: Fields, grasslands with taller vegetation
on which the whistling male perches.

Nesting: 3–7 white, brown-spotted eggs in a
dome-shaped nest hidden in grass.

Range: Southeastern Canada through all eastern
states, and from Arizona southeast
through Mexico all the way to Brazil.

The Eastern and Western meadowlarks
are so similar that at a distance only
their songs and calls distinguish them.
Moreover, the two may even learn each
other's song where their ranges overlap.
Meadowlarks are shaped like Starlings.
In flight they keep their wings stiff,
typically fluttering them a few times
and then sailing.

---

469 Scissor-tailed Flycatcher
(*Muscivora forficata*)
Tyrant Flycatchers (Tyrannidae)

Description: 11–15″ (28–38 cm). A light gray
flycatcher with *scissor-like, deeply forked*

tail twice as long as the body. Pearl gray head and back, lighter breast with salmon pink underlining of wings, flanks, body, and undertail coverts. Blackish wings and tail edged with white feathers. Adults have reddish crown patch (usually concealed). Juveniles gray, shorter-tailed, with little or no salmon pink coloration. Tail length (8–10″; 20–25 cm), shortest in yearlings, longest in adult males.

Voice: A repeated *ka-quee;* in flight display a stuttering series with an emphatic ending.

Habitat: Open country: mesquite and partly open, sparsely populated areas where fences and power lines provide high perches.

Nesting: 4–6 creamy white, spotted eggs in a shallow saucer nest of twigs and grass; in a tree or bush or on a telephone pole.

Range: Southwest-central United States: Kansas, Oklahoma, Texas, and the Mississippi Valley. Winters in Mexico and Central America.

It is often seen perching on a telephone wire with its extraordinarily long tail hanging down. I have seen a flock of over 200 feed, like Barn Swallows, on a swarm of insects. Like a kingbird, it erects its crest, emits harsh cries and fiercely attacks hawks, crows, or other large birds that invade its nest area.

472 Loggerhead Shrike
(*Lanius ludovicianus*)
Shrikes (Laniidae)

Description: 8–10″ (20–25 cm). Mockingbird-sized. Gray above, white below with *wide black face mask* which meets over the strong hooked bill. Small white patch on rump and on back adjacent to wing; black wings with small white window at base of primaries. Juveniles are brownish, with barring below.

Voice: A harsh, scolding *bzeee, bzeee*. Song is a series of coupled phrases, such as *queedle-queedle.*

Habitat: Roadside vegetation, thickets, savanna, desert, or any open country with high perches as lookouts.

Nesting: 4–8 yellowish-white speckled eggs in a well-lined twig nest built near the trunk of a tree or thorny bush.

Range: North America south of the coniferous forest region into Mexico. Winters in southern United States.

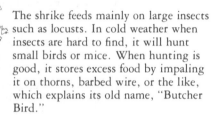

The shrike feeds mainly on large insects such as locusts. In cold weather when insects are hard to find, it will hunt small birds or mice. When hunting is good, it stores excess food by impaling it on thorns, barbed wire, or the like, which explains its old name, "Butcher Bird."

474 **Eastern Kingbird**
(*Tyrannus tyrannus*)
Tyrant Flycatchers (Tyrannidae)

Description: 8–9″ (20–23 cm). Blackish head, dusky mantle and wings, black tail *with white terminal band;* white below. Red feathers in middle of crown usually concealed. Long crown feathers and upright posture give the flycatcher a distinctive silhouette. Sexes similar.

Voice: The common call is *dzee* or *dzeet*. Cry is a series of harsh, rapid, crescendo *kits* and *kitters*.

Habitat: Savanna, rangeland, forest edges, riverside groves, and even city parks and roadsides.

Nesting: 3–5 white, spotted eggs in a large, bulky nest consisting of heaps of twigs, straw, and twine lined with hair and rootlets. Nests are built on the horizontal limbs of trees.

Range: Basically an eastern bird but widespread in the Rocky Mountain states and western provinces, reaching the coast in

southern British Columbia and Washington and the western valleys of Oregon. Migrates sparingly through the Pacific and southwestern states.

It perches on treetops, fences, and power-line poles; when a bird—often much larger than itself—flies into its territory it attacks fiercely, uttering a piercing cry. When one sex starts the battle, the other usually joins in. Its aggressive behavior has earned this bird its name.

560, 622 Brewer's Blackbird
(*Euphagus cyanocephalus*)
Orioles (Icteridae)

Description: 8–10″ (20–25 cm). Spring male has iridescent purple-black head, green-violet *glossy body,* and conspicuous *yellow eyes.* Glossy sheen absent in males in autumn. Female light gray-brown with brown eyes.

Voice: Call is *check.* Courting male utters a creaking *k-seeee* with tail spread and head lowered.

Habitat: Brushy savanna, irrigated pastures, roadsides, streamside thickets, towns, feed lots.

Nesting: 4–6 light gray, blotched eggs in a nest of twigs and grasses plastered with mud or cow dung and lined with fine materials in low shrubs or on the ground. In loose, small colonies. The male guards the female and the nest, but once the female is settled on the eggs, this polygamous bird may entice another female to nest within his territory.

Range: From southwestern British Columbia and Manitoba east to the Great Lakes, south to northern Baja California and western Texas.

Following man and his cattle, the Brewer's first pushed north into

Washington State around the turn of the century. Later it traveled northeastward, reaching Wisconsin, and it is still spreading in Ontario, Canada. A very social species, it mixes not only with its own kind but with other blackbirds such as the Red-winged or the Brown-headed Cowbird.

568 Grasshopper Sparrow
(*Ammodramus savannarum*)
Finches (Fringillidae)

Description: 4½–5″ (11–13 cm). Small flat-headed sparrow, with short tail. Dark brown crown has *buffy median stripe*. Chestnut- and black-striped back, *buffy unstriped* breast, lighter belly. Yellowish bend of wing not always visible. Juveniles have pale stripes on breast.

Voice: Song faint, high-pitched, somewhat like song of the Savannah Sparrow, but grasshopper-like and buzzing. Female also sings a buzzing song, probably a locational call used to find her mate in the dense grass.

Habitat: Grassland, fallow fields with tall grass, prairies.

Nesting: 4 or 5 creamy white, spotted and speckled eggs in a well-concealed ground nest in the grass.

Range: From coast to coast south of the belt of boreal forest and mainly north of the southwestern desert. Also southern Arizona, central Florida, West Indies and Central America. Winters from the southern U.S. southward.

When flushed, this sparrow flies a short distance and drops out of sight, into tall grass. Although widespread, it is secretive and often overlooked.

Botteri's Sparrow
(*Aimophila botterii*)
Finches (Fringillidae)

Description: 5¼–6¼" (13–16 cm). *Reddish-brown* with some blackish streaks on forehead and back; narrow eye-stripe separates gray eyebrow-stripe from similarly colored face and neck; unstreaked *pale buffy to whitish below*. Rounded brown tail. Slight rust-colored tones in wings and tail.

Voice: Song consists of several short trills often introduced by a couple of *clips* and *che-licks*, but is variable.

Habitat: Open arid country of a grassland, savanna, or desert-scrub character.

Nesting: 2–5 white eggs. Apparently builds nests on the ground, but little else is known about its breeding habits.

Range: Mexico, extending north to southeastern Arizona and southern Texas in summer rainy season.

An entirely terrestrial bird that lives and feeds on the ground and hides in thick vegetation. It is distinguished from the similar Cassin's Sparrow by its song.

Cassin's Sparrow
(*Aimophila cassinii*)
Finches (Fringillidae)

Description: 5¼–5¾" (13–15 cm). Fine brown streaking on *grayish-brown head* and *back*; dingy buff unstreaked underparts with faint streaking on lower flanks occasionally visible. Sexes look alike. Young streaked on breast as well.

Voice: 4 loud, melodious, clear whistles, uttered from the top of tall grass and also in flight. Second note is prolonged and quavering; third note is lowest.

Habitat: Semi-desert; arid uplands such as those with yuccas and tall grass.

Nesting: 3 or 4 white eggs in a deep, almost

tunnel-like cup on the ground, or at base of bush or cactus.

Range: Arizona to Colorado and New Mexico; Mexican states along the United States border, where it also winters.

Very secretive except when the male is on its breeding ground. There it steadily proclaims its territory with its lark-like flight song. Rival males often hold song duels from grass tops just 20 feet apart. The Great Plains population is believed to migrate southwestward, after breeding into the grassy deserts of Arizona and Mexico.

Rufous-winged Sparrow
(*Aimophila carpalis*)
Finches (Fringillidae)

Description: 5–5½″ (13–14 cm). Resembles Rufous-crowned Sparrow, but is lighter with finer streaking on back and more pronounced whisker mark. Rufous crown divided by gray median stripe. *Rufous eye-line and shoulder patch.* Unstreaked whitish below with light wing bars and rounded tail. Juveniles lack rufous markings and wing bars but display double whiskers with finely streaked, light brown upper breast and sides.

Voice: Sharp *seep* call is characteristic; song is variable but always ends in a trill of rapid *chips*.

Habitat: Grassland mixed with thorn bushes, mesquite trees, or cholla patches.

Nesting: 4 or 5 light bluish-white eggs in a cup of coarse grass lined with finer grasses, placed low in a bush, young mesquite, or cactus, not well hidden. It nests at the end of summer when rains come.

Range: Southeastern Arizona south through Sonora to northern Sinaloa, Mexico.

An important habitat requirement for this very restricted species seems to be

tall sacaton grass. Its range was
formerly more widespread in Arizona,
but areas heavily grazed by cattle have
seriously reduced its habitat and it has
all but disappeared. It lives in small,
scattered population in isolated areas
and expert guidance is necessary to
locate it.

Baird's Sparrow
(*Ammodramus bairdii*)
Finches (Fringillidae)

Description: 5–5½" (13–14 cm). *Broad ocher median
stripe through crown* and narrow band of
fine streaking across breast. Streaked
flanks and back tail feathers edged with
buff; corners of tail light-grayish.

Voice: Song is a low trill introduced by two or
more *zip* notes. Call note is a high *chip*.

Habitat: Prairies.

Nesting: 4 or 5 white, blotched eggs in a grassy
nest well hidden in tall grass.

Range: Alberta, Saskatchewan, and Manitoba
and Montana to South Dakota. Winters
in southern prairies including southern
Arizona, southern New Mexico and
northern Mexico.

Of all grassland sparrows, this bird is
the most reluctant to fly, and when
flushed, slips through the grass like a
mouse. Its numbers have declined with
the plowing of the prairie.

569 Savannah Sparrow
(*Passerculus sandwichensis*)
Finches (Fringillidae)

Description: 4½–5¾" (11–15 cm). Streaked
brownish above, *heavily striped below;*
light median crown stripe; *eyebrow stripe
is light* (usually accompanied in some
subspecies by yellowish lores). Short
notched tail, pale pink legs.

Voice: Song is a series of high-pitched *chips* and trills, starting slowly and ending in a rapid slur, sometimes followed by a descending *ciaaa . . .* Call is a thin *tsit.*

Habitat: Open grassland, savannas, tundra, salt marshes.

Nesting: 4–6 whitish eggs, spotted with brown or purple, in a shallow grass-lined ground nest.

Range: Aleutians, northern Alaska and Canada south to Mexico and Guatemala. Northern populations are migratory. It does not breed in the Southeast and is only a visitor in Savannah, Georgia, from which its name is derived.

Sixteen subspecies are recognized, each slightly different in coloration and song. The formation of many subspecies usually indicates that the birds are faithful to their native area.

570, 606 Lark Bunting
(*Calamospiza melanocorys*)
Finches (Fringillidae)

Description: 6–7½″ (15–19 cm). Spring *male black with large white wing patch.* Female, immature, and winter male streaked sandy buff above, white below; white eye-line, faint mustache stripe; *white wing patch* (not always visible); rounded, white-tipped tail feathers.

Voice: A Canary-like song with loud bubbling sequences and trills, interspersed with harsher notes. Call is a two-noted whistle.

Habitat: Dry plains and prairies; open sagebrush.

Nesting: 4 or 5 light blue eggs in a loose grass nest in a scrape with rim flush with the ground; often protected by weedy patch.

Range: Prairies of southern Canada and west-central United States. Winters southward into Mexico.

The spectacular black-and-white male is one of the most conspicuous birds of the prairies. In giving its flight song it rises almost vertically, then drops back to its original perch.

---

577 **Lark Sparrow**
(*Chondestes grammacus*)
Finches (Fringillidae)

Description: 5½–6¾" (14–17 cm). Well-defined *chestnut ear patches and crown striping;* white cheek and black whiskers; *central black spot on unstreaked buffy breast.* Long dark tail slightly graduated, with prominent white corners and margins. Sexes look alike. Young less colorful, with lightly streaked breast.

Voice: Song consists of various trills interspersed with low *churr* notes. Call is a *tsip.* The male sings incessantly both day and night, from the ground, a wire, or a fence post.

Habitat: Dry fields, savanna, oak or coniferous woodlands, farmland, city parks.

Nesting: 3–5 white, spotted eggs in a grassy ground nest lined with fine fibers and hair; also found in low bushes or vines.

Range: Southern Canada to northern Mexico, from the Okanagan Valley of British Columbia and the west coast of the United States almost to the Atlantic Coast. Winters south to Guatemala.

Male may be monogamous or may have two females with nests close together. He defends his nests but not a large territory. Lark Sparrows are very social, crowding together for feeding even during the nesting season.

578   Clay-colored Sparrow
(*Spizella pallida*)
Finches (Fringillidae)

Description: 5–5½″ (13–14 cm). Streaked brown
above, buffy breast, whitish belly, two
light wing bars; *crown divided in middle
by white streak surrounded by buff-brown
ear patch;* pale eye-line and cheek, dark
mustache stripe; brown rump.
Immature has more buff on breast,
wing, and mantle and a less distinct
mid-crown streak.

Voice: 4 or 5 loud monotone buzzes, each
starting low and ending at high
intensity. Call is a soft *tsee*.

Habitat: Around taller shrubby vegetation in
prairies; also open brushland.

Nesting: 3–5 bluish, sparsely marked or
unmarked eggs in a well-built nest on
or near the ground, lined with hair.

Range: Breeds from northeastern British
Columbia and southern Mackenzie east
into southern Ontario, south through
Montana, Wyoming, and Colorado,
east into Iowa, Wisconsin, and
Michigan. Winters in Texas and
Mexico.

The plowing of the prairies reduced its
habitat, but with the clearing of forests
it has extended its range northeastward;
it has recently been found nesting in
eastern Canada near Ottawa.

581, 607   Bobolink
(*Dolichonyx oryzivorus*)
Orioles (Icteridae)

Description: 6–8″ (15–20 cm). Breeding male has
black crown, face, and underparts; buffy
nape. Large *white patches in shoulder
region and on rump;* back, wings, and
pointed tail black with buff edges.
Female and winter male buffy below
with buff-and-black stripes on head.

Voice: The male sings, among other melodious

and "twanging" phrases, his own name, *bob-o-LINK.* Call is a sharp *wenk.*

Habitat: Originally tall-grass prairie, now open hayfields, meadows, and farmland.

Nesting: 4–7 pale gray, blotched eggs in a flimsy grass-lined nest in a grassy area.

Range: From interior British Columbia east to the Maritime Provinces, south to northeastern California, Utah, Arizona, and the Colorado prairies. Breeding range has diminished in the East and the Great Lakes area, but has spread west with an increase in irrigation and agricultural development.

A polygamous bird, the male Bobolink courts with the basic blackbird stance: head down, neck feathers ruffled, tail fanned, and wings arched downward, displaying his prominent white shoulder patches. In fall Bobolinks join with other blackbirds and are often seen in rice fields or other agricultural areas.

595 McCown's Longspur
(*Calcarius mccownii*)
Finches (Fringillidae)

Description: 5¾–6″ (14–15 cm). Brown above, white below; breeding male has *black crown, whisker mark, and central breast blotch.* Gray ear patch; white markings on the gray of head, neck, and nape are highlighted by white throat and eye-line. Rust-colored patch at bend of wing in both sexes not always visible. Black inverted "T" pattern on white tail. Female and winter male buffy brown, with heavier streaking above than below.

Voice: Flight song is series of rapid tinkling warbled notes, difficult to transcribe. Call is a dry rattle.

Habitat: Short-grass prairie.

Nesting: 3 or 4 white or pale greenish eggs, with brown and purplish streaking, in a small grass-lined ground depression.

Range: From southern Alberta and Manitoba
south through northern Colorado and
Nebraska. Winters in prairies from
southern Colorado to northern Mexico;
in small numbers west to California.

In courting, the male sings and raises
one wing straight up, displaying its
silvery white lining to his mate. The
first description of this species was
written during the Lewis and Clark
expedition by Captain Meriwether
Lewis in his journal entry of June 2,
1805: ". . . small bird which in action
resembles a lark; the male rises into the
air with a brisk motion of the wings,
sings very sweetly, has several shrill soft
notes rather of the plaintive order
which it frequently repeats and varies;
after remaining stationary about a
minute in his aerial station he descends
obliquely, occasionally pausing and
accompanying his descent with a note
something like *twit twit twit* . . ."

597   Chestnut-collared Longspur
(*Calcarius ornatus*)
Finches (Fringillidae)

Description: 5½–6½" (14–17 cm). Breeding male
has buffy brown back, *black cap, eye-
line, and underparts* with white lower
belly. White cheek, buffy-tinged white
throat and ear stripe. Broad chestnut
patch on nape; black-and-white tail
feathers with black triangle in middle.
Female and winter male similar to a
grayish-buffy sparrow.

Voice: Like other longspurs, it gives a rapid
warbling song in flight on the breeding
grounds. Flight note is a finch-like *kit-
tle;* also a thin *buzz.*

Habitat: Short-grass prairie (a thicker, taller
growth than that preferred by
McCown's Longspur).

Nesting: 3–5 greenish-white, speckled eggs in a
grass-lined scrape, usually next to a

small stone or bush.

Range: Prairie provinces of Canada south to
west-central United States, where it is
found in Colorado, Nebraska, and
Minnesota. Winters on grassy areas of
the southwestern states and Mexican
Plateau.

This is the common longspur of
the prairies. In spring males are
conspicuous as they give their flight
song and, descending, perch on a
prominent plant or hillock.

603 Horned Lark
(*Eremophila alpestris*)
Larks (Alaudidae)

Description: 7–8″ (18–20 cm). Pale brown, with
black bib, yellow wash on throat and face;
black whisker marks, black "horns"
(difficult to see in the field). Black tail
feathers with white margins. Young
lack the black face pattern and have
silver-speckled back.

Voice: The male often sings his tinkling song
from a mound of earth or as he circles
high above his territory. Each phrase
accelerates to an emphatic close. Calls
include a thin *tsee-eep* and a *buzz.*

Habitat: Open patches of bare land alternating
with low vegetation, such as on the
tundra, alpine meadow, and sagebrush
plains.

Nesting: 3–5 gray, dark-spotted eggs in a grass-
lined depression on the ground.

Range: Widespread in Arctic and mountain
tundras of the Northern Hemisphere,
extending south to grasslands in
northern Africa and South America. In
North America, except the southeastern
seaboard, in all suitable habitats and
fields.

The Horned Lark walks or runs instead
of hopping; when feeding, it moves in
an erratic pattern. On its breeding

territory and when it flocks during winter, it feeds on seeds and ground insects. This bird is philopatric, or faithful to its birthplace, where it returns after every migration. Consequently, each local population adapts to the color of its habitat; fifteen distinct subspecies have been described in the western region.

Sprague's Pipit
(*Anthus spragueii*)
Pipits (Motacillidae)

Description: 6¼–7" (16–18 cm). Same size as Water Pipit but with longer bill, *buffy black-streaked back, lighter buff-streaked underparts,* and pale, *straw-colored legs.* Both pipits have white throat and outer tail margins. Large dark eye stands out from buffy face.

Voice: Its beautiful flight song on the breeding territory is reminiscent of the Old World Skylark: the bird describes a great arc in flight, singing a series of descending two-note phrases as it flies upward until it is out of sight, but is silent on the downward plunge. Call is a thin *tseep.*

Habitat: Short-grass prairie; shuns burned or plowed land.

Nesting: 4 or 5 grayish-white, spotted eggs in a grass nest, sometimes partially domed, placed on the ground.

Range: Breeds in the prairie provinces and states from Alberta to Manitoba south to Montana, the Dakotas, and Minnesota. Winters in southern Arizona, east to Texas, and in Mexico.

More secretive and solitary than the Water Pipit, Sprague's does not run in the open when disturbed but tries to hide in dense grass. When flushed, it flies low for a short distance and then drops down. Since it has not adapted to grassland converted to cultivation, its

range and numbers are now much
reduced.

616 Yellow-billed Magpie
(*Pica nuttalli*)
Crows (Corvidae)

Description: 16–18″ (41–46 cm). A slightly smaller
version of the Black-billed Magpie, but
with *yellow bill and bare yellow area of
skin behind eye.* Large white wing
patches and long wedge-shaped,
iridescent greenish-black tail. Juvenile
has blackish beak and lacks bare face
patch.

Voice: A raucous *qua-qua-qua* and a querulous
quack.

Habitat: Oak savanna, oak woods, riverside
growth, ranches, and suburbs.

Nesting: 5–8 olive green, blotched eggs in a
large, domed stick nest; breeds in
colonies in tall trees usually so
overgrown with mistletoe that it is
often hard to detect the nest. The
American Kestrel often usurps its nest.

Range: Only in California, where it lives in the
Central Valley, southern foothills, and
coastal valleys. Ranges of Yellow-billed
and Black-billed magpies do not
overlap.

The colony lives communally the year
round, feeding, socializing, and
collectively mobbing predators. This
magpie has found in vacant city lots
and weedy storage yards a substitute for
habitats it lost to intensive agriculture.
It has become a city bird but keeps
away from places where people gather.

617 **Black-billed Magpie**
(*Pica pica*)
Crows (Corvidae)

Description: 17½–22" (44–56 cm). Large *black and white bird* with *long tail and dark bill*. Bill, head, breast, and underparts black, with green iridescence on wings and tail. White belly, shoulders, and primaries which are conspicuous as white wing patches in flight.

Voice: A rapid, nasal *mag? mag? mag?* or *yak yak yak*.

Habitat: Open savanna, brush-covered country, streamside growth.

Nesting: 6–9 greenish, blotched eggs in a neat cup nest within a large, bulky, domed structure of strong, often thorny twigs, with a double entrance, in a tree or bush.

Range: Northern part of the Northern Hemisphere. In North America from Alaska south to eastern California, and east to Oklahoma.

Magpies generally nest individually but can sometimes be found in loose colonies; they are social when feeding or after the breeding season. Those living in western rangeland appear shy of man, but their behavior in the Old World is very different. In northern Finland, magpies live in the middle of settlements and place their nests low. In Hungary, a bounty is placed on them because they damage the broods of partridges and other gamebirds; as a result, they nest out of reach in the tallest trees.

619 **Great-tailed Grackle**
(*Quiscalus mexicanus*)
Orioles (Icteridae)

Description: Male, 16–17" (41–43 cm); female, 12–13" (30–33 cm). *Almost crow-sized male* is iridescent, glossy green-black and purple, with *yellow eyes*. In display flight, the long *keel-shaped* tail is fanned so that from the side it appears as a wide, triangular flag. Female and immatures are brown, dark-eyed, with pale brown eye-stripe and underparts.

Voice: A variety of whistles and clacking noises, and a harsh *chack, chack*. The Spanish call the male *clarinere,* the clarinet player.

Habitat: Grassy or marshy country with tall trees; partial to human habitations, where it may nest as well as feed.

Nesting: 3–5 bluish eggs, covered with brown scrawls, in a big, bulky, grass-lined nest in a tree, bush, or marsh reeds; in colonies and, to the south, in heronries.

Range: Widespread in the tropics, occurring from the western Gulf Coast of the United States to South America. The Great-tailed has recently expanded from southern Texas and Arizona to the north and west; it reached California in 1964 and was found nesting there in 1967.

Like magpies, these noisy, opportunistic birds feed on a great variety of food: fruits, grain, insects, garbage, and offal. They are usually bold, but become cautious and wary when in danger. The polygamous male is more cunning and shy than the females; he often remains safe in a treetop until all his females are feeding on the ground. He will then join them.

Alpine Meadows

Lush green mountain meadows found in
large areas of the western mountains,
above timberline or on the steep slopes
of valleys.
Relatively few species of birds live in
these meadows or in the boulder fields
or talus slopes that may surround them.
In wet meadows, small deciduous
shrubs provide habitats for a few other
species (White-crowned Sparrow,
Wilson's Warbler), but these are
treated in their primary habitat.

273, 275   **White-tailed Ptarmigan**
(*Lagopus leucurus*)
Grouse (Tetraonidae)

Description: 12–13″ (30–33 cm). Smallest of the
ptarmigans. In winter, *pure white* except
for black bill and eyes. In summer,
mottled-barred *brown head, breast,* and
back, with *white wings, belly, and tail
remaining.* Red combs above eyes on
spring male.

Voice: Soft, low hoots and low clucking notes.

Habitat: Alpine meadows, avalanche breaks,
rocky open areas above timberline.

Nesting: 6–8 buff, faintly spotted eggs in a
scrape sparsely lined with grass, leaves,
and feathers.

Range: Rocky Mountains from Alaska south to
New Mexico, and coastal ranges south
to Washington.

Open-country grouse such as
ptarmigans—especially the displaying
male—fly a great deal more than forest
grouse but still prefer running to
flying. White-tailed Ptarmigans
probably lived in California during the
Ice Ages but died out there. They have
recently been reintroduced and
re-established in the High Sierras.

393, 402   **Broad-tailed Hummingbird**
(*Selasphorus platycercus*)
Hummingbirds (Trochilidae)

Description: 4–4½″ (10–11 cm). Resembles Ruby-
throated Hummingbird (*Archilochus
colubris*) of the eastern United States but
male's gorget rose rather than red and tail
rounded rather than forked. Both sexes
metallic green above, white below.
Female, similar to Rufous and Allen's
females, has green central tail feathers;
outer tail feathers rust-colored at base,
black in middle, and white on outer
tips.

Voice: Call is a sharp *chick.* Adult male makes

a *unique loud musical trill with wings* in flight, which distinguishes it.

Habitat: Varies widely from mountain meadows, pinyon-juniper woodland, dry ponderosa pine, to fir or mixed forest and canyon vegetation.

Nesting: 2 white eggs in a woven cup nest of lichen and plant down.

Range: Mountainous areas from eastern California to northern Wyoming, the Great Basin, and Rocky Mountain states, south through the Mexican Plateau. Winters in Central America.

Accounts of this species mention that it nests in the same tree or bush year after year, a phenomenon known as philopatry—faithfulness to the previous home area. It will return to the same branch and even build a new nest atop an old one.

398 Black-chinned Hummingbird
(*Archilochus alexandri*)
Hummingbirds (Trochilidae)

Description: 3¼–3¾″ (8–10 cm). Small hummingbird. Male green above with black chin, underlined by *violet-purple throat band.* Female green above with white throat and breast, buff sides, and white-tipped outer tail feathers.

Voice: Calls are a low *tup* and a buzz. Male makes a dry buzz with wings in flight.

Habitat: Mountain and alpine meadows, woodlands, canyons with thickets, chaparral, and orchards.

Nesting: 2 white eggs in a nest of fluffy plant wool and lichens woven together with spider webs in a shrub or low tree.

Range: British Columbia south throughout the West to Mexico and western Texas; absent from humid northern Pacific Coast. Winters in Mexico.

The male Black-chinned, like all hummingbirds, maintains a mating and

feeding territory in spring. He courts his female with a dazzling aerial display involving a pendulum-like flight pattern. When mating interest wanes, the male often takes up residence elsewhere, near a good food supply. Later, when the blooming season and insect swarming subside, both male and female move south. Details of their migration are not yet well understood.

Black Rosy Finch
(*Leucosticte atrata*)
Finches (Fringillidae)

Description: 5½–6½″ (14–17 cm). *Dark blackish-brown* with *conspicuous gray cap* in male; black forehead and much pink on belly, rump, wings, and tail. Female is browner, showing some pink, and may not have gray cap. Bill yellowish in both sexes.

Voice: A variety of low *cheep* notes are used in various situations: as a contact call in flight, and in proclaiming an occupied nesting territory.

Habitat: Alpine tundra and meadows; winters in nearby lowlands.

Nesting: 3–5 white eggs in a cup nest in a hole in a vertical cliff.

Range: Rocky Mountains of southwestern Montana, Idaho, Wyoming, northeastern Nevada, and northern Utah. Winters south to northern Arizona and New Mexico.

Experts have not determined whether the three forms of Rosy Finches—the Brown-capped, Black, and Gray-crowned—are distinct species. Although typical males are distinctly colored within their breeding ranges, there are areas where two of the forms, the Black and the Gray-crowned, overlap and hybridize. In winter, when mixed flocks roam the highlands of the Great Basin, Blacks and Gray-crowneds are seen together roosting in caves or abandoned mine shafts, in barns, or under bridges.

459 Gray-crowned Rosy Finch
(*Leucosticte tephrocotis*)
Finches (Fringillidae)

Description: 5¾–6¾" (15–17 cm). *Dark brown back* and *underparts* with black forehead, gray nape and crown; *pink shoulder and rump; face gray* in *coastal* birds, *brown* in *interior populations.* Female is similar but less colorful.

Voice: Flying flocks give harsh *cheep, cheep* notes.

Habitat: Alpine tundra and high snowfields; winters in nearby lowlands.

Nesting: 3–5 white eggs in a bulky nest placed in a rock cavity.

Range: Aleutians. Scattered in alpine areas at low elevation in Siberia and Alaska but high in the mountains of Canada and the United States. Extends south through the Oregon Cascades to the Sierra Nevada of California. Descends to lower elevations in winter.

During breeding, both the male and the female grow a pair of "gular pouches" opening from the floor of the mouth, which they use to carry food to the young. This species feeds mainly on minute alpine plant seeds and insects wind-borne from lower elevations. The Gray-crowned Rosy Finch is found farther to the west than the similar Brown-capped Rosy Finch and Black Rosy Finch. The ancestors of the Rosy Finches came from Asia. The mosaic distribution of forms in the West may result from the splitting of one population during glacial periods, or from multiple invasions from Asia.

465 **Brown-capped Rosy Finch**
(*Leucosticte australis*)
Finches (Fringillidae)

Description: 5¾–6½" (15–17 cm). Mostly *light brown, without gray crown patch* of the closely related Gray-crowned Rosy Finch and Black Rosy Finch. Its rump, wing, and belly are pinkish-rose. Female chiefly brown. Both sexes have blackish bills.

Voice: A series of low *cheep* notes are uttered to maintain contact in the flock. In the mating season the male gives a similar song during a long, circular, undulating flight.

Habitat: Alpine tundra and meadows; winters in nearby lowlands.

Nesting: 3–5 white eggs in a cup nest in a rock crevice or on a hidden, covered ledge.

Range: Southern Rocky Mountains from southeastern Wyoming to northern New Mexico.

Winter flocks are noisy with the sound of twittering; upon alighting, these finches hop over the ground looking for seeds. Trusting birds, they let observers come close.

---

571 **Water Pipit**
(*Anthus spinoletta*)
Pipits (Motacillidae)

Description: 6–7" (15–18 cm). Resembles a sparrow in color and ground-dwelling habits. *Slender* body and *bill, light buff with* fine breast and side *streaks;* buffy eye-line and white throat. *Dark legs* and *white tail margins.* Tail jerks nervously.

Voice: It flies up unexpectedly, calling *jee-et*. Utters a melodic, tinkling song in display flight, executed low above the ground, similar to a lark.

Habitat: In North America, Arctic and alpine tundra; in winter meadows, beaches, open land.

Nesting: 4–7 grayish or buffy eggs thickly
spotted with dark brown in a grassy
nest on ground under shelter.

Range: Aleutians and in tundra and uplands
from northern Alaska across Canada,
and, in the West, south through the
mountains to New Mexico. Winters in
mild areas from coastal British
Columbia south to Guatemala.
Widespread in Eurasia.

In the North the Water Pipit feeds on
the countless insects on the edges of
tundra puddles, whereas in alpine
meadows it visits unmelted snowbanks.
Warm air rising from valleys below
transports many insects to high
altitudes; most of these die and are
frozen in snowbanks, providing food for
the pipits.

Fields

Cultivated or abandoned arable land.
Abandoned fields quickly revert to
weedy vegetation, then to low bushes,
seedlings, and saplings. Many field
birds find shelter in hedgerows; others
frequent roadside weeds, bushes, or
trees. Drainage ditches may attract
marsh or water birds during migration.
Such typical field visitors as Brewer's
Blackbird, House Sparrow, and House
Finch are described in other primary
habitats because fields cover a relatively
small area in the West.

233 **Mountain Plover**
(*Charadrius montanus*)
Plovers (Charadriidae)

Description: 8–9½" (20–24 cm). Sandy brown
above, *white below* with traces of
incomplete sandy breast band. *Black
crown patch* offset by white forehead and
eyebrow and less distinct dark eye-line.
Thin white wing-line more apparent in
flight, as is white-edged tail with
broad, "smudgy" dark terminal band.
In nonbreeding plumage, face pattern
less white and more buffy, as are breast
markings. Legs are pale flesh
color.

Voice: A single-noted harsh *krrrr* is given in
flight.

Habitat: This upland bird is found in areas away
from water such as dry short-grass
prairie or plains.

Nesting: 3 dark olive, heavily brown-spotted
eggs in a ground scrape; no nest.

Range: Prairie and sagebrush country of eastern
Montana, Wyoming, and eastern
Colorado. Winters from central
California along southern half of border
states and southward into Mexico.

With the intense cultivation of the
prairie belt, the nesting habitat of this
plover has been drastically reduced. It
feeds in small flocks, mostly on insects.
In winter, larger concentrations can be
seen.

265, 267 **Ring-necked Pheasant**
(*Phasianus colchicus*)
Pheasants (Phasianidae)

Description: Male, 30–36"; (76–91 cm); female, 21–
25" (53–64 cm). A spectacular bird.
Both sexes have long, pointed, cross-
barred tail, but male's is much longer.
Male has iridescent *green-black head with
two feathered tufts* above its scarlet
wattles. Coloration variable and white

neck ring occasionally lacking. Body deep tawny-chestnut with blue-black belly and rich golden, mottled flanks. Rump most often pale green-gray but may be rust-colored. Female light brown with darker mottling.

Voice: The male gives a double-noted crowing call, with the first note stressed.

Habitat: Farmland, with adjacent brushy growth of woodlands for cover; roosts in orchards, roadside trees, or marsh reedbeds in winter.

Nesting: 6–14 buffy or pale olive eggs in a grass-lined scrape in grassy or weedy protective vegetation.

Range: Widespread from Europe throughout southern Asia. Introduced from China and England, it thrives in southwestern Canada, most of the western United States, the grain belt, and the Northeast. Does not frequent the southern states where spring and summer are too hot for it and render the males infertile.

A fast runner with strong, noisy, short-distance flight, this pheasant feeds primarily on grains, seeds, and berries. It lives in harems, one male attracting several females. Early-laying females often drop eggs anywhere on the feeding field or in another nest, often of a partridge or other pheasant, that they encounter on the way to their own.

285 **Gray Partridge**
"Hungarian Partridge"
(*Perdix perdix*)
Pheasants (Phasianidae)

Description: 12–14" (30–36 cm). Low, stocky, has outline of a quail. Rusty brown face and throat surrounded by brown cap, *gray* neck and breast. Rufous diagonal barring on flanks and outer tail feathers; conspicuous chestnut *horseshoe* on *lower breast,* smaller in female than in male and lacking on fall chicks.

Voice: A hoarse, double-noted *kur-rik*.

Habitat: Open farmland with weeds for shelter; grainfields.

Nesting: 10–16 olive eggs in a grass-lined ground depression under brush, grass, or crops such as alfalfa, corn, or wheat. Both male and female raise the chicks.

Range: Mainly prairie states and provinces but widely introduced to North America from the wheat fields of the Hungarian plains (hence its alternate name "Hungarian Partridge").

Truly birds of open country, they never perch and seldom fly great distances when flushed. They survive on bare stubble except in the snowy winter, when they form small coveys and frequent brushy shelter where they bed down in the snow and huddle for warmth. Harsh winter conditions may take a large toll of these birds, but their large clutches enable them to rebuild their population.

408, 430 **American Goldfinch**
(*Carduelis tristis*)
Finches (Fringillidae)

Description: 4½–5½″ (11–14 cm). Breeding male *bright yellow* with *black cap,* white rump, and *white* edges on *black wings and tail*. Female and winter birds dull olive-yellow with no black cap. Immatures mostly buffy tan.

Voice: The song is a prolonged jumble of short trills and thin twittering notes. Flight notes are *per-chic-oree* or *potato-chips* and *yip, yip*.

Habitat: Weedy, shrubby, grassy areas, orchards and meadows with some deciduous trees; openings in coniferous forests, cultivated valleys, and second growth.

Nesting: 3–6 pale bluish eggs in a small, well-built cup nest of grass, plant down, and bark in a tree or bush.

Range: Southern British Columbia through the
Pacific states and in mountains south to
the desert; also widespread in the
Northeast but does not breed in the
South. The northernmost populations
are migratory.

They migrate in compact flocks with an
erratic, "roller coaster" flight. Studies
of their winter migrations from
Vancouver, British Columbia, and
Washington State showed that these
birds hesitated before flying across
water. In one instance, some returned
to the mainland. One by one, the
whole flock followed suit. Ten minutes
later they returned to the waterside,
chattering noisily. Many birds then
continued on. Those remaining
repeatedly took wing only to veer off
and again return to land. Finally, a
sharp drop in temperature forced the
birds to complete their migration.

559, 621 Bronzed Cowbird
(*Molothrus aeneus*)
Orioles (Icteridae)

Description: 6½–8¾" (17–22 cm). *Male is all black,
with bronze, iridescent sheen; red or orange
eyes;* thick, rather conical bill. Smaller
female is blackish, and has red eyes,
but lacks sheen.

Voice: Bubbling, mechanical, squeaking
notes, similar to song of Brown-headed
Cowbird, but higher-pitched and more
prolonged. Call is a rattling sound.

Habitat: Fields, pastures, savannas, and feedlots.

Nesting: 1–4 pale blue-green eggs. Parasitic,
laying in the nests of orioles or other
birds of similar size, one egg to a nest.

Range: From the southwestern United States,
along the Mexican border, in southern
Arizona and Texas, south to Panama.

A strongly social bird, it associates with
blackbirds as well as its own species and

roosts in huge flocks, often in city parks. During the courtship display, the male raises the ruff on his neck; he also leaves the ground in front of the female and hovers one or two feet in the air.

574 Skylark
(*Alauda arvensis*)
Larks (Alaudidae)

Description: 7–7½″ (18–19 cm). *Light earth brown above,* with heavy, dark streaking. Buff below with lighter streaking. Outer tail feathers and belly white. Crown feathers are elongated and may be raised into a small rounded hood.

Voice: Calls *trly* or *prrit*. Utters a beautiful song high in the sky. Rising in arcs ever higher until almost out of sight, the songster flutters and gives a clear, trilling, often Canary-like song, or mimics other birds. His song sounds continuously for 3 or 4 minutes until he folds his wings and falls like a stone toward the center of his territory.

Habitat: Grasslands and fields.

Nesting: 3 or 4 whitish, brown-spotted eggs in a grass nest in a ground scrape.

Range: Eurasia, northern Africa. Introduced to the Saanich Peninsula, just north of Victoria, British Columbia, in the early 1900s and now has a steady population of some 1000 individuals there.

The dense rain forest habitat of much of the Northwest prevents the Skylark from spreading farther south; it has attempted to colonize only a few leeward, grassy slopes on the San Juan Islands in Washington State.

589 **Tree Sparrow**
(*Spizella arborea*)
Finches (Fringillidae)

Description: 5½–6½" (14–17 cm). Similar to
Chipping Sparrow—brown above,
white below—but with distinctive *dark
central breast spot.* Solid *chestnut cap, eye-
line,* and *faint mustache.* Two-toned bill
dark above, yellow below; two wing
bars and dark legs.

Voice: Call is a *tseet.* In winter, flocks also
utter a twittering sound, *teedle-eet,*
sometimes described as a "tinkle of
icicles."

Habitat: Brushy willow thickets, scrub, and
clearings near northern treeline. In
winter, weedy fields and roadsides.

Nesting: 4 or 5 pale blue, speckled eggs in a
feather-lined cup on or near the
ground.

Range: Breeds in the tundra zone of the Far
North from Alaska to Newfoundland;
in winter south to California,
northwestern Texas, and North
Carolina.

These birds can tolerate subzero
temperatures if they get sufficient
calories from their seed diet; thus they
are able to winter in open country
where snow does not entirely cover the
weeds and grasses. They are more
commonly seen in brushy pastures at
the edge of fields and woods.

Cities, Parks, Suburbs

Partly paved urban or suburban areas as well as parks, suburban gardens, orchards, and areas around industrial plants, farms, and ranches. All of these areas support birds that tolerate man's settlements, but such species occur in other habitats as well.

345 Inca Dove
(*Scardafella inca*)
Pigeons (Columbidae)

Description: 7½–8″ (19–20 cm). Small pale dove somewhat larger than Ground Dove. Rufous primaries, *long, narrow tail with white sides; upperparts look scaled.* At a distance it seems paler, with less rust color showing than on Ground Dove.

Voice: A monotonous *coo-hoo,* repeated; first note higher.

Habitat: Suburban gardens, city parks, ranches, fields.

Nesting: 2 round, whitish eggs in a compact nest of rootlets, twigs, and weeds placed low in a tree or bush.

Range: Southeastern California, southern Arizona, New Mexico, and Texas and south to Costa Rica.

This tropical bird has become a city dweller, its spread made possible by watered "oases"—cities and suburbs.

346 Rock Dove
(*Columba livia*)
Pigeons (Columbidae)

Description: 13″ (33 cm). The familiar Domestic Pigeon. Varies from snow white to brown-red, slate black, and piebald, but most common is the color of the wild form: blue or ash gray with white rump, dark terminal band on tail, and two dark crossbars on each wing. Iridescent green and violet-purple area on neck.

Voice: A deep, rolling series of *coos.*

Habitat: Cities, towns; also rocky canyons or sea cliffs.

Nesting: 2 white eggs in a sheltered niche on buildings or cliffs, even in palm trees of cities in the West. Gathers sticks and other materials haphazardly for its flimsy nest.

Range: Cosmopolitan; North America except

the far northern taiga and tundra region.

This city bird was introduced from Europe, where the wild ancestral stock lives on rocky cliffs of the Atlantic and Mediterranean coasts. Wintering hawks sometimes prey on pigeons, especially on defective or conspicuously marked individuals.

350 Ringed Turtle Dove
(*Streptopelia risoria*)
Pigeons (Columbidae)

Description: 10–12" (25–30 cm). Like a pale, whitish Mourning Dove but tail rounded rather than pointed. *Light tan with narrow, black collar* on hind neck.

Voice: Quite different from that of other doves in the West; a purring cooing, *cuck-currooo*, uttered repeatedly by the male almost all year round. Also a nasal *wheez*.

Habitat: Suburbs, gardens, parks.

Nesting: 2 white eggs in a flimsy stick platform in a tree.

Range: Los Angeles, California. Escaped from captivity. Also established locally in southern Florida.

This southern Asian species has been a cagebird in Europe and the Orient for centuries. The small population in downtown Los Angeles has apparently not spread and is localized in a few parks and tree-lined streets.

351 Spotted Dove
(*Streptopelia chinensis*)
Pigeons (Columbidae)

Description: 13" (33 cm). Larger and stockier than Mourning Dove. Dark cinnamon-gray above, buffy below. Light gray head and *wide black collar with white spots on hind neck. In flight, its long, blunt tail looks black, with flashy white corners.* Juveniles lack the "necklace."

Voice: A 3-syllabled cooing, uttered from a high perch; rendered as a rolling *coo-coo-cooooo.*

Habitat: Suburbs and gardens in the West.

Nesting: 2 white eggs in a flimsy stick platform in a tree.

Range: Introduced from southeastern Asia to Los Angeles, some have spread to neighboring southern California towns.

This dove seems to be a harmless addition to the southern California garden avifauna, feeding on seeds and nesting quite secretively. The courting male may be observed bowing rhythmically, then flying up with tail spread wide.

435, 447 **Hooded Oriole**
(*Icterus cucullatus*)
Orioles (Icteridae)

Description: 7–7¾" (18–20 cm). Breeding male is *orange below* with *orange cap,* black back, wings and tail; large *black bib* from face to upper chest. Female olive green above, olive-yellowish below. Both sexes have two white wing bars. Immature male is like the female, but has a small black bib.

Voice: Call is a whistled *wheet?* Also a series of deliberate chattering notes. The song is a series of jumbled phrases including whistles, guttural trills, and rattling notes.

Habitat: Originally streamside growth, but it quickly adapted to tree plantations, palm rows, city parks, and suburbs with palm or eucalyptus trees and shrubbery.

Nesting: 3–5 bluish or grayish-white, spotted eggs in a long, hanging basket nest which it enters from the top; preferably in palm fronds and eucalyptus trees.

Range: Central California, central Arizona, New Mexico, southernmost Texas, and south to Central America.

This oriole is easy to observe as it moves slowly through the taller trees in search of insects. Its nest is often parasitized by cowbirds, the aggressive young cowbird usually receiving the most food and starving the oriole nestlings.

445, 543 **American Robin**
"Robin"
(*Turdus migratorius*)
Thrushes (Turdidae)

Description: 9–11" (23–28 cm). Perhaps the best known of all North American birds. Puffed-out breast is *a fox-red or orange color;* gray-brown upperparts; throat white, head and tail blackish, paler in the female. Juveniles may be difficult to identify because they are slender-looking birds, brown-spotted below, and lack the characteristic red breast of adults.

Voice: Many regard the rich caroling of the male, uttered from a high perch, as the true herald of spring. It consists of clear rising and falling phrases recalling the words "cheer-up, cheerily," etc. The call note is a vibrant *weep.* It also gives a loud *put-put-put* and, in flight, a lisping *see-lip.*

Habitat: Lawns and parks in suburbs; any wooded habitat. Also mountain meadows interspersed with woods.

Nesting: 3 or 4 blue eggs in garden shrubbery or boulevard trees in a cup-like nest of roots and small twigs, reinforced with mud and lined with fine material. Early in spring, when cold threatens the brood, it hides its nest low in densely needled branches of a cedar or a juniper bush. During later broods, when summer heat may prostrate an incubating female, the nest is placed high in a maple or sycamore where leafy branches evaporate moisture and cool the surrounding air. The amount of mud in the insulating wall is also varied according to the season.

Range: Most of North America between the tundra and the desert. In winter, they leave most parts of Canada and the colder northern United States and fly to the southern states to harvest winter berries.

Their mainstay is earthworms, which they hunt on lawns, standing stock-still with head cocked to one side as though listening for their prey but actually discovering it by sight. Formerly simply called "Robin."

460, 585   House Finch
(*Carpodacus mexicanus*)
Finches (Fringillidae)

Description: 5–5¾" (13–15 cm). Sparrow-sized. Most adult *males shiny red on crown, breast, and rump* but less extensively so than males of Cassin's and Purple finches. Female has plain, unstriped head and heavy streaking on light underside. Immature males less highly colored, often orangish or yellowish on head and breast.

Voice: A *chirp* call like that of a young House Sparrow. The song is an extensive series of warbling notes ending in a *zeee*, Canary-like but without the musical trills and rolls. Sings from a high tree, antenna, or similar post for prolonged periods.

Habitat: Chaparral, deserts, and orchards, as well as coastal valleys that were formerly forested with redwood, cedar, or Douglas fir but have now become suburbs.

Nesting: 3–5 bluish, lightly streaked or spotted

eggs, with each pair breeding two to four times a summer; tightly woven, compact nest set anywhere from a bush to a building.

Range: Throughout the West, from southern Canada to southern Mexico, and east to Nebraska. Introduced and now widespread in Eastern United States.

These are social birds, and by placing plastic strawberry baskets under the eaves of my California patio, I induced nine pairs to nest there. House Finches are omnivorous, gleaning insect pests and, in winter, grass and weed seed. Garden-bred birds join large field flocks during the fall, often feeding in farmers' fields, and may become agricultural pests.

475 Mockingbird
(*Mimus polyglottos*)
Mockingbirds (Mimidae)

Description: 9–11″ (23–28 cm). Robin-sized. *Gray above, white below;* white wing bars, and nervous motion of tail. *In flight,* tail is black with striking white borders, and *wing flashes white.* Characteristic sudden opening and closing of wings when on a lawn perhaps scares hidden insects into movement. Also a sideways flicking motion of the tail.

Voice: A persistent bubbling, sometimes gurgling or fluty song, consisting of stanzas of repeated phrases. This bird is famous for imitating many other birds as well as the noises of cars, tractors, sirens, and other objects. Call notes include a harsh *chock.*

Habitat: Originally found in scrubby woodland, canyons, and the like, it is now also a common garden bird.

Nesting: 3–6 blue-green eggs with dark spots in a nest lined with fine plant material, placed low in a shrub.

Range: From southernmost Oregon through

northern Utah to Newfoundland and south to southern Mexico and the West Indies.

At mating time, the male becomes increasingly exuberant, flashing his wings as he flies up in aerial display, or singing while flying from one song post to another. After breeding, each parent establishes and vigorously defends its own winter territory. Mockingbirds require open grassy areas for their feeding; thick, thorny, or coniferous shrubs for hiding the nest, and high perches where the male can sing and defend his territory. Suburban gardens provide ideal habitats.

555, 611 Starling
(*Sturnus vulgaris*)
Starlings (Sturnidae)

Description: 7½–8½"(19–22 cm). Chunky; with short tail. In spring *black with iridescent green-purple gloss* and yellow bill. In winter duller, heavily speckled with light spots; dark bill. Fledged young, which roam together in flocks, look like a different bird: grayish-brown above, lighter below.

Voice: A simple, low-pitched, chirpy chatter without musical quality, interspersed with whistles, clicks, and mimicked songs and calls. Call note is a loud grating *veer*.

Habitat: Cities, fields, orchards, and woodlands.

Nesting: 5 or 6 pale blue eggs in natural cavities, woodpecker holes, nest-boxes, kingfisher or Bank Swallow holes, niches in buildings, and even in the sides of large hawks' nests. In the West, two broods are raised if the season is long enough.

Range: Another success story of an unpopular exotic. About 100 starlings were released in New York's Central Park in 1890. It arrived in California in the

1940s and in British Columbia in 1947. Now found from Alaska and southern half of Canada south to the Gulf Coast and northern Mexico.

Hordes of these birds damage vegetable or fruit crops and do considerable damage around orchards and feedlots, consuming and fouling the feed of domestic cattle. They join blackbirds and feed on locusts, ground beetles, and the like. Starlings compete with native hole-nesters for woodpecker holes and natural cavities.

Crested Myna
(*Acridotheres cristatellus*)
Starlings (Sturnidae)

Description: 10½″ (27 cm). Chunky, Robin-sized bird. All *black with prominent bushy crest*. In flight, shows large, *white patch* on *each wing*. Eyes, bill, feet yellow. White corners to tail.

Voice: Song consists of a variety of rich or harsh phrases with much repetition. It is an excellent mimic.

Habitat: Cities, suburbs, farms.

Nesting: 4 or 5 greenish-blue eggs in a large nest of grass, string, etc., in holes or cavities in trees or buildings and in boxes.

Range: Introduced from southeastern Asia to Vancouver, British Columbia, in 1897, whence it spread through the lower Fraser River Valley; it is seen sporadically in neighboring Washington State.

Mynas roost in colonies, but the flocks are small compared with those of the Starlings. Bold and fearless, they waddle on streets amid traffic, and pick food from lawns, roadsides, and gardens.

580, 592   House Sparrow
(*Passer domesticus*)
Weaver Finches (Ploceidae)

Description: 5¾–6¼″ (15–16 cm). Male has brown and black striping on wings and mantle, *gray crown, chestnut stripe* behind white face, and large *black bib*. In October just after the molt, black and chestnut marks are almost completely obscured by dingy gray feather margins which wear off by spring. *Female* is dusky brownish-*gray above* and plain gray below.

Voice: Variations on the themes of *chirp* and *cheep* monotonously repeated.

Habitat: Cities, suburbs, ranches.

Nesting: 5 or 6 pale greenish-white speckled eggs, two or three times a season. It is usually a hole-breeder and builds a huge, loose, untidy straw and grass nest in closed niches in buildings and on lampposts, signs, and the like.

Range: Early colonists introduced it mainly from England (hence its alternate name "English Sparrow"), releasing a few birds in Central Park, New York City, in 1850. It reached California some 20 years later, the Northwest by the late 1890s, and spread north as far as grain was grown. It slowly adapted to the South and by 1940 was south of the Mexican Plateau. It now ranges from Alaska to southernmost South America.

Within a short time after their introduction, these sparrows adapt to the local environment. Thus the sparrows of the rainy climate of Vancouver, British Columbia, are plump, dark birds, whereas those inhabiting Death Valley, California, are slim, pale sand-colored birds. These changes took less than 60 years, influencing our ideas about the speed of evolutionary change in birds.

Chaparral

A uniquely western habitat of low, broad-leafed, evergreen shrubs interrupted by open, barren areas or by low, creeping vegetation. Occurs on windswept coasts and the hot, dry hillsides of the California–Arizona area. Also in alpine meadows above the tree limit. More than 20 species of scrub or forest-edge birds also occur in the chaparral, some even breeding there (Scrub Jay, Sage Sparrow, Rufous-crowned Sparrow, Lawrence's Goldfinch, Bushtit, and others).

277   Mountain Quail
(*Oreortyx pictus*)
Pheasants (Phasianidae)

Description: 10½–11½" (27–29 cm). Largest North
American quail. Similar to California
and Gambel's quails: grayish-blue head,
neck, and breast; chestnut throat patch
framed by creamy forehead and side
streak. Olive-brown back, heavy white
diagonal markings on chestnut flanks.
Female duller. Both sexes have *long,
straight, black head plume*.

Voice: Its frequent call is a single haunting,
low, owl-like, slightly ascending
whistled: *woook?* "Conversational" notes
include a series of soft whistles.

Habitat: Dry mountains; brushy wooded areas
and chaparral.

Nesting: 8–12 light reddish eggs in a scrape
lined with dry grass and leaves, hidden
among protective rocks, logs, or thick
vegetation.

Range: Washington, Idaho, Oregon, and
California. Introduced to southern
Vancouver Island, British Columbia.

This quail migrates on foot from high
territory where it breeds to protected
valleys, where it winters in coveys of 6–
12 birds. They are difficult to flush, since
they persistently run through the
thickest cover.

278, 279   California Quail
(*Lophortyx californicus*)
Pheasants (Phasianidae)

Description: 9–11" (23–28 cm). Colorfully and
intricately patterned. Small·and plump
with *black forward-curving plume arising
from chestnut crown.* Creamy forehead
and black throat. Crown and throat
edged in white. Grayish-blue breast
and softly mottled nape; unstreaked
brown back and creamy belly scaled with
brown markings. Creamy diagonal flank

streaking. Female less boldly marked than male.

Voice: A loud, distinctive *ka ka kow,* the second note highest. Sometimes expressed as *chi-ca-go* or *who are you?* Often with 2-noted "warmup" phrases. Calls include a series of loud *pit!* notes.

Habitat: Brush with open areas such as coastal or foothill chaparral and live oak canyons; also adjacent desert and suburbs.

Nesting: 10–15 pale brown, spotted eggs in a shallow, grass-lined scrape. Downy chicks grow wing feathers first; just ten days after hatching they can fly when in danger.

Range: Originally, both California and Baja California. Introduced to southern Vancouver Island, British Columbia; also found in southern Oregon and northern Nevada.

Perched on tree or fence post, the male claims his territory by cackling and posturing; the entire family takes to trees for roosting as well as for safety. After the breeding season, these birds become gregarious and gather in large coveys, often visiting city parks, gardens, and yards.

281 Chukar
(*Alectoris chukar*)
Pheasants (Phasianidae)

Description: 13–15½" (33–39 cm). Similar in size and shape to Gray Partridge. Light brown back and wings with gray-tinged cap, breast, and rump. *White cheek and throat framed by broad black band.* Bold chestnut-and-black diagonal striping on flanks, creamy white belly, and bright rufous outer tail feathers. Bill and legs orange-red. Sexes look alike.

Voice: A low, harsh cackling *chuk-karr,* often repeated for long periods.

Habitat: Arid mountainous areas, canyons, and grassy slopes with rock outcroppings.

Nesting: 8–15 buffy, brown-spotted eggs in a grass- and feather-lined scrape in the shelter of rocks or bush. Both male and female care for the young.

Range: Mainly the Great Basin, from southern British Columbia south to Baja California and east to Colorado.

The Chukar partridge was successfully introduced to the West from the "Mediterranean" dry belt of Eurasia. It is a hardy gamebird that can outrun a hunter (first running uphill, then flying downhill). Its loud calls and colorful coveys enliven desolate country.

390, 392   **Allen's Hummingbird**
(*Selasphorus sasin*)
Hummingbirds (Trochilidae)

Description: 3–3½″ (8–9 cm). Small hummingbird. Male has iridescent green crown and back; rufous rump and tail. *Bright* iridescent *copper-red gorget* (appears dark when not in direct sunlight), white breast, rufous sides. Female bronze-green above, including central tail feathers, with white-tipped rufous outer tail feathers, flecked throat, white underparts with rust tinge on flanks.

Voice: Adult male produces a musical buzz in flight. Calls include a variety of buzzy notes, a low *chup,* and an excited *zeeee chuppity-chup.*

Habitat: Coastal chaparral, brushland, and edges of redwood forests.

Nesting: 2 white eggs in a tiny, tightly woven cup placed on a sheltered branch.

Range: Along the Pacific Coast, from southern Oregon to southern California, but males and migrants occur from midsummer to fall elsewhere in California, as well as in Mexico and Arizona. Birds living on islands off southern California coast are thought to be resident. Winters in northwestern Mexico.

The incredibly fast flight of this tiny bird is associated with its rapid metabolism and high body temperature, around 108° F (42° C). Experiments I have conducted at my feeder show that when the air is cool the bird conserves body heat by withdrawing its feet into the patch of down that covers its belly. In warmer weather, the toes are unfolded from the downy "muff." When the air is hot the hovering bird cools itself by dangling feet and toes.

399 Anna's Hummingbird
(*Calypte anna*)
Hummingbirds (Trochilidae)

Description: 3½–4" (9–10 cm). Medium-sized hummingbird. Both sexes metallic green above; male has *dark rose-red crown and gorget* and grayish chest. Female has spotted throat with central patch of red spots, grayish-white underparts, and white-tipped outer tail feathers. Throat of juveniles frequently unmarked.

Voice: Song of male is a series of coarse squeaking notes continuing in a definite pattern for several seconds; delivered from a perch. Common calls include a sharp *chip* and a rapid *chee-chee-chee-chee-chee*. When displaying, the male climbs high in the air and plummets rapidly earthward, giving an explosive *peeep!* as he levels off just above the ground. This sound issues from the specialized, narrow tail feathers spread out during the descent.

Habitat: Chaparral, brushy oak woodland, and gardens.

Nesting: 2 white eggs in a tiny woven cup of small twigs and lichen fastened onto a sheltered horizontal limb.

Range: Principally from northern Baja California and coastal foothills up to southern Oregon; summer pioneers

reach Vancouver Island, British Columbia. With the planting of eucalyptus trees and increased use of window feeders in California's Central Valley, food is always available and this species now stays year round. Other inland populations are migratory.

Anna's and other hummingbirds vigorously defend their feeding territories, which although often as small as a few clumps of fuchsias provide adequate nectar and small nectar-feeding insects. From July to late fall, however, transient and juvenile birds disregard territorial claims, and competition at feeders increases greatly.

442 Rufous-sided Towhee
(*Pipilo erythrophthalmus*)
Finches (Fringillidae)

Description: 7–8½″ (18–22 cm). Smaller than a Robin. Male has *black hood, wings, and back with white wing bars and spots.* Black tail has white edging on outer feathers. White breast and belly with *bright rufous sides.* Female has same pattern but is brown where male is black. Both sexes have red eyes.

Voice: The song varies, often with a few introductory notes and usually ending with a long trill, such as *drink-your-teeaaa* or *to-wheeeee*. On the Pacific Coast, the buzzy trill makes up the entire song. Call is an inquisitive *meewww?*

Habitat: Forest edges, thickets, woodlands, gardens, and shrubby park areas.

Nesting: 3–6 white eggs with reddish-brown and lilac spots in a loose cup nest built in a dense bush, such as cedar or juniper hedge, close to or on the ground if sheltered by tall planting.

Range: Southern Canada to southern United States and northern Central America.

Widely distributed except for the dense
forests of the Alaskan and northern
British Columbian coasts and treeless
prairies. In winter northwestern and
mountain area towhees migrate to the
lowlands of the southwestern states and
Mexico.

Suburban gardens as well as chaparral
perfectly suit this towhee, which is not
as secretive as other towhees in the
West.

---

484 Wrentit
(*Chamaea fasciata*)
Wrentits (Chamaeidae)

Description: 6–6½" (15–17 cm). *Uniformly brown*
with streaked breast and *conspicuous
white eyes*. Its name is apt, for its head,
beak, and eyes resemble those of a tit,
whereas the long cocked tail and
secretive habits remind one of a wren.

Voice: An accelerating series of musical notes
running together into a trill and
dropping slightly in pitch toward the
end: *peep peep peep-pee-pee-peepeepepeprrrr*.
Call is a prolonged dry "growling"
note. Far more often heard than seen.

Habitat: Chaparral, shrubs, and brush.

Nesting: 3–5 greenish-blue eggs in a neat cup
nest of bark fiber, held together by
cobwebs and hidden in a low bush.

Range: From the Columbia River, on the
northern border of Oregon, south along
the coastal chaparral into Baja
California, and in the foothills of the
Central Valley of California.

The Wrentit spends all its adult life
within the territory chosen in its first
year. Individuals hesitate to cross open
spaces of even 30–40 feet, and it is
believed that the wide Columbia River
effectively stops it from entering
Washington, even though that side of
the river offers suitable habitat.

524 **Green-tailed Towhee**
(*Pipilo chlorurus*)
Finches (Fringillidae)

Description: 6¼–7″ (16–18 cm). Ground finch,
smaller than other towhees. Sexes
similar; *rufous cap, olive green above,* with
white throat and belly, gray breast.
White lores and dark mustache stripe.
Yellow wing linings.

Voice: Song loud and lively, consisting of
slurred notes and short, buzzy trills,
usually delivered from atop a shrub or
young conifer. Call is a short, nasal
mew.

Habitat: Sagebrush, mountain chaparral,
pinyon-juniper stands, and thickets
bordering alpine meadows.

Nesting: 4 white, heavily spotted eggs in a
rather loosely constructed nest on the
ground or in low, protected sites such
as chaparral, juniper, and yucca.

Range: Central Oregon south through
mountains to southern California and
the Great Basin to southeastern New
Mexico. Winters at lower elevations
and south to southern Arizona, south
central Texas and into Mexico.

This shy bird hops and scratches for
food under low cover, flicking its tail
and erecting its rufous cap into a crest.
It prefers low scrub and occurs in
brushy openings in boreal forests on
western mountains, as well as in
sagebrush habitats.

536 **California Thrasher**
(*Toxostoma redivivum*)
Mockingbirds (Mimidae)

Description: 11–13″ (28–33 cm). Large thrasher
with *long, deeply curved bill.* Dark brown
above with lighter gray-brown breast;
cinnamon belly and undertail coverts. Dark
brown eye; indistinct light brown
eyebrow-stripe.

Voice: Sings for prolonged periods atop a shrub. Song recalls that of a Mockingbird, but harsher, more halting, and less repetitious. An expert mimic. Call is a low harsh *cheik* and a throaty *prrip.*

Habitat: Chaparral, foothills, dense shrubs of parks or gardens.

Nesting: 2–4 pale blue-green, speckled eggs in a bowl-shaped nest of sticks and roots lined with finer materials and placed in a shrub.

Range: Only in California west of the Sierras, south into northern Baja California.

It feeds on the ground under the shelter of bushes and uses its heavy, curved bill to hoe the soil and turn over leaf litter in search of food. Its wings are shorter than those of the desert thrashers and it often escapes by scurrying rather than flying.

546 Dusky Flycatcher
(*Empidonax oberholseri*)
Tyrant Flycatchers (Tyrannidae)

Description: 5¼–6″ (13–15 cm). Back *gray with slight olive tinge;* buffy breast with light throat and very pale yellow belly. Narrow white eye-ring and wing bars.

Voice: Song similar to that of Hammond's Flycatcher: a staccato series of chirps, transcribed as *se-lip, churp, treep.* Call is a sharp *wit.*

Habitat: Woodland containing tall trees and tall undergrowth; mountain chaparral and open, brushy, coniferous forests.

Nesting: 3–5 white eggs in a neat twiggy cup low in the crotch of a shrub or small tree.

Range: From the southern Yukon through most of the western mountains, excluding the coastal forest of the Pacific Northwest, and as far south as southern California and New Mexico. Winters in Mexico.

Hammond's and Dusky flycatchers are closely related, very similar in appearance and voice, and difficult to distinguish. The populations were probably separated when the ice fields of the North advanced and the forests were divided into western and eastern refuges. When the flycatchers returned to the newly forested northern half of the continent, each had developed differing habitat needs, allowing them to coexist without competing for nesting sites and food. The Dusky usually nests in the lower ranges of the forest, preferring chaparral; the Hammond's chooses higher levels of tall fir trees.

563 Brown Towhee
(*Pipilo fuscus*)
Finches (Fringillidae)

Description: 8–10″ (20–25 cm). *Earth brown above* with buffy, faintly streaked throat, light brown underparts, and *rust-colored undertail coverts*. Birds of the Southwest are paler and grayer and have a rufous cap.

Voice: Song is a series of squeaky *chips* on the same pitch, accelerating into a rapid trill. The pattern varies according to the area. The call is a sharp *chink* and thin *tseeee*.

Habitat: Shady underbrush, open woods, pinyon-juniper woodlands, and suburban gardens.

Nesting: 3 or 4 bluish-green eggs, lightly spotted or scrawled with blackish-brown markings, in a cup nest low in a bush or young tree. The female incubates; the male sings his territorial song from a nearby perch.

Range: Coastal and foothill chaparral from Oregon to southern Baja California; brush country of the southwestern states of Arizona, Colorado, Oklahoma, and Texas to southern Mexico.

The Brown Towhee is rarely noted because it often forages quietly among chaparral bushes or garden cover. Although its range in the chaparral overlaps during winter with that of the Rufous-sided Towhee, it lives in low scrub, whereas the Rufous-sided keeps to scrub oaks and other taller "forest edge" areas.

591 Rufous-crowned Sparrow
(*Aimophila ruficeps*)
Finches (Fringillidae)

Description: 5–6" (13–15 cm). *Rufous crown with darker rufous eye-stripe* on gray head; conspicuous black whisker mark. Mantle gray with rufous-brown streaks; underparts unstreaked gray. Juveniles have buffy breast with faint streaking and little, if any, rufous markings.

Voice: Song is a rapid, pleasing jumble of notes, recalling that of the House Wren, but with "sparrow quality." Distinctive call is a downslurred *dear dear dear* and a thin, plaintive *tseeee.*

Habitat: Open oak woodland; on treeless dry uplands with grassy vegetation and bushes, often near rock outcrops.

Nesting: 3–5 white or slightly bluish eggs in a neat nest of plant fiber and grasses on or near the ground.

Range: From California, southern Arizona, and southern New Mexico east to Texas and central Oklahoma, and south to south-central Mexico.

A secretive bird, the male in spring sings in the early morning from the tops of boulders, but otherwise it is usually on the ground. If disturbed, it will fly to a nearby rock for a short survey, then return to the grass.

601   **Black-chinned Sparrow**
(*Spizella atrogularis*)
Finches (Fringillidae)

Description: 5–5½" (13–14 cm). A gray sparrow
with *black chin and eye smudge, pink bill,
chestnut-streaked mantle, white belly.* Thin
white wing bars. Female and juveniles
lack black facial markings.

Voice: The beautiful song is a series of slurred
notes, either *swee? swee?* or *chew chew
chew,* running together into a rapid
Canary-like trill.

Habitat: Low, dense chaparral on arid mountain
slopes; sagebrush.

Nesting: 3 or 4 pale blue, plain or spotted eggs
in a grass-lined cup well concealed in a
low bush.

Range: Central Plateau of the western United
States and highlands of northern
Mexico; coastal, foothill, and subalpine
areas of southern California and Baja
California. Winters from southern
Arizona and western Texas southward.

Very little is known about the habits of
this sparrow. Singing males are
conspicuous when they sit on top of
high bushes; their song carries well
through the narrow, brushy canyons
they inhabit, but in general the species
is shy and secretive.

Sagebrush

The cold winter desert of the Great
Basin Plateau, covered mainly with a
gray-green fragrant bush, the evergreen
Sagebrush (*Artemisia tridentata*). Only
the occasional salt pan or rocky
outcropping is truly desert. Several
species are adapted to living, hiding,
and even feeding in sagebrush; others,
such as the Crissal Thrasher and the
Black-throated Sparrow, range in both
this area and the hot desert of lower
elevations. Others are also found in the
pinyon-juniper woodland habitat,which
merges with the sagebrush habitat.

249 Poor-will
(*Phalaenoptilus nuttallii*)
Nightjars (Caprimulgidae)

Description: 7–8½″ (18–22 cm). Smallest nightjar.
Its mottled, gray-brown body serves as
camouflage; *no white mark on wings* but
whitish collar separates black throat
from mottled underparts. Dark outer
tail feathers are tipped with white,
more conspicuously in male; *tail is
rounded.*

Voice: Rarely seen or heard during the day
unless flushed, but on warm nights in
the breeding season this bird reveals its
presence by uttering a melancholy call,
the first note lower than the second;
this sounds like its name, *poor-will*. In
flight it utters a low *wurt, wurt*.

Habitat: Desert, chaparral, sagebrush, and other
arid uplands.

Nesting: 2 pinkish-white eggs on bare ground.

Range: Breeds from southeastern British
Columbia and Alberta south throughout
the western United States. Winters in
southern United States and Mexico.

The Poor-will has been discovered
hibernating in the desert in California,
surviving a long cold spell in torpid
condition without food and with its
body temperature lowered almost to
that of the environment. Swifts and
other birds may also undergo torpor.

253, 257 Sage Grouse
(*Centrocercus urophasianus*)
Grouse (Tetraonidae)

Description: Male, 26–30″ (66–76 cm); female, 22–
23″ (56–58 cm). *Both sexes streaked gray
above with a black belly.* Male has a long
pointed tail; black throat, white collar,
and white breast flanked by elongated
neck plumes. Female's head, back, and
breast uniformly barred. In courtship
display male's tail is fanned and tilted

forward; white neck and breast are inflated by pair of naked yellowish-green air sacs.

Voice: When flushed, it may give a chicken-like *cluck cluck cluck;* courtship calls described below.

Habitat: Open country, plains, foothills, sagebrush semi-deserts.

Nesting: 7 or 8 or more olive-buff, lightly spotted eggs in a well-concealed grass-lined depression.

Range: From southern British Columbia, Alberta, and Saskatchewan south to western Colorado, Utah, Nevada, and eastern California.

As its name suggests, this grouse feeds on sagebrush buds and leaves, where it also nests and hides. The males gather each spring on a traditional display ground, or lek, for the courtship ritual, each male occupying a small area. After strutting with neck feathers raised and wings and tail spread out, the male stops with head thrust forward and breast inflated, making popping and burbling noises by alternately inflating and deflating his air sacs. Females crisscross the male's territories, squatting before the mate of their choice. The most dominant males are polygamous.

490 Gray Flycatcher
(*Empidonax wrightii*)
Tyrant Flycatchers (Tyrannidae)

Description: 5½" (14 cm). *Gray above,* white below. *Lower mandible flesh-colored.*

Voice: Song is in two parts, rising in tone: *chiwip* (or *chi-bit*) *cheep.* Call is a soft *wit.*

Habitat: Sagebrush and pinyon-juniper woodland.

Nesting: 3 or 4 white eggs in a grass-woven cup nest, low in sagebrush or a small tree.

Range: Great Basin states.

This flycatcher lacks the olive and yellow tinges to the back and underparts that mark the Willow, Hammond's, Dusky, and Western flycatchers. Its color blends with the blue-gray hues of the sagebrush and helps conceal it from predators.

533 Sage Thrasher
(*Oreoscoptes montanus*)
Mockingbirds (Mimidae)

Description: 8–9" (20–23 cm). Robin-sized; smaller than other thrashers. *Grayish-brown above,* light underparts with heavy brown streaking. White wing bars and yellow eyes. *White-tipped outer tail feathers.*

Voice: Song is a rich pattern of various musical phrases not unlike the song of the Mockingbird. Call is a low blackbird-like *chuck.*

Habitat: Sagebrush, and rabbit-brush cover in cold winter deserts of the West.

Nesting: 4 or 5 glossy blue, boldly spotted eggs in a bulky twig nest on the ground or well hidden in brush.

Range: South-central British Columbia to southern Nevada, Utah, through Texas and Oklahoma, and in the San Joaquin Valley of California. Winters from central California to northern Mexico.

A good songster from a conspicuous perch or in flight, it is a less repetitious mimic than the Mockingbird. It feasts on fruits and vegetables in gardens of desert towns, but also eats many damaging insects in alfalfa fields near its sagebrush nesting area.

575 Vesper Sparrow
(*Pooecetes gramineus*)
Finches (Fringillidae)

Description: 5–6½″ (13–17 cm). Streaked brown above, with streaked head, throat, and breast. Light, narrow eye-ring, *chestnut bend of wing,* and *white outer tail feathers.*

Voice: A finch-like song, with variations similar to Song Sparrow's: 2 introductory notes followed by 2 or 3 short higher trills, ending in a rapid melody.

Habitat: Open grassy areas with some elevated song posts; hayfields and grainfields, meadows, roadsides.

Nesting: 3–6 creamy white, spotted eggs in a grass-lined ground nest in low vegetation.

Range: Coast to coast from Canada to south-central United States. Winters to southern Mexico.

The name Vesper Sparrow (the Latin word *vesper* means evening) is a misnomer, as it does not sing more often in the evening than other sparrows. Since this open-country bird accepted cultivated land as a habitat, its populations have been thriving.

600 Brewer's Sparrow
(*Spizella breweri*)
Finches (Fringillidae)

Description: 5″ (13 cm). Light brown upperparts with black streaks; unmarked pale underparts. Resembles Clay-colored Sparrow but has *solid, finely streaked crown.* Well-defined darker ear patch bordered by fine black eye-line and two parallel whisker marks. Unstreaked breast; darker, finely streaked back with buff wing bars.

Voice: Alternating trills, musical or buzzy, often quite prolonged. Call note is a soft *seep,* most often given in flight.

Habitat: Sagebrush and alpine meadows.
Nesting: 3–5 bluish, brown-spotted eggs in a grass nest on or near the ground.
Range: From British Columbia east to Saskatchewan south to New Mexico, Arizona, and southern California. Absent from the cool Pacific coastal belt.

This sparrow is unusual in having two distinct nesting populations, one in the alpine meadows of the Rocky Mountains of the Yukon and the other in the sagebrush deserts.

602 Sage Sparrow
(*Amphispiza belli*)
Finches (Fringillidae)

Description: 5–6" (13–15 cm). Gray above; *white belly with small black midbreast spot.* Back and sides striped, wings lighter with buffy feather edges that also form two wing bars. *Pronounced white eye-ring.* Gray cheek, white eyebrow stripe, black mustache stripe. Immatures browner and have white throat and fine dark streaking on buff breast and belly.
Voice: Song is a short pattern of finch-like jumbling notes, rising, then falling. Call is a soft tinkling.
Habitat: Sagebrush, chaparral, dry foothills.
Nesting: 3 or 4 bluish-white, speckled eggs in a loose cup built of sagebrush pieces, lined with fur and well hidden in sagebrush or other scrub.
Range: From Washington south to Baja California, and throughout the Great Basin. Winters in small flocks in the low desert of southern California, Arizona, New Mexico, and Mexico.

The Sage Sparrow is secretive, moving under cover rapidly when approached, except during the spring breeding season, when males sing from a sagebrush perch to announce their territory. It has a habit of flicking its tail while hopping around on the ground.

Pinyon-Juniper Woodlands

Above the sagebrush desert the mountain slopes have a scattering of pine trees and juniper bushes amid grass or sagebrush. In some places the trees form extensive stands of woodland. The large, tasty, and calorie-rich pine nuts attract many birds, and a few specialized birds prefer this habitat.

427, 437   Scott's Oriole
(*Icterus parisorum*)
Orioles (Icteridae)

Description: 7½–8¼″ (19–21 cm). Male has *black head, mantle, throat, and central breast area, bright lemon-yellow underparts,* rump, and outer tail feathers. Wings, central tail feathers, and wide terminal band are also black. Male has one slender white wing bar. Female lime-yellow with dusky streaks on back; two wing bars. First-year male resembles female, but with small faint black throat and bib.

Voice: The song, a series of rising and falling flute-like notes, resembles that of a Western Meadowlark; it is delivered from atop a yucca, juniper, or other tree. Call is a harsh *chuck*.

Habitat: Breeds in the pinyon-juniper woodland of montane semi-desert areas; yucca trees or palms in deserts; sycamores or cottonwoods in canyons.

Nesting: 3–5 bluish-white, irregularly spotted eggs in a grassy hanging pouch nest often skillfully hidden among dry yucca fronds, pines, or live oaks.

Range: Desert region from southeastern California, southern Nevada, Utah, and Arizona's Chihuahua Desert through southern New Mexico and western Texas. South of the border, found in the deserts of northwestern Mexico and Baja California.

Besides gleaning insects, this fine songster feeds on available fruits, including those of cacti, and has been observed taking nectar—a habit practiced by many tropical orioles. Like most orioles, it skillfully climbs drooping branches and twigs as well as delicate yucca flowers.

507 Pinyon Jay
(*Gymnorhinus cyanocephalus*)
Crows (Corvidae)

Description: 9–11¾" (23–30 cm). Robin-sized. Long, slender bill gives it a resemblance to the nutcrackers. *Gray-blue, darkest on head*, with white streaking on throat. Rather short tail. Crow-like flight and flocking habits. Yearlings gray.

Voice: A high-pitched *caaa*, often quavering at the end to resemble a laughing *haa-a-a-a*.

Habitat: Ponderosa pine, pinyon-juniper, and forests of mixed pine and oak.

Nesting: 3 or 4 greenish-white, speckled eggs in a twiggy cup nest; in loose colonies.

Range: Central Plateau area, extending to Oklahoma, eastern California, and northern Baja California.

Although they sometimes pull up earthworms from lawns in the fashion of Robins, Pinyon Jays feed principally on pine nuts, which they store in fall and consume during winter and spring. Their local abundance varies from year to year with the success of the nut crop. They nest early after a good harvest; in poor years they delay breeding until August.

548 Ash-throated Flycatcher
(*Myiarchus cinerascens*)
Tyrant Flycatchers (Tyrannidae)

Description: 7½–8½" (19–22 cm). Smaller than a Kingbird. Slender bill and *gray-white throat. Olive-brown* above, light yellow underparts, with *cinnamon-rust primaries and tail feathers.* Two white wing bars.

Voice: Common call is a rolling *quee-eerr* suggestive of a low-pitched playground whistle. Also various *pip* or *pwit* notes and various croaking sounds.

Habitat: Open woodland, pinyon-juniper,

chaparral, oak canyons, deserts, and riverside groves.

Nesting: 4 or 5 creamy, streaked eggs in a cup that usually includes pieces of shed snakeskin, placed in woodpecker holes or knotholes.

Range: Southern Washington and Idaho south into California and Mexico, east to Colorado and Texas. Winters from extreme southern California and Arizona southward.

These birds launch their pursuit of insects from the dead upper branches of mature trees at the edge of woodlands. Trunk rot in these trees creates cavities useful as nesting sites. Open nests would be too exposed in the sparse foliage of this dry habitat, transitional between woodland and open range. Although this flycatcher has become a hole breeder, it still builds a nest and has streaked, camouflaged eggs like its open-nesting ancestors.

Gray Vireo
(*Vireo vicinior*)
Vireos (Vireonidae)

Description: 5–5¾" (13–15 cm). *Gray above, whitish below, with faint white eye-ring and lores;* single, indistinct wing bar. The *sideways twitching of its tail* is unique among vireos and reminiscent of gnatcatchers.

Voice: Song is a series of 4–6 phrases with a pause between each phrase and a much longer pause between stanzas; e.g., *cheerio . . . che-whew . . . chireep? . . . cheerio.*

Habitat: Dry brush, especially juniper in the pinyon-juniper-covered slopes of the southwestern mountains; scrub oak and other types of chaparral.

Nesting: 3 or 4 white eggs, lightly spotted with brown, in a nest hung from a forked branch in a bush.

Range: Southern California east to Utah, south to western Texas and Baja California. Winters south to central Mexico.

This bird's overall gray blends with the blue-gray of the junipers. Even the bunchgrass and sagebrush have the same pale grayish color, a feature of the vegetation widespread on the arid mesas, slopes, and plateaus of the West. The Gray Vireo needs this camouflage when it searches for food near the top of the low cover it prefers.

608 Black-throated Gray Warbler
(*Dendroica nigrescens*)
Wood Warblers (Parulidae)

Description: 4½–5" (11–13 cm). *Head striped black and white, black bib on throat, white below* with black stripes on sides, *blue-gray back* with black striping; yellow spot between bill and eyes. Two white wing bars and white outer tail feathers. Winter male, female, and juveniles lack black bib.

Voice: The song is a series of buzzes, rising in pitch and intensity, then falling: *zee zee zee zee bzz bzz.* Call is, a dull *tup.*

Habitat: Shrubby openings in coniferous forest or mixed woods, dry scrub oak, pinyon and juniper, chaparral, and other low brushy areas; also in forests.

Nesting: 3–5 creamy white eggs, splashed with brown, in a tightly woven plant-fiber cup in a bush or tree, usually below 10 feet.

Range: Coastal forests from southern British Columbia (except Vancouver Island) to northern Baja California. Also found in the Great Basin states. Winters in the Southwest and northern Mexico, but mainly in central Mexico.

This bird resembles Townsend's Warbler in every respect except that it lacks the green and yellow colors of the latter. Whereas the bright plumage of Townsend's blends well with the bright green of the spruces and pines of the coast forest, the drab appearance of the Black-throated Gray is a good adaptation to the bluish gray-green of western junipers.

Oak Woodlands

Western oaks, seldom taller than 50–60' (20 m), form groves interrupted by grassy or bare areas. These groves cover large expanses from Oregon (and on a small scale, from the extreme southwest of British Columbia) to Baja California and Texas, and south into Mexico. Live oaks (i.e., evergreen oaks) are mainly found in California. Deciduous evergreen oaks that shed their leaves but quickly acquire new verdure occur in southern Arizona and southwestern New Mexico (see coniferous forests habitat for mixed oak and pine woods). A large group of birds (Long-eared Owl, Band-tailed Pigeon, Northern Oriole, House Wren, and many others) are commonly found in oaks but just as often in other deciduous-tree habitats and are treated in such habitats.

266 **Turkey**
(Meleagris gallopavo)
Turkeys (Meleagrididae)

Description: Male, 48″ (122 cm); female, 36″ (91 cm). Naked head bluish with red wattles which brighten in spring display; dusky brown body with bronzy iridescent sheen. In courtship, male spreads tawny tail in a fan, revealing a broad black subterminal band with white or buffy edge (chestnut in eastern population). Male has spurs and long dangling tuft of feathers (called the "beard") in middle of breast. Female considerably smaller, less iridescent, and frequently lacks beard.

Voice: Gobbling calls similar to those of domestic turkey.

Habitat: Oak woodlands, pine-oak forests.

Nesting: 8–15 buffy, spotted eggs in a shallow depression lined with grass and leaves and cared for by the female.

Range: Eastern and southwestern United States and Mexico; introduced to many western states, including California.

The Turkey was formerly abundant throughout eastern forests but has decreased drastically and disappeared from much of its former range through destruction of its woodland habitat and overhunting. Game management and restocking have helped it make a comeback in some areas. In spring the older males gather a harem of females, attracting them with gobbling calls. Wild turkeys are extremely wary.

---

283 **Montezuma Quail**
"Harlequin Quail"
(Cyrtonyx montezumae)
Pheasants (Phasianidae)

Description: 8–9½″ (20–24 cm). Male's *face has striking black-and-white marking*, with elongated pale *buffy* feathers forming a crest; *sides and flanks bluish-black with heavy white speckling.* Female is mottled brown.

Voice: A soft, whinnying call.

Habitat: Grassy and brush-covered ground in pine-oak woodlands.

Nesting: 8–14 white eggs in a grass-lined depression, concealed in dense grass. After incubation, the male shares in brooding and leading the family.

Range: Southern Arizona to western Texas and south to Oaxaca.

This bird relishes berries and acorns as well as its winter staples, tubers and bulbs, which it scratches out with its sturdy feet. By the time it breeds in summer, the rains have come and insect food is abundant. Formerly known as the "Harlequin Quail."

286, 287 **Screech Owl**
(*Otus asio*)
Owls (Strigidae)

Description: 7–10" (18–25 cm). Small owl with *ear tufts* and *camouflage coloring;* color ranges from gray to brown to rusty.

Voice: Varies geographically. In the West, the call is an accelerating "bouncing ball" series of 6–8 low whistles, often dropping in pitch toward the end. Also a quick series on one pitch.

Habitat: Woodlands, orchards, back yards with many trees.

Nesting: 4 or 5 white eggs in a natural or woodpecker cavity, or even a nesting-box.

Range: Throughout most of North America except boreal and montane forests.

This common owl incubates each egg as it is laid. Thus the eggs hatch in sequence and the young within a brood vary widely in size and age. This allows the parents to raise all their young if

food is plentiful, or only the first few if food is scarce. This pattern is widespread among owls and birds of prey that feed on mice and meadow moles, which fluctuate widely in abundance.

Whiskered Owl
(*Otus trichopsis*)
Owls (Strigidae)

Description: 6½–8″ (17–20 cm). Almost identical to gray form of Screech Owl, but with longer bristles at base of bill and larger *white spots on scapulars*. Identified by call.

Voice: A series of low whistles in a distinctive pattern: *hoo-hoo hooo hoo, hoo-hoo hooo hoo,* etc. Also a rapid series: *hoohoohoohoohoo.*

Habitat: Pine-oak woods, oaks, and sycamores.

Nesting: 3 or 4 white spherical eggs in a deep tree cavity or a flicker hole.

Range: Mountain canyons of southern Arizona and New Mexico between the Sonora and Chihuahua deserts and just north of the Mexican border, through the mountains of the Mexican Plateau to Honduras.

This common owl of the oak canyons of southeast Arizona is virtually indistinguishable from the gray form of the Screech Owl, except at night when its distinctive voice identifies it. Birders in the Tucson area make night trips to find this and many other species of owls in the nearby canyons and mountains. The owls respond readily to imitations or recordings of their calls, often coming close enough to be seen with a spotlight.

367, 369 Nuttall's Woodpecker
(*Picoides nuttallii*)
Woodpeckers (Picidae)

Description: 7–7½" (18–19 cm). Small *"ladder-backed"* woodpecker. Black head with white markings; male has red cap on midcrown; light side spotting on otherwise unstreaked white underparts. Where its range overlaps that of the Ladder-backed Woodpecker, its voice distinguishes it.

Voice: Rolling call, *prreep,* often expanded into a long, rolling *prree-prree-prrrreeeee.* Drums frequently in spring.

Habitat: Canyon scrub oaks, oak woodlands, and streamside growth.

Nesting: 3–6 white eggs in a hole excavated in a thin dead branch of an oak or cottonwood, or even a large, thick-stemmed elderberry bush.

Range: California with a slight extension to southern Oregon and Baja California.

Although some sources indicate that this California species is restricted to interior and coastal foothills containing extensive stands of oaks, I have found it nesting in suburban Sacramento and in cottonwood trees along California's Feather River.

376 Acorn Woodpecker
(*Melanerpes formicivorus*)
Woodpeckers (Picidae)

Description: 8–9½" (20–24 cm). Smaller than Robin. *Male has yellowish-white forecrown;* red crown, light eyes, black nape, back, wings, and tail. Black chin, yellowish-white throat and sides of head with heavy dark streaking on breast and flanks; white belly, wing patches, and rump. *Female has black forecrown;* otherwise identical to male.

Voice: This noisy woodpecker gives a variety of calls, including a distinctive *JA-cob,*

JA-cob or *WAKE-up, WAKE-up.* Also a rolling drum with bill against a dead limb.

Habitat: Open oak and pine-oak forests.

Nesting: 4 or 5 white eggs in a hole in a tree. In colonies. All members of the colony share in excavating holes—mostly in dead oak branches—feeding young, and possibly incubating.

Range: Southern Oregon through California, and Arizona; New Mexico, and western Texas south to Colombia.

This well-named woodpecker harvests acorns, and in agricultural or suburban areas almonds and walnuts as well. In autumn the birds store their crop of nuts tightly in individual holes so that no squirrel can pry them out. The storage trees are usually mature or dead pines, or Douglas firs with thick, soft bark, but dead oak branches and fence posts are also used. The holes made by a colony are re-used year after year. Acorns seem to be emergency provisions; on mild winter days these birds may be observed catching flying insects.

377 Lewis' Woodpecker
(*Melanerpes lewis*)
Woodpeckers (Picidae)

Description: 10½–11½" (27–29 cm). Smaller than a flicker. Metallic *greenish-black above; collar and breast gray, pinkish-red belly;* dark red face framed with greenish black. Sexes look alike.

Voice: Usually silent; it occasionally gives a low, churring note.

Habitat: Open pine-oak woodland, oak or cottonwood groves in grassland, ponderosa pine country.

Nesting: 6–8 white eggs in a cavity in a dead stump or tree limb, often at a considerable height; in colonies.

Range: The dry West, from southern British

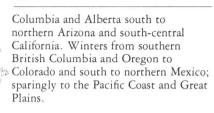

Columbia and Alberta south to northern Arizona and south-central California. Winters from southern British Columbia and Oregon to Colorado and south to northern Mexico; sparingly to the Pacific Coast and Great Plains.

Unlike most woodpeckers, Lewis' does not peck at wood for food and is seen more often on top of a fence post than clinging to it vertically. As with the Acorn Woodpecker, its main method of getting food is catching flying insects; both species also use and store acorns and other nuts for winter, sometimes damaging fruit orchards. Lewis' is the common woodpecker of mountain ranchland, and some ranchers call it the "Crow Woodpecker" because of its dark color, large size, and slow flight.

380 Arizona Woodpecker
(*Picoides arizonae*)
Woodpeckers (Picidae)

Description: 7–8" (18–20 cm). Unstreaked, *brown-backed* woodpecker; brown crown and ear patch on white face. Underparts spotted and barred with brown. Male distinguished by *red nape*.

Voice: Call is a sharp *peek!* or a rasping *jee jee jee*.

Habitat: Dry live oak and pine-oak woodland; slopes at elevations up to 7000 feet.

Nesting: 3 or 4 white eggs in a cavity in a dead branch of a live tree.

Range: Restricted to the mountains of south-eastern Arizona and southwestern New Mexico south to south-central Mexico.

Shy birds, their habits are little known. Like other woodpeckers they lay round white eggs in cavities, without nests. Other hole-breeders such as chickadees and some flycatchers, which build nests and lay patterned eggs, probably evolved the hole-breeding habit more recently and may lose these traits.

---

456 Painted Redstart
(*Myioborus pictus*)
Wood Warblers (Parulidae)

Description: 5" (13 cm). *Black* "hood" and *upperparts* accentuated by large white wing patch and outer tail feathers. Bright *red breast* and *white belly*. Sexes look alike.

Voice: Song is a rich, chanting *cheery cheery cheery chew*. Call is a *cheereo*, different from calls of other warblers.

Habitat: Pine or pine-oak woods, oak canyons, pinyon-juniper-covered high slopes.

Nesting: 3 or 4 creamy white, finely speckled eggs in a grass nest, with fine grass or hair lining, in a ground hollow.

Range: Southern Arizona, New Mexico, and western Texas south into the mountains of Central America.

This bird flits energetically, drooping its wings and fanning its tail in typical redstart fashion. It catches flying insects, much like the American Redstart. The two birds are not closely related but have evolved in a similar way and fill the same ecological niche in the forest.

---

478 Virginia's Warbler
(*Vermivora virginiae*)
Wood Warblers (Parulidae)

Description: 4–4¼" (10–11 cm). Male *gray above*, with *yellow breast, rump, and undertail coverts*. Throat and belly white. Chestnut crown patch and white eye-ring visible at close range. Female is duller.

Voice: The male delivers a *seedle seedle seedle sweet sweet* from a high perch. Call is a sharp *plink*.

Habitat: Scrub oak and other chaparral, pinyon-juniper brushland, pine and oak.

Nesting: 3–5 white, finely speckled eggs in a loosely built cup nest on the ground.

Range: Southern parts of the Central Plateau and the Rockies, from Nevada to Colorado, and extreme eastern California to New Mexico. Winters in Mexico.

This warbler forages for insects and spiders in scrub oaks near the ground. Though the male occasionally uses a song post such as the top of a juniper, he also sings while feeding in the middle of the chaparral. It closely resembles three other warblers: the Nashville, Lucy's, and the rare Colima.

486 Plain Titmouse
(*Parus inornatus*)
Titmice (Paridae)

Description: 5–5½" (13–14 cm). Sparrow-sized. *Gray with small crest,* usually erect, and lighter underparts.

Voice: A harsh, fussy *see dee dee* or *chica-dee-dee.* A variety of other repeated notes, such as *teed le-doo.*

Habitat: Live oaks and deciduous growth of all kinds; oak woodlands, streamside cottonwoods, forest edges, and oak-juniper woodlands.

Nesting: 5–8 white eggs, with brown spotting, in tree cavities, fence-post holes, or crevices of old buildings. The cavity nest is composed of grasses, fur, and some feathers.

Range: From southern Oregon, northern Nevada, Utah, and southwestern Wyoming, east to Oklahoma and south to Baja California, Arizona, southern New Mexico, and western Texas.

Whereas chickadees gather into winter flocks, the related Plain Titmouse is usually found singly or in pairs. This bird is conspicuous, for it calls often as it feeds among juniper and elderberry bushes or high in the spring growth of freshly sprouted oaks. It also frequents gardens in suburbs of western towns adjacent to its native habitat.

489 Bridled Titmouse
(*Parus wollweberi*)
Titmice (Paridae)

Description: 4½–5" (11–13 cm). Warbler-sized. Gray above, whitish below with *black crest and "bridle" joining eye-line and chin marking.*

Voice: Its many vocalizations are similar to calls of other chickadees and titmice, but are more rapid and on a somewhat higher pitch. The song is a 2-syllable phrase, resembling that of the Plain Titmouse, repeated several times. One of its common calls is a variant of the familiar *chick-a-dee.*

Habitat: Deciduous and mixed woods in the mountains.

Nesting: 5–7 white eggs in a tree hole.

Range: Highlands of western Mexico, extending into southern Arizona and New Mexico.

Its range overlaps with that of the Mountain Chickadee, but the unique face and crest pattern distinguish it. It accepts nesting holes made or used by other species, and even settles in breeding boxes.

495 Blue-gray Gnatcatcher
(*Polioptila caerulea*)
Old World Warblers (Sylviidae)

Description: 4–5" (10–13 cm). Small, slender bird. *Bluish-gray above, white below; long black tail with white outer tail feathers is* cocked like a wren's. Male's crown and forehead bordered with black. Female less bluish and lacks black markings on head. Narrow white eye-ring and white edging of secondary wing feathers conspicuous in both sexes.

Voice: Call is a thin *speeeee*. Song is a jumble of fussing, warbled notes.

Habitat: Deciduous woodland, streamside thickets, live oaks, pinyon-juniper, chaparral.

Nesting: 4 or 5 pale blue, blotched eggs in a tiny, tightly woven cup; bits of lichen camouflage the outside and the supporting branch.

Range: From northern California east to western and southern Colorado, southern Ontario, and New York south to Central America. Winters in southern United States and Central America.

These gnatcatchers are lively birds, constantly flicking their conspicuous long tails upward while gathering insects from the branches of trees or bushes. Gnatcatchers and kinglets are the North American representatives of the Old World Warbler family.

---

500 Western Bluebird
(*Sialia mexicana*)
Thrushes (Turdidae)

Description: 6–7" (15–18 cm). Long-winged, rather short-tailed. Male has *deep blue hood and upperparts; rusty red breast and crescent mark across upper back;* white belly. Female sooty gray above, with dull blue wings and tail. Juveniles like female but grayer, with speckled underparts.

Voice: Soft calls sound like *phew* and *chuck*. Song is a short, subdued *cheer, cheer-lee, churr.*

Habitat: Open woodland and pasturelands where old trees provide nest sites.

Nesting: 4–6 pale blue eggs in a grass nest

in a tree cavity or woodpecker hole.
Range: From southern half of British Columbia
and western Alberta south to Baja
California, central Mexico; west along
the Rocky Mountains to west Texas.

Females are attracted by the vivid blue
of the male and by the availability of
nesting holes, which are often in short
supply. Once the male secures a nesting
hole he entices the female with a
colorful display that serves to repel
rivals. His red breast, like that of the
Robin, is a signal of aggression toward
other males.

505   **Scrub Jay**
(*Aphelocoma coerulescens*)
Crows (Corvidae)

Description: 11–13″ (28–33 cm). Robin-sized, but
large, strong bill and long tail make it
appear larger. *Head, wings,* and *tail blue*
(conspicuous when it glides after a
long, undulating flight); *back dull brown*
and underparts light gray; *white throat*
offset by incomplete blue necklace.
Voice: Call is a loud, throaty *jayy?* or *jree?* In
flight, a long series of *check check check*
notes.
Habitat: Woodland and chaparral, but does not
breed in low scrub because it needs
watch posts; also inhabits suburban
gardens.
Nesting: 3–5 eggs, spotted on darker, greenish
or reddish base, in a twiggy cup well
hidden in a tree or dense shrub. The
western Scrub Jay is territorial and only
moderately social.
Range: Washington east to Wyoming, south to
Texas, California, and Mexico; also in
Florida.

Like all jays, it may be secretive and
silent around its nest or while perching
in a treetop in early morning but is
frequently noisy and conspicuous. Many

condemn it as a nest robber, although in summer it is mainly insectivorous. These birds also eat acorns and have been described as "uphill planters," counterbalancing the tendency of acorns to bounce downhill. The jays bury many more acorns than they consume and help regenerate oak forests that have been destroyed by fire or drought.

506 Mexican Jay
(*Aphelocoma ultramarina*)
Crows (Corvidae)

Description: 11½–13″ (29–33 cm). Similar to Scrub Jay but larger and more muted, without white markings on throat or above eyes. Dull blue head, rump, wings, and tail; gray back and dusky ear patch.

Voice: Calls are high-pitched and inquisitive: a loud *shrink?* or *wenk?* often repeated.

Habitat: Oak forests and wooded canyons.

Nesting: 4 or 5 green eggs in a twig bowl lined with horsehair low in a tree.

Range: Southern Arizona, New Mexico, and western Texas south into Mexico.

Nesting territories of Mexican Jays are small and adjacent; when a predator approaches, an entire colony moves to the defense, scolding loudly from a safe distance. Acorns are their staple diet, but they also glean insects and rob eggs and young from nests.

Olivaceous Flycatcher
(*Myiarchus tuberculifer*)
Tyrant Flycatchers (Tyrannidae)

Description: 6½–7″ (17–18 cm). Smallest crested flycatcher, with much *brown but little rufous on tail.* Pale olive, brown above, *grayish throat* and breast with very pale yellow belly.

Voice: Common note is a long, mournful
whistle in a minor key, rising, then
falling in pitch. Also a plaintive,
rolling *prree pree prreeerr*.

Habitat: Scrub oak thickets and canyon growth.

Nesting: 4 or 5 creamy white, finely marked
eggs in a tree cavity.

Range: Western Mexico, extending north to
the mountain slopes of southeastern
Arizona and southwestern New Mexico.

Small groups of these flycatchers have
been observed "sunning" on the steep,
bare slope of an arroyo, or dry wash,
with wings and tails spread wide, face
down. Several other species, including
Ground Doves, also indulge in this
activity, which is still not understood.

Buff-breasted Flycatcher
(*Empidonax fulvifrons*)
Tyrant Flycatchers (Tyrannidae)

Description: 4½–5″ (11–13 cm). Olive above with
rich, *buffy underparts, lighter on throat
and belly;* white eye-ring and wing bars.

Voice: Song is a quick *chicky-whew*. Call is a
dull *pit*.

Habitat: Open canyon growth and pine-oak
forests.

Nesting: 3 or 4 creamy white eggs in a well-
camouflaged nest saddled at the base of
a horizontal branch.

Range: A Mexican and Central American
species extending to the southern corner
of Arizona and New Mexico.

This bird characteristically hunts from a
low perch, often launching its pursuit
from the top of weeds. However, it can
also be seen hovering over a pine
branch, picking insects from the
needles.

Deciduous Woods

The West has little of the dense deciduous forest found in southeastern Canada and the eastern United States. The commonest deciduous growth occurs along river bottoms and consists mainly of willow and cottonwood, mixed in the extreme South with sycamore and walnut. In the northern prairie region and Rockies, aspens are the dominant deciduous tree. The northwestern rain forest is replaced, when logged or burnt, by stands of fast-growing alders. North of the treeline, stunted birches dot the tundra. Other deciduous trees such as alder and dogwood grow along the edges of coniferous forests.

Such mixed woods harbor birds of both deciduous and coniferous habitats. Because of their varied nature and extent, the deciduous woods are utilized by many species that are found primarily in other areas.

248 **Whip-poor-will**
(*Caprimulgus vociferus*)
Nightjars (Caprimulgidae)

Description: 9–10" (23–25 cm). Its mixture of
mottled gray, brown, black, and tan
provides it with excellent camouflage
among litter on the forest floor. Male's
blackish throat and breast separated by
white semi-collar; two-thirds of outer
tail feathers white. Female's semi-collar
and outer tail feathers buff-colored.
Tail rounded, no white on wings. Both
sexes have large, dark eyes, small bill,
wide gape with stiff sensory hairs
around it to help catch flying moths.

Voice: A rolling *prrip-poor-rrill!* repeated
tirelessly at dusk and before dawn; first
and last syllables are emphasized. In
flight, a soft *week week.*

Habitat: Forest floor in woodlands; oak or pine
canyons.

Nesting: 2 white, irregularly spotted and
blotched eggs on dead leaves on the
forest floor; no nest.

Range: Deciduous forest areas in the East;
mountains of Arizona, New Mexico,
Mexico, and Central America. Recently
spreading westward, has reached
southern Nevada and California.

Whip-poor-wills, like other night-
flying birds, were once suspected of
witchery. They fly around livestock at
dusk to feed on insects swarming over
the animals. It was believed that they
sucked milk from goats' udders and
caused them to dry up; hence their
family name, Caprimulgidae, from the
Latin *capri* and *mulgus,* meaning goat-
milker. Until recently they were known
as goatsuckers; now the name nightjar
is preferred.

263 Ruffed Grouse
(*Bonasa umbellus*)
Grouse (Tetraonidae)

Description: 16–19″ (41–48 cm). Chicken-sized. Slight crest. Mottled, brownish with buff streaks above, gray-brown cross-barring below. *Fan-shaped tail has contrasting cross-barring* on gray or red base, and broad *black terminal band* emphasized by lighter margins. Male has ruff of erectile black feathers on side of neck. Female is plainer, with smaller ruff and tail.

Voice: The drumming of the male is a hollow-toned, low-pitched accelerating series of beats made with the wings. The voice is used only in close communication, as in the soft murmur of a female with chicks, or a series of sharp notes when alarmed on the ground.

Habitat: Deciduous woodland, and edges within the coniferous forest zone.

Nesting: 9–12 buffy eggs, sometimes spotted, in a sheltered scrape.

Range: From the northern tree limit across North America south to the limit of good coniferous growth: northeastern California, northern Utah and Colorado, and from the Great Lakes forest south along the Appalachian chain.

The male's spring display consists of the "drumming" described above. The female raises the chicks alone. In summer the birds feed on berries and fruits; in winter they take to the tree tops and forage on buds, catkins, and twigs, preferring aspen and poplar.

---

288 Great Horned Owl
(*Bubo virginianus*)
Owls (Strigidae)

Description: 18–25″ (46–64 cm). *Large owl. Ear tufts set wide apart, yellow eyes.* Mottled gray-

brown above with fine dark gray
horizontal barring below.

Voice: A deeply resonant hooting, *hoo, hoo-hoo-hoo, hoo;* also 3 hoots.

Habitat: In all habitats, even deserts, as long as shelter such as woods or cliffs is close.

Nesting: 2 or 3 white eggs in an old nest, such as that of a heron or hawk, in a tree, crevice, or cliff.

Range: Common in all of North America up to the northern tree limit.

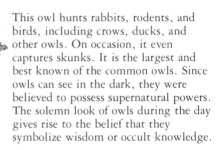

This owl hunts rabbits, rodents, and birds, including crows, ducks, and other owls. On occasion, it even captures skunks. It is the largest and best known of the common owls. Since owls can see in the dark, they were believed to possess supernatural powers. The solemn look of owls during the day gives rise to the belief that they symbolize wisdom or occult knowledge.

289 Long-eared Owl
(*Asio otus*)
Owls (Strigidae)

Description: 13–16″ (33–41 cm). Similar to but smaller than the Great Horned Owl. It lacks the white throat, has *vertical chest markings* rather than horizontal, and its *long, dark ear tufts,* when raised, are much closer together than those on other "eared" owls.

Voice: In spring its hooted *hoooo,* repeated at intervals, and its cat-like calls reveal its presence in woods.

Habitat: Deciduous and mixed woods, conifer groves, near open country, and even sagebrush desert.

Nesting: 3–8 white eggs in a crow, magpie, or hawk nest, which it occupies in early spring before the original nesters start their breeding season.

Range: In temperate areas of North America from Canada to Baja California; also in Eurasia and northern Africa.

This forest owl is strictly nocturnal; during the day it rests near the trunk of a tree, where its camouflage makes it hard to detect. It is sometimes mobbed by other birds, but seldom attacks them. It feeds mainly on rodents, like other owls locating prey more by hearing than sight. It can even catch mice tunneling under snow.

312, 313 Red-shouldered Hawk
(*Buteo lineatus*)
Hawks (Accipitridae)

Description: 17–24″ (43–61 cm). W. 36–48″ (0.9–1.2 m). *Rufous shoulder patch, rust red body and underwing lining* identify adults. Translucent "window" at base of primaries frequently visible. *Heavily banded tail* apparent from both above and below. Immatures have brown streaked, whitish underparts and less apparent red on shoulders.

Voice: A rapid series of slurred whistles uttered in flight: *peeer-peeeer-peeer-peeer*.

Habitat: Prefers wet meadows and bogs, moist woodlands; especially river-bottom woodland across the treeless plains.

Nesting: 2–4 dull white, blotched eggs in a large flat stick nest in a tall woodland tree along a river or other watercourse.

Range: The California lowlands, along the Central Valley and the southern coast to Baja California, form an isolated part of its range. Widespread in the eastern United States and adjacent eastern Mexico.

This hawk seems to have a more restricted hunting area than other *Buteos*. It defends its territory at nesting time with loud calls and conspicuous soaring displays. In fall and winter, when frogs, snakes, and crayfish cannot be obtained easily, its staple food is the meadow mouse. Then it frequents drier areas, mingling with Red-tailed and

other hawks. In some regions such as
Sacramento, California, it tolerates
gardens and suburban areas.

327   Cooper's Hawk
(*Accipiter cooperii*)
Hawks (Accipitridae)

Description: 14–20″ (36–51 cm). Similar to the
Sharp-shinned Hawk, but larger, with
rounded (not square) tail and slower
wingbeat. Male slate blue above, *barred
rusty below,* female larger and brownish-
blue above. Immatures brown above, *streaked
with brown below.*

Voice: A rapid series: *kek kek kek kek kek.*

Habitat: Woodlands, forest edges, river groves,
and even wooded city areas.

Nesting: 3–5 bluish-white eggs; incubated
chiefly by the female. A stick platform
nest, lined with bark; built by the male
with the female's assistance.

Range: Widespread from southern Canada to
northern Mexico; winters as far south as
Costa Rica.

This still is a relatively common bird of
prey in most parts of the West. A fast
and powerful flier, this hawk hunts by
flying low over trees, traveling short
distances at a time, and using the
terrain for concealment. It feeds mainly
on small birds and mammals.

339   Black Hawk
(*Buteogallus anthracinus*)
Hawks (Accipitridae)

Description: 20–23″ (51–58 cm). *Black* with wide
wings and *broad white band across
middle of tail* (narrow terminal band
not easily seen). Cere and legs yellow,
latter visible in flight. When soaring, it
holds its wings flat, shows light spot on
underwing at base of primaries, and

somewhat resembles Black Vulture. Immatures look like a different species: dark brown with tawny barring above, light buff with darker streakings below, strongly banded tail.

Voice: Gives nasal, high-pitched alarm cry.

Habitat: Wooded canyons, river-bottom forests in the United States; varied, semi-open tropical woods farther south.

Nesting: 1–3 white, somewhat spotted eggs in a large stick platform used over and over but each time lined with fresh leafy branches.

Range: From southernmost Utah, Arizona, New Mexico, and Texas south through Central America and northern South America.

These birds are sluggish, sitting for long periods on trees, then gently dropping down on their prey. They feed on crabs, frogs, fish, even birds and mammals. Since there are so few pairs in the United States, birders should not disturb them by venturing too close to the nest.

340 Gray Hawk
(*Buteo nitidus*)
Hawks (Accipitridae)

Description: 16–18″ (41–46 cm). W. 36″ (0.9 m). Small hawk. *Pale gray above with gray-white barring on underparts,* white rump, and *three wide conspicuous black bands on tail.* Immatures have pale striped, buffy underparts and narrowly banded tail.

Voice: A clear downslurred whistle.

Habitat: Deciduous growth along stream beds that have sufficient open space for hunting.

Nesting: 2 or 3 whitish eggs in a small twig nest lined with fresh green branches in a tall tree, such as a cottonwood, when available; otherwise, mesquite.

Range: From southern Arizona and northern

Mexico, as far south as Brazil and Argentina.

Birds of prey living in deciduous woods often line their nests with leafed branches. The male brings in fresh branches even after the nest is finished and throughout the incubation period. Gray Hawks feed mainly on lizards, swooping on them from a perch.

341 Zone-tailed Hawk
(*Buteo albonotatus*)
Hawks (Accipitridae)

Description: 18½–21½" (47–55 cm). W. 48" (1.2 m). *Black Buteo* with same dihedral (i.e., with wings tilted slightly upward) soaring pattern as Turkey Vulture. *Two-toned black-and-gray wings* longer and narrower than in most of *Buteos*. Adult's *tail has white banding below*. Immatures have several narrow light tail bands, wide dark terminal tail band, and small white spotting on black breast.

Voice: Like many other *Buteos*, this species gives loud, downslurred whistles.

Habitat: Arid country with deciduous woods, low scrub or desert mountains.

Nesting: 2 or 3 white eggs, frequently slightly marked, on a rather large platform nest of sticks and green branches in a tall tree or cliff. The nest is enlarged and used year after year.

Range: From central Arizona, southern New Mexico, and western Texas through Central America to South America.

This black long-winged *Buteo* bears a superficial resemblance to the much larger Turkey Vulture, except for the light-banded tail. It may be that this resemblance deceives small birds and other prey who allow it to approach, thinking they have nothing to fear from a "carrion-eater."

361 Chimney Swift
(*Chaetura pelagica*)
Swifts (Apodidae)

Description: 4¾–5½" (12–14 cm). Small, but long, sickle-shaped wings make it seem larger. Short tail hardly visible in flight, so that body appears cigar-shaped. Wings seem to beat alternately or are held stiff while sailing. *Dark, sooty brown* with throat somewhat paler.

Voice: Piercing *chips* or *ticks*.

Habitat: Originally woodland, now mainly cities and towns. Forages everywhere in the open sky.

Nesting: 4 or 5 white eggs in a quarter-cup of twigs, glued with saliva. Formerly nested in tree holes; now builds in chimneys.

Range: Eastern Canada and United States, extending a short distance into the West in Saskatchewan and the Rocky Mountain foothills. Expanding westward in small numbers, it has bred in California. Migrates through eastern Mexico to winter in the Amazon basin.

Larger than the western Vaux's Swift. Chimney Swifts may be observed in the western Great Plains states during migration, from mid-August to late September and again in May.

362, 364 Downy Woodpecker
(*Picoides pubescens*)
Woodpeckers (Picidae)

Description: 6–7" (15–18 cm). A smaller version of the Hairy Woodpecker, with bill proportionately shorter and more slender and with barred outer tail feathers. Black forehead, crown, and bridle across the eyes contrast with *white face, underparts, and central part of back;* wings checkered black-and-white. Male has red patch on nape.

Voice: Call is a soft *pik;* also gives a high, descending rattle or *whinny* series: *ee ee ee ee ee ee ee.*

Habitat: Broken or mixed forest; often found in conifers but feeds and nests chiefly in young deciduous trees. Also frequents orchards, city parks, and suburban areas.

Nesting: 4–7 white eggs in a hole in a dead tree.

Range: Woodlands of Alaska and northern Canada south to southern California, the Texas panhandle, and the Gulf Coast.

A familiar bird in the West, especially in the winter, when many move into the suburbs and feed on suet at birdfeeders. One can then learn to recognize its call and its habit of tapping on branches hardly thicker than itself. As with other woodpeckers, the male is larger than the female and has a longer, stronger bill and chisels deep into wood, whereas the female pries under the bark with her shorter bill. Thus a pair shares the food resources without competing with one another.

370, 371, 372, 373 **Common Flicker**
including "Yellow-shafted Flicker"
and "Red-shafted Flicker"
and "Gilded Flicker"
(*Colaptes auratus*)
Woodpeckers (Picidae)

Description: 12½–14" (32–36 cm). A large woodpecker. *Barred cinnamon-brown back* and *white rump.* Brown head, gray face and neck, red mustache of male separated from boldly black-on-white spotted underparts by *black crescent on breast.* Salmon pink wing and tail linings of western flickers are conspicuous in flight.

Voice: A piercing *keee-ar.* Also *flicka-flicka-flicka,* and a loud prolonged series: *wick wick wick wick wick.*

Habitat: Deciduous or mixed woods, semi-open country, edge or replacement growth in northern conifer belt, saguaros and woods along desert washes.

Nesting: 5–10 white eggs in a hole excavated in a tree, post, or cactus.

Range: Woodlands from Alaska to Mexico and coast to coast, even including deserts of the Southwest.

Common flickers occur in three color variants, the "Red-shafted" of the West; the "Gilded," living in the desert; and the "Yellow-shafted," found east of the Rocky Mountains. The "Yellow-shafted Flicker" has a brilliant golden-yellow underside of wings and tail, a red crescent on the nape, and a black mustache in the male. The "Gilded" has wings and tail like the "Yellow-shafted," red mustache like the "Red-shafted." The "Red-shafted" and "Yellow-shafted" hybridize in the Great Plains. The Ice Ages separated the ancestral flickers and kept them scattered in several refuges for thousands of years. Today these barriers are gone, but the "Gilded" has become adapted to desert and no longer seems to mix with its distant cousins, whereas the two northern populations inhabit the same type of woodland habitat and only the Rocky Mountain chain and the treeless Great Plains keep them somewhat apart. Flickers are important in the woodland community, providing nesting cavities for many hole-nesting birds. They feed on ants and other ground insects, and also, in winter, on berries.

374 **Golden-fronted Woodpecker**
(*Melanerpes aurifrons*)
Woodpeckers (Picidae)

Description: 8½–10½″ (22–27 cm). Smaller than a flicker. *Back and wings have "zebra-backed" barring.* Tail black. White rump and wing patch show in flight. Head and underparts pale buff; some yellow on belly. Yellow tuft of feathers above bill in both sexes; *nape patch is bright orange in male* and yellow-orange in female; male has bright red cap edged with gray. Juveniles lack head patches.

Voice: A rolling *churrrr,* similar to that of the other "zebra-backed" woodpeckers.

Habitat: A great variety, including stream woodlands, mesquite, flood-bed growth, thorn forest.

Nesting: 4–6 white eggs in a cavity excavated in a tree or fence post.

Range: Texas and Oklahoma south through Central America, where it is the most common woodpecker.

The range of this species lies between those of two very similar "zebra-backed" woodpeckers. It hybridizes with the eastern Red-bellied Woodpecker (*Melanerpes carolinus*) in Texas. The Gila Woodpecker of the Sonora Desert is isolated and adapted to the driest conditions. The great climatic upheavals of the last Ice Age probably created the barriers that split the range of their common ancestor.

378, 379 **Yellow-bellied Sapsucker**
including "Red-naped Sapsucker"
and "Red-breasted Sapsucker"
(*Sphyrapicus varius*)
Woodpeckers (Picidae)

Description: 8–9″ (20–23 cm). Smaller than a flicker. Three subspecies, sometimes considered different species, are all characterized by a *long white wing patch, barred back,* and *white rump.* Eastern birds ("Yellow-bellied Sapsucker") have *red forehead and throat* (female's throat is white). Rocky Mountain and Great Basin birds ("Red-naped Sapsucker") have *red nape,* forehead, and throat (female's throat is only partly red). Both these subspecies have *black chest band* separating throat from yellowish belly. Northwest coast and Sierra Nevada birds ("Red-breasted Sapsucker") have *entire head, throat, and breast bright red* with *deep yellow belly.* All immatures dusky brown with light spots above, lighter below, with black-and-white checkered wings and tail.

Voice: A soft, slurred *whee-ur* or *mew.* The display communication of the spring pair is not a drum but a tap in a broken series: *prrrrrrrp, prrp, prp, prp.*

Habitat: Edges of coniferous forest; woodlands, groves of aspen and alder.

Nesting: 4–6 white eggs in a cavity drilled in a tree.

Range: In the West, the "Red-breasted" occupies the coastal forest from the Alaskan panhandle to the California redwoods, the Cascades and Sierra Nevada ranges; the Rocky Mountain areas harbor the "Red-naped;" the "Yellow-bellied" occurs in cottonwood and aspen groves of the prairie provinces. All forms winter from southern United States to Central America.

Sapsuckers feed mainly on insects extracted from bark, thus keeping down the number of boring insects that destroy healthy trees. They enjoy sap and drill holes around a tree trunk in horizontal lines or checkerboard pattern.

395, 404 Rivoli's Hummingbird
(*Eugenes fulgens*)
Hummingbirds (Trochilidae)

Description: 4½–5½" (11–14 cm). Large, long-tailed hummingbird. Male is *deep green above, black below, with iridescent purple forehead and crown* and metallic *green gorget.*

Female olive green above, gray below,
with lightly streaked throat and pearly
gray tips on outer tail feathers.
Immature male heavily flecked with
iridescent green below.

Voice: The high-pitched *teek* note is not as
drawn-out as the *seep* of the Blue-
throated Hummingbird.

Habitat: Canyons, deciduous and pine-clad
slopes, and streamsides.

Nesting: 2 white eggs in a tiny nest of lichen
and plant down on a horizontal limb.

Range: Mountains of southeast Arizona,
southwestern New Mexico, and western
Texas south into Central America. The
northern populations are migratory.

Rivoli's Hummingbird flies more
slowly than the smaller hummers,
sometimes sailing on set wings. It is
more of an insect-gleaner than the other
species, though it takes its share of
nectar from flowers and feeders.

396, 403   **Blue-throated Hummingbird**
(*Lampornis clemenciae*)
Hummingbirds (Trochilidae)

Description: 4½–5″ (11–13 cm). Very large
hummingbird. Male green above,
dusky gray below, with *bright blue gorget.*
Blue-black tail with *broad white corners*
of outer tail feathers. Female closely
resembles female Rivoli's but has much
larger white margins on tail feathers.
Both sexes have thin white stripes
above and below the eyes.

Voice: A loud *seep* uttered in flight as well as
when perching. When perched, the *seep*
note may be uttered at one-second
intervals for long periods.

Habitat: Streamside growth in canyons.

Nesting: 2 white eggs in a large cup nest with
green mosses woven into the outside
wall, fastened to a vertical plant stalk;
occasionally in the shelter of cabins, on
electric wires; usually over or near
water.

Range: Southeastern Arizona, southern New Mexico, and western Texas, where it breeds at the northern fringes of its otherwise all-Mexican range.

Rapid flyers, their wings make an audible humming sound. They take both nectar and insects. Studies in Mexico show that their nests must be sheltered from rain and sun and be near water where flowering vegetation abounds. The Blue-throated returns to such a site year after year.

397 Violet-crowned Hummingbird
(*Amazilia verticalis*)
Hummingbirds (Trochilidae)

Description: 3¾–4½″ (10–11 cm). *Bronze above, white below, including throat;* no gorget. *Crown violet-blue;* bill red with dark tip. Sexes look similar.

Voice: A loud chatter.

Habitat: Canyons, streamside growth.

Nesting: 2 white eggs in a downy, lichen-covered nest on a horizontal branch. A few nests have been found in sycamore trees in Guadalupe Canyon in Arizona and New Mexico.

Range: Western Mexico, extending north to the corner where Arizona and New Mexico meet. Accidental in California.

Although rare in its very limited range in southeastern Arizona, this bird is common in its Mexican range from Sonora south to Colima. It is a conspicuous bird and behaves aggressively toward other hummers.

White-eared Hummingbird
(*Hylocharis leucotis*)
Hummingbirds (Trochilidae)

Description: 3½" (9 cm). Small hummingbird. Both sexes have *long broad white ear-stripe* and *red bill with dark tip.* Male green above and below with purple crown and iridescent blue-green chin; female lacks these and is whitish below with *green spotting and barring on throat and sides.*

Voice: Breeding males utter a long, monotonous clinking *tink-tink-tink.* During the nonbreeding season, the male also sings a low song.

Habitat: Mountain woodlands.

Nesting: 2 white eggs in a moss nest interwoven with needles, lichens, and twigs, in a small tree.

Range: From extreme southeastern Arizona through Mexico and mountainous Central America.

Early in the year males establish individual feeding territories. As the breeding season approaches, several males gather in an area where they will court vigorously. Females with a nest visit these groups and return to their nesting area with a male.

409, 439   Wilson's Warbler
(*Wilsonia pusilla*)
Wood Warblers (Parulidae)

Description: 4½" (11 cm). Male is olive green above with *black cap, underparts yellow.* Female similar but lacks black cap.

Voice: Song is a rapid series of light *chips,* accelerating in tempo and increasing in intensity: *chip chip chip chip chip chip chip.* Call is a soft *timp.*

Habitat: Deciduous shrubbery or thickets; in the Northwest, windfall openings, cuts and burns growing up in shrubs and second-growth alders, poplars, or other trees at the edge of woods; elsewhere, streamside growth and alpine willow-fir thickets in the mountains.

Nesting: 3–6 white, spotted eggs in a leaf-lined rootlet nest in dense vegetation near or on the ground.

Range: From Alaska across Canada to New England in the boreal forest zone; in the West, widespread north of the desert areas. Winters from Mexico to Central America.

It is easy to observe this common warbler because it has little fear of man and because it searches the outside of leafy branches, often catching flying insects on the wing. During early summer, the foraging male utters long bursts of vivid song.

410 Yellow Warbler
(*Dendroica petechia*)
Wood Warblers (Parulidae)

Description: 4½–5¼" (11–13 cm). The only *overall yellow* warbler in North America. Male has chestnut striping on breast and flanks. Female and young have fainter breast streaking or sometimes none at all and look more olive green than yellow.

Voice: 8 or so quick notes with an emphatic ending *sweet-sweet-sweet-sweet-setta-see-see-whew!* proclaim the male as he patrols his newly established territory. Call, a loud downslurred *cheep*. Flight note, as in many wood warblers, a thin buzzy *zeet*.

Habitat: Edges of open mixed deciduous and coniferous woodlands as well as city parks and suburbs. Low, shrubby vegetation of bogs and river edge is preferred.

Nesting: 4 or 5 whitish eggs spotted with brown around the large end, in a down-lined deep cup nest in the crotch of a tree or shrub.

Range: Common from the treeline of Alaska

and Canada south to southern California and the subtropical Florida Keys and from coast to coast. Tropical subspecies live in Mexico, Central America, and northern South America.

Warblers are favorite hosts of cowbirds, and some warbler populations are in danger from such pressure. A cowbird lays only one egg per foster nest, but she may lay eggs in four or five nests in a short time, thus jeopardizing many broods. If the female Yellow Warbler discovers a cowbird parasitizing her nest, she quickly covers the alien egg with a new foundation and lays another clutch. One nest was found to be five layers deep.

---

411   MacGillivray's Warbler
(*Oporornis tolmiei*)
Wood Warblers (Parulidae)

Description: 4¾–5½" (12–14 cm). *Slate gray hood extending from mantle to breast,* where it darkens to black. *Olive green above, yellow below;* female slightly paler. Both sexes have *broken white eye-ring.* In fall, hood lighter, with little or no eye-ring.

Voice: Song, a chanting *tree tree tree tree sweet sweet!* Call is a loud *tik,* sharper than the calls of most other western warblers.

Habitat: Coniferous forest edges, burns, brushy cuts, or second-growth alder thickets and streamside growth.

Nesting: 3–5 white eggs with brown spotting in a grassy cup nest close to the ground in a bush or tall weeds.

Range: From the Pacific coastal forest of southeastern Alaska eastward to the Rocky Mountains and the prairies, and south to the desert. Winters in Mexico and South America.

A common western warbler. Two similarly hooded warblers occur east of

the Rockies, the Connecticut Warbler (*Oporornis agilis*) and the Mourning Warbler (*Oporornis philadelphia*). No doubt these all originated from a common "hooded warbler" forebear during the vicissitudes of the past Ice Age, when during warm interglacials the forests expanded, only to be split again when the cold grip of the glaciers returned.

412 Nashville Warbler
(*Vermivora ruficapilla*)
Wood Warblers (Parulidae)

Description: 4–5" (10–13 cm). Male has *gray head, olive green upperparts, bright yellow chin, throat, and underparts* fading into whitish on belly. Distinctive *white eye-ring.* Chestnut crown patch sometimes visible. Female, immatures, and fall male somewhat duller olive green above, bright yellow below.

Voice: Song is a rapid series of sweet 2-part notes, followed by a short trill of single notes: *see-pit see-pit see-pit see-pit titititi.* Call note is a sharp *plink.*

Habitat: Sparse second growth, burns, edges of deciduous woodland, particularly aspens and cottonwoods; also bogs.

Nesting: 3–5 reddish-brown, speckled eggs in a nest of rootlets, grass, and soft vegetation recessed into the ground, usually on a steep slope.

Range: Southern British Columbia east to western Montana and south through the Cascades and Sierras to southern California, avoiding coastal forests. In the East from southern Manitoba to Newfoundland and south into the northeastern states. Winters in Mexico.

The Rocky Mountains and the prairies form a barrier between the western and eastern races of this species. The two populations show minor differences in color but have similar habits. The

western race was once called the
"Calaveras Warbler."

Colima Warbler
(*Vermivora crissalis*)
Wood Warblers (Parulidae)

Description: 5″ (13 cm). Larger than Virginia's
Warbler and lacks yellow on breast.
Gray above, with chestnut crown patch
and *olive-yellow rump*. *Whitish below*,
with yellow undertail patch. Narrow
eye-ring, no wing bars.

Voice: Like that of Virginia's Warbler, its call
is *plisk*. Song is a short musical trill
ending with two lower notes.

Habitat: Deciduous and mixed montane forest.

Nesting: 4 creamy white, spotted and splashed
eggs in a cup nest built on the ground.

Range: The Chisos Mountains of western Texas
and adjacent Mexico.

This bird has one of the most restricted
ranges of any American bird,
comparable to the similarly local
Kirtland's Warbler (*Dendroica
kirtlandii*), which breeds only in central
Michigan. However, because of its high
mountain home, this warbler is not as
well known. It is a rather slow-moving
warbler that feeds in the low canopy of
bushes or scrub oaks, although the male
sings his territorial song from a high
perch.

413 Yellow-breasted Chat
(*Icteria virens*)
Wood Warblers (Parulidae)

Description: 6½–7½″ (16–19 cm). The largest
warbler, size of a large sparrow. Olive-
brown above; gray head with *conspicuous
white spectacles* bordering eye and black
eye patch. Bright *yellow throat and
breast*, white belly. Stout bill and

relatively long tail. Sexes look similar.

Voice: Song is a disjointed series of loud clucks, rattles, and repeated whistles, often given from a conspicuous perch or on a short flight. Sings its harsh, nonmusical, thrasher-like song day and night. Call is a short *airr*.

Habitat: Streamside willow thickets, wet meadows with tall shrubs.

Nesting: 3–5 white, spotted eggs in a grass cup nest, low in a bush or thicket.

Range: Coast to coast, from southern Canada to northern Mexico. Winters from Mexico to Panama.

The Chat is an atypical wood warbler. Its large size and bill, long tail, and distinctive display flight (hovering with slow, deep-flapping wings and dangling feet) make it seem like one of the Mimidae family—mockingbirds and thrashers. Since it prefers brushy tangles and is relatively shy, it is more often heard than seen.

418, 431 Lawrence's Goldfinch
(*Carduelis lawrencei*)
Finches (Fringillidae)

Description: 4–4½" (10–11 cm). Male has *black cap* and throat; pale pink bill; *gray nape, cheek,* and *mantle; yellow* breast, lower back, and rump; white undersides and belly. Female lacks black facial markings. Both sexes have dark wings and tail with bright yellow wing bars. In winter, the blacks and yellows are paler. Juveniles are streaked buffy or light brownish on back.

Voice: Song, typical of goldfinches, is a hurried jumble of melodious and scratchy notes, often incorporating both its own call notes and those of other species. Flight note, often revealing its presence high overhead, is a high *tin-kle,* the first note higher. Also *per-kloony.*

Habitat: Dry grassy slopes with weed patches,

chaparral, and open woodlands.

Nesting: 4 or 5 bluish-white eggs in a tightly woven cup nest in a low tree or bush.

Range: Central and southern California, west of the Sierra Nevada and south into Baja California. Winters south to western Texas and northern Mexico.

Goldfinches are late nesters, waiting until plants and weeds have grown, bloomed, and gone to seed so the soft fresh seeds can be fed to the young. Lawrence's nests late in May. It breeds erratically; one year many may be found in an area, the next, when the seed crop fails, few may be seen. After breeding, they feed in flocks on the abundant chamise chaparral. They appear even in the driest washes and slopes, as long as they have access to water.

---

420 Tropical Kingbird
(*Tyrannus melancholicus*)
Tyrant Flycatchers (Tyrannidae)

Description: 8–9½″ (20–24 cm). Resembles the Western Kingbird. Gray head, olive back, and *brown notched tail with no white*. White throat and *bright yellow upper breast, belly, and undertail coverts.*

Voice: The call, an insect-like sputtering trill, does not carry far. Eastern Mexican birds (north to southern Texas) give a *chi-queer* call.

Habitat: Woodland borders, savannas, riverside groves.

Nesting: 3–5 buff, spotted eggs in a cup nest on a horizontal branch.

Range: From southern Arizona and southern Texas through the tropical Americas. Stragglers are often found along the Pacific Coast in fall, and sometimes north to British Columbia.

This species is one of a group of Mexican birds that make a post-breeding reverse migration in the late summer and fall northward along the Pacific Coast. Because of its similarity to the Western and Cassin's kingbirds, its presence was overlooked until recently.

Thick-billed Kingbird
(*Tyrannus crassirostris*)
Tyrant Flycatchers (Tyrannidae)

Description: 9" (23 cm). *Brownish above* with darker head; tail *uniformly gray-brown. Throat and breast whitish* with pale yellow tinge on lower belly. Large bill and crest give it "bull-headed" appearance.

Voice: Loud *kiterreer* and high-pitched *bur-ree.* Said to be quite noisy.

Habitat: Streamside growth, sycamore canyons.

Nesting: 3 or 4 white eggs spotted with brown in a cup of twigs and weed stems in a sycamore or cottonwood.

Range: Mexico. Extremely local in southeastern Arizona and adjacent New Mexico; accidental in Pacific coastal states.

Another of the Mexican birds that cross the United States border and make southeastern Arizona fascinating for birders. These kingbirds perch high in trees and prey on flying insects. They react to predators with loud cries, calls, and attacks.

Sulphur-bellied Flycatcher
(*Myiodynastes luteiventris*)
Tyrant Flycatchers (Tyrannidae)

Description: 7½–8½" (19–22 cm). A heavily streaked large flycatcher. Upperparts buff-brown with brown streaks; *underparts yellow with blackish streaks. Dark line across eye, another like a mustache. Tail and rump rufous.*

Voice: Loud, shrill *peet-chee* calls, sounding like squeaking wagon wheels, are uttered by

single bird or a pair in duet. Male has
soft *tre-le-re-re* song.

Habitat: Wooded canyons; prefers sycamores.

Nesting: 3–5 white or buff eggs, with spots and
blotches, in a nest in a tree hole.

Range: Southeastern Arizona to Costa Rica.
Accidental in Texas and California.

These loud, vividly marked birds are
easily detected when they sally forth
from treetop perches in pursuit of flying
prey, but when sitting still they are
well camouflaged. Like the closely
related kingbirds, they have a brightly
colored crest but it is hidden among
crown feathers.

433, 449, 455 **Summer Tanager**
(*Piranga rubra*)
Tanagers (Thraupidae)

Description: 7½–7¾″ (19–20 cm). Male *rose red;*
yellowish bill. Female olive-yellow
above and orange-yellow below, light
yellowish bill; lighter yellow wing
lining visible in flight. Juvenile males
may have irregular patches of red and
yellow plumage.

Voice: The male's Robin-like song is a series of
rising and falling whistles with a
slightly burry quality: *cheerily, weechew, wee-cher, cheer, cheerily, weechew.*
Call is a quick *chicky tuck* or *chicky-
tucky-tuck.*

Habitat: Cottonwood and willow thickets along
washes and streams.

Nesting: 3 or 4 pale blue-green, brown-blotched
eggs in a shallow cup nest on a
horizontal branch of a tree.

Range: In the Southwest, from the Colorado
River Valley in California and Arizona
across the southern tier of states; more
widespread in the Midwest and the
South. Winters in Central America.

Tanagers eat insects and small fruits
obtained from the canopy of trees,

where they spend most of their time. In this species the adult males remain red all year.

436, 446 **Northern Oriole
including "Baltimore Oriole"
and "Bullock's Oriole"**
(*Icterus galbula*)
Orioles (Icteridae)

Description: 7–8½" (18–22 cm). Includes the eastern "Baltimore Oriole" and the western "Bullock's Oriole." Male Bullock's is *orange-yellow with black crown, nape, and mantle;* narrow black eye-stripe and *narrow black bib.* Wings have *broad white patch* and white edges on flight feathers. Central tail feathers and tips of outer tail feathers are black. Female unstreaked olive-gray above with yellow throat and chest and white belly. Male Baltimore has solid-black head, throat, and mantle, lacks white wing patch, and color pattern of outer tail feathers is reversed. Female has faintly streaked back and brighter orange underparts.

Voice: The western form, Bullock's, gives a loud series of whistles: *chuk chucky wheew wheew wheew.* Call is a rolling chatter.

Habitat: Woodland and savannas, streamside growth, farms and ranches, oak woods, city parks and suburbs with tall shade trees.

Nesting: 3–6 whitish eggs, with scrawled markings, in a finely woven basket often overhanging a stream or road.

Range: Across wooded areas of southern Canada and the United States south into Mexico. Also Great Plains (see below). Winters in Central America.

Despite marked differences in coloration of the males, the Bullock's and Baltimore orioles interbreed freely. Since the once treeless prairies have been broken with towns and other settlements, Baltimore Orioles have spread westward, and Bullock's eastward, into areas formerly occupied by neither. They hybridize freely along rivers and in plantings on the Great Plains. For this reason they are considered one species, the Northern Oriole.

438, 441 **American Redstart**
(Setophaga ruticilla)
Wood Warblers (Parulidae)

Description: 4½–5¾" (11–15 cm). Male *black,* with white belly and *orange patches on outer tail feathers,* wings, and sides. Female is gray above, white below, with yellow tail, wing, and side patches. Immature male resembles female, with faint black markings and variable yellow-orange patches.

Voice: Song, a thin high-pitched series of notes often slurred at the end. Variable. Call, a thin, slurred *tseep.*

Habitat: Open deciduous woods, streamside growth with some tall trees.

Nesting: 3–5 white, creamy, or bluish, spotted eggs in a well-constructed twiggy cup nest in an upright crotch, in a tall shrub or deciduous tree.

Range: Basically an eastern bird, but occurs in openings in the boreal forest zone of Canada almost to the Pacific Coast, and in adjacent western states south to Utah and Colorado. Winters from Mexico to northern South America.

Its flashy color and constant movement while frequently drooping its wings and fanning its tail to expose its bright signal patches make this flycatching warbler unmistakable.

443, 582 Black-headed Grosbeak
(*Pheucticus melanocephalus*)
Finches (Fringillidae)

Description: 6½–7¾" (17–20 cm). *Plump finch.*
Male has *black head,* large pale bill,
rusty orange collar, breast, sides, and
rump, yellow belly and wing linings.
*Black-and-white-patterned wing and tail
prominent in flight.* Female and yearling
male are buff with fine black streaking
on crown, back, and undersides.
Prominent black-and-white face pattern
and sparsely streaked buffy breast
distinguish it from other female grosbeaks.

Voice: Song, delivered from a high perch and
occasionally in flight, is a rapid,
melodious series of rising and falling
whistles interspersed with low *whirr*
notes. Call is a sharp *eek!* Young birds
give a complaining *whee-oh.*

Habitat: Dense woods along rivers, edges of
second-growth deciduous woods, stands
of tall oaks, mountain forest edges;
orchards and gardens.

Nesting: 3–5 pale blue, spotted eggs in a loose
shallow nest in a tree fork, tall shrub,
or crown of a sapling.

Range: From southern British Columbia and
Saskatchewan south to its wintering
grounds in western Mexico.

The Black-headed hybridizes with its
eastern counterpart, the Rose-breasted
Grosbeak (*Pheucticus ludovicianus*), along
their mutual boundary. This situation
arose when the treeless prairies, which
once formed a barrier between the two
species, became dotted with towns and
homesteads, providing suitable habitats
for both species. The Black-headed
Grosbeak is a rather still and secretive
bird throughout the summer.

448, 467   **Cardinal**
(*Cardinalis cardinalis*)
Finches (Fringillidae)

Description: 7½–9" (19–23 cm). Male *brilliant red,*
crested, with black face and throat
framing conical red bill; female olive-
buff with some red showing on crest,
wings and tail. Immatures drab buff.

Voice: Whistles a loud, melodious *cheer, cheer,
cheer,* followed by a rapid *woight-woight-
woight-woight.* Calls are soft *tsip* and *pink*
notes.

Habitat: Gardens, streamside thickets, mesquite
patches, mixed woodland margins.

Nesting: 3 or 4 pale green eggs, with dark spots,
in a loosely constructed cup nest low in
shrubs or thickets.

Range: From the Colorado River Valley of
California through southern Arizona to
Baja California and Mexico. Introduced
in the Hawaiian Islands and around Los
Angeles. Widespread in the eastern
United States.

Feeding mainly on the ground in the
open and nesting in thickets, it is well
suited to a garden area. Nonmigratory,
it stays around bird feeders even in the
snowy winters of southern Canada and
the northeastern states, but it does best
where winters are milder.

457   **Coppery-tailed Trogon**
(*Trogon elegans*)
Trogons (Trogonidae)

Description: 11–12" (28–30 cm). Robin-sized.
Unmistakable combination of stout,
hooked yellow bill, *upright posture,* and
*long, square-cut tail. Male glossy, dark
emerald-green on upperparts,* head, and
upper breast; white breast band; *crimson
belly* and undertail coverts. *Copper-red
tail* has black terminal band, but
viewed from below it is gray with broad
white bars. Female plain brown where

male is green, with white patch on cheek; pink where male is crimson, with white and light coffee bands on breast.

Voice: The calls, described as *ko-ah ko-ah ko-ah* and *kum! kum! kum!*, carry quite far but are hard to locate even when the bird sits close by, because it usually stays in the middle level of the forest canopy.

Habitat: Thick deciduous mountain growth; sycamore canyons.

Nesting: 3 or 4 white eggs in a woodpecker hole, termite nest, or other cavity; no nest.

Range: From southeastern Arizona to Central America.

This beautiful trogon is related to the bird of the Maya emperor-gods, the Quetzal. Finding it is a prime objective of birders since its range barely extends into the United States. Trogons are insectivorous, but their diet also includes small fruits.

477 Gray Catbird
"Catbird"
(*Dumetella carolinensis*)
Mockingbirds (Mimidae)

Description: 8–9¼" (20–24 cm). Towhee-sized. *Slate gray with black cap* and chestnut patch under tail.

Voice: Mewing calls, hence its name. Its pleasant loud song incorporates several mewing notes and some mimicry. Phrases not repeated.

Habitat: Deciduous thickets, forest edges, underbrush of stream borders.

Nesting: 3–5 blue-green eggs in a cup lined with twigs and fine roots, hidden in a low bush.

Range: Though uncommon, it reaches the Pacific in the Puget Sound lowlands of British Columbia and Washington; thence southeastward to eastern Arizona. Much commoner east of the Rockies to the Atlantic Coast.

This bird is often seen in suburban gardens. It forages mainly on the ground, gleaning insects from litter and low bushes, and eating fallen berries during late summer and fall. It does not uncover litter with its feet like a finch but pokes with its bill, turning leaves and twigs to find the food underneath. Formerly called "Catbird."

485 **Bushtit**
including "Common Bushtit"
and "Black-eared Bushtit"
(*Psaltriparus minimus*)
Titmice (Paridae)

Description: 3¾–4" (10 cm). Gray above with light underparts, small bill, and relatively long tail. Pacific Coast birds have brown crown, pale ear patch; Rocky Mountain birds have gray crown, brown ear patch. Birds in mountains near Mexican border with black ear patch formerly called "Black-eared Bushtit."

Voice: Contact calls are light *tsip* and *pit* notes, constantly uttered. Alarm call, warning of an approaching predator, is a high trill.

Habitat: Deciduous growth, usually streamside. In the coastal forest, it lives in second-growth alder thickets, or edges of coniferous forest composed of maple, dogwood, and birch; also in oak woodland, chaparral, and juniper brush.

Nesting: 5–15 white eggs in a hanging gourd-shaped nest with a side entrance near the top, made of soft plant wool and lichens, suspended in a bush or tree. Family flocks remain together until spring mating season.

Range: In the West, from extreme southwestern British Columbia down the Pacific states to southern Baja California; in the Southwest, from the southern Rockies (extending south to Sonora) east to Oklahoma.

Bushtits flock in small bands, flitting nervously through trees and bushes, hanging, prying, picking, and gleaning, and keeping contact through a constant banter of soft chirps. They pervade a small area, then vanish, and reappear a couple of hundred yards away.

---

487 Black-capped Chickadee
(*Parus atricapillus*)
Titmice (Paridae)

Description: 4¾–5¾" (12–15 cm). *Black throat patch and cap,* white face. *Gray above,* creamy below, with *buff flanks.*

Voice: The rapid, nasal *chickadee-dee-dee* call instantly identifies it. The spring song of the male is a slow, melancholic two-toned *fee-beee,* the *beee* at a lower pitch.

Habitat: Deciduous woods and edges of coniferous forests within the range of the boreal forest.

Nesting: 4–7 white eggs, lightly spotted with rust-colored dots, in a nest in a tree hole.

Range: Found across North America, it has a close relative in the Old World. In the West it breeds south to northern California, northern Nevada, southern Utah, and New Mexico.

These birds are constantly active, hopping, clinging, and hanging from twigs and branches, often near the ground. Black-capped Chickadees usually prepare their own nesting hole in soft, rotting tree stumps. Enticing them into breeding boxes is difficult unless the boxes are filled with sawdust, which deceives the chickadees; they carry the sawdust out piece by piece and accept the box for nesting.

Gray-headed Chickadee
(*Parus cinctus*)
Titmice (Paridae)

Description: 5–5½" (13–14 cm). Plumper than the
Black-capped Chickadee and larger than
the Boreal Chickadee. *Large cap and
mantle gray-brown; black triangular throat
patch;* light underparts with *pale buff
flanks.*

Voice: Hoarser, shorter *chickadee-dee* than the
call of the Blackcap; often only the *dee-
dee* is heard.

Habitat: Aspen, spruce, willow, and sometimes
coniferous thickets, near the northern
or altitudinal tree line.

Nesting: 6–9 white, finely spotted eggs, in a
nest of moss and hair, in a tree hole or
rotten stump.

Range: From Lapland in the north of Europe
across the forest-tundra to Alaska and
into the northwestern Canadian Arctic.

The similar Gray-headed and Boreal
chickadees probably evolved into
separate species during the later stages
of the Ice Age, the former remaining in
northern Eurasia, the latter in the
boreal forests of North America. Then,
quite recently, the Gray-headed
Chickadee seems to have crossed the
Bering Strait and is now found in the
western North American Arctic.

493 Rose-throated Becard
(*Platypsaris aglaiae*)
Cotingas (Cotingidae)

Description: 6" (15 cm). Resembles a flycatcher with
its relatively *large head and thick bill.*
Male dark gray above with pearly gray
underparts and *rosy throat.* Female and
juveniles have dark, dusky cap, are
reddish-brown above, with buffy
underparts and buff collar that encircles
neck.

Voice: Call is a thin, squeaky *speee-er.*

Habitat: Wooded canyons, river groves with deciduous growth.

Nesting: 4–6 white, delicately speckled eggs in a large, loosely knit, hanging ball suspended from the end of a branch of a forest tree, often a sycamore.

Range: From mountains of southeastern Arizona and adjacent areas and the lower Rio Grande Valley of Texas south to Costa Rica.

It is the only North American member of the cotingas, a large tropical family, which varies greatly in coloration, behavior, and nesting patterns. This bird habitually sits quietly for a long time on a terminal twig in the lower canopy, then darts out after flying insects. It also eats berries.

498, 550 Blue Grosbeak
(*Guiraca caerulea*)
Finches (Fringillidae)

Description: 6–7½″ (15–19 cm). Smaller than other American grosbeaks but with same large conical bill. Male *dark blue with two rusty wing bars;* female and juveniles tan with lighter buff underparts and faintly blue-tinged primaries and rump and rust-colored wing bars.

Voice: The male's song is a simple warble, rising and falling in pitch and lasting from two to five seconds. Call is a sharp *pink.*

Habitat: Streamside woodlands with much open area; marshy meadows with tall vegetation and hedgerows; overgrown fields.

Nesting: 3 or 4 pale bluish eggs in a loose twiggy cup in a low shrub or tree.

Range: Breeds from California, southern Colorado, and South Dakota, east to New Jersey, and south to Costa Rica. Winters from northern Mexico to Panama.

After breeding, small flocks feed
together or mix with other seed-eating
finches and sparrows. They also search
out insects, especially grasshoppers,
that live in the grassy vegetation of
open fields.

501 Lazuli Bunting
(*Passerina amoena*)
Finches (Fringillidae)

Description: 5–5½" (13–14 cm). Male has *bright
turquoise hood, back, rump; cinnamon
breast and sides; white belly.* Wings dark
with two *white wing* bars. Female is
light brown above, unstreaked buffy
below with paler throat and belly; blue
tinge on primaries, rump, and tail;
light wing bars.

Voice: The territorial male sings a typical finch
song: a sequence of 10–12 beats,
beginning at a high pitch and falling
toward the end, with some of the beats
repeated, such as *sweet-sweet chew-chew
seet chew.* Where it overlaps with the
Indigo Bunting, the songs are mixed,
the young males incorporating phrases
of both songs. Call is a soft *chip.* In
flight, a dry buzz.

Habitat: Deciduous brushland and edges,
clearings in woods, chaparral,
streamsides.

Nesting: 3 or 4 pale bluish-white eggs in a
neatly woven cup nest low in a bush.

Range: Southern British Columbia to North
Dakota south to Oklahoma and
northern Baja California. Winters
in extreme southern Arizona and in
Mexico.

The Lazuli hybridizes with its eastern
counterpart, the Indigo Bunting
(*Passerina cyanea*), in the Great Plains,
where their ranges overalp. A diligent
songster, the male patrols the perimeter
of his territory, spending much time on
his song perches.

Arctic Warbler
(*Phylloscopus borealis*)
Old World Warblers (Sylviidae)

Description: 4¾" (12 cm). Medium-sized warbler. *Olive green* above with dark line through eye and light *greenish-yellow eyebrow-stripe*. Whitish throat and belly; sides olive-gray; indistinct single wing bar. Pale legs.

Voice: A quick trill, introduced by a *zick* or *zick-zick zick*. The call is also *zick* or *zirrup*.

Habitat: Birch woods, willow thickets.

Nesting: 5–7 white, pink-speckled eggs in a domed cup nest in grass on the ground.

Range: From Norway to Siberia, and in western Alaska, whence it migrates southwest through the Asian mainland, from which its ancestors came after the last glacial period.

This bird is the only North American pioneer from a large genus of similarly colored Old World warblers. It most resembles the Tennessee Warbler, whose range it does not overlap.

508 Bell's Vireo
(*Vireo bellii*)
Vireos (Vireonidae)

Description: 4¼–5" (11–13 cm). *Small, olive-gray vireo*. Light underparts with pale buffy yellow sides. Indistinct white eye-ring and narrow wing bars. Very nondescript.

Voice: Easily identified by its song, a rapid series of coarse *chips,* increases in tempo and intensity toward a rapid climax which is alternately slurred upward (as if asking a question) and downward (as if answering it).

Habitat: Deciduous thickets along streams, ravines, and forest edges; in mesquite in the Southwest.

Nesting: 3–5 white, brown-spotted eggs in a

hanging cup suspended from a low tree.

Range: Breeds in the southern coastal areas of California, along the southwestern states, skirting the open prairies, north to Colorado, eastward to Indiana; south through Mexico. Winters in Mexico.

Incubating Bell's Vireos, like other vireos, are so fearless around their well-camouflaged nests that an observer may photograph them from a few feet away. Their strong, somewhat curved beak, with a slight hook at the end, like a miniature of a shrike's beak, reminds us that these birds, however gentle they seem, are determined predators. They feed on caterpillars, aphids, various larvae, and spiders.

---

511 Orange-crowned Warbler
(*Vermivora celata*)
Wood Warblers (Parulidae)

Description: 4½–5½″ (11–14 cm). *Olive green above* with orange crown feathers, which usually remain hidden. Olive-yellow underparts with very faint breast streaking. *No eye-ring or wing bars.*

Voice: Song is a simple trill going up or down the scale toward the end. Call is a sharp *stick.*

Habitat: Forest edges, especially in low deciduous growth, burns, clearings, and thickets. In migration often seen in riverside willows and in scrub oak chaparral.

Nesting: 4–6 white eggs, with reddish or lavender spots often concentrated around the large end, in a rather large nest of grass and other plant fibers, lined with fur or feathers, usually on the ground or in a low shrub.

Range: Breeds from Alaska east to Labrador and Quebec, and south to Baja California, Arizona, and New Mexico.

Winters from the southern United
States to Central America.

The Orange-crowned Warbler is one of
the commonest western warblers. Its
very lack of conspicuous field marks is
an aid to its identification. Like other
birds with concealed crown patches,
this warbler displays the crown only
during courtship or when alarmed.

514 Warbling Vireo
(*Vireo gilvus*)
Vireos (Vireonidae)

Description: 4½–5½" (11–14 cm). Small,
inconspicuous vireo. Olive-gray above,
lighter below; *white eye-stripe; no wing
bars.*

Voice: A long, variable, languid warble
similar to that of the Purple Finch. Call
note is a soft *vit.*

Habitat: Deciduous and mixed woods, from
mature stands to low thickets.

Nesting: 3–5 dull white, heavily spotted eggs in
a suspended cup nest woven around a
forked branch of a tree. As with all
vireos, both parents share nest-building
and caring for the young.

Range: Throughout wooded North America
from Canada to Mexico and Central
America. Winters in Mexico and
Central America.

Since this bird is common, its song is
part of our image of the spring and
early-summer woods. It is often heard
in cities and towns with wooded gardens
or park-like surroundings. The
unrelated Garden Warbler (*Sylvia borin*)
of Europe is found in the same habitat
as the Warbling Vireo and has evolved
an almost identical song.

515 **Red-eyed Vireo**
(*Vireo olivaceus*)
Vireos (Vireonidae)

Description: 5½–6½" (14–17 cm). A large vireo.
Greenish above and white below with
eyes red in adults, brown in immatures.
Gray crown, with white eyebrow-stripe,
accentuated by black bordering lines. No
wing bars. Moderately heavy bill with
slightly curved upper mandible.

Voice: A tireless singer on its breeding
grounds. Song consists of short phrases,
loud and melodious, uttered from high
in the canopy. One interpretation is *See*
me? Here I am! Up here. See? Vireo! Call,
a nasal *chway.*

Habitat: Wherever deciduous trees grow; in
second-growth woods along streams and
rivers; parks and other shade tree
habitats.

Nesting: 3 or 4 whitish eggs lightly spotted with
dark brown; in a small, well-woven
nest suspended from a fork in a
deciduous tree.

Range: Common in all Canadian provinces and
in parts of Washington, Idaho,
Montana, and the eastern Rocky
Mountain states, eastward to the
Atlantic Coast and south to the Gulf
Coast.

The Red-eyed Vireo may become a
fierce fighter around its nest and can
intimidate even the large Pileated
Woodpecker. Its horizontal perching
stance and slow movement through the
understory of deciduous woods make it
an easy bird to study.

516 **Solitary Vireo**
(*Vireo solitarius*)
Vireos (Vireonidae)

Description: 5–6" (13–15 cm). Gray crown, olive
green back, *white throat and underparts.*
Two broad *white wing bars and large*

white spectacles. The olive-backed birds of the Pacific states have yellowish flanks; those in the Rocky Mountains are gray-backed with no yellowish tinge below.

Voice: Loud, rich, slurred notes with pauses between notes usually longer than the duration of the notes themselves: *chu-wee, cheereo, bzurrp, chuweer.* Scolding call is a harsh *chv chv chv·chv.*

Habitat: Deciduous or mixed woodland, second growth or streamside groves in the West; junipers and yellow pine stands in the southern Rockies.

Nesting: 3–5 creamy white, spotted eggs in a nest of grasses and long fibers hung from a prong near the end of a limb low in a tree or bush (conifer where available). The nest basket is composed of grasses and long fibers woven around the branch. A marvel of avian architecture, it has most of its strongest fibers at the point of greatest stress. The outside is camouflaged with bark chips, leaves, catkins, and lichens; the inside is lined with soft material.

Range: Widespread in wooded areas of the West; also in most parts of the East. Winters in Mexico and Central America, where breeding populations are also found.

The song of most vireos consists of a variety of staccato notes, the basic theme being *vi-rio, vi-reii, vi-reyo,* with the accent on the second syllable. Those who named the genus in 1807 heard in the song the Latin word *vireo,* meaning "I am green"—as are most species of these foliage-inhabiting birds.

518 **Willow Flycatcher**
"Traill's Flycatcher"
(*Empidonax traillii*)
Tyrant Flycatchers (Tyrannidae)

Description: 5¼–6¾″ (13–17 cm). *Olive-brown above, darkest on head, light throat* and belly with pale olive dusting across breast. Pale eye-ring. Dusky wing has two whitish bars.

Voice: *Weep a dee ar* or *fitz-bew*, uttered explosively. Call is a sharp *pwit*.

Habitat: Willow or alder thickets along streams, bogs, muskeg; also edges of mountain meadows in the southern parts of its range.

Nesting: 3 or 4 white eggs, usually spotted with brown, in a neat but loosely woven cup nest in an upright crotch of a low shrub.

Range: Breeds from southern British Columbia east through Alberta, North Dakota, and western New York to Maine, and south to California, Arkansas, and Virginia.

The seven western species of the genus *Empidonax* are so similar in appearance that only an expert can tell them apart by sight alone. During the breeding season, each species lives in its characteristic habitat; but during their journey north we may encounter migrants of different species resting in a habitat where they are not usually found. Thus, the only sure way to identify the breeding male is by the voice, which is different in each species. In other seasons when the male does not sing, all that can readily be told is that they are Empidonaces. This bird was formerly called "Traill's Flycatcher."

519 Alder Flycatcher
"Traill's Flycatcher"
(*Empidonax alnorum*)
Tyrant Flycatchers (Tyrannidae)

Description: 5¼–6" (13–15 cm). *Olive-brown above, whitish throat,* light undersides, two light wing bars, light eye-ring. Alder and Willow flycatchers are so similar that they were formerly considered one species, "Traill's Flycatcher."

Voice: Song is a monotonous 3-syllable *fee-bee-o.* Call is a short, sharp *whit* or *wee-o.* The Willow has a less musical *fitz-bew.*

Habitat: Alder and willow thickets along streams, second-growth alder woods, brush-filled clearings, aspens, bogs.

Nesting: 3 or 4 white eggs, with fine brown spots, in an untidy cup of rootlets lined with horsehair and fine fibers, set in an upright fork of a tree or bush.

Range: Breeds from Alaska, Manitoba, and Quebec south to British Columbia, Minnesota, Ohio, and New York.

These birds hunt in the airspace below the canopy of tall alders in a swamp or creek bottom. They sit erect on a twig, then dart out after flying insects. The Alder came to be considered distinct from the Willow when studies revealed that the song patterns and breeding habits of these species differed. In the fall, when they do not sing, they are indistinguishable and are called by the former name of both, "Traill's Flycatcher."

Beardless Flycatcher
(*Camptostoma imberbe*)
Tyrant Flycatchers (Tyrannidae)

Description: 4–4½" (10–11 cm). *Smallest flycatcher;* warbler-sized. Grayish-olive above, pale gray below, *pale brownish wing bars.*

Voice: Call is *pee-ut* or *pee-yerp*. Particularly diagnostic is a series of 3–5 clear but faint whistles: *see-see-see-see-see.*

Habitat: Deciduous groves, mesquite, streamside stands.

Nesting: 2 or 3 white, finely spotted eggs in a domed nest in a protected spot on a tree, such as in a mistletoe tangle.

Range: From southern Arizona, New Mexico, and Texas through most of Mexico and Central America.

This very small bird acts more like a vireo or a Verdin than a typical flycatcher; it moves through the foliage gleaning insects rather than sallying out to capture flying insects. Because it is small, nondescript, and inhabits thickets it is most often located by its distinctive shrill call.

522, 525   Painted Bunting
(*Passerina ciris*)
Finches (Fringillidae)

Description: 5–5½" (13–14 cm). Male is perhaps most colorful North American bird. *Indigo-blue head, chartreuse-green mantle, bright red underparts and rump;* dusky wing and tail. Female is bright lime green above, yellower lemon green below. Yearling males resemble females.

Voice: A lively warbling whistle composed of single and double phrases and trills.

Habitat: Brushy field borders, clearings, stream edges.

Nesting: 3 or 4 grayish-white, spotted eggs in a woven cup nest lined with fine grass or hair, in the low shelter of bushes.

Range: Breeds from New Mexico and Oklahoma east to Missouri and North Carolina, and south to Mexico. Winters from the Gulf states through Central America.

Though the Painted Bunting's song is not particularly musical, males used to be favorite cagebirds because of their beautiful coloration; they are still sold in Mexico. The male sings all year round except during late summer, when it molts.

---

526 Bewick's Wren
(*Thryomanes bewickii*)
Wrens (Troglodytidae)

Description: 5–5½" (13–14 cm). Slightly larger than House Wren. Plain, unpatterned *warm brown* above, *white or grayish-white below,* with distinct *long white eyebrow-stripe.* When tail is fanned, *white outer tips of tail feathers* are conspicuous, as is its unique slow flicking of tail sideways.

Voice: The loud, cheerful song usually begins with a soft buzz, as if the bird is inhaling, followed by a trill and a series of slurred notes. As in many birds, its singing perches are often higher than its foraging areas. Scold notes include a harsh *vit vit vit* and a harsh, drawn-out buzzing note.

Habitat: On or near the ground in a brush-covered, partly open area, including the edge of deciduous forest, coniferous woods with underbrush, chaparral, and pinyon-juniper woodland.

Nesting: 4–7 white or pinkish, finely speckled eggs in a down-lined nest in a hole, cavity, or breeding box, much like the House Wren.

Range: Locally from British Columbia east to the Appalachians and south to southern Mexico.

Bewick's Wren uses its long, narrow, slightly downcurved bill for scavenging on the ground and picking in crevices for insects and spiders. Searching for food, it may venture into hollow trunks, rock crevices, or barns.

529 House Wren
(*Troglodytes aedon*)
Wrens (Troglodytidae)

Description: 4½–5" (11–13 cm). A small *gray-brown
wren with faint eye-stripe,* light
crossbarring on otherwise plain back;
long, slightly curved bill and short tail,
which it frequently cocks.

Voice: A tireless singer in spring and early
summer, it delivers a rapid bubbly trill
that rises and falls in pitch. Scolding
call, a loud *trrrrr* and a harsh buzz.

Habitat: Deciduous woodlands and edges, brush
areas created by burn or windfall,
willows sprouting up along meandering
streams of mountain meadows, pine
and oak woods at high elevations in
Arizona.

Nesting: 5–8 pinkish-white eggs faintly dotted,
in a simple nest built in a natural tree
cavity, woodpecker hole, or nest box.

Range: Southern Canada from British
Columbia to the Atlantic Coast, and
through most of United States. Winters
from the southern United States to
southern Mexico.

When competing for a nest site, the
House Wren may throw out the nest,
eggs, and even the young of other hole-
breeding birds. In the process it may
kill its competitors, or if they are more
powerful, it harasses them by filling the
hole with its own nest material.

538 Swainson's Thrush
(*Catharus ustulatus*)
Thrushes (Turdidae)

Description: 6½–7¾" (17–20 cm). *Olive-brown above,*
whitish below with dark spots on buff
breast; *buff eye-ring and cheek.* Tail and
back are uniformly colored. Similar
Hermit Thrush has fox red tail.

Voice: Song is a quick series of fluty notes,
starting with a clear long note on one

pitch, then spiraling up the scale, becoming fainter until the last notes fade out. Call note is a *whit*.

Habitat: Deciduous and mixed forest undergrowth, dense second-growth thickets, and streamside maples and willows.

Nesting: 3–5 blue eggs, with pale brown markings, in a cup nest of mixed leaf, twig, and roots, often with moss, usually located low in a coniferous tree.

Range: Coast to coast in the boreal forest of Alaska, Canada, and the Great Lakes region; in the rain forest and mountains of the Northwest and California and in the northern Rocky Mountains of the United States. Migrates to South America.

Because each bird's territory is small and the species abundant, one may hear a chorus of males sing briefly every morning and evening. It sings, feeds, and breeds in shady thickets; migrants fly at night, feed and rest during day.

540 **Veery**
(*Catharus fuscescens*)
Thrushes (Turdidae)

Description: 6½–7¾″ (17–20 cm). Small thrush. *Tawny brown above, with trace of buff spotting on breast.* Lacks distinctive eye-ring.

Voice: Song is a downward-spiraling series of trilling *veeeer* notes. Call is a whistled *whee-ou*.

Habitat: Deciduous woodlands and shrubs; it prefers a wetter habitat than do other thrushes.

Nesting: 3–5 blue, unmarked eggs in a soft cup nest of leaves and grasses, on or near the ground at the base of a bush or in a brush pile.

Range: From British Columbia across southern Canada and northern half of United States, extending south in the

Appalachians to Georgia and Rocky Mountains to Arizona. Winters in South America.

The Veery, a secretive bird, lives in dense shade. Experiments on other thrushes show that their vision in shade or twilight is better than that of most other birds. In autumn the Veery migrates to South America. It migrates at night, the flock keeping together in dark skies by means of a "contact call" characteristic of the species.

---

542 **Northern Waterthrush**
(*Seiurus noveboracensis*)
Wood Warblers (Parulidae)

Description: 5½–6½" (14–17 cm). A *thrush-like* warbler, olive-brown above, with a *creamy eye-stripe*. Creamy yellow or whitish underparts with brown streaks from chin to abdomen. It walks with bobbing motion like a Spotted Sandpiper.

Voice: The song is a sequence of quickly uttered, identical, short, chattering phrases repeated many times and speeded toward the end. Call is a loud, sharp *chink*.

Habitat: Bogs, thickets beside streams and lakes, and woods.

Nesting: 4 or 5 white, spotted eggs in a moss-lined cup nest in a ground cavity or among roots in a streambank.

Range: Northwestern Alaska south to Montana, and east to the Atlantic Coast. Winters from Mexico to northern South America.

Ornithologist E. H. Forbush's statement over a half century ago still applies: "It is a large wood warbler disguised as a thrush and exhibiting an extreme fondness for water."

558, 620 Brown-headed Cowbird
(Molothrus ater)
Orioles (Icteridae)

Description: 6–8" (15–20 cm). Smallest North
American blackbird. Small finch-like
bill. *Male is metallic green-black with
coffee-brown head;* female lighter gray-
brown overall. Juveniles like female,
with lightly streaked breast, and
"scaled" upperparts, caused by gray
margins of feathers.

Voice: The courting male delivers a variety of
high, squeaking whistles and gurgling
notes accompanied by head-throw
postures and spread tail; females,
commonly a rattling call and soft *tsip*.

Habitat: During breeding season, woodlands,
light stands of trees along rivers,
suburban gardens, city parks, and
ranches. At other times, in mixed
flocks with other blackbirds in fields
and pastures.

Nesting: 4 or 5 eggs, usually white, lightly
speckled with brown (but color is
highly variable), laid one at a time in
the nests of other songbirds, especially
finches, warblers, and vireos.

Range: Widespread from southern Canada to
the Mexican Plateau, but a newcomer
to the Northwest, expanding as the
virgin forest was opened up in the last
few decades. Winters in milder areas of
United States.

Cowbirds are promiscuous; no pair
bond exists. In late spring the female
cowbird and several suitors move into
the woods. The males sit upright on
treetops, uttering sharp whistles, while
the female searches for nests in which to
lay her eggs. Upon choosing a nest, she
removes one egg of the host's clutch,
and deposits one of her own in its
place. The young cowbird is so much
larger than the young of the host that it
crowds and starves them out.

562 Yellow-billed Cuckoo
(*Coccyzus americanus*)
Cuckoos (Cuculidae)

Description: 11–13½" (28–34 cm). Long, slender
bird. Rather long, curved bill with
yellow lower mandible. Olive-brown
above, contrasting white below, with
bright rufous primaries, most noticeable
in flight. Large white spots on ends of
black outer tail feathers.

Voice: The song is a long series of hollow
"wooden" notes decelerating toward the
end: *kakakaka ka ka ka ka ka, ka, ka-
oh, ka-oh, kka-oh, kow, kow;* unlike the
melodious *coo-coooo* of its Old World
relative, which gave the family its
name.

Habitat: Deciduous woodland with large trees;
riverside woods, mesquite.

Nesting: 2–4 light blue-green eggs in a frail
twig nest in a low tree or bush.

Range: The only cuckoo nesting west of the
Rockies. In the West, generally
uncommon, and entirely absent from
the Rocky Mountain and Central
Plateau areas. Widespread in Midwest
and East from southern Canada to the
Caribbean. Winters in South America.

Cuckoos sit quietly, watching and
listening for moving insects, and are
helpful in combating forest defoliation
caused by infestations of hairy
caterpillars, which few other birds eat.

572 Fox Sparrow
(*Passerella iliaca*)
Finches (Fringillidae)

Description: 6–7¼" (15–18 cm). A chubby, large
sparrow, dusky brown, fox red, or
slaty, often so dark that no back pattern
can be discerned; *heavy streaking of
underparts* converges at midbreast into a
large brown spot. Heavy bill with
lighter-colored lower mandible, slightly

notched *rust-colored tail,* and rounded head outline.

Voice: A lively song that opens with one or more clear whistles and follows with several short trills or *churrs.* Call, a sharp *chink.*

Habitat: Thickets and edges of coniferous, mixed, or second-growth forest or chaparral. On islands off the coast of the Pacific Northwest in chaparral-like low shrub cover.

Nesting: 4 or 5 pale green, speckled eggs in a cup, low in a bush or on the ground.

Range: Widespread in the Far north from the taiga-tundra transition region of Alaska to Unalaska Island in the Aleutians and the Canadian Northwest Territories east to New England; south to the coast of the Pacific Northwest and to southern California, the central Rockies, and other western mountains at timberline.

It spends much time in the shade of shrubs and bushes, scratching in fallen litter for insects and seeds. It sings from a rather high but not prominent post, and nests near the ground.

---

573 **Song Sparrow**
(*Melospiza melodia*)
Finches (Fringillidae)

Description: 5–7" (13–18 cm). Heavy brown streaking on white underparts with prominent *central breast spot* (sometimes lacking in juveniles). Variation in size of subspecies is considerable and colors range from pale sandy to deep black-brown. "Pumps" its relatively long, rounded tail in flight.

Voice: Cheerful song often begins with 3 clear piping notes, followed by a lower note and a rapid jumble of notes. Call is *chimp.*

Habitat: Forest edges, clearings, thickets and marshes with open grassy feeding areas,

low dense scrub for nesting, and some
high vantage points for singing.

Nesting: 3–6 pale greenish-white, heavily
marked eggs in a neat, well-hidden
grassy cup nest in a bush or on the
ground. Up to three clutches are laid in
one season.

Range: The Aleutians east to Newfoundland
below the Arctic tree-line scrub and
south to Baja California, central
Mexico, Nebraska, and North Carolina.

One of the most widespread, diverse
and geographically variable of North
American birds. The 34 recognized
subspecies range from very large, dark-
colored, large-billed birds on the rocky
beaches of the humid Aleutian Islands
to small, sandy, short-billed birds in
scrub desert areas in the Lower
Colorado River Valley. Other subspecies
are found in coastal salt marshes,
freshwater marshes, humid coastal
belts, and the dry, sagebrush-covered
regions.

586 **White-crowned Sparrow**
(*Zonotrichia leucophrys*)
Finches (Fringillidae)

Description: 5½–7″ (14–18 cm). *Crown white,*
bordered by black stripes. Eyebrow white
with narrow black line behind eye.
Cheek, neck, and breast are gray; belly
whitish. Back streaked gray and brown;
white wing bars. First winter birds
have brown-and-buff crown pattern.
Bill pink or yellowish.

Voice: The song is variable geographically but
basically consists of a clear introductory
whistle followed by 4–8 whistles or
wheezy trills on different pitches. Call
note is a metallic *chink* or *pink*.

Habitat: Forest edges and clearings, often found
along streams or surrounding bogs;
alpine meadows; brushy burns, fields,
parks, and suburban gardens. Essential

for its breeding habitat are patches of grass and open ground for foraging, with low shrubbery nearby for escape and nesting.

Nesting: 3–5 pale bluish, dark-spotted eggs in a neat cup nest of fine grasses on or near the ground.

Range: Widespread across Alaska and Canada, south in western United States, to California and New Mexico. Winters in the Southwest and Mexico, though some coastal breeding populations are not migratory.

The northern, northwestern, and mountain subspecies have slightly different head patterns and songs. Song dialects vary locally as well. In the Arctic, where the sun does not set during the breeding season, these sparrows sing all night long; however, White-crowns farther south—e.g., in the Pacific Northwest—also sing frequently during the dark May nights. This conspicuous and abundant sparrow is one of the most studied birds in the West.

599 Lincoln's Sparrow
(*Melospiza lincolnii*)
Finches (Fringillidae)

Description: 5–6" (13–15 cm). Resembles Song Sparrow, but *cheek gray, mustache stripe pale buffy,* and *buffy breast finely streaked with brown.* Central breast spot usually missing.

Voice: Wren-like song; a low gurgling stanza that ends after some rising phrases. Calls are *tik* and a buzzy *tzeee.*

Habitat: Moist and brush-covered bogs, meadows; also mountain meadows with willow thickets or other dense clumps of vegetation.

Nesting: 4 or 5 greenish-white eggs, with dark markings, in a well-hidden grass cup nest on the ground in bog or muskeg.

Range: Breeds in the boreal forest from coast to coast, and along western mountain chains to southern California and New Mexico. Winters from the southwestern states to Central America.

When not singing, it is wary and secretive. In winter, a lone Lincoln's Sparrow is often seen amid other sparrows wintering on the Pacific Coast and in bushy areas inland.

---

618 Common Grackle
(*Quiscalus quiscula*)
Orioles (Icteridae)

Description: 11–13½" (28–34 cm). Jay-sized. *Long, keel-shaped tail. Black with bronze sheen;* green or purple sheen on head and breast. Female smaller, not as shiny. Both sexes have yellow-white eyes; dusky brown juveniles have brown eyes.

Voice: A loud squeak that sounds like an unoiled wheelbarrow, and a *chuck* call.

Habitat: Marsh borders, wet woodlands, farms, parks.

Nesting: 4–6 greenish, blotched eggs in a bulky nest in an evergreen tree, in woods, or around a farmhouse; in colonies.

Range: Breeds across Canada from southern Mackenzie and the foothills of the Rockies in Alberta, Montana, and Texas east to Newfoundland and south to Florida. Winters from New England, the Ohio River Valley, and Kansas south. Casual west of the Rockies; accidental in California.

It is an opportunistic feeder, varying an insect and grain diet with both the eggs and the young of small birds. During courtship, it jerks its body, lowers wing, tail, and head, and squeals. It also exhibits its long, conspicuous tail in display flight. This species is smaller and lacks the strong sex differences of the Great-tailed Grackle.

625 Common Crow
(*Corvus brachyrhynchos*)
Crows (Corvidae)

Description: 17–21″ (43–53 cm). Smaller than
Raven, with *shorter, less powerful bill.*
Black overall.

Voice: The *caw* call is not as hoarse as that of
the Raven.

Habitat: Deciduous growth, along rivers and
streams; orchards and city parks. Also
mixed and coniferous woods, but avoids
closed coniferous forests and desert
expanses.

Nesting: 4–6 greenish, spotted eggs, in well-
constructed bowl-shaped stick nest,
often well lined with plant material, in
trees; often breeds in loose colonies. A
very social bird, as many as two or
three hundred will roost together in
winter.

Range: Coast to coast wherever trees grow,
thus from the northern treeline to the
desert belt; but not in the Pacific
Northwest.

An opportunist in its feeding, it will
consume a great variety of plant and
animal food: seeds, garbage, insects,
mice. In orchards and fields it destroys
many injurious insects. Its nest
plundering is decried; however, the
labeling of birds as either "harmful" or
"useful" is misleading and antiquated.
Crows do destroy many eggs and
nestlings of woodland and meadow
birds, but they also weed out the weak
and feeble and they alert the animals of
a neighborhood when danger
approaches.

626 Common Raven
(*Corvus corax*)
Crows (Corvidae)

Description: 21½–27″ (55–69 cm). Large, black
bird. *Thick bill,* shaggy ruff at throat,

and *wedge-shaped tail*. Alternately flaps and soars like a hawk, flapping less and soaring more than Common Crow.

Voice: Utters a hoarse, croaking *kraaak* and a variety of other notes, including a hollow, knocking sound and a melodious *kloo-klok,* usually in flight.

Habitat: A great variety, including deserts, mountains, canyons, boreal forests, Pacific Coast beaches.

Nesting: 4–7 green, spotted eggs in a large loose nest of sticks, bones, and some soft material, often wool, on a cliff face, tree, or saguaro cactus.

Range: Aleutians and throughout Alaska and Canada to Greenland. South, in the West, to Central America and east to the foothills of the Rockies. Also widespread in the Old World.

A very "intelligent" bird, it seems to apply reasoning in situations entirely new to it. Its "insight" behavior at least matches that of a dog. It is a general predator and opportunistic feeder, like other members of the crow family, and often feeds at garbage dumps.

Coniferous Forests

The belt of forest covering northern North America and Eurasia is called boreal forest or taiga. It consists of coniferous trees such as spruce, pine, hemlock, and tamarack. It has southern extensions in the Rocky Mountains and the Sierra Nevada of California in the form of mountain coniferous forest. Higher up, subalpine forests of firs and pines form the treeline. The mountains of the Southwest have another type of coniferous forest—pine-oak woodland with coarse grasses covering the forest floor. Finally, the densest coniferous forest is the coastal rain forest, dominated by gigantic Douglas fir in the north and equally huge Redwood in the south. Although this habitat includes many species of birds, because it ranges from the woods of wet lowlands to dry uplands and from the Arctic almost to the tropics, species from other habitats also occur in it—for example, goldeneye ducks, Marbled Murrelets (which are pond and seabirds respectively), and crows, ravens and flickers (which are found in all wooded habitats).

206, 209 Lesser Yellowlegs
(*Tringa flavipes*)
Sandpipers (Scolopacidae)

Description: 9½–11″ (24–28 cm). Smaller version of
the Greater Yellowlegs, with shorter,
straight dark bill. Mottled gray above,
white tail with dusky bars, *white rump,*
and dusky wing; faint white eye-line;
long, bright yellow legs. Birds in spring
plumage are generally much darker
than those seen in the fall.

Voice: 1 or 2 whistles, *yew* or *yew-yew,* without
loud, ringing quality of Greater
Yellowlegs' voice. On nesting ground it
utters a torrent of such calls as long as
an intruder is near.

Habitat: Muskeg, bogs, ponds in coniferous
woodlands.

Nesting: 4 buff, blotched eggs in a nest of plant
material in a depression on the ground.

Range: From Alaska to James Bay in the forest
and forest-tundra zones. Migrates
southeastward through the West Indies
to South America. Transient in the
West, mainly on coastal mud flats and
flooded fields. Some remain in the
Southwest in winter.

This bird is fearless not only on its
nesting grounds but even on migration.
It was formerly considered a delicacy
and hunted widely, but now enjoys full
protection.

207 Greater Yellowlegs
(*Tringa melanoleuca*)
Sandpipers (Scolopacidae)

Description: 12½–15″ (32–38 cm). Large sandpiper.
Long neck and slightly upturned bill;
long bright yellow legs. Grayish overall
with black-and-white mottling above,
white below; *white rump* and barred tail.

Voice: A ringing *kyew-kyew-kyew,* the second
note often emphasized.

Habitat: During the breeding season, muskeg,

wet meadows in the taiga, or boreal
forests of Canada; in winter, marshes,
edges of large inland bodies of water,
along irrigation canals.

Nesting: 4 grayish-white or buffy tan eggs, with
heavy brown splotches, in a shallow
unlined scrape in woodland; not
necessarily near water.

Range: All along the northern fringes of the
taiga belt, from Alaska to
Newfoundland. In winter in California,
southern Arizona, and the Gulf and
south Atlantic states, but a common
transient in most western wetlands,
indeed in all of North, Central, and
South America.

While watching yellowlegs gathered for
fall migration at a Canadian lake, I
observed their display, each showing
the white rump and tail pattern to a
rival whom the bird wanted to supplant
on the feeding ground. Each turned the
tail slightly toward his rival and
lowered the wing closest to the other;
both held this posture for several
seconds.

260, 261 **Blue Grouse**
(*Dendragapus obscurus*)
Grouse (Tetraonidae)

Description: 15½–21″ (39–53 cm). Large grouse.
Male *dusky gray or bluish gray overall* with
orange-yellow comb over the eyes, some
mottling on wings. *Light gray terminal
band on dark tail* may be lacking in
birds in the northern Rockies. Females
and immatures mottled brown with
dark tail.

Voice: A deep series of hoots: *whoop, whoop,
whoop . . .* increasing in volume and
tempo toward the end of the series.
Calling birds are often extremely
difficult to find.

Habitat: Burns, edge brush in coastal rain forest;
Rocky Mountain montane forests,

	slashes, and subalpine forest clearings.
Nesting:	5–10 creamy, lightly spotted eggs in a scrape lined with pine needles and grass, usually sheltered by a stump or rock.
Range:	Coastal forest area from southeastern Alaska to San Francisco Bay; the Sierra Nevada and Rocky Mountains.

The spring display of the territorial male is an imposing sight. Perched on a stump or fallen log, the male produces "booms" or "hoots" by inflating and deflating the sound-magnifying pouches on each side of his neck. The yellow or purple featherless pouch is ringed by the white downy bases of surrounding feathers. In winter this grouse feeds exclusively on pine needles; its summer diet consists of insects, seeds, and berries.

---

262 Spruce Grouse
(*Canachites canadensis*)
Grouse (Tetraonidae)

Description:	15–17" (38–43 cm). Darker than Blue Grouse. *Slate gray above, black below,* with a red comb above the eye. White line around throat, white-spotted flanks; *tail black with chestnut terminal band.* (Franklin's form in northern Rockies and Cascades has large white spots on black tail.) Females and immatures mottled and barred light brown.
Voice:	Similar to the hooting series of the Blue Grouse, but even lower in pitch. In display, flies up with a loud clap of wings.
Habitat:	Coniferous woodlands, edges of deep forests.
Nesting:	8–12 buffy, spotted eggs in a plant-lined scrape.
Range:	Across Alaska and Canada south to New England; south in the Rockies to northeastern Oregon and northwestern Wyoming.

The male Spruce Grouse displays with tail fanned, the rust band or white spots making a beautiful semicircular row. This species is dwindling rapidly due to its loss of habitat and a tameness that have made it an easy mark for hunters.

290 Great Gray Owl
(*Strix nebulosa*)
Owls (Strigidae)

Description: 24–33" (61–84 cm). Largest owl in North America. Large *rounded head lacks ear tufts; enormous pale facial disk patterned* in *concentric gray circles* with *yellow eyes* and bill and *black chin spot*. Mottled gray and brown above, grayish lengthwise streaking below. Relatively *long tail*.

Voice: Very deep *hooo* note at irregular intervals.

Habitat: Bogs and forests of the taiga; in the southern fringes of its range, montane conifers where openings and alpine meadows provide good hunting grounds.

Nesting: 2–5 white eggs in an abandoned hawk or crow nest in a tall tree, frequently pine, or cliffside.

Range: From Alaska to Ontario, south along mountains east of the coastal ranges from British Columbia to central California (the Sierra Nevada) and from the northern Rockies to Yellowstone. Rare and local in the United States; common only in the Far North.

Like most large owls, it has a remarkably small body within a large mass of feathers that provide excellent insulation in the rugged climate it prefers. It often hunts in the late afternoon.

292 Hawk-Owl
(Surnia ulula)
Owls (Strigidae)

Description: 14½–17½" (37–44 cm). Crow-sized.
With its *long tail* and swift flight it
resembles a short-winged hawk, hence
its name. *Mainly brown* with white
blotches and dots above, broad white
cross-barring below, narrow light bars
on tail. Facial disk and throat outlined
in white, as are *dark chin, eyebrows, and
prominent cross-bar from eyebrow through
ear region* and side of breast. Eyes
yellow. Juveniles, lacking most of the
white cross-barring, are plainer.

Voice: A hawk-like cry, described as *ki-ki-ki-
ki*.

Habitat: Boreal forests, including tundra forests.

Nesting: 3–7 white eggs in a stump, snag, or
nest of another bird.

Range: Across the boreal forest zone from
Alaska and northern British Columbia
to Newfoundland (as well as from
Norway to Siberia), but not in montane
extensions of the boreal forest toward
the south, such as the Rockies,
Appalachians, etc. Thus a truly
northern owl. An occasional winter
visitor in the northern United States.

In its northern domain the sun seldom
sets during the summer half of the year.
Adapted to these conditions, it is the
most diurnal of all North American
owls. It feeds on rodents, including
mice and lemmings, that are active
throughout the 24-hour day. In winter
when rodent runways are deep beneath
the snow, it takes more birds,
including grouse, than mammals. Like
many northern birds that have rarely
seen humans, it can be exceedingly
tame.

293 Spotted Owl
(*Strix occidentalis*)
Owls (Strigidae)

Description: 16½–19″ (42–48 cm). Medium-sized owl. *Dark brown with white spots above; brown barring below; dark eyes. Strix* owls are round-headed, fluffy birds with no ear tufts.

Voice: The most common call is 2 or 3 short hoots followed by a louder, more prolonged *hooo-ah*. The quality suggests a barking dog. Also a series of notes on one pitch gradually increasing in volume, and a whistled *gueee-ah* note.

Habitat: Coniferous forests, densely wooded canyons.

Nesting: 2 or 3 white eggs, usually in a natural tree or canyon-wall cavity or an abandoned hawk nest.

Range: Rain forests of extreme southern British Columbia to San Francisco Bay; forests of the Sierra Nevada and other western ranges to southern California; the Rocky Mountains from Colorado south into Mexico.

This large rodent-eater is rather rare in much of the West. It lives in dense stands of mature forests. The cutting of roads through forests has been followed by the disappearance of the Spotted Owl in the area. Simultaneously, larger Horned Owls have moved in, but whether or not they killed off the Spotted Owl has not been ascertained. The status of the Spotted Owl is under study to see what additional protection it needs beyond that which covers all owls.

295 Pygmy Owl
(*Glaucidium gnoma*)
Owls (Strigidae)

Description: 7–7½″ (18–19 cm). Sparrow-sized. Small round head and *long, finely barred tail,* often cocked at an angle. Varying shades of brown with fine buff spotting above; buff with bolder brown streaks below; two white-edged black spots at back of neck suggest "eyes." Undulating flight.

Voice: Most common call is a series of hollow whistles on one pitch. Also a thin rattle around the nest.

Habitat: Open coniferous forests or mixed aspen and oak woods; dense canyon growth.

Nesting: 3–6 white eggs in an abandoned woodpecker hole.

Range: From southeastern Alaska throughout the West, with the eastern limit formed by prairies adjacent to the Rocky Mountain forest; south to the mountains of Mexico and Guatemala.

This small owl sometimes hunts by day, attacking birds even larger than itself. In spring the male is conspicuous, uttering a staccato whistle every few seconds, while flicking his long tail upward and sideways. In response, the small forest birds sound an excited alarm, scolding and mobbing this tiny owl, just as they would any larger owl.

297 **Flammulated Owl**
(*Otus flammeolus*)
Owls (Strigidae)

Description: 6–7″ (15–18 cm). Slightly larger than a sparrow; similar to but smaller than a Screech Owl, with small, indistinct *ear tufts* and *dark* rather than yellow *eyes.* Grayish above, light below, with white and rust-colored markings. Sexes look similar but female larger than male.

Voice: A monotonous low hoot, single or double, is repeated almost endlessly, and sounds as mechanical as the time signals of a radio station.

Habitat: Coniferous woodlands and forest edges

in the Northwest; dry ponderosa pine woods in the Southwest.

Nesting: 3 or 4 white eggs in a tree hollow or deserted woodpecker hole.

Range: From the interior forest of British Columbia through the Rocky Mountain and Pacific states (but not to the coast), south to the mountains of the Mexican Plateau.

As with other owls, the Flammulated male supplies food and protection, while the female is the chief nest-tender. Mice and similar prey are usually decapitated, the male feeding on the head, the female and young getting the softer body. Later the female leaves the nestlings and shares the hunting grounds with her mate.

298, 299 Saw-whet Owl
(*Aegolius acadicus*)
Owls (Strigidae)

Description: 7–8½" (18–22 cm). Small owl. *Brown above,* lightly streaked with white on the forehead and crown; *white below* with broad reddish-brown streakings. Lacks ear tufts; has *yellow eyes, dark bill,* and short tail. Immatures are tawny-rust with broad white eyebrows that form a "V."

Voice: A monotonous series of low, whistled notes on one pitch. Also an upslurred whistle.

Habitat: Coniferous or deciduous woodlands, from bogs and moist alder thickets to drier ponderosa pine slopes.

Nesting: 4–7 white eggs in a woodpecker hole or other tree cavity.

Range: Breeds in southeastern Alaska and southern Canada east to the Atlantic Coast; in the West southward along all wooded mountain ranges into Mexico. Also appears in winter on the forested lowlands across North America.

A nocturnal hunter of forest rodents and large beetles, it is tame and approachable during the day while resting. Though widespread in Canada and all of the northern and western United States, its distribution is spotty. This pattern may be attributable to uneven or inadequate food supplies in areas with severe winter conditions.

---

300 Boreal Owl
(*Aegolius funereus*)
Owls (Strigidae)

Description: 8½–12″ (22–30 cm). Robin-sized. Short-tailed, flat-headed, chubby owl. *Chocolate brown* with thick *white spotting on head,* sparsely spotted elsewhere. Large facial disk is grayish with dark border. *Eyes and bill yellow.*

Voice: Spring call is compared to the tolling of a soft bell. Also a series of high-pitched whistles.

Habitat: Coniferous woodlands.

Nesting: 4–7 white eggs in a tree hole.

Range: Circumpolar. From Alaska east to Newfoundland in the boreal forest belt of the North; similarly across Eurasia. Rare visitor in the northern United States.

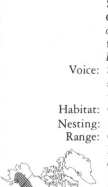

This small mouser of the twilight nights of the North is so tame that in Europe I have caught dozens (for banding) with my bare hands. The incessant calling of the amorous male keeps one awake in subarctic campsites.

324, 325 Sharp-shinned Hawk
(*Accipiter striatus*)
Hawks (Accipitridae)

Description: 10–14″ (25–36 cm). Similar in color to Cooper's Hawk, but *smaller with square rather than rounded tail;* tail often

notched. Head and neck
proportionately shorter than in Cooper's
Hawk. Slate blue above, white below
with rich rusty cross-barring. Plumage
of sexes similar, but female is larger.
Immatures brown above with brown
streaks on whitish underparts.

Voice: A high *ke-ke-ke-ke* may be heard near
the nest.

Habitat: Forests or edges of woods.

Nesting: 3–5 bluish, spotted eggs on a twiggy
platform in a dense conifer, live oak, or
other woodland tree. The young fledge
after two months. Laying is timed so
that the fully fledged young leave the
nest early enough to sharpen their
hunting skills on less experienced
fledgling songbirds.

Range: Coast to coast and from the northern
tree limit to the savannas of the
southern states. Also breeds in forested
highlands of Mexico and Caribbean
islands.

Accipiters (Goshawk, Cooper's, and
Sharp-shinned hawks) are recognized by
their long, thin, cross-barred tails and
short, broad, rounded wings. This
combination of tail and wing shape
enables the *Accipiter* to maneuver in
closed woodlands to capture birds,
squirrels, and other small mammals.

326 **Goshawk**
(*Accipiter gentilis*)
Hawks (Accipitridae)

Description: 20–26″ (51–66 cm). W. 42–48″ (1–1.2
m). Uniformly *gray* above, white with
light gray cross-barring below. Dark gray
crown and ear patch separated by *white
eye-stripe*. Flies with several short, rapid
flaps followed by a glide. As in most
birds of prey, female is larger and
stronger than male. Goshawk is
chunkiest of *Accipiters*, resembling
Red-tailed Hawk in shape. Juveniles

brown above with brown-streaked
creamy underparts and light eye-stripe.

Voice: A repeated *kek kek kek* and a harsh
scream are given around the nest site.

Habitat: Taiga; the northern coniferous forests
and western extensions.

Nesting: 3 or 4 whitish eggs in a stick platform
nest built in a tall tree in a dense
coniferous forest. In Colorado and
Wyoming, often nests in aspen trees.

Range: Circumpolar. In the West, from Alaska
through the Rocky Mountains to New
Mexico; also the mountains and forests
of Washington, Oregon, and interior
California. Migrates and winters in
lowlands as far south as northern
Mexico.

The male supplies food while the
female incubates and broods. As the
young grow and demand more food,
both parents hunt. Although Goshawks
can kill animals as large as jackrabbits
and geese, they feed mainly on grouse
and smaller birds.

328, 329 Merlin
"Pigeon Hawk"
(*Falco columbarius*)
Falcons (Falconidae)

Description: 10–13½" (25–34 cm). W. 24" (61
cm). Small, stocky falcon with *pointed
wings* and long, narrow *banded tail*.
Male is blue-gray above with black tail
bands; female and immatures are brown
above with buff tail bands. All are buff
with light brown streaking below.
Adults have yellow cere and skin around
eyes; immatures blue. Well-defined
dark facial marks typical of falcons
are lacking.

Voice: Generally silent. However, on its
breeding grounds it may give a quick
kik-kik-kik . . . high in pitch.

Habitat: Open parkland, coniferous forests, and
taiga; frequently found in open country

and foothills in winter.

Nesting: 3–6 rust-colored, dark-spotted eggs in a tree hollow, on the ground, or in an abandoned nest of a larger bird.

Range: Nests in the boreal forest south of the treeline from coast to coast and along the western mountains south to Oregon, Idaho, Montana. Also northern Eurasia. Winters south of the breeding range to northern South America.

This falcon, formerly called "Pigeon Hawk," flies low, with a steady wingbeat. It feeds mainly on small birds of open country but also takes rodents and large insects such as dragonflies. In the West it is mostly seen in migration or wintering, scaring flocks of field birds or shorebirds.

347 Band-tailed Pigeon
(*Columba fasciata*)
Pigeons (Columbidae)

Description: 14–15½" (36–39 cm). Larger than the Domestic Pigeon. *Dark gray above; tail has pale gray terminal band.* Head and underparts purplish-plum, whitening toward vent. Adults have *narrow white semi-collar at nape.* Yellow bill is tipped with black; yellow legs.

Voice: A deep, owl-like *whoo-hoo.*

Habitat: Coniferous forests along the northwestern Pacific Coast, but in the southwestern part of its range it prefers oak woodlands or pine-oak forests where it can feed on acorns.

Nesting: 1 white egg in a loosely constructed platform nest of twigs in a tree.

Range: From southern British Columbia to Baja California in and near coastal forests and hills; in mountain chains extending from Utah and Colorado south through Mexico to Central America; also in oak woods of Colombia.

This shy forest pigeon is adapting to parks and gardens, where it feeds on lawns and ornamental berries, especially holly. Already a city bird in the Northwest, it has spread from natural redwood pockets to conifer plantings in suburbs of Santa Barbara and other California towns. In fall these birds gorge themselves on acorns.

357 **Violet-green Swallow**
(*Tachycineta thalassina*)
Swallows (Hirundinidae)

Description: 5–5½" (13–14 cm). Dark metallic *bronze-green upperparts,* iridescent violet rump and tail, the latter slightly forked; *white underparts. White cheek* extending above eye and white on the sides above rump distinguish it from the Tree Swallow.

Voice: A high *dee-chip* given in flight. Also a series of varying *tweet* notes.

Habitat: Breeds in forests, wooded foothills, mountains, suburban areas.

Nesting: 4 or 5 white eggs in a grass-and-feather nest in a woodpecker hole, a natural cavity, under the eaves of a building, or in a nest-box.

Range: From Alaska east to South Dakota, south to Baja California, Texas, and central Mexico. Winters south to Central America, and irregularly in coastal southern California.

Like many other swallows, it lives in colonies, basically because of its feeding needs; where one finds food there is usually enough for all, and when feeding communally these birds can more readily detect and defend themselves from hawks.

358, 359 Purple Martin
(*Progne subis*)
Swallows (Hirundinidae)

Description: 7¼–8½" (18–22 cm). Largest swallow in North America. Adult male *glossy blue-black;* wings and forked tail duller black. Female and yearling birds dusky black above, light below with smoky gray throat and breast.

Voice: A rich, low *chew* note. Song is a series of rich gurgling notes.

Habitat: Open woodlands, burns with snags, edges, hollow trees, and city buildings.

Nesting: 3–5 dull white eggs in a nest of grasses, leaves, stalks, feathers, and even mud, in a tree hollow, an abandoned woodpecker hole, the eaves of buildings, or even an eroded gopher hole; frequently near water.

Range: Southern Canada to northern Mexico; scarce in the West. Still largely a bird of wooded areas, it is not found in the Central Plateau and its mountain-chain rims. Winters in South America.

In much of the West it is becoming scarcer, probably due to competition with Starlings for nest sites. Unlike the eastern birds, it does not occupy "martin houses" placed in gardens, preferring the open countryside or downtown areas.

Vaux's Swift
(*Chaetura vauxi*)
Swifts (Apodidae)

Description: 4–4½" (10–11 cm). *Tiny* swift, slightly smaller than its eastern, darker counterpart, the Chimney Swift. Dark overall with *dingy lighter underparts.* Long, stiff, gently curved wings with slightly rounded tail.

Voice: A bat-like chipping instead of the piercing cry of the Chimney Swift.

Usually silent on migration.

Habitat: Breeds in forests. An aerial feeder, often found away from woods, especially in adverse weather, feeding on insects low, near, or over water. Frequently seen with flocks of Black Swifts.

Nesting: 3–5 white eggs in a nest of small sticks cemented together with saliva and attached to the inside surface of a hollow tree. The "edible bird's nest" of Southeast Asia is a swift's nest of pure saliva, a protein glue resembling egg white, which hardens to a nest, but can be boiled and eaten in soup.

Range: From the southern tip of the Alaskan panhandle to central California (largely confined to the coastal ranges) and south discontinuously, in Central and South America.

The eastern Chimney Swift is better known because the dwindling of the eastern forests has forced it to use chimneys for nesting, whereas the Vaux's is still mainly a forest dweller. Both species have a stubby tail, every feather ending in a naked shaft with a hard spine that helps to support the bird as it clings to vertical surfaces, such as its nesting cavity walls. Its fast flight is characterized by sailing glides between spurts of rapid flapping.

363, 365 Hairy Woodpecker
(*Picoides villosus*)
Woodpeckers (Picidae)

Description: 8½–10½" (22–27 cm). Medium-sized. Larger than its relative the Downy. White head with black crown, eye-mask, and "whiskers." Male has *red patch* at base of crown; light underparts; *white back;* black wings with white spots. Tail black with *white outer tail feathers.* Female similar but lacks red patch.

Voice: A loud, sharp *peek!*

Habitat: Deciduous trees; coniferous stands, especially in montane forests and river groves.

Nesting: 3–6 white eggs on wood chips in a previously used tree hole or newly excavated cavity.

Range: All of wooded North America from the subarctic treeline of Canada to the tropics of Panama, where it is a highland bird.

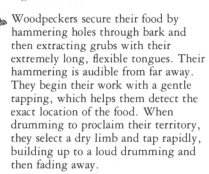

Woodpeckers secure their food by hammering holes through bark and then extracting grubs with their extremely long, flexible tongues. Their hammering is audible from far away. They begin their work with a gentle tapping, which helps them detect the exact location of the food. When drumming to proclaim their territory, they select a dry limb and tap rapidly, building up to a loud drumming and then fading away.

381 Pileated Woodpecker
(*Dryocopus pileatus*)
Woodpeckers (Picidae)

Description: 16–19½" (41–50 cm). Almost *crow-sized. Male predominantly black with red crest and mustache;* white face, black eye-mask and long white throat stripe. White flanks and underwing linings flash in flight. Female similar, but red less extensive on crest and absent on mustache.

Voice: A loud *kak kak kak kak . . .* , similar to the call of a Common Flicker, but louder and slightly higher in pitch.

Habitat: Mature stands of coniferous and mixed woods, where dead stumps abound.

Nesting: 3–5 white eggs in a bare hole excavated by the pair.

Range: Breeds across the continent in the Canadian taiga; coastal forest down to central California, the Sierra Nevada, and the Cascades of Oregon. Rare in

the Rocky Mountain states, but widespread in the East.

With the probable extinction of the Ivory-billed Woodpecker, this is now the largest woodpecker in America. Its staple food consists of carpenter ants living in fallen timber, dead roots, and stumps. The woodpecker excavates thumb-sized rectangular cavities, then uses its enormously long, sticky tongue to reach the ant burrows.

382 Northern Three-toed Woodpecker
(*Picoides tridactylus*)
Woodpeckers (Picidae)

Description: 8–9½" (20–24 cm). Smaller than the Black-backed Three-toed Woodpecker. *Yellow cap,* black head with white facial stripes; black-and-white-barred "ladder back"; black wings, rump, and tail; barred flanks and white underparts. Female lacks yellow cap.

Voice: Call is a sharp *pik* or *kik.* Drums like the Black-backed Three-Toed Woodpecker.

Habitat: Coniferous forests; from light woodland muskeg or burns to open pine woods and dense stands.

Nesting: 4 white eggs in a cavity in a dead tree, usually a conifer. When the nestlings are well grown, their presence can be detected by tapping the tree: a loud buzzing, squealing chorus answers at once.

Range: In the North, from Alaska across the Canadian taiga belt to Newfoundland, south along the western mountains to the Oregon Cascades in the West, and east to Arizona and New Mexico.

The theory of a "double invasion" may explain why the Old World taiga belt harbors only this species of three-toed woodpecker whereas North America has two species. One Old World invader probably crossed the Bering Strait in the remote past, when it was a dry land bridge. The American pioneer population then probably underwent a slight accommodation in behavior and appearance, so that when a second invasion followed, the two were sufficiently different to remain separate species.

383 Black-backed Three-toed Woodpecker
(*Picoides arcticus*)
Woodpeckers (Picidae)

Description: 9–10″ (23--25 cm). Medium-sized. Dark-patterned; male has *yellow cap*. *Black above,* white below, with narrow white line behind eye, and wide mustache. White underparts framed by *heavily barred flanks*.

Voice: Call is a sharp *kyik* or *tschik*. Drums frequently, the "drum roll" increasing in tempo toward the end.

Habitat: Coniferous woodlands; fir or lodgepole pine burns with tree snags.

Nesting: 4 or 5 white eggs in a hole chiseled in a stub, snag, or living coniferous tree.

Range: Boreal forests across the Canadian taiga, with an extension through the mountain ranges of the West down to the Sierra Nevada.

Dead conifers with large areas of scaled bark generally indicate the presence of this uncommon woodpecker. When alarmed, it quickly sidles to the far side of the tree and reappears cautiously. If frightened, the bird flies away, often calling sharply. Unlike other woodpeckers, which have four toes, these birds have only three.

384 Williamson's Sapsucker
(*Sphyrapicus thyroideus*)
Woodpeckers (Picidae)

Description: 9½″ (24 cm). Male has *black head, breast,* and *back,* white facial stripes, bright red throat, and large white wing and rump patches. *Lemon yellow belly* is bordered with black-and-white-barred flanks. Sexes very dissimilar: female has brown head, dark brown and white zebra stripes above and on flanks; large dark bib and smaller, less brilliant yellow area on belly.

Voice: A soft nasal *churrr,* descending in pitch. Drum has an intermittent cadence.

Habitat: Ponderosa pine forests and open coniferous forests; subalpine forests of the Southwest.

Nesting: 3–7 white eggs. Prefers pine or fir snags; may reuse a nesting tree, but each time it chisels a new hole, leaving the abandoned one for Violet-green Swallows or other hole-nesting birds.

Range: Throughout the West in drier forests from southeastern British Columbia to New Mexico; not found in coastal ranges. Winters in southern Pacific states from Arizona to central Mexico.

The distribution of this woodpecker, like that of many birds, is tied to a certain climatic belt. In southern areas, cool climates occur at high elevations, whereas in northern latitudes such conditions occur closer to sea level. The type of pine forest in which this bird thrives covers valley benches in British Columbia.

---

385 White-headed Woodpecker
(*Picoides albolarvatus*)
Woodpeckers (Picidae)

Description: 9″ (23 cm). Small woodpecker. Black overall with *white head, throat,* and *wing patch.* Male has red patch on nape.

Voice: Calls include a sharp *pee-dink* and a more prolonged *pee-dee-dee-dink*. Drum is a short, even series.

Habitat: Ponderosa pine belt of the mountains; also in subalpine belt of firs.

Nesting: 3–5 white eggs in a self-excavated nesting hole often close to the ground in a pine stub or snag.

Range: Extreme south-central British Columbia, northeastern Washington and Idaho, south to southern California and just across the Nevada line, but avoids the Pacific Coast rain forest.

An inconspicuous bird, hard to find due to its silent habits, it rarely taps or drums, vocalizing only around the nest. It feeds by scaling bark off the tree to reach the insects underneath. Although its black-and-white pattern is striking in flight, it provides excellent camouflage when the bird perches in a shady forest.

386 Red-breasted Nuthatch
(*Sitta canadensis*)
Nuthatches (Sittidae)

Description: 4½–4¾" (11–12 cm). *Blue-gray above,* with black cap bounded by white line above broad *black eye-stripe. Rusty breast,* belly, and undertail coverts. Female and juveniles have slate gray cap and are paler below.

Voice: A high, nasal *yank-yank-yank;* its nasal quality recalls the tooting of a tin horn.

Habitat: Coniferous or mixed woods.

Nesting: 4–7 white eggs, with reddish-brown spots, in an excavated cavity lined with feathers, moss, grass, and shreds of bark, in a dead coniferous tree or stump, frequently identifiable by its pitch-smeared entrance.

Range: Northern coniferous forests from coast to coast, south along the coastal interior and Rocky Mountain chains to California in the West, and to the Appalachians in the East.

Nuthatches hoard excess food and will transport seed from a tree heavily laden with mature cones to their distant larders. In years of bad harvest, they migrate in large numbers to more southerly forests. They also feed on bark insects, maneuvering with agility around the tips of small, outer branches or in tree tops.

387   White-breasted Nuthatch
(*Sitta carolinensis*)
Nuthatches (Sittidae)

Description: 5–6" (13–15 cm). Sparrow-sized. *Blue-gray above, white below, crown and nape black;* the only nuthatch with a wholly white face.

Voice: A low *yank* or *yair.* Song is a nasal, whistled series on one pitch: *whee, whee, whee, whee . . .*

Habitat: Widespread in various habitats: western birds prefer coniferous forests as well as oak woods and pinyon-juniper woodlands; eastern birds live in mature hardwood forests.

Nesting: 5–9 white, spotted eggs in a natural or excavated tree cavity lined with bark chips and fur.

Range: Southern Canada, coast to coast in the United States and in Mexico. Absent in large areas where suitable forested habitat is unavailable.

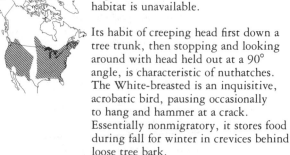

Its habit of creeping head first down a tree trunk, then stopping and looking around with head held out at a 90° angle, is characteristic of nuthatches. The White-breasted is an inquisitive, acrobatic bird, pausing occasionally to hang and hammer at a crack. Essentially nonmigratory, it stores food during fall for winter in crevices behind loose tree bark.

388 Brown Creeper
(*Certhia familiaris*)
Creepers (Certhiidae)

Description: 5–5¾" (13–15 cm). Small, slender bird
with *mottled brown upperparts,* a whitish
eyebrow, and white underparts. Long
downcurved bill; stiff tail braces it like a
woodpecker.

Voice: High-pitched song consists of about 6
notes falling and then rising: *see-see-see-whee-see-see.*

Habitat: Mature coniferous or mixed forests.

Nesting: 4–8 white eggs, with reddish-brown
speckles, in a nest of twigs, bark, and
moss held together by cobwebs, usually
built low behind overhanging loose
bark of a coniferous tree.

Range: Mainly in the taiga belt, in North
America from Alaska to Newfoundland;
has also spread south into the montane
conifer groves, as far as Central
America.

As it searches for bark insects the
Brown Creeper always moves in an
upward direction, circling tree trunks
in spirals, then plunging to the base of
the next tree.

389 Pygmy Nuthatch
(*Sitta pygmaea*)
Nuthatches (Sittidae)

Description: 3¾–4½" (10–11 cm). *Small* nuthatch.
Bluish-gray above, with *gray-brown cap*
terminated by indistinct black eye-line.
Faint white smudge at base of nape.
Creamy white below. Usually in flocks.

Voice: A monotonous *peep, peep-peep.*

Habitat: Primarily ponderosa pine forests with
undergrowth of bunchgrass. Less
common in stands of other pines,
Douglas fir, and western larch.

Nesting: 5–9 white eggs with reddish-brown
speckles; nest is a quantity of soft
material, often vegetable down,

amassed in the cavity of a dead pine or stump approximately 15 feet from the ground.

Range: Widespread from southern British Columbia eastward through the Black Hills, and south to Baja California, mainland Mexico, including the scattered pine-capped desert mountains of the Southwest.

The three nuthatch species in the West live in separate wooded habitats. The White-breasted is found mainly in the lowland oaks and riparian forests, through the foothills into mixed woods, though it also extends into the mountaintop pine forests. The Pygmy Nuthatch keeps mostly to pine woodlands. The Red-breasted Nuthatch is found in the firs of the subalpine forests. All feed on bark and twig insects, as well as stored nuts, seeds, eggs, and hibernating larvae in winter.

391, 406 **Rufous Hummingbird**
(*Selasphorus rufus*)
Hummingbirds (Trochilidae)

Description: 3–4″ (8–10 cm). Male's non-iridescent, *rufous upperparts and sides* contrast with *bright orange-red gorget* and white breast. Female is green above, with rufous on sides and at base of tail feathers; very similar to female Allen's and Broad-tailed hummingbirds.

Voice: Low chipping and buzzy notes, similar to those of the Allen's. An excited *zeee-chuppity-chup* is often heard. The wings of adult males may produce a musical buzz in flight.

Habitat: Forest edges, thickets in coniferous or deciduous forests, woodlands, mountain chaparral, and alpine meadows.

Nesting: 2 white eggs in a well-constructed nest insulated with mosses and lichen. In the southern part of its range it chooses two nest sites. The first nest, built in

April on a low branch of a conifer, offers more protection from wind and chilly nights. The second, in June, mainly in broadleaf trees, is set higher up, where evaporation from leaf surfaces cools the air around the nest and compensates for summer midday heat.

Range: The Pacific Northwest, northward through interior valleys and coastal slopes to the Alaskan panhandle. To the south, in California's redwood forests, Allen's Hummingbird predominates. In migration, both species can be seen everywhere in southern California and later wintering in Mexico.

The first bird to discover a source of food defends it. Although satiated, it perches nearby and intercepts an intruder in the air with angry buzzing. If a female is disturbed when feeding, she gives a "no trespassing" signal by fanning and waving her tail. Females, therefore, have developed distinct tail patterns, whereas males, facing the opponent, signal with their brilliant throat patches, called gorgets. The sexes have separate territories; the female visits the male at mating time, the male ignoring the female's territory and moving away after the mating season.

400, 407 **Calliope Hummingbird**
(*Stellula calliope*)
Hummingbirds (Trochilidae)

Description: 2¾–4" (7–10 cm). Smallest North American hummer. Male metallic *green above, gorget white with purple-violet* rays, which can be raised to give a whiskered effect. (All other North American hummers have solid-colored gorgets.) Female *green above, white below,* with dark streaks on throat, buffy flanks, and white-tipped tail corners; resembles female Rufous but smaller, with smaller bill and paler flanks and less rufous at base of tail.

Voice: A series of light *chip* notes. Displaying male utters a high *see-ree* note as it dives over female.

Habitat: Breeds and feeds in montane and subalpine forest clearings, brushy edges, and alpine meadows.

Nesting: 2 bean-sized white eggs, surprisingly large for such a tiny bird, in a small lichen-and-moss nest covered with cobwebs on a limb of a bush or well-protected small tree.

Range: From interior and southern coastal British Columbia to Baja California in the West, and from Alberta to Wyoming in the Rocky Mountains. Winters in Mexico.

In mating display or in defending their feeding flowers, male hummers (and occasionally females) put on a striking spectacle, rising out of sight and then swooping down to buzz the female or their opponent. Each species has its own flight pattern.

Olive Warbler
(*Peucedramus taeniatus*)
Wood Warblers (Parulidae)

Description: 4½–5″ (11–13 cm). *Tawny orange head, nape, and breast;* broad *black eye-line* extends from bill to neck. Gray above, white below, with dark wings and tail, and broad white wing bars. Female has olive-gray crown, nape, and ear patch; upperparts gray; eye-stripe, throat, and upper breast have dingy yellowish wash; belly white. Duller plumage in fall; juvenile males resemble female.

Voice: Song is a titmouse-like series of whistled phrases: *peter, peter, peter . . .* Call is a downslurred *kew*.

Habitat: High pine and subalpine fir belts of southwestern mountains.

Nesting: 3 or 4 grayish-white to bluish eggs, heavily speckled with black markings, in an intricate cup nest of fine rootlets, grasses, moss, and lichens, high in a conifer near the end of a horizontal bough or fork.

Range: Southern Arizona and New Mexico south to Nicaragua.

The habits of this warbler are not well known since it lives in tall trees, often in inaccessible mountains.

Magnolia Warbler
(*Dendroica magnolia*)
Wood Warblers (Parulidae)

Description: 4½–5″ (11–13 cm). Spring male is gray with black markings above, white line behind eye, and large white patches on wings and tail. Rump and *underparts yellow,* the latter *with heavy black breast streaks.* Female and fall male are olive rather than gray, with sparse flank markings.

Voice: Both the *chip* call and the striking song of the male are typical of warblers. Song is a rising *wisha-wisha-wisha-witsy* or *pretty-pretty-Rachel.*

Habitat: Moist coniferous forests and mixed stands.

Nesting: 3–5 creamy white eggs, spotted and usually wreathed at larger end, in a loose, shallow grass- and root-lined cup nest low in a small conifer.

Range: Across the boreal forest belt from interior British Columbia and Mackenzie to the East coast, and from the Great Lakes south along the Appalachian Mountains. Casual during migration in the western states. Winters in Central America.

This beautiful warbler received its name when it was discovered on a magnolia tree in Mississippi on spring migration to its northern breeding grounds.

414, 552   **Yellow-rumped Warbler**
including "Myrtle Warbler"
and "Audubon's Warbler"
(*Dendroica coronata*)
Wood Warblers (Parulidae)

Description: 5–6" (13–15 cm). *Bright yellow cap,*
flanks, and rump. Dark gray above with
black streaks, white belly; in spring
and summer, males have black breast.
Conspicuous white eye-ring and tail
spots. The white-throated northern
population with two white wing bars
was formerly known as the "Myrtle
Warbler"; the western race, with
yellow throat and one broad white wing
bar, was called "Audubon's Warbler."
The two have been found to interbreed
and are now considered one species, the
Yellow-rumped Warbler. Females in all
plumages as well as fall and winter
males are brownish-beige with two
light wing bars, faintly streaked
underparts, and some yellow on throat,
flanks, and rump.

Voice: Song of the male is a loud trilling,
rising or falling at the end. Flocks that
winter in desert oases, live oak canyons,
and parks and gardens of the Southwest
utter a sharp *chep* or *chip*.

Habitat: Coniferous forests in open areas, even
when mixed with such deciduous edge
growth as dogwood, maple, and alder;
in winter, in any kind of woodland.

Nesting: 4 or 5 white eggs with brown and gray
specks in a feather-lined cup nest in a
conifer, ranging from low elevations to
as high as 50 feet.

Range: The "Myrtle Warbler" lives in the
boreal forest across North America; in
the West, south to north-central
British Columbia and southern Alberta,
north of dotted line on map. It
migrates partly through the western
region but, mostly, to the southeastern
United States. The "Audubon's
Warbler" lives in coniferous forests of
the West, south into Mexico in the
mountains, south of dotted line. They

winter in the Southwest and in Central America.

Yellow-rumped Warblers are vivid and conspicuous birds that search for food both high and low in Douglas firs or pines. They most often sing from the high canopy of trees. During winter they disperse in loose flocks, so two or three birds at most are observed at a time. The birds constantly chirp a "contact call" that keeps the flock together.

---

415 Townsend's Warbler
(*Dendroica townsendi*)
Wood Warblers (Parulidae)

Description: 4¼–5" (11–13 cm). Adult male has black crown and nape, ear patch, throat, and bib. *Face and breast bright yellow;* sides heavily streaked with black; white belly. Wings and tail dusky with two white wing bars and white outer tail feathers. In winter black bib of male, female, and immatures is replaced by dark streaking; black elsewhere becomes dusky olive. Back is green in all plumages.

Voice: A rising series of notes, usually with 2 phrases, the first repeated three or four times, the second once or twice: *weazy weazy weazy weazy twea* or *dee dee dee-de de.* Call is a soft *chip.*

Habitat: Coniferous forests; in old stands of Douglas firs, where it forages in the upper canopy.

Nesting: 3–5 white eggs, wreathed and speckled with brownish markings, in a well-concealed shallow cup in a conifer.

Range: Coastal forests of the Pacific Northwest from Alaska and British Columbia to northern Washington; Idaho, Montana, and Wyoming. Winters to Central America.

This warbler is a darker counterpart of the Black-throated Green Warbler, (*Dendroica virens*), which breeds east of the Rocky Mountains. The pattern of Townsend's plumage is similar to that of the Hermit, Black-throated Gray, and Golden-cheeked warblers; all these warblers are believed to have developed from one ancestral stock.

416 Hermit Warbler
(*Dendroica occidentalis*)
Wood Warblers (Parulidae)

Description: 4½" (11 cm). *Yellow head,* with *black chin and throat, gray back;* white underparts with black-streaked flanks. Gray wings and tail with white wing bars and outer tail feathers. Female and immatures have little or no dark throat markings; gray of back extends to top of crown. No other western warbler is as white underneath.

Voice: A series of high notes, somewhat less buzzy than the song of a Townsend's Warbler; recalls a Yellow Warbler in pattern but less emphatic. Call is a soft *chup.*

Habitat: Mature coniferous forests.

Nesting: 3–5 creamy white eggs, speckled and wreathed with light brown markings, in a neat shallow cup nest of rootlets, bark, and pine needles, "saddled" on a conifer branch, usually 20–40 feet high, but occasionally near the ground.

Range: Pacific coastal states from Washington to northwestern California and the Sierra Nevada. Winters in Mexico and Central America.

This species lives high in the canopy of the tallest redwoods and Douglas fir trees and is therefore difficult to observe. It has been occasionally found to hybridize with Townsend's Warbler. The similarity in their songs indicates that the two species are close relatives.

Grace's Warbler
(*Dendroica graciae*)
Wood Warblers (Parulidae)

Description: 4½–5″ (11–13 cm). Bright *yellow eye-stripe, chin, throat, and breast;* upperparts *gray* streaked with black; underparts white with black striping on sides; wings and tail dark with two white wing bars and whitish outer tail feathers. Sexes similar, though female and juveniles may be paler.

Voice: Repeated song is a short musical trill, faster toward the end: *che che che che che-che-che-che.* Call is a soft *chip.*

Habitat: Montane stands of pine or mixed pine-oak forests.

Nesting: 3 or 4 white or creamy eggs, finely spotted with reddish-brown, in a small cup nest of rootlets and bark shreds lined with hair or feathers, well concealed in a conifer, some 20–60 feet above the ground.

Range: Central Utah and Colorado south along the mountains of the Southwest (but not California) to Honduras and Nicaragua.

Because this small bird lives high up in pine trees and is difficult to observe, little is known of its life history. It moves from treetop to treetop with a quick erratic flight, darting out of the canopy to catch prey in midair. During migration it prefers mountain forests similar to those in which it breeds, but in winter, in Central America, it also frequents lowland pine savannas with stands of tall pines.

426, 429 **Evening Grosbeak**
(*Hesperiphona vespertina*)
Finches (Fringillidae)

Description: 7–8½″ (18–22 cm). A plump bird, with *heavy conical bill. Wings and tail black, large white wing patch. Body dark yellow,* with yellow on forehead and eyebrows; head, neck, and breast dark olive-brown. Bill yellowish-green in breeding birds; ivory in winter. Female and immatures dusky, wings and tail marked with white.

Voice: Calls incessantly to maintain contact within the flock. In flight, *tchew tchew tchew* or a shrill *p-teer.* Also a clear, downslurred *tew.*

Habitat: For breeding, coniferous and mixed forests. In fall, large flocks gather in woods where seeds or fruits are available, remaining into late spring.

Nesting: 3 or 4 bluish-green eggs with fine markings in a flimsy stick nest high in a conifer. Several pairs may nest close together.

Range: In the West, the southern part of the coniferous forest belt in the Canadian provinces; the coastal forest and the mountain chains, through the latter south to Mexico. It spread eastward during the last half century into the Great Lakes region and even farther east.

Major Delafield, an explorer of the 1820s, was the first to write about this grosbeak. He sighted some of these birds near his tent at twilight, and believed that they hid in dark shade during the day and dispersed at sunset; this led to its subsequent Latin designation by Cooper: *Hesperiphona vespertina,* "Evening Night-singer." The misnomer stuck both in Latin and in English. When winter food gets scarce, the flocks, numbering from scores to hundreds, wander far in the valleys and plains in search of maple or dogwood seeds, wild cherry pits, buds, and other fruits and seeds.

432, 450 Hepatic Tanager
(Piranga flava)
Tanagers (Thraupidae)

Description: 7–8″ (18–20 cm). Male is a subdued *orange-brick color,* darker than Summer Tanager. Both sexes have *dark bill* and *ear patch.* Female olive green above, deep yellow below, with more orange tint to throat than other female tanagers.

Voice: Strong, short phrases, whistled vireo-fashion at even intervals; each phrase may rise, fall, or remain on the same tone. Call notes are a low *chup* and an inquisitive *wheet?*

Habitat: Mountain coniferous forests; live oaks.

Nesting: 3–5 bluish eggs, with fairly heavy overall blotches, in a shallow nest of rootlets and weeds on a low horizontal branch.

Range: Northwestern Arizona, New Mexico, southern Nevada, southeastern California, and Texas. Breeds farther south from Mexico to South America.

Though insect-feeders during the nesting period, these tanagers eat figs, ripe guavas, and other fruits on their winter grounds in Central America.

434, 454 Western Tanager
(Piranga ludoviciana)
Tanagers (Thraupidae)

Description: 6–7½″ (15–19 cm). Adult male has *brilliant red head, bright yellow body, with black back, wings, and tail.* Two wing bars; smaller uppermost bar yellow, lower white. Female is yellow-green above, yellow below; wing bars similar to male's.

Voice: Song is strong and carries far; Robin-like in its short fluty stanzas rendered with a pause in between. The quality is much hoarser, however. Call is a dry *pit-r-ick.*

Habitat: Open coniferous forests.

Nesting: 3–5 bluish-green, speckled eggs in a frail, shallow saucer nest of woven rootlets, weed stalks, and bark strips, "saddled" in the fork of a horizontal branch of Douglas fir, spruce, pine, or occasionally oak, usually at a low elevation.

Range: Widespread in the West, from Alaskan panhandle and southern Mackenzie south to northern Baja California, skirting the deserts; in the mountains of the Southwest. Winters in Mexico and Central America.

In late spring and early summer it feeds on insects, often like a flycatcher from the high canopy; later it feeds on berries and other small fruits.

444 Varied Thrush
(*Ixoreus naevius*)
Thrushes (Turdidae)

Description: 9–10″ (23–25 cm). Similar to Robin. Upperparts are *slate gray; rusty orange throat and breast* interrupted by broad *slaty or black breast band;* off-white belly. Female is similar but paler. Juveniles' breast band incomplete, frequently with orange and dusky speckles. Flight more undulating than Robin's.

Voice: Song is not melodious, but is nevertheless remarkable. Whistles 2 or 3 buzzy notes, each drawn out until it fades away, followed by a short silence. The thrush sings concealed high in a tree, its song echoing in the dark of the silent forest. Calls are a low *took* and a soft buzz.

Habitat: Dense coniferous or deciduous forests with abundant water sources.

Nesting: 3–5 pale blue, spotted eggs in a moss-lined twig cup in a small tree, sapling, or bush.

Range: In the coastal rain forest of the Pacific

Northwest from central Alaska south to northern California. Winters in great numbers in the madrona forests of southwestern British Columbia and southward.

This thrush lives on the shaded floor of coniferous forests. Like the Robin, it feeds on earthworms and insects in open, bare areas. In winter it migrates to lowlands or flies south to California parks, habitats it shares with Robins.

452, 553 Red Crossbill
(*Loxia curvirostra*)
Finches (Fringillidae)

Description: 5¼–6½" (13–17 cm). Sparrow-sized finch with *crossed mandibles.* Head and body of male *dusky brick red,* wings and tail dark. Female is drab olive-gray with dull yellow on rump and underparts. Immature males have orange tint with dusky streaks on mantle and breast. Plumage of both sexes has overall mottled appearance.

Voice: A repeated *kip-kip* or *jeep-jeep* betrays its presence. Song is a short series of chipping and tinkling notes.

Habitat: Coniferous forests, favoring pines.

Nesting: 3–5 light bluish-green eggs, wreathed at the large end with brown markings, in a neat shallow nest of dry twigs, moss, and rootlets, lined with lichens and fur placed at any height on a fork in a conifer.

Range: Resident throughout the boreal coniferous forests of Eurasia, North Africa, and North America where it extends from Alaska to Newfoundland and south to Baja California, Nicaragua, and the southern Appalachians.

The bill of these unusual birds is specialized for opening pine cones. Holding the cone with one foot, the bird inserts its closed bill between the cone and the scales, pries the scales apart by opening its bill, and extracts the seed with its flexible tongue. Because of its dependence on pine seeds, the Red Crossbill is an erratic and nomadic species. When cone crops fail, these birds gather in flocks and may wander far from their normal haunts. They may breed almost anywhere, and at any season, so long as the food supply is adequate.

453, 554   **White-winged Crossbill**
(*Loxia leucoptera*)
Finches (Fringillidae)

Description: 6–6¾" (15–17 cm). Slightly larger than the more common Red Crossbill; plump finch with crossed mandibles. Male is *pink;* dark wings and tail. *prominent white wing bars.* Female olive-gray with dusky streaking, *yellowish rump,* and dark wings and tail with *white wing bars.* Tail notched.

Voice: The flight call is a soft *twee* or a loud, harsh *cheet cheet.* Song is variable, melodiously canary-like, with warbling trilling.

Habitat: Coniferous woodlands.

Nesting: 3 or 4 greenish-white, spotted eggs in a deep nest of rootlets, twigs, mosses, and bark strips lined with fine grasses and feathers, in a coniferous tree, frequently spruce.

Range: Resident in the boreal forest across Eurasia and North America and south in the mountains to central British Columbia and New England. Also on the West Indian island of Hispaniola.

The White-winged Crossbill with its smaller, slimmer bill is more dependent upon spruce cones than pines, but like the Red Crossbill it wanders widely and irregularly in search of cones and may breed at any month of the year. During its wanderings it feeds on a great variety of other seeds or fruits and even insects. At such times it may be seen in association with Red Crossbills.

458 Red-faced Warbler
(*Cardellina rubrifrons*)
Wood Warblers (Parulidae)

Description: 5¼" (13 cm). Gray above, white below with bright *red forehead, throat, and breast;* black crown and ear patch; white nape patch and rump.

Voice: Song is a series of rich notes: *sweet-sweet-sweet-weeta-see-see-see,* similar to that of the Yellow Warbler. Call is a loud *chup.*

Habitat: Montane coniferous forests.

Nesting: 3 or 4 white, marked eggs in a loosely assembled ground nest of rootlets and grasses sheltered by a log, rock, or patch of weeds.

Range: South-central Arizona and southwestern New Mexico to the Mexican Sierra Plateau; winters in Mexico and Central America.

Active and energetic like most warblers, it keeps to the outside canopy of tall trees. This warbler has the characteristic habit of flicking its tail sideways.

461, 583 Purple Finch
(*Carpodacus purpureus*)
Finches (Fringillidae)

Description: 5½–6¼" (14–16 cm). Larger and stockier than the House Finch, but smaller than Cassin's and darker than both. *Dusky rose red of male* extends from upperparts to *breast* and *flanks,* brightest at *crown and rump.* Off-white below, mantle streaked with brown, wings and notched tail brown. *Female has pronounced light stripe behind eye, dark stripe on jaw,* and more heavily streaked breast than female House or Cassin's.

Voice: Full song is a complicated prolonged warble with less variation in pitch than that of the House and Cassin's finches. Call is a rich *cheer-lee* and, in flight, a sharp *pit.*

Habitat: Prefers edges of coniferous forests, but may also frequent mixed woods and second-growth alder thickets.

Nesting: 4 or 5 pale bluish eggs, with brown and black spots and scrawls, in a neat shallow cup nest of twigs, strips of bark, and rootlets, lined with grasses and hair, on a horizontal conifer branch, sometimes as high as 60 feet above ground.

Range: Coastal rain forest; montane coniferous forest of the Far West; coast to coast in northern boreal forest. Migratory in the North, but moves only to the southern United States.

During the breeding season, pairs are territorial, the male displaying in front of the female with his loud warbling song. After the clutch is raised, they may be seen in large flocks visiting orchards, parks, and other woodlands.

462, 584 **Cassin's Finch**
(*Carpodacus cassinii*)
Finches (Fringillidae)

Description: 6–6½" (15–17 cm). Larger than both House and Purple finches. Male's breast coloration *paler rose red* than that of the Purple Finch; brown-streaked nape and mantle make rosy crown and rump, especially *crown,* appear more *brilliant.* Unstreaked flanks and belly pale pink to whitish. Female resembles female Purple Finch but more finely streaked above and below, with less distinct eye-line and jaw stripe. House Finch smaller, slimmer, the male is redder and has brown-streaked belly.

Voice: Song is a series of warbles, similar to the Purple Finch's but flutier and more varied. Call note, a high *pwee-de-lip,* is diagnostic.

Habitat: Open conifer stands at high elevations.

Nesting: 4 or 5 bluish-green eggs, with dark brownish spots, in a cup nest of twigs and rootlets, in a conifer.

Range: Interior mountain ranges or valleys of the West, from the southern Canadian Rockies and the Selkirks to the mountains of Baja California and, farther east, to the southern rim of the Central Plateau. Northernmost populations migratory; in winter many are found in northern Mexico.

The closely related Cassin's, House, and Purple finches are each found in different altitudes and habitats; thus there is no competition among them. In California the House Finch is common in the arid, hot plains, deserts, and the foothills, nesting widely in chaparral and oak woodland. In the montane forest belt, the Purple Finch is found at the edges of coniferous stands and the shady oak growth of canyons. Cassin's is found higher up in firs and yellow pines.

466, 481 **Pine Grosbeak**
(*Pinicola enucleator*)
Finches (Fringillidae)

Description: 8–10″ (20–25 cm). Large, plump finch. Stubby, strongly curved black bill. *Dull rose red body* with dark streaking on back, dark wings with two white wing bars; dusky, notched tail. *Juvenile* male *dull pinkish-red* on head and rump with gray body. *Females* similar to first-year males in pattern, with *dull mustard head* and rump markings.

Voice: A 3-noted whistle similar to that of the

Greater Yellowlegs.

Habitat: Coniferous forests.

Nesting: 2–5 pale blue-green, blotched eggs in a bulky nest of grasses, rootlets, and moss lined with hair, low in a coniferous tree, usually no more than about 10–12 feet from the ground.

Range: Circumpolar. Breeds across the northern forest belt of Europe, Asia, and North America; in the West extends south into the pine and fir forests of high mountains from the northern Sierra Nevada and Rockies to New Mexico.

During snowy winters these grosbeaks can be located in scattered open forests by the feeble calls that keep the flock together. They settle in a tree and feed, snapping off buds or seeking the pits in fruit, until sated or disturbed. When food is scarce, they may descend from mountains into woods at sea level.

---

470 **Clark's Nutcracker**
(*Nucifraga columbiana*)
Crows (Corvidae)

Description: 12–13″ (30–33 cm). Almost crow-sized, with flashing black, white, and gray pattern. *Light gray* with dark eye and long, sharply pointed bill. Black wing with large white wing patch at trailing edge; black tail with white outer tail feathers. Face white from forehead to chin, white belly. Crow-like flight.

Voice: A guttural *kraaaa* . . .

Habitat: Stands of juniper and ponderosa pine, or whitebark and larch, on high mountain ranges, near the treeline.

Nesting: 2–6 green, spotted eggs in a deep bowl nest of sticks in a coniferous tree. Nests very early.

Range: From the Great Basin area, including southern British Columbia and Alberta,

throughout the pine-clad western mountains south to California and to northern Baja California.

An erratic winter wanderer, this nutcracker's periodic irruption in great numbers, bringing it all the way to the Pacific Coast, is related to failure of the pine seed crop. Near camps and picnic sites it begs and steals food scraps. It can hold several nuts in a special cheek pouch under the tongue in addition to those it holds in the beak.

471 Gray Jay
(*Perisoreus canadensis*)
Crows (Corvidae)

Description: 10–13″ (25–33 cm). *Dark gray above*, with narrow, light band across back; *light below*. Blackish nape contrasts with almost white forehead and face. Juveniles are dark slaty overall, with light whisker.

Voice: A whistled *pwee-ah* note. Also a great variety of other notes, some harsh and grating.

Habitat: Northern coniferous forests.

Nesting: 3–5 greenish-gray, spotted eggs in a bowl of twigs lined with feathers or other soft material. An early nester, this jay often incubates with snow on its back.

Range: Taiga from Alaska to the Atlantic Coast, the coastal rain forest to northern California, and the interior and Rocky Mountain ranges to extreme northeastern California, Arizona, Colorado, and northern New Mexico.

Anyone who has camped in the mountains of the northern forests is familiar with this bird, formerly called "Canada Jay" and popularly known as the "Whiskey Jack" or "Camp Robber." This bird is attracted to campsites, where it appropriates as much food as possible. It stores scraps of frozen meat, suet, or hide, gluing them into balls with its saliva and hiding them among the needles.

473 Northern Shrike
(*Lanius excubitor*)
Shrikes (Laniidae)

Description: 9–10¾" (23–27 cm). Robin-sized. Hooked bill, *lower mandible pale.* Light gray above, white with fine dusky barring below. *Black mask,* wing, and tail; white throat, rump, and outer tail feathers; large white wing patches. Slightly smaller Loggerhead Shrike has less heavy bill and face mask that meets over bill. White side patches and undertail coverts distinguish both shrikes in flight from Mockingbird. Brown immatures have more pronounced breast barrings and less defined face mask.

Voice: Warning note is *sheck-sheck;* in alarm, a mewing *jaaeg.* Song is a subdued, varying warble often mimicking other birds, uttered by both sexes. Usually silent in winter.

Habitat: Coniferous woodlands, bogs; in winter, partly open country with some trees used as watching posts.

Nesting: 4–9 grayish-white, brown-blotched eggs in a bulky nest of twigs, lined with feathers, in a conifer or bush.

Range: Circumpolar. In North America it breeds in the Far North of the boreal forest belt, from Alaska east to Labrador. Winters south of the breeding range; in the West, in the Central Plateau and Rocky Mountain states, rarely farther south.

The Northern Shrike sits quietly, often in the top of a tree, before swooping down after insects, mice, and small birds. It kills more than it can eat, impaling the prey on a thorn or wedging it in a forked twig. On lean days it feeds from its larder.

476 Townsend's Solitaire
(*Myadestes townsendi*)
Thrushes (Turdidae)

Description: 8–9½″ (20–24 cm). More like Mockingbird than a thrush. It sits upright, usually high on a branch; *overall gray,* unstreaked, slightly darker above, with thin *white eye-ring and white outer tail feathers; pale rusty wing patch.* Juveniles are mottled gray and white.

Voice: Usually utters the loud, melodious, fluty rising and falling phrases of its somewhat thrush-like song from a high perch, but it may also fly up and sing over the nesting territory. Call is a bell-like *heep.*

Habitat: Open coniferous forests, edges, or burns with single standing trees in the mountains.

Nesting: 3 or 4 grayish-white eggs, with light brown spots concentrated at the large end of the egg, in a large, loosely built nest of weeds, lined with rootlets, on the ground, in holes, among roots, in road cuts, old mine shafts, and rocks of talus slopes.

Range: From the high mountains of the West to the Sierra Madre ranges of Mexico and the ranges of northern Baja California. In the North, it reaches Alaska and northern British Columbia. Usually winters in lowlands.

This is the northernmost of a number of mountain-forest thrushes (solitaires) of the New World and the only species north of Mexico. Like other thrushes, it forages on the ground for berries and insects; in winter, it descends to lower elevations, and may even occur in desert oases.

479 **Yellow-eyed Junco**
(*Junco phaeonotus*)
Finches (Fringillidae)

Description: 5½–6½" (14–17 cm). Unique *bright yellow-orange eye* and black lores. Bill has *dark upper mandible* and *pale lower mandible. Gray above* with *bright rusty mantle* and white outer tail feathers. Underparts lighter.

Voice: Song is more highly patterned than that of the Dark-eyed Junco. One representation is *chip-chip, seedle-seedle, chee-chee-chee,* although it is variable.

Habitat: Coniferous forests; pine-oak woods.

Nesting: 3 or 4 bluish-white, spotted eggs in a slight cup nest of small rootlets and fine grass lined with horsehair, on the ground under the protection of a log, a stump, or grass tufts, or in a low tree.

Range: Southeastern Arizona and southwestern New Mexico south through the high mountains of Mexico to Guatemala.

This junco is slower, more deliberate in its movements than the Dark-eyed Junco; it walks, rather than hops, on the forest floor.

480 **Gray-headed Junco**
(*Junco caniceps*)
Finches (Fringillidae)

Description: 5½–6" (14–15 cm). *Ash gray head, neck, sides, rump, and tail; rufous back;* white belly and outer tail feathers; eyes dark. Sexes look alike.

Voice: Song is a loose rolling trill on one pitch. Note is a sharp *tic* or *chip.*

Habitat: Coniferous forest edges and light stands where the ground is mostly open but shaded, with nearby ground cover for shelter; also aspen groves; pine-oak forest in the South.

Nesting: 3–5 white eggs spotted with brown, in a grass nest on the ground.

Range: Northwestern Nevada, southern Idaho,

and Wyoming south through the mountains to southeastern California, northern Arizona, southern New Mexico, and western Texas. Winters at lower elevations, and south to northern Mexico.

In appearance this junco seems to be an intermediate form between the Dark-eyed and Yellow-eyed juncos. Its plumage is similar to that of the Yellow-eyed, but it has dark eyes. In birds from the northern part of its range both mandibles of the bill are pale as in the Dark-eyed, while in birds to the south the upper mandible is dark like that of the Yellow-eyed.

483 **Dark-eyed Junco**
including "Oregon Junco"
and "Slate-colored Junco"
and "White-winged Junco"
(*Junco hyemalis*)
Finches (Fringillidae)

Description: 5–6¼" (13–16 cm). This species shows much geographic variation in color. Typically, males of western populations ("Oregon Junco") have *black hood, chestnut mantle,* white underparts with buff sides. Eastern males ("Slate-colored Junco") are *dark slate gray on head,* upper *breast, flanks and upperparts,* with white lower breast and belly. Both forms have pink bill and dark gray tail with *white outer tail feathers.* The pine forests of the Black Hills in western South Dakota and eastern Montana have an isolated population ("White-winged Junco") similar to the eastern form with two white wing bars and extensive white outer tail feathers. Western females have gray hood; females of all forms less colorful.

Voice: Ringing metallic trill on the same pitch. Members of a flock may spread out widely, keeping in contact by

constantly calling *tsick* or *tchet*. Also a
soft buzzy *trill* in flight.

Habitat: Openings and edges of conifers and
mixed woods; in winter, roadsides,
parks, suburban gardens.

Nesting: 3–6 bluish-white eggs, with variegated
blotches concentrated at the larger end,
in a compact nest of rootlets, shreds of
bark, twigs, and mosses, lined with
grasses and hair, on the ground,
protected by a rock ledge, mudbank,
tufts of weeds, or fallen log.

Range: In wooded regions of North America
from Alaska to Newfoundland, and
south across northern United States. In
the West, south through the coastal
rain forest and the mountain forests of
the northwestern states to Baja
California. Western birds winter mostly
in Pacific coastal areas, occasionally
wandering to the East coast. A few
eastern birds occur on the West coast
in winter.

This lively territorial bird is a ground
dweller and feeds on seeds and small
fruits in the open. It also moves
through the lower branches of trees and
seeks shelter in tangles of shrubs.

Mexican Chickadee
(*Parus sclateri*)
Titmice (Paridae)

Description: 5″ (13 cm). Black cap, *extended black
bib, and gray flanks.*

Voice: Its *chick-a-dee* call is huskier and lazier
than that of the Mountain Chickadee.

Habitat: Coniferous or pine-oak forests at high
altitudes.

Nesting: 5–8 whitish eggs, frequently with
reddish-brown spotting, in a fiber nest
lined with grass, feathers, or fur in an
excavated hole in a dead branch. The
incubating bird covers the eggs with
nest material when disturbed.

Range: From the adjacent southern corners of

Arizona and New Mexico south throughout the mountains of the Mexican Plateau.

This bird feeds along the outer tree canopy, often hanging upside down to pluck small insects from conifer needles. Like other chickadees, it has an ingenious arrangement of leg tendons which enables it to pull close to a branch while upside down. Vireos, warblers, and kinglets must hover above branches, and are unable to reach the undersides, so that chickadees can exploit this feeding opportunity without competition.

488 Mountain Chickadee
(*Parus gambeli*)
Titmice (Paridae)

Description: 5–5¾" (13–15 cm). Gray above, paler below. *White eye-stripe, black cap and bib; pale gray flanks.*

Voice: A hoarse *chick-a-zee-zee, zee.* Spring song is similar to that of the Black-capped Chickadee, but 3-toned: *fee-bee-bee,* the *bees* at a lower pitch.

Habitat: High-altitude coniferous forests.

Nesting: 7–9 white, sometimes spotted eggs in a hair- or fur-lined natural cavity or woodpecker hole; like other chickadees, it sometimes excavates a hole in soft, rotten wood.

Range: In the mountains of interior British Columbia south through the Rocky Mountain and Cascade-Sierra chains to Baja California to western Texas.

A fearless, constantly active insect-gleaner of the mountain forest, it frequently descends into the lowlands in winter. In November an occasional flock can be found near sea level in desert oases containing conifers such as Palm Springs, California, while other flocks will still be at 8500 feet in the subalpine forest of adjacent Mount San Jacinto.

496, 497   Mountain Bluebird
(*Sialia currucoides*)
Thrushes (Turdidae)

Description: 6½–8" (17–20 cm). Male *turquoise blue* with *lighter blue breast* and white belly. Female gray-brown with trace of blue on wings, rump, and tail. *More erect, less hunched* posture than that of the Western Bluebird and Eastern Bluebird (*Sialia sialis*). Juveniles are brown above, lightly spotted below, with pale blue wash on the wings and tail.

Voice: A quiet warbling dawn song. Calls, which vary with the species, include a soft *phew, ior,* and *terr.* This bluebird's notes are somewhat harsher and more nasal than those of other species.

Habitat: Open areas where mountain meadows and pastures are interspersed with loose stands or single coniferous trees. In the North, nests at low elevations in pine woodlands and wooded areas; farther south, in subalpine forests among alpine meadows, aspen groves, and other montane woodlands.

Nesting: 4–6 pale greenish-blue, unmarked eggs, in a grass nest lined with feathers or bark chips, in a tree cavity, usually an abandoned woodpecker hole, or even a nest-box.

Range: From Alaska, northern British Columbia and Alberta, and central Manitoba south to the mountains of southern California and to western Oklahoma. Winters in southern part of its breeding area at low elevations and in Mexico.

These birds hover low over the ground and drop down to catch insects, or dart out from a branch, flycatcher-fashion, and then return to another perch.

502 Steller's Jay
(Cyanocitta stelleri)
Crows (Corvidae)

Description: 12–13½" (30–34 cm). *Only western jay with crest.* Front half of bird sooty black, rear dark bluish-gray, with tight black cross-barring on secondaries and tail. Lightly streaked eyebrow, chin, and forehead markings vary considerably.

Voice: A harsh *shack-shack-shack-shack* or *chook-chook-chook* call reveals its presence. May also mimic the screams of hawks.

Habitat: Coniferous forests: pine and oak woods in the South, small groves and stands of mixed oak and redwood in northern California. In the Northwest, a bird of dense coniferous forests. In fall it moves to oak trees at lower elevations, often leaving the conifers it prefers at nesting time.

Nesting: 3–5 greenish, spotted eggs in a neat twiggy bowl lined with small roots and fibers, well hidden in a shady conifer.

Range: Throughout the West, from coastal Alaska to the prairies and from the Rocky Mountains down to southern California and into Central America.

Somewhat more reticent than the Gray Jay, it nevertheless quickly becomes accustomed to campsites and human providers. It is often seen sitting quietly on treetops, surveying the surroundings. Near the nest site, it is silent and shy.

509 Golden-crowned Kinglet
(Regulus satrapa)
Old World Warblers (Sylviidae)

Description: 3¼–4" (8–10 cm). One of the smallest North American birds. Olive green above, dirty white below, with small, slender bill, white wing bars, and

slightly notched tail. *White eyebrow;*
black-bordered orange-yellow (male) or
yellow (female) crown.

Voice: A high-pitched *see-see-see.*

Habitat: Dense, first-growth conifer stands.

Nesting: 5–11 grayish-white eggs, heavily
spotted with pale brown and mauve, in
a delicate oblong nest with high walls,
thickly lined with moss and feathers,
and with a small opening at the top;
suspended from twigs, high in a
densely needled conifer, frequently
spruce.

Range: Coast to coast across the boreal forest
zone from southern Alaska and Canada
south, in the East, into the northern
Appalachians; in the West, southward
through the Douglas fir and subalpine
fir zones of the western mountain chains
and the cool, wet coastal rain forest.
Winters as far south as Central
America.

Outside the breeding season, these
tiny, energetic birds are frequently seen
in the company of Ruby-crowned
Kinglets, creepers, nuthatches, and
chickadees. These feeding flocks move
as a group through the trees, searching
out the greatest abundance of insects
and larvae.

510 Ruby-crowned Kinglet
(*Regulus calendula*)
Old World Warblers (Sylviidae)

Description: 3¾–4½" (10–11 cm). Olive-gray
above, shaded white below, with white
wing bars. It is distinguished from
Golden-crowned Kinglet by *incomplete
white eye-ring,* and small, *scarlet crown
patch* of male (frequently concealed);
crown patch lacking in female.
Differentiated from warblers and vireos
by its smaller size; short, slightly
forked tail; continuous, rapid
movements and nervous wing-flicking

habit (a habit shared by Golden-crowned).

Voice: Call is a harsh *ji-dit*. Song begins with several high, thin notes followed by loud, whistled phrases.

Habitat: Coniferous forests in summer; mixed coniferous and deciduous thickets in winter.

Nesting: 5–10 creamy eggs, finely speckled; its carefully woven nest very similar to that of the Golden-crowned; suspended near the outermost tip of a conifer branch; prefers spruce.

Range: Coast to coast in the taiga, from Alaska through Canada; along the Rocky Mountains to Arizona, and along the Pacific coastal mountains to the mountains of southern California. Winters south to Gulf states and Central America.

Because kinglets weigh little, they are able to feed on the tips of branches of conifers. The Ruby-crowned feeds lower in the canopy than the Golden-crowned and characteristically hovers above a twig looking for caterpillars, aphids, and other insects. The Ruby-crowned is not as social in its winter range as the Golden-crowned and occurs more often singly than in flocks.

Hutton's Vireo
(*Vireo huttoni*)
Vireos (Vireonidae)

Description: 4¼–4¾″ (11–12 cm). Small, grayish-olive vireo with *partial white eye-ring below, incomplete spectacle,* and two white wing bars.

Voice: The territorial male announces his presence by a series of loud, short whistles and chatter. A monotonous 2-part phrase, either upslurred or downslurred: *chu-whe, chu-wee . . .* or *che-eer, che-eer . . .* Call is a harsh *chit-chit.*

Habitat: Deciduous and mixed forests, primarily
            oak woodlands, live oak tangles in
            canyons of the Southwest.

Nesting: 3 or 4 white eggs, with scattered brown
            spots, in a hanging cup nest lined with
            feathers and moss suspended from a
            shrub branch or young tree.

Range: Spotty from southern Arizona and
            Texas south to Central America. Arid
            deserts and highlands separate the pale
            olive-colored, migratory populations
            from the darker birds found in Pacific
            coastal forests from southern British
            Columbia to northern Baja California,
            where it is a year-round resident.

            This bird moves slowly, almost
            sluggishly through the canopy, halting
            after every move to forage for insects
            among the foliage. During winter,
            Hutton's Vireo may join a mixed flock
            where it may be mistaken for the
            similar Ruby-crowned Kinglet, but the
            vireo is distinguishable by its heavier
            bill, incomplete spectacles, and duskier
            throat and breast.

512 Tennessee Warbler
(*Vermivora peregrina*)
Wood Warblers (Parulidae)

Description: 4½–5″ (11–13 cm). *Gray crown* and
               nape, olive green above, whitish below,
               with *black eye-line and white eye-stripe*.
               Female lacks pronounced gray crown
               and has pale yellow underparts and
               yellowish eye-stripe. Fall adults and
               juveniles are plainer olive green with
               white undertail coverts.

Voice: A short twitter repeated 4 or 5 times,
               followed by another higher or lower,
               with the two sequences sometimes
               separated by a third, shorter one,
               sometimes interpreted as *ticka, ticka,
               ticka, ticka, ticka, swit, swit, chew-chew-
               chew-chew-chew-chew*. Call note is a thin
               seet.

Habitat: Northern boreal forests or taiga; mixed deciduous woodlands and brush.

Nesting: 4–7 white eggs, often lightly spotted with reddish-brown, in a hair-lined nest of grasses and fibers, on or near the ground, often in peat moss in bogs, in the shelter of tall cover such as a clump of grass or low bush.

Range: From southern Yukon and northwestern British Columbia across Canada to the New England states. Winters around the Caribbean from Guatemala to Venezuela. Scarce migrant through the West.

It feeds and sings at medium to low height in needled or broadleaved trees. The coloration of this warbler resembles that of some vireos, but it has more slender body and bill and the nervous, searching habit common to all warblers.

Coues' Flycatcher
(*Contopus pertinax*)
Tyrant Flycatchers (Tyrannidae)

Description: 7–7¾" (18–20 cm). *Large-headed dark flycatcher* with slight crest. Olive-brown above, slightly lighter below. Small light gray throat patch, yellow lower mandible, and indistinct wing bars.

Voice: Song is a plaintive *Jo-sé-Ma-rï-a.* Call note is a repeated *pwit*.

Habitat: Highland coniferous forests, favoring pine and pine-oak areas.

Nesting: 3 or 4 dull white, spotted eggs in a compact, woven, grass-lined cup nest, camouflaged outside, set high in the prong of a horizontal limb and secured with cobwebs.

Range: Mexico and Central America, reaching the United States in southern Arizona and New Mexico.

Flycatchers sit upright on prominent posts, watching for insects. When they

spot prey, they dart out, catch it in flight, and return in an arc-shaped flight to the same or nearby perch. This species was named for the famous 19th century American ornithologist Elliott Coues.

513 Western Wood Pewee
(*Contopus sordidulus*)
Tyrant Flycatchers (Tyrannidae)

Description: 6–6½" (15–17 cm). *Dark olive-gray above* with slightly lighter breast and sides. Light yellowish chin and belly and *two whitish wing bars.* No eye-ring.

Voice: Once heard, easy to recognize. Mainly in the morning and at twilight, it utters a *pee-wee* rather strong and harsh as compared with the more feeble, sibilant *pee-a-wee* given by the Eastern Wood Pewee (*Contopus virens*).

Habitat: Coniferous, deciduous, or mixed woods near water.

Nesting: 3 or 4 creamy white, spotted eggs in a tightly built cup nest, usually on a horizontal branch, at least 20 feet above the ground.

Range: Throughout the West, from southern Alaska through the Mexican highlands to Central America. Northern populations are migratory.

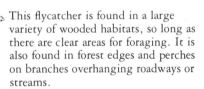

This flycatcher is found in a large variety of wooded habitats, so long as there are clear areas for foraging. It is also found in forest edges and perches on branches overhanging roadways or streams.

517 Hammond's Flycatcher
(*Empidonax hammondii*)
Tyrant Flycatchers (Tyrannidae)

Description: 5–5½" (13–14 cm). *Olive-gray above;* light throat, gray breast, pale yellow belly. Throat not as white as Alder's and breast darker than Dusky's but field identification is very difficult. Thin white eye-ring and wing bars. Bill narrower and shorter than Dusky's. *Flicks wings and tail more vigorously than other similar species.*

Voice: Song is *seweep tsurp seep,* the last part rising. Calls are a high *peep* (like the note of a Pygmy Nuthatch) and a soft *wit.*

Habitat: Mature coniferous forests at high altitudes.

Nesting: 3 or 4 white eggs, occasionally spotted, in a well-built cup nest "saddled" on a branch 15–60 feet high in a coniferous tree.

Range: Central Alaska south and west, including the Rocky Mountains, to northern California and central Colorado. In winter, northern Mexico to Central America.

Since conditions at sea level in the North are repeated at higher elevations farther south, this flycatcher frequents boreal forest on the low plains of Alaska as well as the subalpine forest, at around 10,000 feet, in the southern Rocky Mountains.

---

527 **Winter Wren**
(*Troglodytes troglodytes*)
Wrens (Troglodytidae)

Description: 4–4½″ (10–11 cm). Tiny dark, *reddish-brown* wren. Indistinct light eye-line; barred both above and below, more heavily on belly. *Short, often uptilted tail,* which it flicks conspicuously.

Voice: A clear, trilling, musical song, high in pitch, lasting for several seconds and repeated often; its quality is akin to a bubbling stream rushing over stones. Call is a double *chimp-chimp.*

Habitat: Shady secluded underbrush in coniferous forests.

Nesting: 4–7 white eggs, finely spotted with reddish-brown, in a protected cavity lined with moss, on or near the ground, often among roots in a storm-felled tree, or in a road cut or the side of a bank.

Range: All other wrens are found exclusively in the Americas, but this species breeds from the British Isles across northern Asia and from Alaska to the Atlantic Coast. In North America, its range extends south of the boreal forest in two areas: the Appalachian chain in the East and the coastal forest and Sierra Nevada forest in California.

In the open the male builds a large, elaborate (though unlined), domed structure with a side entrance. This mock or dummy nest is not used for nesting and is thought to be a diversionary tactic against would-be nest robbers.

---

539   **Gray-cheeked Thrush**
(*Catharus minimus*)
Thrushes (Turdidae)

Description: 7–8″ (18–20 cm). Bluebird-sized. Dull *olive-brown above, white below,* with heavy *dark spots* on *breast. Gray face.* In winter, darker below.

Voice: Song, thin and nasal, is rendered as *wee-oh, chee, chee, wee-oh,* rising at the end. Call is *wee-a,* and, when alarmed, *chuck.*

Habitat: In tundra forest or woodlands; coniferous stands, dense alders or willows.

Nesting: 3–5 greenish, brown-dotted eggs in a neat cup nest low on a tree or in a bush.

Range: Alaska and northern British Columbia east to Newfoundland and New England. In the northernmost taiga and the tundra woodland belt. Migrates east of the Rocky Mountains.

A reticent bird, it keeps mostly under cover. It searches for food on the ground. This thrush is one of the few American birds that have spread to northeastern Siberia in the scrub tundra but migrate back through North America to tropical Central and South America.

---

541 Hermit Thrush
(*Catharus guttatus*)
Thrushes (Turdidae)

Description: 6½–8" (17–20 cm). *Olive-brown above, with rufous tail;* whitish below, with streaked throat; blackish-brown spots on breast. Flicks its wings and tail nervously.

Voice: Loud, slow, repetitive phrases spiraling down the scale carry and echo in the still of the evening forest; it also sings at dawn. Many consider this the most beautiful bird song in America. Call note is a soft *chup* or *chup-chup*.

Habitat: Mixed woods or open coniferous forests. In the Northwest, mostly at timberline but nests along ocean shores on the Queen Charlotte Islands.

Nesting: 3–5 bluish-green eggs in a neat cup nest of grasses, rootlets, moss, and leaves, on or just above the ground.

Range: Breeds from Aleutians west to Unimak Island, Alaska to Newfoundland, south to California in the West, to Maryland in the East. Winters mainly in southern United States.

These thrushes forage on the ground, most of the time under dense cover, hopping around and then watching in an upright position like a Robin.

544   Boreal Chickadee
(*Parus hudsonicus*)
Titmice (Paridae)

Description: 5–5½" (13–14 cm). *Dark brown cap,*
black bib, rusty brown sides, grayish-
brown mantle, and dirty white
underparts.

Voice: Call is a wheezy *shisk-ka-day-day,* lazier
and less patterned than the calls of the
Mountain and Black-capped chickadees.

Habitat: Coniferous and mixed woodlands; edges
of coniferous forests.

Nesting: 5–9 white, faintly brown-spotted eggs
in a fur-lined nest in a tree cavity, often
self-excavated.

Range: Across the taiga of the northland,
extending south in the British
Columbia–Washington Cascades, the
Rocky Mountains to extreme
northwestern Montana, and the
northern Appalachians.

During late summer and early fall,
when there is an abundance of
caterpillars and seeds, northern
chickadees store food for winter among
needles, or under the bark of branches
at a height that will be above the
winter snow cover but below branches
exposed to blizzards.

545   Chestnut-backed Chickadee
(*Parus rufescens*)
Titmice (Paridae)

Description: 4½–5" (11–13 cm). Dusky, black-
capped and black-bibbed chickadee
with *chestnut flanks and back.*

Voice: Its *chick-a-dee* call is somewhat shriller
and the beat faster than in other
chickadees. Often simply utters a thin
tsee-deee and thin lisping notes.

Habitat: The Pacific rain forest; moist areas
containing conifers.

Nesting: 5–8 creamy white, lightly spotted eggs
in a natural cavity or woodpecker hole;

much like the Black-capped Chickadee, it often excavates rotten stumps and then builds a nest of moss and hair.

Range: From coastal Alaska south to the redwood pockets of central California; in the western ranges of the Rocky Mountains in southern British Columbia and western Montana.

In the coastal forest of the Northwest, where the Chestnut-backed and Black-capped chickadees overlap, the former prefers the top half of conifers, while the latter feeds in the lower half of trees, very frequently oaks. Thus they do not compete for space even within the same area.

---

547 Olive-sided Flycatcher
(*Nuttallornis borealis*)
Tyrant Flycatchers (Tyrannidae)

Description: 7–8″ (18–20 cm). Large, stocky, thick-headed flycatcher. Dark brownish-gray above, broad *olive-gray flanks that almost meet* in center of dusky white chest. *White "downy" tufts* on lower back frequently visible behind folded wing.

Voice: Song is a clearly whistled *whip-three-beers!*, the middle note highest in pitch. Call is an incessant *pilt, pilt.*

Habitat: Northern coniferous woodlands, burns, and clearings. Also favors eucalyptus (in California), aspens, birches, and maples.

Nesting: 3 or 4 creamy white to light buff eggs, with a wreath of small blotches around the larger end, in a shallow saucer-shaped nest of stalks and roots on a high branch of a conifer.

Range: Across the boreal forest from Alaska through Canada, and south through the forested West to Baja California, Nevada, Arizona, and New Mexico. Winters in South America.

This flycatcher hunts insects from a high branch of a conifer. Analysis of stomach contents shows that everything it eats is winged; it takes no caterpillars, spiders, or other larvae.

549 Western Flycatcher
(*Empidonax difficilis*)
Tyrant Flycatchers (Tyrannidae)

Description: 5½–6″ (14–15 cm). Olive-brown above, with *yellow throat* and belly separated by dusky olive breast; white eye-ring and light wing bars. Fall birds may be duller. Bill long and wide, lower mandible *bright yellow*.

Voice: Quite distinct, rising *pseet, ptsick, seet*. First part alone is often used as a call, or is repeated on a drawn-out, almost sibilant high pitch. Second part is rapid and louder.

Habitat: Moist, shaded coniferous or mixed forests; canyons.

Nesting: 3 or 4 white eggs, spotted with brown, in a moss-lined cup nest of small twigs and rootlets, built against a tree trunk where the bark has split, among the roots of a wind-felled tree, in a bank, or under the eaves of a forest cabin.

Range: From Alaska to Baja California, and through forests of the western mountains to Montana and New Mexico. Winters in Mexico and Central America.

The Western Flycatcher utilizes shady airspace between tangled ground cover of huckleberry and salmonberry and the low branches of the towering Douglas firs, cedars, or redwoods. It is the most frequently observed *Empidonax* in most of its western range.

561, 623 Rusty Blackbird
(*Euphagus carolinus*)
Orioles (Icteridae)

Description: 8½–9¾" (22–25 cm). Breeding *male black* with some dull metallic green sheen and *yellow-white eyes.* Female in spring is *slate gray* with *yellow eyes. Winter* adults of both sexes and juveniles are *light rust-brown* with finely barred underparts.

Voice: Call is a harsh *chack.* The short song sounds like a squeaky hinge.

Habitat: Boggy, wet woods and edges of the taiga.

Nesting: 4 or 5 light bluish, blotched eggs in a bulky nest low in tree or bush or on the ground near water.

Range: Across the northern, boreal forests of Alaska and Canada. Winters in the eastern United States. Occasionally individuals or small flocks are seen in fall and winter in the Pacific and Rocky Mountain states and it is a regular migrant through central British Columbia.

In the breeding season, the Rusty is the only blackbird in most of its range and is easily identified. In autumn, the rusty tinge to the mantle and light eyes of both sexes distinguish this species from the similar Brewer's Blackbird, which is abundant in most of the West.

565 Bohemian Waxwing
(*Bombycilla garrulus*)
Waxwings (Bombycillidae)

Description: 7½–9" (19–23 cm). *Larger* and *heavier* than the Cedar Waxwing. Lighter cinnamon-gray above; dove gray rather than yellow below; *white and yellow wing markings* and *rusty-red vent area.* Both species have a frequently *inconspicuous crest, yellow terminal tail band,* black mask partially edged in white, and bright red spot on each wing. Sexes similar. Immatures have indistinctly streaked underparts.

Voice: A rasping *sr-r-r-r-ee,* lower in pitch than the calls of the Cedar Waxwing, with the individual notes more discernible.

Habitat: Edges of taiga and openings in boreal forests. Winters, often in large flocks, in any habitat with berry-bearing trees or shrubs.

Nesting: 4–6 eggs, more bluish than those of the Cedar Waxwing, in a moss-lined twiggy nest high in a spruce or other conifer.

Range: Northern Eurasia and from Alaska through western Canada to the northwestern United States.

This species occurs in the northern United States in numbers only about once in a decade. Its occasional erratic movements southward in winter are thought to be caused by food shortages in the north.

566 Cedar Waxwing
(*Bombycilla cedrorum*)
Waxwings (Bombycillidae)

Description: 6½–8″ (17–20 cm). Trim, crested bird. Grayish-brown, with black mask and chin; yellow belly, white undertail coverts; *yellow terminal tail band.* Juveniles have indistinct gray-streaked breast.

Voice: A high, sibilant *see-e-e-e.* Voice is often the only means of detecting its presence.

Habitat: Edges of coniferous or mixed forests; orchards or fruiting trees where second-growth stands, such as alders, maples, and dogwoods, follow a watercourse; city parks with berry-bearing trees and shrubs.

Nesting: 3–6 blue-gray, dotted eggs in a loose nest of twigs and grass woven onto a horizontal branch and bolstered with mosses and lichens.

Range: Breeds from coast to coast in deciduous or mixed forest and around parks and gardens from southeastern Alaska to central California in the West and from Newfoundland to Georgia in the East. Winters in most of its range and southern United States.

In summer Cedar Waxwings are rather inconspicuous, but in winter they travel in flocks of 40 or more, incessantly calling, turning, and twisting in flight, and frequently alighting in the same tree. Berries are their main food source in winter, but they revert to flycatching in milder seasons.

587 White-throated Sparrow
(*Zonotrichia albicollis*)
Finches (Fringillidae)

Description: 6–7″ (15–18 cm). Similar to White-crowned Sparrow. Chestnut brown above with black-and-white crown striping, and bright *yellow lores;* gray cheek and breast, *white throat.* Two narrow white wing bars. Bill is always dark, never pink as in White-crowned Sparrow. Birds in nonbreeding plumage are duller. Juveniles have brown and buff head stripes, light throat, and fine breast streaking.

Voice: A common contact call is a drawn-out *tseep.* The much studied musical song starts with 2 high, steady whistles, followed by repeated "triplets." The song has been described as: *Old Sam Peabody, Peabody, Peabody* and *Oh sweet Canada, Canada, Canada.*

Habitat: Coniferous and mixed woodlands, openings, and burns; winters in streamside brush; often found at feeders.

Nesting: 3–5 greenish-white eggs, with heavily spotted brown markings concentrated at larger end, in a cup nest of mosses, coarse grasses, rootlets, bark fibers lined with fine grasses or hair, hidden on or close to the ground.

Range: East of the Rocky Mountains across Canada's boreal forest and south along the Appalachians. Winters abundantly in the South and East, but less commonly in the West.

This upright, large-headed sparrow is usually found on the ground. In winter it may join mixed flocks of White-crowned and Golden-crowned sparrows.

---

588 Golden-crowned Sparrow
(*Zonotrichia atricapilla*)
Finches (Fringillidae)

Description: 6–7″ (15–18 cm). Similar to White-crowned Sparrow. Male's *gold crown* bordered by *wide black cap*. Dusky bill. Brown above with gray unstreaked breast, cheek, and collar; two white wing bars. Fall immatures have two dark-brown crown stripes with dusky yellowish central area and a trace of mustache stripe.

Voice: Song, often given throughout the winter, consists of 3 descending, plaintive notes sounding like *oh, dear me.* Calls are *tseet* and *chink.*

Habitat: Alpine meadows and coniferous forest clearings; winters in coastal brushland and chaparral.

Nesting: 4 or 5 bluish, speckled eggs in a neat cup nest well hidden in a dense weed clump or bush.

Range: Alpine meadows of the far northwestern coast of Alaska and British Columbia, extending across the northernmost Rockies. Winters along Pacific Coast.

One or two of these sparrows often join winter flocks of White-crowned Sparrows. They live with the flock but feed more in the shelter of bushes and visit open lawns less often.

590 Chipping Sparrow
(*Spizella passerina*)
Finches (Fringillidae)

Description: 5–5¾" (13–15 cm). *Rufous cap bordered by white eyebrow-stripe;* black eye-line. Cheek, collar, and underparts are unstreaked gray. Mantle brown with dark streaking; two white wing bars. Sexes similar. Winter adults have duller rufous cap and eye-stripe with brown-tinged gray areas. Immatures have light median stripe through crown, brownish cap, buffy eye-stripe and underparts.

Voice: An insect-like trill on one pitch. Call is a high, sweet *seep.*

Habitat: Coniferous and deciduous woodland edges; orchards and parks.

Nesting: 3–5 light blue eggs, with brown, black, and purple markings primarily at the large end, in a neat cup nest of dead grasses, rootlets, and weeds, lined with hair, in a conifer, bush, or vine.

Range: Widespread in the boreal forest as well as the eastern deciduous forest, and lowland montane areas of the West, southwest to Mexico and the mountains of Central America.

This sparrow is inconspicuous even when it feeds in the open, for it moves slowly among the grass or litter. The singing territorial male is also hard to find as he sits quietly among the branches of a conifer.

594 Harris' Sparrow
(*Zonotrichia querula*)
Finches (Fringillidae)

Description: 7–7¾" (18–20 cm). Largest sparrow. *Solid-black crown, forehead, and bib offset pink bill;* light gray eye-stripe, ear patch, and nape; underparts buffy brown with dark streaking; belly white. Crown of winter adults is grayish;

juveniles have buffy head, white throat, and dark blotching on chest.

Voice: In alarm, *cheenk* or *weenk*. Call is a single or repeated *tchip*. Song, voiced in spring on the winter grounds, is loud and melancholic: 2 or 3 notes whistled on the same pitch, followed by 2 or 3 higher or sometimes lower notes; on breeding grounds males sing in chorus.

Habitat: Timberline bordering the tundra, in woodland broken by open expanses; in winter, in hedgerows, open woodlands, weedy places.

Nesting: 4 pale blue, spotted eggs in a grass cup on the ground.

Range: In the Mackenzie and Keewatin districts and in northern Manitoba. Winters mainly in south-central prairie states.

In winter, Harris' mixes with and generally dominates flocks of the more numerous White-crowned and Golden-crowned sparrows. When the flock is disturbed it often flies up to the top of a nearby bush. It is more shy and wary in its northern breeding territory.

598 Pine Siskin
(*Carduelis pinus*)
Finches (Fringillidae)

Description: 4½–5¼″ (11–13 cm). Grayish-brown above, buffy below, with *dusky streaking overall; yellow on wing and tail.* Sharp, slender bill and deeply notched tail. Sexes look similar, but females have less yellow.

Voice: In flight, a scratchy *shick-shick* and a thin *tseee*. Also a rising, buzzy *schhrreeee*.

Habitat: Coniferous forests; second-growth alders, aspens, and broadleaf trees along the fringes of boreal forests.

Nesting: 3–6 pale blue, spotted eggs in a grass-lined cup nest usually about 10 feet from the ground on a horizontal limb of a conifer. Erratic breeder; often in loose colonies.

Range: From southern Alaska and Canada, south through the western United States and across the Mexican border; north-central and northeastern United States. Found irregularly farther south in winter.

Siskins, redpolls, and goldfinches are a closely related group of seed specialists. All have short, conical beaks, short, slightly forked tails, bright wing markings, and "nervous" behavior. They feed in flocks, which, after breeding, may contain hundreds of birds. They are all acrobats, often hanging upside down, like titmice and chickadees, plucking seeds from hanging seed pods and catkins.

609 Blackpoll Warbler
(*Dendroica striata*)
Wood Warblers (Parulidae)

Description: 5–5¾" (13–15 cm). Spring male has *black cap* and nape, white ear patch; *black-streaked olive-gray above,* black-streaked sides and *white underparts.* Female lacks the contrasting cap and face, is duller overall. Fall male is dull olive green above, yellowish below with faint dusky streaking and light eye-stripe. Fall female and immatures are similar to fall male, with more streaking below. In all plumages has distinctive white wing bars and white undertail coverts.

Voice: Song is insect-like, extremely high-pitched, first rising, then falling; some hear it as *zi-zi-zi* repeated 6 to 12 times. Calls are a low *chip* and a thin *zeep.*

Habitat: Coniferous forests.

Nesting: 4 or 5 creamy white, spotted eggs in a feather-lined, cup-shaped nest, low on, or under, a spruce.

Range: Across the boreal forest from Alaska to
the New England mountains. Winters
in South America.

This bird breeds in the Far North. In
August it takes off toward the
Southeast, across the Atlantic states,
through Florida, and returns by the
same route in April and May. It is
rarely seen west of the Rockies in
spring, but in fall small numbers occur
regularly along the Pacific Coast. These
are mostly young birds.

---

624   Northwestern Crow
(*Corvus caurinus*)
Crows (Corvidae)

Description: 16–17″ (41–43 cm). Black, smaller
than Common Crow, its close relative.
Voice: Calls resemble those of the Common
Crow but are somewhat hoarse.
Habitat: Shorelines, tidewater areas, edges of the
coastal forest.
Nesting: 4–6 greenish, brown-spotted eggs in a
bowl-shaped stick nest in a tree. Except
when suitable nest sites are crowded, it
nests singly. On offshore islets, where
seabird concentrations attract this crow,
trees are often lacking, and it may nest
in low bushes or even on the ground.
Range: Coastal southern Alaska, British
Columbia, and Washington.

In tidal marshes Red-winged
Blackbirds attack these crows, just as
inland blackbirds harass the Common
Crow. This mobbing behavior distracts
the crows from their habitual
plundering and prevents them from
discovering nests; thus broods of marsh
birds remain largely unmolested. At
cormorant or gull colonies, however,
crows walk all day among incubating
and brooding birds and quickly snatch
any egg or hatchling accidentally
exposed and left unprotected.

Upland Tundra

A dry, Arctic habitat either in the
North or in alpine areas. The growth
here is stunted willow and birch and
includes such shrubs as Arctic
crowberry; grassy patches or expanses
also occur. Hilly areas are often covered
with frost-split barren rocks and have
little or no vegetation. Many tundra
nesters such as Snow Buntings, Water
Pipits, Whimbrels, and Rough-legged
Hawks are common winter visitors in
open areas of most of the West.

54 Long-tailed Jaeger
(*Stercorarius longicaudus*)
Jaegers (Stercorariidae)

Description: 20–23″ (51–58 cm). Size of a small gull
but has long pointed wings and very
long tail. White flash at base of
primaries. *Dark gray above; whitish
below.* Black cap, white face and neck;
yellow near ear. Elongated central
feathers of adults extend 6–10″ beyond
rest of tail. Blue-gray legs. Juveniles
lack long tail, are dark, barred and
mottled. The Long-tailed is the
slimmest and smallest of the jaegers;
its flight is remarkably graceful and
buoyant.

Voice: Mostly silent, but on the tundra it cries
kree kree.

Habitat: Tundra breeder; otherwise open oceans.

Nesting: 2 olive-brown, brown-spotted eggs in a
scrape in the moss on the tundra.

Range: Circumpolar. Breeds on coasts of Arctic
Ocean, including northern Alaska and
Canada. Winters in the oceans of the
Southern Hemisphere. Thus transient
in the latitudes of Pacific North
America.

Migrating mainly on the high seas, it is
virtually never seen by bird-watchers on
the shore. In summer on the tundra it
feeds on lemmings, insects, fish, and
even small birds; toward the end of the
Arctic summer it may also eat
crowberries before starting south on its
long migration. The Long-tailed robs
other seabirds less frequently than other
jaegers.

189, 235 American Golden Plover
(*Pluvialis dominica*)
Plovers (Charadriidae)

Description: 9½–11″ (24–28 cm). Robin-sized;
somewhat smaller than more common
Black-bellied Plover. In spring, *mantle*

dotted with golden yellow, *underside black,* with broad white margin around black face from forehead through ears and hind neck. In flight, light underwing, not black as in Black-bellied Plover. In fall and winter, light brown with buffy forehead, eyebrow-stripe, and underparts, but grayish barring on neck and flanks, light buff barring and spotting on darker mantle.

Voice: A falling *que-e-e-a* or *pee-u-u-u* flute tone, or repeated *coodle, coodle* whistles. In flight, a soft *que-eep.*

Habitat: Nests on dry, upland tundra; gathers in winter and on migration on mud flats and grassy open habitats.

Nesting: 4 buff, spotted eggs in a scrape lined with lichens, on the tundra.

Range: Tundra in the western Arctic of Siberia and North America. Winters mostly on Pacific and South Sea islands and in southern Asia, Australia, and South America. Uncommon transient in the West.

Plovers run a short distance before taking off; this habit was utilized in a famous study of the directional movements of American Golden Plovers. In the experiment, the center of a circular cage was covered with an ink pad while the outer floor, which sloped toward the center, was covered with blotting paper. Baby Golden Plovers were removed from their nests in Alaska and taken to experimental cages in California, Wisconsin, and Florida. Though they had not flown south to where they were confined, as spring arrived and the urge to migrate north arose, each bird showed by the concentration of its tracks on the blotting paper an inborn orientation toward its original home—Alaska.

190, 234   **Black-bellied Plover**
(*Pluvialis squatarola*)
Plovers (Charadriidae)

Description: 10½–13½" (27–34 cm). In spring, top
of head and back checkered gray and
buff; face, neck, breast, and belly
black. Broad white stripe from eye to
side of breast. In winter, mottled
grayish buff upperparts, pale grayish
underparts. In all plumages, *whitish
wing-stripe, rump, and tail,* and *black
patch under the wing* visible in flight.
American Golden Plover is slightly
smaller, dotted with golden spots above
(except in winter), has a dark wing,
rump, and tail, and lacks the dark
underwing patch.

Voice: A rising and falling whistle of haunting
quality: *ker-loo-ee.* The American
Golden utters a loud, falling *que-e-e-a.*

Habitat: Tundra; winters on seashores, mud
flats, and coastal marshes.

Nesting: 4 buffy, blotched eggs in a scrape lined
with lichen, on the tundra.

Range: Northern Siberian, Alaskan, and
Canadian tundra. Winters in southern
continents, but enough remain on
North America's Pacific Coast to be
common in winter there.

When the tide recedes and a broad mud
flat is exposed, shorebirds spread out to
feed. The smaller sandpipers, such as
the Least, Western, Dunlin, and
Sanderling, remain in loose flocks,
while the plovers spread out along the
beach. The wary Black-bellied Plover is
the first to take flight when an observer
approaches; on its tundra nesting
ground it allows a close approach. It
does so not because it trusts man, but
because on the tundra the safest course
is to remain still and well camouflaged,
whereas on a tidal flat the surest escape
is flight.

194 **Western Sandpiper**
(*Calidris mauri*)
Sandpipers (Scolopacidae)

Description: 6–7" (15–18 cm). *Long black bill,
slightly decurved at the tip. Rusty red above
in spring,* white below; *some reddish on
shoulders* even *in fall.* Legs and feet are
black. In fall, gray above, white below.

Voice: A grating and rather high *keeep* note,
often with a squeaky quality.

Habitat: Upland tundra in summer; seacoast in
winter.

Nesting: 4 creamy eggs, with profuse reddish-
brown markings, in a depression on dry
tundra.

Range: Breeds in the coastal tundra of Alaska.
Winters on the Pacific Coast from
California to Peru and on the Atlantic
Coast from New Jersey to Venezuela.
Great numbers move through British
Columbia, Washington, and Oregon,
mainly along the coast; rare in the
interior states.

This is the western counterpart of the
Semipalmated Sandpiper, the common
"peep" of the Atlantic and Gulf coasts.
The flocks of these "peeps" that spread
out on mud flats during fall and winter
take to flight readily when an intruder
nears. When the tide covers their
shallow feeding grounds, the flocks
move to higher ground; there they
preen themselves and wait for the next
low tide, when they can resume
feeding.

197 **Baird's Sandpiper**
(*Calidris bairdii*)
Sandpipers (Scolopacidae)

Description: 7–7½" (18–19 cm). One of the
"peeps," as the smaller sandpipers are
called. Back feathers are dark brown
with buffy edge, giving it a scaly

appearance. *Breast buffy with faint lines across upper part.* Wings very long, and when folded, their crossed tips extend noticeably beyond tail. *Black bill and feet.*

Voice: Call is a sharp, low-pitched *kreep,* often doubled.

Habitat: Nests on the tundra; the rest of the year on the shores of ponds and lakes, and grassy pools.

Nesting: 4 buffy, brown-spotted eggs in a scrape on the dry tundra.

Range: Northeastern Siberia through the high Arctic to northwestern Greenland. Migrates through the West, mainly across the plains, during both fall and spring, to and from its wintering areas in southern South America.

Recent research shows that in the fall the adults fly rapidly along a narrow route across the High Plains of North America, while juveniles move over a broad front extending from coast to coast. It is suspected that they may cover up to 4000 miles nonstop. Migratory birds metabolize fat stored under their skin.

216 Whimbrel
(*Numenius phaeopus*)
Sandpipers (Scolopacidae)

Description: 15–18¾" (38–48 cm). Large gray-brown sandpiper with *long, decurved bill; crown striped;* legs and feet blue-gray. Smaller than Long-billed Curlew, paler, with shorter bill.

Voice: Flight call is a loud, whistled *whi whi whi whi whi.* Does not give the bugling call of the Long-billed Curlew.

Habitat: Nests on the tundra; during migration mainly on sea beaches, tidal flats, and large, partly flooded fields.

Nesting: 4 olive, blotched eggs in a grass-lined scrape on upland tundra.

Range: Breeds in northern Eurasia, Alaska, and
Canada. Regularly winters from
California and Florida coasts south to
southern South America.

In migration they occur along sandy
beaches, in salt marshes, and even on
rocky coasts. The larger the bird, the
more space it needs. Thus a lone
Whimbrel usually stands amid several
dowitchers and numerous smaller birds;
however, when feeding or resting in
salt marshes and coastal meadows
Whimbrels occur in flocks. This
species feeds on large insects, berries,
and aquatic invertebrates while on its
tundra nesting grounds.

Bristle-thighed Curlew
(*Numenius tahitiensis*)
Sandpipers (Scolopacidae)

Description: 17″ (43 cm). Large shorebird. Mottled
gray-brown; long decurved bill, long
neck and legs. Like the Whimbrel, this
curlew has four black and three white
stripes on head but *rump is tawny and
without barring.* Bill usually paler than
that of Whimbrel.

Voice: A plaintive, drawn-out whistle, unlike
the ringing call of the Whimbrel.

Habitat: Mountain tundra in summer; island
beaches in winter.

Nesting: 4 greenish, brown-spotted eggs in a
depression lined with tundra
mosses.

Range: One of the rarest of American birds, its
breeding is limited to a small
mountainous area of western Alaska.
Winters on mid-Pacific tropical islands,
migrating directly over water to Hawaii
and other islands. Does not visit the
mainland south of Alaska.

The first nest of this little-known bird
was found by Cornell ornithologist

Arthur A. Allen in June 1948 on the lower Yukon River. Its population is small, and although it is not yet threatened on its breeding grounds, its Pacific island habitats are becoming more and more settled.

223, 230 **Red Knot**
"Knot"
(*Calidris canutus*)
Sandpipers (Scolopacidae)

Description: 10–11" (25–28 cm). Among the largest of beach sandpipers, *with bill as long as head*. Breeding birds mottled *gray-brown above, reddish below*. In fall and winter pale gray on back, white belly. Immatures buffy-gray. Best identified by stout proportions, moderate-sized bill. Rump and tail grayish at all seasons.

Voice: A low-pitched *tu-whit*. Also a nonmusical *wunt wunt*.

Habitat: For nesting, drier tundra; in winter, mud flats, estuaries, and open areas in coastal salt marshes.

Nesting: 4 buffy, brown-marked eggs in a scantily lined scrape, in a gravel-covered open area of the coastal tundra.

Range: Circumpolar in the High Arctic tundra. Migrants from northern Alaska or Siberia go south along the Pacific Coast in August and September, returning in April or early May. Winters locally along the coast of California and south to southern South America. Also found in migration along the Atlantic Coast.

This species, the dowitchers, Willet, and Marbled Godwit are the large birds most commonly seen on mud flats. The Red Knot resembles the small sandpipers in shape and coloration, but is much larger. Formerly called the "Knot."

268, 269, 270,   **Willow Ptarmigan**
271   (*Lagopus lagopus*)
Grouse (Tetraonidae)

Description: 15–17" (28–43 cm). Rather large, variable colored grouse with red comb over eyes. *In winter, entirely snow white* except for *black tail*. In summer, male is rusty red with white wings and belly; female is mottled and barred *brown* except for white wings. Spring and fall molting plumages show a variety of checkered patterns. Other summer male ptarmigans are more grayish-black. Willow lacks black lores of male Rock Ptarmigan in winter plumage.

Voice: In flight, courting males call a noisy series of gruff notes. Also a bark-like challenge from the ground. When alarmed, both sexes fly up with a loud guttural cackling.

Habitat: Tundra; also thickets of valleys and foothills; muskeg.

Nesting: 7–10 eggs, pale with red-brown markings, in a scrape often sheltered by vegetation, rocks, or logs.

Range: Circumpolar Arctic. In the West, from the extreme northern coasts to the southern limit of forest tundra and open muskeg flats as far south, along alpine tundra, as central British Columbia.

The common ptarmigan of the Far North, its numbers increase tremendously during some years but in others it is very scarce. While the female incubates, the male guards the territory. When the chicks grow up, several families gather in large flocks and often migrate southward together when freeze-up sets in. In summer, ptarmigans feed on green shoots, buds, flowers, and insects; in winter, they take mainly twigs and buds of dwarf willows.

272, 274   Rock Ptarmigan
(*Lagopus mutus*)
Grouse (Tetraonidae)

Description: 13–14″ (33–36 cm). Smaller than
Willow Ptarmigan. *In winter, entirely
white* except for partly *black tail* and
black lores in male. In summer, male is
mottled dark brown-gray with white
wings and belly; female is lighter, with
gray, whitish, and brown on most
feathers. Male has scarlet combs over
eyes.

Voice: Courting male utters a growling *kurr-
kurr*. Alarm note is a noisy cackle on
taking off.

Habitat: This is the grouse of the alpine zone of
barren, rocky land near the permanent
snows of the Far North and the
ecologically similar flat, far northern
tundra.

Nesting: 6–9 (but up to 16) buffy eggs, with
dark brown marbling or spotting, in a
sheltered scrape.

Range: Circumpolar; in western North America
mainly on Arctic tundra but extending
southward to Aleutians, mountain
tundra of Alaska and British Columbia.

White winter plumage is good
camouflage in a world of snow. It also
provides thermal insulation, since white
feathers have empty cells filled with air,
whereas colored feathers contain
pigments. Ptarmigans plunge into the
snow to roost. In winter, "snowshoes,"
the long, thick feathering on their feet,
facilitate movement on the snow. Their
winter food consists mainly of buds and
twigs; special bacteria help them digest
woody material of low caloric value.

303 Snowy Owl
(*Nyctea scandiaca*)
Owls (Strigidae)

Description: 20–27″ (51–69 cm). W. 55″ (140 cm).
Very large owl. Round head and yellow
eyes; *white body* is spotted gray-brown
above and lightly barred below. Female
more spotted and immatures more
heavily marked with brown.

Voice: Silent in winter. Gives loud croaks and
harsh whistles on its far northern
breeding grounds.

Habitat: In summer, upland tundra; in winter,
fields, marshes, beaches, and other open
country.

Nesting: 5–7 or more white eggs in moss and
grass-lined depression on dry ground in
the tundra.

Range: Circumpolar; nests in the Eurasian and
North American tundra. During
winters of food shortage it may invade
southern latitudes, reaching Oregon,
northern California, Utah, Colorado,
and northern states farther east.

Snowy Owls depend on lemmings as
their major food. The lemming
population fluctuates from year to year,
and when the supply gets too low, the
owls migrate southward in great
numbers. At such times observers in
the south note an irruption of Snowy
Owls.

310, 316 Rough-legged Hawk
(*Buteo lagopus*)
Hawks (Accipitridae)

Description: 19–24″ (48–61 cm). W. 48–54″ (1.2–
1.4m). Large hawk. Legs feathered to
talons. In light phase, has buffy head,
chest, and leg feathers with dark
streaking; *broad black belly band, wrist
patch,* and *broad terminal tail band* edged
with white. Primary tips and trailing
edge of wing are black. In dark phase

(rare), head, body, and underwing coverts dark; white flight feathers with dark edge; dark tail band.

Voice: Silent on its wintering grounds. Around the nest it may give a mewing squeal.

Habitat: Nests in upland tundra; in winter, open plains or marshes with elevated lookout posts.

Nesting: 2–6 greenish, variously marked or blotched eggs in a bulky nest of sticks and moss on a cliff.

Range: Circumpolar. Winters in southern Canadian provinces south to southern California (uncommon), Arizona, and Texas and to central states in the East.

Hovers above its prey like a Kestrel. Lemmings and ptarmigans are its main sources of food on its breeding grounds; on its wintering grounds, it takes larger rodents and upland birds. In snowy areas it is usually the only large *Buteo*, with the exception of a few Red-tailed Hawks. It is unafraid, since it does not often meet humans in its nesting area.

---

425 **Yellow Wagtail**
(*Motacilla flava*)
Pipits (Motacillidae)

Description: 6½″ (17 cm). Small and dainty, its tail makes up half its total length. Adult olive-gray above, *bright yellow below. White eye-stripe,* wing bars, and outer tail feathers, which flash in flight. Immatures are olive-gray above with buffy underparts, buffy eye-stripe, and dusky throat collar.

Voice: Rarely sings, but often utters a call: *tsweep.* Alarm note sounds like *ple-ple-ple.*

Habitat: Willow tundra of western Alaska; elsewhere any open, wet, vegetated area. Inhabits marshes more often than the streams and villages preferred by the White Wagtail.

Nesting: 4–7 buff or greenish eggs, heavily mottled and spotted; usually hidden in a sheltered place on the ground.

Range: All of Eurasia. Winters mostly in Africa. The Alaskan population seems a recent arrival from Siberia; it is now common on St. Lawrence Island, Alaska's North Slope and westernmost flatlands.

Though very limited in North America, this wagtail is easy to locate during its short Arctic breeding season. When a ground predator (including humans) appears, several males gather, fly up, and circle the intruder.

White Wagtail
(*Motacilla alba*)
Pipits (Motacillidae)

Description: 7″ (18 cm). Slim, small-bodied. *Long, slender tail* which *wags constantly* and is half the bird's total length. In summer, *black crown, nape, and extensive bib;* black back, white face and underparts, black wings and tail with large white wing patch and white outer tail feathers. In fall, adult's black areas muted to grays. Immatures have olive-gray head and back with dark throat band; white eye-stripe, underparts, wing bars, and outer tail feathers.

Voice: Call constantly uttered in flight is a 2-toned *tschizzik* or *tzilip*. Warning call is *zipp*. After a hawk has passed, it often utters a soft, warbling song that may be a "danger over" signal.

Habitat: Open country with short vegetation; frequently near water: streamsides, riverbanks, seacoasts. Also about towns and villages.

Nesting: 5 or 6 grayish-white eggs, finely speckled with blackish-brown especially around the larger end, in a nest of grasses, rootlets, and leaves, near or on the ground in an earthen bank, rock crevice, stone wall, or niche of an old building.

Range: Widespread in the Old World. Breeds in western Alaska and Greenland; stragglers found on the Aleutians; accidental along the Pacific Coast of North America.

A lively ground bird which bobs its head in dove-like fashion and walks rather than hops; it flies in uneven arcs, calling as it flies. Except when breeding, it is very social.

Red-throated Pipit
(*Anthus cervinus*)
Pipits (Motacillidae)

Description: 6" (15 cm). Sparrow-sized; slim, long-legged ground bird; erect stance. *Light brown above* with *dark streaking on mantle;* indistinct white wing bars. In winter, buffy white below, *heavily streaked on sides of neck and breast,* extending to flanks. In summer, face, throat, and breast washed with *wine red or pink.*

Voice: Call is a sharp *speeez,* or *bee-iis.*

Habitat: Shrubby tundra or open areas of forest tundra; in winter, fallow agricultural fields, meadows, or beaches.

Nesting: 5–7 bluish eggs spotted with brown in a grass nest lined with fine material, on the ground sheltered by a tussock.

Range: A sparse breeder in western Alaska, its tundra range continues across northern Eurasia to Norway. Fall stragglers are occasionally identified flocking with Water Pipits along the Pacific Coast.

A ground feeder in its territory, this pipit sings from the top of shrubs but mostly in the air as it rises slowly and then silently falls with wings and tail spread out.

463 Common Redpoll
(*Carduelis flammea*)
Finches (Fringillidae)

Description: 5–5½" (13–14 cm). Small finch. Gray-brown above, with brown streaks above and on flanks; *black chin, bright red forehead,* and white wing bars. Male shows pink wash on breast and rump; female's underparts whitish. Juveniles lack red and black markings and are heavily streaked below.

Voice: Call is a loud *chit-chit-chit-chit,* often given in flight. Also various twittering notes.

Habitat: Areas of stunted tree growth in the low Arctic tundra where dwarf birches and willows have taken over the sheltered places.

Nesting: 3–6 light green, lightly speckled eggs in a nest of fine rootlets and grass lined with feathers, on the ground or at low elevation in a bush or small tree.

Range: Low Arctic, circumpolar. Irregular winter migrant to northern tier of states (occasionally farther south), ranging from East to West coasts.

These are lively birds, extremely social and constantly moving; even when resting at night members of the flock fidget and twitter. During the long Arctic night, redpolls sleep in snow tunnels to keep warm. They are able to hang upside down—like chickadees—and pry the birch seed from hanging catkins. They are somewhat nomadic; where the birch crop is good they settle in numbers, but may move away with their fledglings and attempt a second brood elsewhere if they find another area with ample food supply.

464 Hoary Redpoll
(*Carduelis hornemanni*)
Finches (Fringillidae)

Description: 5–5½″ (13–14 cm). Resembles
Common Redpoll but paler; male
pinker on breast; feathers have a
"frosty" edge. *Light grayish-brown above,*
with pale dusky streaks; red cap and
black chin; *white unstreaked rump.*
Juveniles lack red and black markings
and rosy wash on breast and are
streaked below.

Voice: A goldfinch-like call: *swee-e-et.* A
rattling *chit-chit-chit-chit* and a
twittering song are identical to those of
the Common Redpoll.

Habitat: Scrubby tundra; in winter, open fields,
grasslands, also catkin-bearing
deciduous trees.

Nesting: 3–6 light green, lightly speckled eggs
in a nest of fine rootlets and grass lined
with feathers, on the ground or at low
elevation in a bush or small tree.

Range: High Arctic, circumpolar. In winter,
Alaskan and Canadian populations
occasionally descend to southern Canada
and border states.

The Hoary Redpoll generally breeds
and winters farther north than the
related Common Redpoll, only
occasionally reaching the northern
United States. In areas where their
ranges overlap, they do not interbreed
although some experts consider them
two forms of a single species.

482 Wheatear
(*Oenanthe oenanthe*)
Thrushes (Turdidae)

Description: 5½–6″ (14–15 cm). Size of a small
bluebird, but with upright posture and
shorter tail. Gray above, buffy below.
Male has broad black eye-line and
contiguous black ear patch; black wings

and inverted "T" pattern on tail; *rump and base of outer tail feathers white.* Female and winter male are drab, light ocher but retain distinctive black-and-white tail pattern. A nervous, restless bird, it flicks and fans its tail while bobbing and darting among the rocks.

Voice: In breeding season, the male selects a prominent perch close to the ground, from which he calls persistently: a short, abrupt twitter, sounding like an ungreased door hinge. Alarm call is *tuck, tuck.*

Habitat: Open country broken with rocks, ravines, shrubs; in Alaska above timberline, on rocky ridges.

Nesting: 5–7 pale greenish-blue eggs, occasionally lightly speckled. A hole-nester, it builds a loose nest of weeds, moss, and grasses lined with hair or feathers in a rock crevice, ground hole, or breeding box.

Range: Widespread in the Old World, from the desert borders to the Arctic. In the West, it breeds from northern Alaska to northwestern Mackenzie; in the East, from Ellesmere Island to Greenland. Accidental in California (Farallon Islands); rare along the East coast.

Two geographically separate populations of Wheatears breed in North America. The western population migrates in fall southwestward to southern Asia. The eastern population migrates southeastward to winter in the Middle East. Thus the New World has been colonized by Wheatears from both East and West; they maintain their ancestral distinction by continuing to follow separate migratory routes.

499   Bluethroat
(*Luscinia svecica*)
Thrushes (Turdidae)

Description: 4¾" (12 cm). Wren-sized. Brown
above, white below. Male has *striking
blue throat and breast with rusty red "star"
in the middle;* black, white, and red
bands across breast; white neck stripe
and eyebrow-stripe. Female and
juveniles have light buff throat
bordered with dark brown feathers. All
plumages have *rusty red patches at base of
brown tail* (similar to that of American
Redstart) displayed during nervous tail-
flicking.

Voice: The territorial male sings a loud, varied
song introduced by a repeated *dip, dip,
dip.* Sometimes the Bluethroat, like its
close relative, the nightingale, mimicks
the song of other birds. Alarm call is
huyt-tock.

Habitat: Shrubby tundra in the breeding season.

Nesting: 4–7 green, brown-dotted eggs in a cup
nest well hidden on the ground.

Range: Widespread in the Old World, in
marshes and in birch and dwarf shrub
belt flanking the tundra. Breeds in
extreme northwestern Alaska.

One of the most recent arrivals among
North American birds. As Siberian
populations of this handsome songster
have increased with the recent warming
trend, the species has been able to
spread across the Bering Strait into
Alaska.

579, 605   Snow Bunting
(*Plectrophenax nivalis*)
Finches (Fringillidae)

Description: 6–7¼" (15–18 cm). Summer male
white with black mantle, tips of flight
feathers, and central tail feathers.
Winter male *white* with buffy crown,
ear patch, collar, and mantle; *black*

central tail feathers, primaries, and
shoulder. Female and immatures more
rusty tan than white. Both sexes have
large white wing patches.

Voice: Song is a short, musical warble, often
with some phrases repeated; it is given
on the far northern breeding grounds
from an exposed perch or in flight.
Common calls are a high *chee* and a low,
twittered *pirrr-rit*.

Habitat: Upland tundra in summer, preferably
with rock outcroppings, rocky slopes,
and cliffs; beaches, short-grass prairies,
fields, and roadsides in winter.

Nesting: 4–6 whitish, heavily spotted eggs in a
depression lined with moss and
feathers, on the tundra among rocks.

Range: Circumpolar Arctic breeder. Winters in
southern Canada and the northern
United States.

Often seen in large mixed flocks with
Horned Larks and longspurs, they
descend on snow-covered fields and
prairies in search of seeds.

596 Smith's Longspur
(*Calcarius pictus*)
Finches (Fringillidae)

Description: 5¼–6½" (15–17 cm). Breeding male
has *deep buffy orange unstreaked*
underparts, with *orange collar* setting off
white head patterned with black crown,
eye-line, and connecting mustache.
Winter male is *buffy orange* with faint
breast streaking, heavier on back; light
eye-stripe, *white patch at shoulder* and
white outer tail feathers. Female similar
but with colors more blended. As in all
longspurs, hind toe has an elongated
claw resembling that of larks.

Voice: Rattling noise on ground or at takeoff,
similar to that of Lapland Longspur but
drier. Warbler-like song of sweet notes.

Habitat: Tundra in summer; fields, prairies, and
airports in winter.

Nesting: 3–5 pale bluish eggs, speckled with brown, in a grass nest on the ground.

Range: Alaskan and Canadian treeline tundra belt east to James Bay. Winters in the south-central United States, mostly west of the Mississippi.

This beautiful longspur breeds at the treeline. Unlike the Lapland Longspur, which is truly a bird of open tundra, Smith's does not have a flight song but marks its territory by singing from the top of a small tree or hillock.

---

604 **McKay's Bunting**
(*Plectrophenax hyperboreus*)
Finches (Fringillidae)

Description: 7″ (18 cm). Similar to but whiter than the widespread Snow Bunting. Breeding male *snow white,* except for *dark bill, black tips of primaries and tips of central tail feathers.* Female has darkish areas on back but *head is pure white.* In winter, both sexes have light brown areas on head and back, more so on female.

Voice: A loud, warbling song reminiscent of the goldfinch. Call is a musical rattle.

Habitat: Tundra; coastal shores in winter.

Nesting: 3 or 4 light green, brown-dotted eggs in a grass-lined scrape on the ground in a rock crevice.

Range: Breeds on Hall and St. Matthew islands in the Bering Sea. Winters to the coast of western Alaska and Nunivak Island.

McKay's Buntings may represent the last survivors of a population of large white buntings north of the ice sheet of the last Ice Age. The more common Snow Bunting occupies adjacent breeding territory on all surrounding Arctic mainlands, but McKay's seems to hold its ground on its tiny and remote nesting islands.

Inland Cliffs and Canyons

The steep, barren slopes of inland cliffs
and canyons provide shelter and nesting
areas for a wide variety of birds—from
the giant California Condor to tiny
swifts. Few species, however, are able
to subsist on the meager resources
there and must forage in other habitats
nearby, where they are most often
encountered.

320 Prairie Falcon
(*Falco mexicanus*)
Falcons (Falconidae)

Description: 17–20″ (43–51 cm). W. 42″ (1.1 m).
Commonest of the three large falcons of
North America. *Pale sandy-brown above,*
with lighter feather edging; *creamy with
fine streaking below. Black wing pits.*
Narrow brownish mustache. Immatures
show less contrast and are more
streaked.

Voice: A loud *kree-kree-kree,* most often heard
around the eyrie.

Habitat: A variety: open mountains, dry plains
and prairies.

Nesting: 3–6 reddish, spotted eggs in an eyrie
set on a protected cliff ledge. Falcons
frequently re-use previous nest sites;
they seldom build a nest.

Range: In the West, from the Canadian prairies
and southern valley of British Columbia
to the Mexican border. Winters farther
south.

Its staple foods are ground squirrels and
other rodents and ground birds of the
prairie. Though it flies faster than the
Peregrine and can overtake any bird its
own size, it is not as spectacular a
hunter, and falconers turned to it only
when the Peregrine became scarce.
Now its numbers are declining, due to
rodent-poisoning programs and nest-
robbing by falconers.

321, 323 Peregrine Falcon
(*Falco peregrinus*)
Falcons (Falconidae)

Description: 15–21″ (38–53 cm). W. 39–45″ (1–1.1
m). Male *slate gray above,* with heavy
dark mustache. Pale below with white
unstreaked throat and fine barring on
buffy breast. Female browner. Juveniles
darker buff, with heavy streaking on
underparts.

Voice: Usually silent. Around the eyrie, a shrill *kek-kek-kek* is heard.

Habitat: Open country. Also river and sea cliffs and islands.

Nesting: 2–4 reddish eggs, flecked and stippled darker red, in a hollow on inaccessible cliff ledges. It has also been known to nest on ledges of buildings in big cities, where it feeds mainly on pigeons.

Range: Cosmopolitan; coast to coast in North America, but now scarce in the western United States and absent from the eastern states. Northern birds winter sparingly along coasts.

Its fast flight and dramatic stoops after prey are legendary and have made it the most sought-after bird of prey by falconers in the northern continents. Pesticide accumulation has brought this falcon near extinction; however, experimental breeding programs in captivity are proving successful.

337 California Condor
(*Gymnogyps californianus*)
Vultures (Cathartidae)

Description: 45–55" (114–140 cm). W. 102–114" (2.5–2.9 m). Largest bird of prey in North America. Black with bare head (reddish-orange in adults, black in young), black ruff, *conspicuous white underwing linings, pale feet.*

Voice: Usually silent.

Habitat: Mountains and surrounding open, sparsely covered brush country where it can easily detect and safely approach carrion.

Nesting: 1 white egg placed in an inaccessible cave or cavity on a cliff. The last known nesting population is in the mountains in Los Padres National Forest, east of Santa Barbara, California. This condor raises only one young every other year and the development of the immature is slow. At 10 months the young are still apprentices at flying, and do not breed until 5 or 6 years old.

Range: Almost extinct, presently found only in mountainous parts of southern California, though in historical times it lived as far north as Oregon and south into northern Baja California.

Probably fewer than 50 of these condors are left, according to the California Condor Recovery Team. More public support is needed to save the last American condors.

---

352   **Barn Swallow**
(*Hirundo rustica*)
Swallows (Hirundinidae)

Description: 5¾–7¾" (15–20 cm). *Very long, deeply forked tail.* Blue-black above, light cinnamon-rust below, with richer chestnut-red throat and forehead. *White undertail spots.* Juveniles have rust-colored throat and buffy underparts, shorter tail, less graceful flight.
Voice: A series of soft, twittering notes. Also a sharp *pit-vik* note.
Habitat: Open country often near water.
Nesting: 4–6 white eggs, with brown or reddish spots, in an open nest of mud pellets and straw, heavily lined with feathers; attached to a wall or other vertical surface. Prefers an elevated nest site, often on a bridge or building, and rarely nests away from man-made structures.
Range: Throughout the Northern Hemisphere. In North America in Aleutians west to Unalaska Island and from north-central Alaska through southwestern United States, except in the Gulf and southeastern seaboard states. In winter, migrates to South America.

These swallows usually nest in colonies. Once several pairs nest together they will hunt and rest communally, and

will also noisily mob an approaching hawk. Because it nests under the eaves of cottages as well as palaces, the Barn Swallow (or "Swallow" as it is called in the Old World) is the most popular bird in Europe. Destruction of its nest is believed to bring harm—fire, lightning, death—to the house and its inhabitants.

353 Cliff Swallow
(*Petrochelidon pyrrhonota*)
Swallows (Hirundinidae)

Description: 5–6" (13–15 cm). *Tail slightly notched, not forked, and often appears squarish.* A colorful bird with *light forehead;* blue-black crown and back with white stripes on back; *rust-colored rump,* dark wings and tail. *Chestnut throat and cheek,* buffy collar and whitish belly.

Voice: A rolling *churr* note, quite different from the notes of other swallows. Song is a series of squeaking and grating notes given in flight.

Habitat: Open, vegetated areas often near water.

Nesting: 4–6 creamy, spotted eggs in a gourd-shaped mud nest lined with grass and feathers with a protruding entrance neck on the side, under the eaves of a building, a bridge, or natural cliff face; in large colonies of up to several hundred.

Range: Coast to coast, and from the southern limit of the tundra to tropical Mexico and the southeastern United States. Winters in South America.

Cliff Swallows feed on small swarming insects, whose appearance depends on sunny, dry days. In California they frequently return in early spring to ancestral colonial breeding sites. If it turns chilly, however, they will abandon the area until weather and feeding patterns are more favorable, and return "on schedule" for their

publicized arrival on March 19 at the
San Juan Capistrano Mission.

Cave Swallow
(*Petrochelidon fulva*)
Swallows (Hirundinidae)

Description: 5–6″ (13–15 cm). Steel-blue crown,
dusky above with white streaks on
back, and light chestnut rump; light
below. *Forehead dark chestnut, throat and
cheek buffy.* Cliff Swallow has opposite
pattern: light forehead and dark throat
and cheek. Tail square.

Voice: *Weet, cheweet,* and a loud *chu, chu.*

Habitat: Caves and the dry country around
them.

Nesting: 3–5 spotted creamy eggs in a shallow
nest of mud and straw in a cave,
sinkhole, or culvert; in colonies.

Range: Various separate areas: some caves in
southern Texas and southeastern New
Mexico. Parts of Mexico (Yucatán
Peninsula) and Greater Antilles of the
West Indies.

In Yucatán, the Cave Swallow nests in
ruins of Mayan cities. Elsewhere it is
known to nest in caves and sinkholes,
but recently it has adopted highway
culverts as well. In many cases these
swallows share their caves with bats. In
the morning, as the last bats disappear
into the cave for their daytime roost,
the Cave Swallows fly out to hunt
insects or collect mud pellets for their
nests. In the evening the sequence is
reversed.

White-throated Swift
(*Aeronautes saxatalis*)
Swifts (Apodidae)

Description: 6–7″ (15–18 cm). Barn Swallow–sized, but with the typical *stiff, fast wingbeats* of a swift. Striking *piebald* appearance in the air; seen from below, wings, flanks, and tail *black,* the rest *white.*

Voice: A prolonged series of grating notes, represented as *jee-jee-jee-jee-jee.*

Habitat: Open sky; breeds in dry mountains or other rocky areas with good aerial feeding.

Nesting: 3–6 white eggs in a nest in a cleft of a sea or mountain cliff; in colonies.

Range: Interior valleys from British Columbia through the Rocky Mountains and the Southwest, including California, south to Central America. Moves south in winter.

These common western swifts are often seen in the vicinity of steep cliffs where they may fly in small groups, chattering constantly. Like some other swifts, they mate in flight, gyrating earthward in a "free fall," separating only when about to hit ground.

360 **Black Swift**
(*Cypseloides niger*)
Swifts (Apodidae)

Description: 7–7½″ (18–19 cm). Size of a large swallow but with longer, sickle-shaped wings. *All black,* though whitish forehead is apparent at close range. Longish tail, slightly forked, often fanned. Flies with long glides interspersed with spurts of rapid wingbeats, the wings working alternately. Feathers of immature edged with white.

Voice: More silent than other swifts. Gives a soft, high-pitched twitter: *twit-twit-twit-twit . . .*

Habitat: Mountains and coastal cliffs; most
frequently seen in the open sky.

Nesting: 1 white egg in a moss, grass, and algae
nest well hidden under a waterfall, on a
protected sea cliff ledge, or on a canyon
wall; nests and feeds in colonies.

Range: Narrow Pacific coastal area from the
Alaskan panhandle down to California,
and in the Sierra Nevada and southern
Rockies. Also in Central and South
America.

Swifts, in general, are the most aerial of
all land birds; they feed on aero-
plankton, swarms of tiny insects, and
flies. On sunny days they fly high above
the forest, but when the weather
worsens, they fly at lower altitudes,
following the insects. During a summer
storm of three or four days' chilling
rain, flocks leave the nesting grounds
and may fly hundreds of miles until
they encounter favorable weather.
Following the storm they return in
small groups to the nests. In their
absence, the young survive without
food, becoming torpid: cold,
motionless, and barely breathing.
Lower metabolism prevents starvation,
thus allowing the young to be raised
through alternating periods of plenty
and shortage.

521 **Say's Phoebe**
(*Sayornis saya*)
Tyrant Flycatchers (Tyrannidae)

Description: 7–8″ (18–20 cm). Dusky head, breast,
and back with darker wings and *black
tail. Light rust-colored belly and undertail
coverts.*

Voice: A mellow, whistled *pee-ur* with a
plaintive quality.

Habitat: Plains, sparsely vegetated country, dry
sunny locations, often near ranch
houses, barns, and other buildings.

Nesting: 4 or 5 white eggs in a nest of grass and

wool in sheltered, elevated, dry sites on ledges, rock walls, or buildings.

Range: Widespread in the West from central Alaska, the Yukon, and northern Mackenzie south to central Mexico; not present west of the Cascades and Sierras except locally in south-central California and western Oregon. Winters from southwestern states through Mexico.

Although primarily insect-eaters (as are all flycatchers), Say's Phoebes will eat other foods, such as berries, during long spells of cold, inclement weather when insects are unavailable.

530 Canyon Wren
(*Catherpes mexicanus*)
Wrens (Troglodytidae)

Description: 5½–5¾" (14–15 cm). Finely mottled *brown above with rust-colored rump and tail; pure white throat and breast* with finely streaked *dark chestnut-brown belly.*

Voice: The pleasing song is a descending series of clear, whistled notes, decelerating in tempo: *tee-tee-tee-tee-tee tee-teer teer teer.* Call is a harsh *zzeep.*

Habitat: Canyons and rocky barrens.

Nesting: 4–6 white eggs, with brown spotting, in a small nest of twigs, leaves, and grasses lined with hair or fur, in a rocky crevice.

Range: Resident from southern British Columbia to Montana, and south to southern Mexico.

This wren is found in remote canyons and on rocky mountainsides but has also adapted to man-made structures such as stone buildings and rock walls.

531 **Rock Wren**
(*Salpinctes obsoletus*)
Wrens (Troglodytidae)

Description: 5–6" (13–15 cm). *Finely mottled gray above with rust-colored rump. Light eye-stripe and fine streaking on pale breast; buffy tips of outer tail feathers.*

Voice: Song is a series of 3–5 trilling notes on one pitch, usually cricket-like in quality. Call is a loud *ki-deeeee.*

Habitat: Cliffs, rocks, talus slopes, from desert to coastal islands.

Nesting: 4–7 white, finely brown-speckled eggs in a nest of weeds, grass, bark, and rootlets lined with hair, feathers, and wool, well hidden beneath overhanging rocks or in a crevice of a rocky hillside.

Range: Southern British Columbia east to Saskatchewan and south throughout the West to Central America. Winters from California south.

The Rock Wren frequently constructs a "path" of rock chips leading to its nest. The purpose of this behavior is not understood but it is reminiscent of the bowerbirds' habit of decorating their territory (display ground) with colored pieces of stone, glass, and other objects.

Part III
Appendices

LIST OF ACCIDENTAL SPECIES

Accidental species are those that do not breed regularly or occur annually in western North America. These include birds that stray from their normal routes.

Birds that come from Asia have appeared mainly in Alaska, but a few have been seen elsewhere on the Pacific Coast. Birds that come from Mexico have appeared in various states north of the Mexican border. We do not include the accidental occurrence of eastern North American birds. Every eastern warbler, for instance, save two local species, has been seen in California or elsewhere in the West.

However, we have listed the eastern water and wetland birds that occur regularly even though in very small numbers, in some parts of the West.

Pelagic Wandering Albatross, *Diomedea exulans*
Short-tailed Albatross, *Diomedea albatrus*
White-capped Albatross (also called "Shy Albatross"), *Diomedia cauta*
Cape Petrel, *Daption capensis*
Streaked Shearwater, *Puffinus leucomelas*
Scaled Petrel, *Pterodroma inexpectata*
Cook's Petrel, *Pterodroma cookii*
Galapagos Storm-Petrel, *Oceanodroma tethys*

Wilson's Storm-Petrel, *Oceanites oceanicus*

White-tailed Tropicbird, *Phaeton lepturus*

Asiatic   Chinese Egret, *Egretta eulophotes*
Whooper Swan, *Olor cygnus*
Bewick's Swan, *Olor bewickii*
Bean Goose, *Anser fabalis*
Spot-billed Duck, *Anas poecilorhyncha*
Falcated Teal, *Anas falcata*
Baikal Teal, *Anas formosa*
Garganey, *Anas querquedula*
Common Pochard, *Aythya ferina*
White-tailed Sea Eagle (or "Gray Sea Eagle"), *Haliaeetus albicilla*
Steller's Sea Eagle, *Haliaeetus pelagicus*
Common Crane, *Grus grus*
European Coot, *Fulica atra*
Little Ringed Plover, *Charadrius dubius*
Mongolian Plover, *Charadrius mongolus*
Dotterel, *Eudromias morinellus*
European Jacksnipe, *Lymnocryptes minimus*
Spotted Redshank, *Tringa erythropus*
Marsh Sandpiper, *Tringa stagnatilis*
Greenshank, *Tringa nebularia*
Wood Sandpiper, *Tringa glareola*
Common Sandpiper, *Actitis hypoleucos*
Terek Sandpiper, *Xenus cinereus*
Black-tailed Godwit, *Limosa limosa*
Far Eastern Curlew, *Numenius madagascariensis*
Polynesian Tattler, *Heteroscelus brevipes*
Great Knot, *Calidris tenuirostris*
Long-toed Stint, *Calidris subminuta*
Curlew Sandpiper, *Calidris ferruginea*
Spoon-bill Sandpiper, *Eurynorhynchus pygmeus*
Ruff, *Philomachus pugnax*
Slaty-backed Gull, *Larus schistisagus*
Black-tailed Gull, *Larus crassirostris*
Black-headed Gull, *Larus ridibundus*
Common Cuckoo, *Cuculus canorus*
Oriental Cuckoo, *Cuculus saturatus*
White-throated Needle-tailed Swift, *Hirundapus caudacutus*
Fork-tailed Swift, *Apus pacificus*
Common Swift, *Apus apus*

Wryneck, *Jynx torquilla*
House Martin, *Delichon urbica*
Fieldfare, *Turdus pilaris*
Eye-browed Thrush, *Turdus obscurus*
Siberian Rubythroat, *Luscinia calliope*
Middendorff's Grasshopper Warbler, *Locustella ochotensis*
Gray-spotted Flycatcher, *Muscicapa griseisticta*
Mountain Accentor, *Prunella montanella*
Gray Wagtail, *Motacilla cinerea*
Indian Tree Pipit, *Anthus hodgsoni*
Pechora Pipit, *Anthus gustavi*
Brambling, *Fringilla montifringilla*
Hawfinch, *Coccothraustes coccothraustes*
Bullfinch, *Pyrrhula pyrrhula*
Common Rosefinch, *Carpodacus erythrinus*
Rustic Bunting, *Emberiza rustica*

Mexican Thick-billed Parrot, *Rhynchopsitta pachyrhyncha*
Groove-billed Ani, *Crotophaga sulcirostris*
Buff-collared Nightjar, *Caprimulgus ridgewayi*
Green Violetear, *Colibri thalassina*
Heloise's Hummingbird, *Atthis heloisa*
Plain-capped Starthroat, *Heliomaster constantii*
Berylline Hummingbird, *Amazilia beryllina*
Nutting's Flycatcher, *Myiarchus nuttingi*
San Blas Jay, *Cissilopha sanblasiana*
Brown-throated Wren, *Troglodytes brunneicollis*
Rufous-backed Thrush, *Turdus rufopalliatus*
Black-capped Gnatcatcher, *Polioptila nigriceps*
Fan-tailed Warbler, *Euthlypis lachrymosa*
Slate-throated Redstart, *Myioborus miniatus*
Rufous-capped Warbler, *Basileuterus rufifrons*
Scarlet-headed Oriole (also called "Streak-backed Oriole"), *Icterus pustulatus*
Black-vented Oriole, *Icterus wagleri*

Five-striped Sparrow, *Aimophila quinquestriata*
Worthen's Sparrow, *Spizella wortheni*

Eastern   Least Grebe, *Podiceps dominicus*
Olivaceous Cormorant, *Phalacrocorax olivaceus*
Anhinga, *Anhinga anhinga*
Little Blue Heron, *Florida caerulea*
Reddish Egret, *Dichromanassa rufescens*
Louisiana Heron, *Hydranassa tricolor*
Yellow-crowned Night Heron, *Nyctanassa violacea*
White Ibis, *Eudocimus albus*
Roseate Spoonbill, *Ajaia ajaja*
Black-bellied Whistling-Duck, *Dendrocygna autumnalis*
Black Duck, *Anas rubripes*
Whooping Crane, *Grus americana*
King Rail, *Rallus elegans*
Purple Gallinule, *Porphyrula martinica*
American Oystercatcher, *Haematopus palliatus*
Piping Plover, *Charadrius melodus*
Wilson's Plover, *Charadrius wilsonia*
Eskimo Curlew, *Numenius borealis*
White-rumped Sandpiper, *Calidris fuscicollis*
Stilt Sandpiper, *Micropalama himantopus*
Buff-breasted Sandpiper, *Tryngites subruficollis*
Hudsonian Godwit, *Limosa haemastica*
Laughing Gull, *Larus atricilla*
Little Gull, *Larus minutus*
Black Skimmer, *Rynchops nigra*
Dovekie, *Alle alle*

BIRD FAMILIES OF WESTERN NORTH AMERICA

Once the reader has become acquainted with the terms "species" and "genus" he will want to know about that more inclusive category, "family." Families are groups of species and genera that are related to each other by aspects of anatomy, sometimes of a minute kind. Each bird family has a Latin name, which is capitalized and ends in the suffix *ae*, e.g. Anatidae, which includes the birds known in English as swans, geese and ducks.

In the following descriptions of the 66 families found in western North America, each opens with the number of species in the world and in North America. These counts are only approximate because occasionally new species are discovered and old species are broken into two species or merged with another species. There is also some disagreement among experts as to whether some families occur in western America.

Accipitridae *Old World Vultures, Hawks, Harriers*
280 species: Worldwide. Twenty-two species in North America, many of them migratory. Sparrow- to turkey-sized birds, female larger than male. Powerful hooked bill; sharp talons. They hunt live animals in the air or on trees or the ground, and also feed on

carrion. Found in all types of habitats.
They build a platform nest on trees or
on the ground, but some do not build
any nest. A few species are colonial.
They are called raptors or birds of prey
and are often unjustly accused of killing
domestic livestock.

Alaudidae *Larks*

75 species: Worldwide. One native,
one introduced species in North
America. Sparrow-sized birds, sexes
alike. They run about on open ground
or in short vegetation; their long, hind
claw and earth colors are suited to their
habitat. They are ground nesters.

Alcedinidae *Kingfishers*

90 species: Worldwide, especially in
the Tropics. Three species in North
America. They migrate where waters
freeze. Warbler to crow-sized birds
with large head, strong, pointed bill,
small feet. Mostly near water but many
live in woodlands or on the edge of
meadows. They hunt moving animals,
chiefly fish, by diving or swooping
down from a perch; land kingfishers
feed on insects, lizards, and frogs.
These birds excavate a deep burrow in
an earthen bank and lay 3–10 eggs in it.

Alcidae *Auks, Murres, Puffins*

22 species: On the cold coasts of the
Northern Hemisphere; twenty breed in
North America, many of them
migratory. Sparrow- to small duck-
sized. Mainly black-and-white or dark-
colored seabirds, with short narrow
wings suited to swimming underwater
as well as swift flight. The bill often
has odd colors and ornaments. They
nest in colonies, breeding on rocky
ledges, crevices or in burrows. On land
many are nocturnal.

Anatidae *Ducks, Geese, Swans*

150 species: Worldwide. Forty-three
species breed in North America. Many

are large; all have webbed feet. Most have a flat, round-tipped bill (some have a hooked bill), and a medium to long neck. Waterfowl nest on or near water, with the young raised mostly on water though adults may range into many types of open habitat. Swans feed in deeper open water, geese graze on marsh and meadow, and ducks are found in all of these. Mostly migratory. Some nest on ground, others on water, still others in cavities; most have a large brood. Males larger than females. In swans and geese the sexes look alike. In ducks the males have very colorful nuptial plumage during the pairing season preceding breeding but later, in eclipse plumage, are plainer and more like the females. They feed on wetland plants and seeds, small aquatic animals, fish, and mollusks.

Apodidae *Swifts*

70 species: Worldwide, but especially numerous in the tropics. Four species, all migratory, in North America. They are aerial birds that never perch; weak feet allow them only to cling to a rock, tree, or wall. Long sickle-shaped wings seem to beat alternately; tail short. Nest of hardened saliva or sticks glued together with saliva, in the shelter of rock walls, waterfalls, caves, hanging fronds, or leaves of trees; 1–3 eggs. All feed on flying insects, soaring and hawking in the air, sometimes at a great height.

Ardeidae *Herons, Bitterns*

64 species: Worldwide. Twelve species, most migratory, in North America. These are wading birds of all wetlands but least often on the seashore. Long legs, long, straight bill, long neck, short tail, feet unwebbed. In flight, the neck is generally held in S-curve and the wings flap evenly; larger species soar at times. Stick or reed nest placed in water, on ground or on a tree. Sexes

look alike and sex roles in pairing
rituals and parental care are nearly
identical. Wading in water they stalk
and eat mainly fish. Some species have
elaborate plumes in breeding season.

Bombcyillidae *Waxwings*

3 species: All migratory. Two species
breed in North America. Plump,
sparrow-sized flycatching birds with
upright stature, soft cinnamon colors
and silky plumage; named for the
bright yellow and/or red waxlike
patches on the wings. Woodland birds
that feed on berries when these are
available, and on insects. They nest in
individual territories, but after
breeding, flocks gather where a supply
of berries is available. Raise 3–6 young
in a cup nest in trees.

Caprimulgidae *Nightjars*

76 species: Worldwide. Six species, all
migratory, in North America. Towhee-
to Robin-sized, earth-colored nocturnal
birds; rest and nest mainly on the
ground, with body posture horizontal.
They are aerial birds that feed on
insects at twilight or at night. Many
have eerie calls. Old wives' tales
alleging that they milk goats gave rise
to their vernacular name "goatsucker."
One or two young are raised on the bare
ground without a nest. Long wings and
tail and swift flight resemble those of
hawks; hence the American name,
nighthawk.

Cathartidae *New World Vultures*

7 species: Found only in tropical and
temperate New World. Three in North
America, partly migratory. Turkey-
sized, large and broad-winged soaring
birds of prey; hooked bill but feet and
talons are weak, unlike those of other
birds of prey. They detect their carrion
food from the air. They congregate
around larger carrion but also search for
food for themselves. Found in various

habitats but mostly open ones. 1–3 young are raised in a sheltered or inaccessible rock ledge, tree hollow, or on the ground, without a nest.

Certhiidae *Creepers*

5 species: Northern temperate regions, mainly in Eurasia. Only the Brown Creeper is found in North America. Sparrow-sized, tree-clinging birds with pointed tail feathers and down-curved bill. They live in forests in crevices in the trunks of old trees, or among rocks in canyons, or on barren mountaintops. 4–8 eggs. Creepers always climb or flutter upward while searching for insect food on a tree trunk or rock wall.

Chamaeidae *Wrentits*

One species: Only in western North America. Sparrow-sized, inconspicuous bird confined to the chaparral habitat where it nests and finds its insect food.

Charadriidae *Plovers*

60 species: Worldwide except Antarctica. Ten species, all migratory, in North America. Sparrow- to pigeon-sized shorebirds with rather short legs and toes, compact body, short neck and bill, rounded head, pointed wings. Some have bold color patterns; sexes look alike. They breed on the ground, in a scrape in sand or gravel. Usually 4 well-camouflaged eggs which both parents tend. Young hatch in down, and can run and feed right off. Not colonial but often unite to defend their brood communally. They feed on animal life in wetlands, running about on beaches, marshes, and meadows.

Ciconiidae *Storks*

17 species: mainly in the warm zones of the world. Only one breeds in North America, and it is migratory. Large, stocky, long-legged, broad-winged, soaring birds with a long, thick,

slightly down-curved bill. They live in wetlands that have trees nearby in which they nest, mostly in colonies. 3–5 eggs. They feed on aquatic animal life mainly by stalking and stabbing, or by probing and catching.

Cinclidae *Dippers*

5 species: In temperate zones of the Old World and the Americas. One in North America, largely nonmigratory. They are stocky, short-tailed, wren-like in appearance and size. These were originally perching birds but are well adapted to run and feed on aquatic animal life around and at the bottom of fast-running mountain streams. 3–7 eggs in a shelter next to the water.

Columbidae *Pigeons, Doves*

290 species: Worldwide but mostly in the tropics. Eight native and three introduced species in North America. Sparrow- to duck-sized. Pigeons have short legs, rounded head, pointed wings, fairly long to long tail; they bob the head when walking, and they drink by pumping water down the throat through the immersed bill. They nest on trees or shrubs, in open country or in deep forests, and feed from the ground to tree canopy on fruits, seeds, and foliage. 1–3, but usually 2, eggs at a time in a flimsy stick nest. Both parents feed what is known as "crop milk" to the naked helpless squabs (as the young are called). The New World species are commonly brown or gray but many Old World species are brightly colored.

Corvidae *Crows, Jays, Magpies*

107 species: Worldwide except for New Zealand and Antarctica. Fifteen species in North America, many of them migratory. Towhee- to duck-sized, with powerful bill and medium to long tail; sexes look alike. The crows are black but many of the jays and magpies

are colorful. Their habitat is extremely
varied but most require trees for
nesting. 3–10 eggs in a cup nest, often
in colonies. They are omnivorous,
feeding on meat (including carrion),
insects, fruits, and some vegetables.

Cotingidae *Cotingas*
90 species: In tropical or subtropical
areas of the Americas. Only one species
(migratory) in the southernmost United
States. Hummingbird- to large-pigeon-
sized, sparrow-shaped with short legs,
slightly hooked bill, many with a short
tail. Mostly colorful with the male
often different from the female. They
live in wooded habitats and glean fruit
and insects from the trees. They build a
mud nest in trees, rocks, or tree
hollows, and raise 1–6 young.

Cuculidae *Cuckoos, Roadrunners, Anis*
125 species: Worldwide; six in North
America, some of them migratory.
Sparrow- to crow-sized, long-tailed
birds, with slender body, slightly
curved and sometimes powerful bill.
They live in various habitats but most
of them in trees or bushes. They feed
on animal matter that they hunt on
trees or on the ground; some cuckoos
concentrate on hairy caterpillars. 2–6
eggs in cup nest. Unlike their European
relatives, American cuckoos are not nest
parasites. Roadrunners are ground
cuckoos; anis are social cuckoos that
live and even nest together. A familiar
American species is the Roadrunner of
the Southwest.

Diomedeidae *Albatrosses*
14 species: Mostly in the oceans of the
southern hemisphere, all distinctly
migratory. Three visit North America
when not breeding. These seabirds are
goose-sized or larger, with a powerful
bill, hooked at the tip, tube-like
nostrils, and very long, narrow wings
that allow them to glide endlessly over

the waves, picking live squid or
floating edibles from the ocean. They
lay one egg in a scrape or mound on the
beach mainly on islands but also on
remote coasts.

Falconidae *Falcons, Caracaras*
60 species: Worldwide. Six, mostly
migratory, falcon species and one
caracara species in North America.
Falcons are birds of prey, from sparrow
to large chicken size, with pointed
wings and long tail, generally with a
mustache stripe, rounded head and
hooked bill with a toothlike notch on
it, with taloned feet. Female much
larger. They are superb flyers, catching
bird prey in the air, or birds and
mammals on the ground or in trees.
Some also feed on bats and smaller ones
take flying insects. Caracaras are large
birds resembling hawks or eagles. They
often feed on fish, and on the carcasses
of fish or other animals. Few falcons
build a nest for their 2–6 eggs, but use
natural niches or cavities and nests built
by other birds.

Fregatidae *Frigatebirds*
5 species: Warm oceans of the world.
One species is an irregular visitor to the
southern coasts of North America, and
local resident on the keys off Florida's
Key West. Duck- or goose-sized birds
with long, slender wings, long, forked
tail, black or black-and-white in color.
These oceanic birds rob other seabirds
of their prey or feed on flotsam and,
rarely, on live prey. They nest together
but not in colonies, on trees and
scrub on islands. They raise one
young.

Fringillidae *Finches, Grosbeaks, Buntings, Sparrows*
Over 500 species: Worldwide except for
Australia and Oceania. Seventy-two
native and one introduced species in
North America; many migratory.
Perching birds with conical bill,

hummingbird- to Robin-sized. The largest bird family in the world, they live in all land habitats and also in wetlands. They feed on seeds and insects which they glean from the ground, plants, or trees. 2–6 young in a cup nest are raised mostly on insect food, some on soft seeds.

Gaviidae *Loons*

4 species: All in the marshes and bogs of the boreal forest and tundra belts of the northern part of Eurasia and North America. Duck-like diving birds (called "Divers" in the Old World) with a heavy, pointed bill; feet set back. Sexes look alike. They feed on fish and aquatic life. They have two young in a mound nest near water, tended by both parents.

Gruidae *Cranes*

15 species: In Eurasia, Africa, and Australia. Two in North America: the nearly extinct Whooping Crane and the more numerous Sandhill Crane. Large, long-legged, long-necked waders, they are among the tallest birds in the world. Long-distance migrants, they have broad wings and do much soaring and gliding. They fly with neck and feet outstretched like storks, but in noisy groups with bugling calls that carry far. Two or three eggs in a mound nest in marshes, bogs, or muskegs. In winter they often feed on grainfields and prairies, taking seeds, insects, mice and the like. Though solitary during nesting, they are very social at other times.

Haematopodidae *Oystercatchers*

7 species: On all temperate coasts, some inland. Two species in North America. Pigeon-sized stocky shorebirds with straight, long, somewhat heavy bill, longish legs, and rather short neck. Mostly black or black-and-white, with reddish bills and legs. They are found

on rocky beaches in the intertidal zone, feeding on marine animals such as shellfish, especially mollusks, which they pry off the rocks and open with their laterally flattened bill. 2–5 downy chicks are hatched in a scrape. After breeding they gather in flocks.

Hirundinidae *Swallows*

80 species: Worldwide. Eight species in North America, all migratory. Warbler- to blackbird-sized birds, with small bill, and often notched or forked tail. They are excellent flyers and feed in the air on flying insect life. They nest in protected ledges or in cavities, sometimes on manmade structures. Many use mud to build a nest cup or sphere. 2–6 eggs. Many of them are very social and nest in colonies.

Hydrobatidae *Storm-Petrels*

21 species: Worldwide. Four in North America, all migratory; several others are accidentals, since these oceanic birds are great wanderers. They are of sparrow to blackbird size, often with black-and-white and gray colors, notched or forked tail, pointed wings, and dainty, hooked bill. They hover and hawk over the ocean surface, searching for edible flotsam, or dive for near-surface plankton. One or two eggs in a sheltered crevice or burrow on an island, which they visit only at night.

Icteridae *Blackbirds, Meadowlarks, Orioles*

94 species: All of them in the Americas, nineteen of them native and one introduced to North America. Sparrow- to crow-sized birds, with a rather powerful bill. Males often larger, brighter, differently colored or with larger tail than females. In various habitats but most of them perch in trees or bushes. Many nest in colonies and raise 2–6 young in a woven cup or hanging basket nest. They feed on insects, fruit, even nectar or seed.

Meadowlarks and Bobolinks live in open country; troupials and smaller but similar orioles inhabit trees; blackbirds and cowbirds feed mainly on the ground but nest in trees, bushes or reeds. The cowbirds are nest parasites.

Laniidae *Shrikes*

74 species: Old World. Only two species live in North America, both migratory. Sparrow- to robin-sized perching birds with a hooked bill. They are territorial birds, living in open, brushy, or wooded habitats and pursue insects or small reptiles, mammals, and birds from watchposts. They are known for impaling their prey on a thorn or pressing it into a tree crotch, often as a food cache. They build a cup nest and lay 2–6 eggs.

Laridae *Gulls, Terns*

80 species: Worldwide. Thirty-one in North America, mostly migratory. Blackbird- to large duck-sized waterbirds. They have strong, long wings, and are excellent fliers. The bill may be slender, stout, pointed, or hooked. Gulls feed on every kind of flotsam, including offal, at the tideline on the beach, but mainly animal matter. Some are accomplished fishers. Terns hover and plunge-dive for fish and other surface animals. They nest in colonies, raise 1–4 young in a nest or scrape, on a safe islet, sand bank, coral bank, rock or ledge.

Meleagrididae *Turkeys*

2 species: One in North America, the other in Central America. Large, colorful gamebirds found in dense forest. The Domestic Turkey stems from the North American Wild Turkey: Bare neck and head with skin red or blue; long legs. They feed and nest on the ground. The male, or gobbler, is polygamous; the female, or hen, raises 7–20 chicks alone. They

feed on insects, worms, lizards, seeds—especially acorns—and foliage. They roost on trees.

Mimidae *Mockingbirds, Thrashers*
30 species: Only in the Americas. Ten mostly nonmigratory species in North America, including such familiar birds as the Catbird and the Mockingbird. Blackbird- to Robin-sized, short-winged perching birds. They live and nest in trees, bushes, or in cacti but feed mainly on the ground. They are distinctly territorial.

Motacillidae *Pipits, Wagtails*
50 species: Worldwide, but mainly in Old World. Five species in North America, all migratory. Warbler- to sparrow-sized ground birds though many require a song perch and roost in tangles and trees. They nest on the ground, in a cavity or high vegetation and lay 2–7 eggs in a cup nest. They feed on the ground in open or grassy areas. As the name suggests, wagtails constantly wag their long tail.

Pandionidae *Ospreys*
One species: Worldwide and truly cosmopolitan. Large, hawk-sized, hook-billed birds of prey. They nest on trees or crags near water, fish by hovering and plunge-diving, and have sharp scales on the bottom of their feet for holding their prey. 2–4 young in a stick nest.

Paridae *Titmice, Verdins, Bushtits*
65 species: Worldwide except for South America. Twelve species in North America, all nonmigratory. Small perching birds of warbler to sparrow size, with rather short bill and wings. They often hang from small twigs. Trees, bushes, or scrub are essential; otherwise their habitat varies widely, from subarctic to desert areas. They feed on insects and, in the North, on

oily seeds and nuts, and store food. 4–15 eggs in a neat nest in a tree hole (titmice and chickadees) or in a domed nest with a side entrance in a tree or cactus (verdins and bushtits).

Parulidae *Wood Warblers*

125 species: The New World. Fifty-two species breed in North America, mostly migratory. Very small to sparrow-sized, slender perching birds with fine slender bill. Mostly bright-colored birds that keep steadily on the move in search of insect food in the foliage of trees or bushes; they also take berries. Cup nest in a tree, bush, or on the ground contains 2–6 eggs. In all wooded or brushy habitats.

Pelecanidae *Pelicans*

8 species: Nearly worldwide. Two species in North America, one white, the other brown, and both migratory. Large, goose-sized waterbirds with huge pouched bill, strong broad wings for soaring, and webbed feet. These seabirds are found inshore or on larger inland lakes and marshes. They feed by diving or plunge-diving on fish. 1–6 eggs in a large platform nest on the ground or a rock or in a tree; in colonies.

Phaetontidae *Tropicbirds*

3 species: In tropical oceans. All three species occasionally visit North American waters but none nests here. Crow-sized white or partly barred birds with long, slender tail like a pheasant's, and gull-like wings. They nest in rock crevices or under brush, laying one egg without a nest. They feed on squid and fish.

Phalacrocoracidae *Cormorants*

33 species: Worldwide. Six species in North America. On ocean shores and inland waters where they dive for fish from the surface of the water. Crow to

small goose size, with long neck,
upright posture, powerful, longish,
hooked bill, webbed feet, black or
black-and-white plumage. 3–6 eggs in
a platform nest in colonies on a tree,
rock ledge or the ground.

Phalaropodidae   *Phalaropes*
3 species: All in North America and all
migratory. Two of these also occur in
Arctic Eurasia. Towhee- to Robin-sized
shorebirds with slender, pointed bill.
They swim on lake or sea, and feed on
planktonic animal life near the surface
of the water. Sex roles reversed:
brighter colored female is territorial,
lays four eggs in a nest on the ground
but leaves the male or males with the
clutch shortly after laying.

Phasianidae   *Pheasants, Partridges, Quail*
189 species: Worldwide. Six native and
three introduced species in North
America; quail are native, but
partridges and pheasants are introduced
from Eurasia. Hen-like birds, sturdy
legs for running and scraping, slightly
curved bill, rounded, short wings.
They feed on the ground on vegetation,
insects, and seeds. Most perch for
roosting but nest on the ground.

Picidae   *Woodpeckers*
210 species: Almost worldwide, except
for Australia, New Zealand, and New
Guinea. Twenty species in North
America, some migratory.
Hummingbird- to crow-sized perching
birds with stiff, pointed tail, short legs,
long toes and claws with which they
cling to the trunks and branches of
trees. They live in all wooded habitats
and in desert cactus. They feed on
insects that they catch by chiseling or
pecking into the bark of trees or glean
on the ground. They also take fruit,
nuts—which they often store—and the
sap of trees. Some are colonial or even
communal. They breed in tree holes

that they dig themselves or take over from other birds. 2–12 eggs without a nest. The sexes usually look alike.

Ploceidae *Weaver, Finches*
143 species: The Old World. Two non-migratory species introduced to North America. Brightly colored perching birds of hummingbird- to Robin-size, some with a very long tail, but all with the short, conical bill typical of seed-eaters. Habitat ranges from grasslands to woods. 2–8 eggs in cone-shaped, domed, or huge communal and often remarkably woven nests. They eat insects as well as seeds. Two species, the House Sparrow and the European Tree Sparrow, have been widely introduced elsewhere.

Podicipedidae *Grebes*
20 species: Worldwide. Six species, all migratory, in North America. Robin- to large crow-sized swimming and diving birds, with slender neck, straight, pointed bill, narrow, pointed wings, feet far back on body. They are waterbirds of lakes, ponds, and marshes, where they dive for polywogs, fish, and other animal food, but they also take vegetation. Male and female look alike. They raise 2–10 young on a floating plant nest.

Procellariidae *Shearwaters, Petrels, Fulmars*
65 species: Worldwide but mainly in the southern hemisphere. Only two species breed in North America. Small gull- to goose-sized. Seabirds resembling gulls but with longer and more slender wings, hooked bill with tube-like nostrils. They are oceanic, gliding over waves on stiff wings, and feeding on fish, plankton, and squid from near the surface. They nest in colonies mostly in burrows they themselves dig. 1–2 young raised by both parents, mostly during nocturnal visits. They make long migrations annually.

Ptilogonitidae *Silky Flycatchers*
4 species: Central America, but one species reaches into the southwestern United States. Slender, crested, short-winged towhee-sized birds. They feed by catching flies or gleaning insects, and also take berries. 2–4 eggs in a cup nest in a tree.

Rallidae *Rails, Gallinules, Coots*
130 species: Worldwide. Nine species, mostly migratory, in North America. Sparrow- to chicken-sized water and marsh birds, with short wings and tails. They bob as they swim and some marsh species such as the gallinules have long toes that enable them to walk on lily pads. Except for the gallinules, these birds have subdued colors that blend with their surroundings. The marsh species feed on aquatic vegetable or animal matter by picking or diving or even by climbing on reeds. 2–16 eggs in a platform or dome nest on water or hidden among reeds. Many flightless rails of oceanic islands are now extinct.

Recurvirostridae *Avocets, Stilts*
7 species: Worldwide in warmer climates. Two species, both migratory, in North America. Medium-sized waders but with very long legs, necks, and bills. The bill of stilts is straight; that of avocets curves upward. They favor open marshes and shores, where they wade, probe for insect food, and lay a clutch of four eggs in a ground scrape.

Scolopacidae *Woodcocks, Snipe, Sandpipers*
90 species: Worldwide. Thirty-five, mostly migratory, in North America, some visiting seasonally from Asia. These wading birds vary widely in size and in the length of bill, neck, and legs. But their plumage generally matches their background, often changing with the season. All nest in a

ground scrape, many of them on the Arctic tundra. The 2–4 eggs are tended by one or both parents, according to the species. Most are gregarious, at least after the breeding season, and all feed on the animal life of marshes, shores, or other open areas. Most of the "shorebirds," with exception of plovers, are in this family.

Sittidae *Nuthatches*

22 species: In many parts of the world. Four species, mainly migratory, in North America. Hummingbird- to bluebird-sized, chunky, short-necked, short-tailed, and short-winged tree-clingers with a straight, long, powerful bill. They are noted for running up or down tree trunks or rocks, gleaning insects and sometimes storing nuts. They nest in trees or ground cavities, and lay 4–10 eggs.

Stercorariidae *Jaegers, Skuas*

4 species: Arctic and Antarctic oceans and coasts. All widely migratory, three nesting in North America and one other visiting there. Crow- to raven-sized, gull-like, slender waterbirds with long, conspicuous tail, darkish coloration, and hooked bill. They have fast, flapping, falcon-like flight. They are predatory when on land, attacking smaller mammals and birds; at sea, parasitic, forcefully taking food from other seabirds. They breed on the tundra and lay 2–4 eggs in a ground nest.

Strigidae *True Owls*

130 species: Worldwide. Seventeen species, some migratory, in North America. Sparrow- to duck-sized, large round head, fluffy plumage that muffles sound, a disk-shaped face with a hooked bill and large eyes, broad, rounded wings, and silent flight. They are nocturnal or twilight hunters of ground mammals and birds in all land

habitats and even marshes. They raise
1–7 young from round, white eggs,
often laid in a cavity, a tree hole, or on
the ground, without a nest except when
adopted from another bird.

Sturnidae   *Starlings*
111 species: The Old World and the
southern continents, two species
introduced into North America.
Sturdy, perching birds of bluebird to
crow size, with a short square tail, a
straight or somewhat hooked bill, and
often with glossy black plumage. They
live in woodlands, grasslands, or near
man. Omnivorous, feeding on insects,
seeds, and fruits, with some of them
doing damage to crops. 3–7 eggs in a
cup nest in a cavity in trees or in niches
of buildings. Strongly social, except
during the breeding season.

Sulidae   *Boobies, Gannets*
9 species: Almost worldwide on
temperate and tropical shores. One
species breeds in North America, and
four others visit there. Duck- to goose-
sized seabirds with long, slender wings,
wedge-shaped tail, longish neck,
webbed feet, and long, straight,
pointed bill. They plunge-dive for fish
and squid in oceanic or offshore waters.
They nest on cliffs or in trees, laying 1–
3 eggs in stick platform.

Sylviidae   *Kinglets, Gnatcatchers, Old World
Warblers*
300 species: Worldwide but mainly in
the Old World and on the southern
continents. Five species in North
America. Very small warbler-sized
perching birds. They feed on insects in
wooded habitats or wetlands and
marshes. 2–10 eggs laid in a nest on
trees, on the ground, or in reeds.

Tetraonidae   *Grouse, Ptarmigan*
18 species: North temperate and Arctic
regions. Ten species in North America,

mainly non-migratory. Hen-like birds, quail- to turkey-sized, male often much larger than female. Rounded wings, sturdy feet suitable for scratching, and slightly curved bill. In various habitats from tundra to sagebrush desert, but American species found chiefly in grasslands. Where possible, they roost on trees, but generally feed on vegetable and animal food on the ground. If the ground is snow covered, northern species feed in the treetops on vegetable matter such as needles, catkins, and twigs. Most species engage in elaborate courtship displays on communal display grounds. Males mostly polygamous; females lays 6–16 eggs in a ground scrape.

Thraupidae *Tanagers*
240 species: In the Americas only. North America has only four native and one introduced species. Brightly colored perching birds of hummingbird- to jay-size, with thick bill or with upper mandible notched. They live mainly in forests, woods, and thickets, and feed on insects, fruit, and nectar. Some feed mainly on mistletoe. 1–5 eggs in a cup nest on a branch.

Threskiornithidae *Ibises, Spoonbills*
33 species: Warmer climates of the world. Four species, all migratory, in North America. Duck or large heron size; long-legged, long-necked, and long-billed waders, with down-curved (ibis) or ladle-shaped (spoonbill) bill. They wade in marshes and ponds, searching for aquatic animals. They nest in colonies on trees, cliffs, or in reeds, and raise 2–5 young in a stick nest.

Trochilidae *Hummingbirds*
320 species: Only in the Americas. Fifteen species, partly migratory, breed in North America. Among the tiniest and most colorful birds, often with

bright metallic colors, especially on the male's head or gorget. They are also known for wings that beat with great rapidity, make a humming noise, and enable them to hover or fly backwards. They use their long slender bills and long brushy tongues to feed on nectar and insects. All lay two large, white eggs in a finely woven cup nest on a branch or root, often sheltered from above.

Troglodytidae *Wrens*

60 species: All in the Americas, with ten in North America. One of these is also found in Eurasia and northern Africa. Mostly small birds, often with an upcocked tail, a mottled or patterned brownish or tan coloration, and a loud song. They have a lively way of searching for food, such as insects in trees, bushes, reeds, or cactus. 2–5 eggs in a woven, domed nest.

Trogonidae *Trogons*

34 species: Tropical areas of America, Asia, and Africa. One species barely reaches the southwestern borders of the United States. Towhee- to crow-sized, long-tailed, slim birds with round head, large mouth, short, hooked bill, short legs, and upright perching stance. They are forest birds that glean insects and fruit. 2–4 eggs in tree holes or termite nests.

Turdidae *Thrushes, Solitaires, Bluebirds*

310 species: Worldwide, except for New Zealand. Thirteen migratory species in North America. Chickadee- to jay-sized perching birds, with narrow, somewhat notched bill, and sturdy feet. They favor wooded, open, or marshy habitats and lay 2–12 eggs in a nest, often reinforced with mud, in the crotch of a tree or in a hole in a tree or rock. They feed on insects but fruit is also a seasonal staple. Most familiar in North America are the American

Robin and the bluebirds. The young of all species have spotted breasts.

Tyrannidae *Tyrant Flycatchers*
300 species: In the Americas only. Thirty-one species in North America, mostly migratory. Hummingbird- to jay-sized, large-headed, short-legged birds with broad flat bill, slightly hooked at the tip. Sexes look alike. They occupy various wooded habitats. In feeding they dart out from a perch to pursue insects in the air, on the ground, or in the forest canopy. A cup nest, sometimes set in a niche or cavity, contains 2–6 eggs.

Tytonidae *Barn Owls*
10 species: Worldwide, except for New Zealand. The one species in North America, the Barn Owl, is non-migratory. These are large-headed birds with a heart-shaped, disk-like face and long, feathered legs. They feed on rodents and birds picked from the ground, a tree, or even from the air at night mostly in forests (but also in grasslands in the Old World tropics). They nest in a hole or niche, laying 4–7 eggs.

Vireonidae *Vireos*
43 species: In the Americas only. Twelve species, all migratory, in North America. Warbler- to finch-sized, greenish or grayish stocky perching birds, with a slightly hooked tip on a straight, sturdy bill. They occupy various wooded or brushy habitats in which they hunt insects in the forest canopy. 2–5 eggs in a woven cup nest suspended from a horizontal crotch in a tree.

BIRD-WATCHING TIPS

Fortunately for bird-watchers, birds occur everywhere. City-dwellers should not refrain from studying birds, for many species frequent urban areas. The back-yard, garden, or farm can easily be made attractive to birds by providing shelter, water, and food for them. Trees, berry-bearing shrubs, a bird bath, flowers rich in nectar, a hummingbird feeder, wren houses, and providing food in winter all help. If you live out in the countryside, your home may become an oasis visited by migrant birds. Most of us will also want to look for new birds away from home, whether in parks, on river banks, or in marshes or forests. Here are a few hints for anyone about to take such a field trip:

You should realize that you will probably do much walking. The more you walk the more birds you are likely to see. Start early. Birds are most active from sunup to about 9 or 10 A.M. Dress for the season, but as lightly as possible. Be prepared to step into mud or push through brush to get a better view of that elusive rail or warbler. Bright-colored clothes make you very conspicuous, so wear them only when you want to be seen—for instance, during the hunting season. Walk quietly, and avoid making sudden movements.

Your essential tools on a bird walk are binoculars, field guide, and notebook. Carry them in a satchel or plastic bag that will protect them from the weather.

Get binoculars with a magnification of 7 or 8 times. Greater magnification is helpful in open areas such as beach, marsh, and sea, but beginners usually have difficulty in focusing and aiming such glasses since the area observed is greatly enlarged. A wide field of view is an advantage and has a direct relation to the size of the objective lens, that is, the lens farthest from your eyes. The size of the objective and the magnifying power can be found engraved on all better brands of binoculars. Thus the figure 7x35 means a magnification of 7 times with an objective 35mm wide. A 7x35 binocular is a convenient size for most birding. When trying out binoculars, step outside of the store and aim at a remote wire or antenna against the sky. When the lenses are in focus, you should see the wire clearly in black. If you change the focus slightly, the picture should become blurry but not colored. If the wire assumes an orange or blue color, don't buy the binoculars; colors of distant birds will be distorted in the same way.

A field guide, such as this book, is the second essential. If an unfamiliar bird has some special characteristic or pattern, you will want to check it out in your guide before you forget what the bird looks like. Not having my field guide handy when I saw my first Sandwich Tern, I tried to memorize its cap and crest pattern because I thought they would be decisive. Later, a look at the guide brought the discovery that the Sandwich Tern has a uniquely colored bill: black with a yellow tip. But I couldn't remember the bill color of the bird I had seen.

Finally, the notebook. Not everyone is disciplined enough to keep regular notes, but those who do often find them invaluable later on. After a day of birding, memory cannot always be trusted to retain all the colors and patterns one has seen.

Advanced birders find a telescope useful for identifying birds a long distance away. It also furnishes an intimate view of the family life of many shy or rare birds without disturbing them. My 9–30X zoom lens telescope has often enabled me to view birds I would not have been able to see with my binoculars.

But a telescope does have disadvantages: It is cumbersome to carry, especially the tripod; and when it is used at the highest powers (which gives it the edge over good binoculars) it vibrates with the slightest wind. A sturdy tripod is essential in this respect, especially when it has rounded, pipe-shaped legs rather than flat surfaced "I-shaped" legs.

GLOSSARY

Accidental A species that has appeared in a given area only a very few times and whose normal range is in another area.

Auriculars Feathers covering the ear opening and the area immediately around it; often distinctively colored. Also called ear coverts.

Boreal forest The northern coniferous forest belt stretching from Alaska to Newfoundland; also called the taiga.

Breeding plumage A coat of feathers worn by many birds during the breeding season; often more brightly colored than the winter plumage.

Casual A species that has appeared in a given area somewhat more frequently than an accidental, but whose normal range is in another area.

Cere A fleshy, featherless area surrounding the nostrils of hawks, falcons, pigeons, and a few other groups of birds.

Circumpolar Of or inhabiting the Arctic (or Antarctic) regions in both the Eastern and Western hemispheres.

Colonial Nesting in groups or colonies rather than in isolated pairs.

Clutch A set of eggs laid by one bird.

Cosmopolitan Worldwide in distribution, or at least occurring on all continents except Antarctica.

Coverts Small feathers that overlie or cover the bases of the large flight feathers of the wings and tail, or that cover an area or structure (e.g., ear coverts).

Crest A tuft of elongated feathers on the crown.

Crown The top of the head.

Cryptic Form or coloring that serves to conceal.

Cup nest A nest built or woven in a cup shape.

Domed cup A cup-shaped nest completely covered or arched over.

Eclipse plumage A dull-colored coat of feathers acquired immediately after the breeding season by most ducks and worn for a few weeks; it is followed in males by a more brightly colored plumage.

Ecosystem An ecological unit consisting of interrelationships between animals, plants, and their environments.

Eyebrow stripe A conspicuous strip of color arching above, but not including, the eye.

Eye-stripe A stripe that runs horizontally from the base of the bill through the eye.

Field mark A characteristic of color, pattern, or structure useful in distinguishing a species in the field.

Flight feathers The long, well-developed feathers of the wings and tail, used during flight. The flight feathers of the wings are divided into primaries, secondaries, and tertials. See also rectrix.

Frontal shield A fleshy, featherless, and often brightly colored area on the forehead of jacanas, gallinules, and a few other groups of birds.

Gorget A patch of brilliantly colored feathers on the chin or throat of certain birds, such as male hummingbirds.

Immature A young bird not under parental care but not yet fully adult in appearance; a juvenile.

Juvenile A bird during the period extending generally from fledging until the first breeding; an immature.

Lek A place where males of some species of birds, such as the Greater Prairie Chicken and the European Ruff, gather and perform courtship displays in a group, rather than courting females individually and in isolation from one another; females visit a lek to mate, but generally they build their nests elsewhere.

Lore The space between the eye and the base of the bill, sometimes distinctively colored.

Mandible One of the two parts of a bird's bill, termed respectively the upper mandible and the lower mandible.

Mantle The back of a bird together with the upper surface of the wings. A term is used for groups of birds (e.g., gulls and terns) in which these areas are of one color.

Molt The process of shedding and replacing feathers; usually after breeding and before the autumn migration.

Mustache A colored streak running from the base of the bill back along the side of the throat.

Naris (*pl.* nares) The external nostril; in birds located near the base of the upper mandible.

Pelagic Of or inhabiting the open ocean.

Phase One of several distinctive plumages worn by members of certain species, such as the Screech Owl and some hawks and herons, irrespective of age, sex, or season. Also called morph.

Platform nest A large, flat-surfaced nest built of sticks and similar material.

Plume A feather larger or longer than the feathers around it; it generally serves for displays.

Primaries The outermost and longest flight feathers on a bird's wing. Primaries vary in number from nine to eleven per wing, but always occur in a fixed number in any particular species.

Race A geographical population of a species that is slightly different from other populations; a subspecies.

Range The geographical area or areas inhabited by a species.

Raptor A bird of prey.

Rectrix (*pl.* rectrices) One of the long flight feathers of the tail.

Resident Remaining in one place all year; nonmigratory.

Riparian Of or inhabiting the banks of a river or stream.

Secondaries The large flight feathers located in a series along the rear edge of the wing, immediately inward from the primaries.

Scapulars A group of feathers on the shoulder of a bird, along the side of the back.

Scrape A shallow depression made by a bird on the ground to serve as a nest.

Shoulder The point where the wing meets the body, as in the Red-shouldered Hawk. The term is also loosely applied to the bend of the wing when this area is distinctively colored.

Spatulate Spoon-shaped or shovel-shaped; used to describe the bill of certain birds, such as spoonbills.

Speculum A distinctively colored area on the wing of a bird, especially the metallic patch on the secondaries of some ducks.

Subalpine The forest or other vegetation immediately below the treeless, barren alpine zone on high mountains.

Subspecies A geographical population of a species that is slightly different from other populations of that species; also called a race.

Taiga The belt of coniferous forest covering the northern part of North America and Eurasia from coast to coast.

Tarsus The lower, usually featherless, part of a bird's leg.

Territory An area defended by the male, by both of a pair, or by an unmated bird.

Tertials The innermost flight feathers on a bird's wing, immediately adjacent to the body. They are often regarded simply as the innermost secondaries. Also called tertiaries.

Tules Certain species of bulrushes abundant in California.

Window A translucent area in the wing of certain birds (such as the Red-shouldered Hawk) visible from below in flight.

Wing bar A conspicuous crosswise wing mark.

Wing stripe A conspicuous mark running along the opened wing.

Winter plumage A coat of feathers worn by many birds during the nonbreeding season, and often less brightly colored than the breeding plumage.

CONSERVATION STATUS OF WESTERN BIRDS

Taking or molesting birds, their nests, eggs, or young is prohibited in the United States and Canada, with the exception of those birds that damage property or agriculture, or are covered by hunting regulations. In addition, rare or endangered birds are protected by special legislation, and their status is carefully monitored by management agencies.

Migratory birds that cross national boundaries are protected by an international treaty between the United States, Canada, and Mexico. Each state also has its own special conservation measures. It should be understood that the status of birds may vary from locality to locality, and interested birders should consult the appropriate federal and state agencies for current information.

Unprotected birds Two introduced and now unwanted species, the Starling and House Sparrow, are not protected in the United States or Canada. The Myna, introduced in British Columbia, is also unprotected. A few others such as Rock Doves and members of the crow and blackbird families may damage crops and therefore are not fully protected in most areas.

Gamebirds These may be hunted during an open season that is regulated by each of the states or provinces. They include the Whistling Swan and all species of brant, geese, and ducks; all species of grouse and quail, the Ring-necked Pheasant and Turkey; also the Sandhill Crane, rails (except Yellow and Black), the Common Gallinule, American Coot; Wilson's Snipe; Band-tailed Pigeon, Mourning Dove, White-winged Dove, Spotted Dove, Ringed Turtle Dove; Common Crow, Black-billed Magpie; and Snowy Owl (in Alaska if taken for food only).

Birds protected by local measures Such birds as House Finches and White-crowned Sparrows cause extensive damage to agricultural crops in California at some seasons and may be controlled by local authorities. Information concerning these measures may be secured from state or provincial authorities. This includes birds that are hunted in some states but are protected in states where they are less common. Also included are many Mexican birds which have small populations in some states along the United States-Mexican border.

Birds protected by general measures Every bird in the United States is so protected except those in group 1, above. In Canada, the Migratory Birds Convention Act protects most species, but not pelicans, cormorants, birds of prey, owls, kingfishers, members of the crow family, blackbirds, Starlings and the House Sparrow. These may or may not be protected by provincial law.

Rare and endangered species or subspecies These species are carefully defined by state or federal law, and are fully protected. These include such birds as the Canada Goose (Aleutian Islands subspecies), California Condor, Bald Eagle, Peregrine Falcon, and Whooping Crane.

PICTURE CREDITS

The numbers in parentheses are plate
numbers. Some photographers have pictures
under agency names as well as their own.
Agency names appear in boldface.

Amwest
Charles Summers (21,
254, 314)

Ardea Photographics
J.A. Bailey (574), Hans
Beste (69) J.B. and S.
Bottomley (238) Donald
Burgess (525) M.D.
England (191) Kenneth
Fink (32, 95, 157, 182,
186, 210, 256, 258,
260, 308, 323) Clem
Haagner (1) Edgar Jones
(411, 544, 609) C.R.
Knights (285) Eric
Lindgren (68, 199) S.
Roberts (62) B.L. Sage
(175) Richard Vaughan
(605) Wardene Weisser
(365, 371, 377, 379,
389, 536, 610) J.S.
Wightman (58)

Peter Arnold
John MacGregor (361)

John Arvin (296) Ron
Austing (289, 311,
326, 327, 330, 331,
372, 381, 474, 495,
503, 594, 596, 607)

Bob Barrett (317, 354,
388, 452) Erwin Bauer
(78) Greg Beaumont
(280, 343) Tom
Brakefield (101, 103,
124, 128, 136, 145,
148, 151, 152, 160,
206, 266, 281, 282,
334) Fred Bruemmer
(83, 86) Ed Bry (154,
200, 203, 553) Steve
Cannings (382, 530,
617) Ken Carmichael
(383) Leslie Chalmers
(477, 515, 590)
Herbert Clarke (52, 64,
66, 70, 77, 79, 81, 87,
113, 140, 170, 171,
178, 179, 194, 198,
211, 217, 221, 222,
223, 232, 242, 276,
277, 278, 279, 294,
346, 351, 357, 366,
368, 369, 391, 398,
412, 413, 415, 418,
434, 435, 436, 439,
440, 454, 456, 475,
476, 480, 494, 507,
508, 511, 513, 516,
521, 526, 548, 572,
588, 599, 600, 603,
616, 623)

Joseph Jehl (17, 39, 55, 65, 72, 225, 226, 601) Isidor Jeklin (408, 410, 430, 438, 448, 566) Stephen Krasemann (271, 426, 445) Carl Kurtz (134, 387, 573, 581, 612) Bob Leatherman (347, 401, 443, 505) Joe McDonald (18, 38, 579) Sam Miller (274) Terrence Moore (322) C. Allan Morgan (119, 173, 345, 556, 557) Alan Nelson (30, 144, 612) Ronald Orenstein (7, 227) Robert Orr (88) O.S. Pettingill, Jr. (129)

Photo Researchers, Inc.
Edmund Appel (3) Tom Branch (303) Ken Brate (34, 364, 487, 587) James Carmichael (286) Steve Coombs (299) Alford Cooper (249) Allan Cruickshank (376, 485, 489, 546) Helen Cruickshank (31, 41, 517) Stephen Dalton (482) Kent and Donna Dannen (465) Harry Engels (378) Kenneth Fink (98, 259, 306) H.F. Flanders (298, 559) George Galicz (309) Patrick Grace (110) Lola Graham (543) B. Griffiths (195, 212, 463, 624) R.F. Head (2) Robert Hermes (13) Robert Hernandez (20) David Hill (75, 89, 168, 459) George Holton (61) Jerry Hout

(425) Paul Johnsgard (123, 142) Levi Keim (268) G.C. Kelley (80, 292) Karl Kenyon (27) Russ Kinne (48, 57, 59, 60, 108, 118, 125, 362, 466) Kirtley-Perkins (498, 614) Stephen Krasemann (115, 290) Calvin Larsen (444) Thomas Martin (185) Karl Maslowski (29, 208, 325, 453) Tom McHugh (320) Anthony Mercieca (141, 163, 283, 417, 468, 500) Alan Nelson (315) Charles Ott (23, 270, 333, 375, 422, 535) O.S. Pettingill, Jr. (462, 464, 519, 529) A.H. Rider (91, 300) Leonard Lee Rue III (248, 313, 481, 583) Philippa Scott (99, 107) J.R. Simon (257, 565, 595) M.F. Soper (70) Alvin Staffan (529) Dan Sudia (429, 512, 558) John Trott (539) M. Vinciguerra (288) Larry West (356) Bill Wilson (193)

Ray Pierotti (82) Ralph Reinhold (467) Richard Robinson (318) Allen Rokach (44) Leonard Lee Rue III (45, 93, 100, 102, 114, 117, 121, 207, 219, 255, 272, 428, 589) Leonard Lee Rue IV (159) Perry Shankle (6) E. Sian (143, 360, 533) Perry Slocum (176, 196, 245, 350, 354, 392, 397, 404, 432, 433, 469,

INDEX

Numbers in bold-face type refer to plate
numbers. Numbers in italic refer to page
numbers. Circles preceding English names
of birds make it easy for you to keep a
record of the birds you have seen.

A

THE AUDUBON SOCIETY

The National Audubon Society is among the oldest and largest private conservation organizations in the world. With over 550,000 members and more than 500 local chapters across the country, the Society works in behalf of our natural heritage through environmental education and conservation action. It protects wildlife in more than seventy sanctuaries from coast to coast. It also operates outdoor education centers and ecology workshops and publishes the prizewinning AUDUBON magazine, AMERICAN BIRDS magazine, newsletters, films, and other educational materials. For further information regarding membership in the Society, write to the National Audubon Society, 950 Third Avenue, New York, New York 10022.

STAFF

Prepared and produced by Chanticleer Press, Inc.

Publisher: Paul Steiner
Editor-in-Chief: Gudrun Buettner
Executive Editor: Susan Costello
Managing Editor: Jane Opper
Project Editor: Susan Rayfield
Associate Editors: Mary Suffudy, Kathy Ritchell
Production: Helga Lose
Art Director: Carol Nehring
Picture Library: Edward Douglas
Drawings and Silhouettes: Paul Singer, Douglas Pratt
Range Maps: Paul Singer
Map of North America:
Herbert Borst, Francis & Shaw, Inc.

Design: Massimo Vignelli

THE AUDUBON SOCIETY FIELD GUIDE SERIES

Also available in this unique all-color, all-photographic format:

Birds (*Eastern Region*)

Butterflies

Fishes, Whales, and Dolphins

Fossils

Insects and Spiders

Mammals

Mushrooms

Reptiles and Amphibians

Rocks and Minerals

Seashells

Seashore Creatures

Trees (*Eastern Region*)

Trees (*Western Region*)

Wildflowers (*Eastern Region*)

Wildflowers (*Western Region*)